# Couple therapy:
# a handbook

**Open University Press**
**Psychotherapy Handbooks Series**
*Series editor*: Windy Dryden

TITLES IN THE SERIES

Published titles:

Individual Therapy: A Handbook
*Windy Dryden (ed.)*

Integrative and Eclectic Therapy: A Handbook
*Windy Dryden (ed.)*

Hypnotherapy: A Handbook
*Michael Heap and Windy Dryden (eds)*

Couple Therapy: A Handbook
*Douglas Hooper and Windy Dryden (eds)*

Child and Adolescent Therapy: A Handbook
*David A. Lane and Andrew Miller* (eds)

Art Therapy: A Handbook
*Diane Waller and Andrea Gilroy (eds)*

# Couple therapy:
# a handbook

Edited by
## DOUGLAS HOOPER
and
## WINDY DRYDEN

Open University Press
Milton Keynes · Philadelphia

Open University Press
Celtic Court
22 Ballmoor
Buckingham
MK18 1XW

and

1900 Frost Road, Suite 101
Bristol, PA 19007, USA

First published 1991
Reprinted 1994, 1996

*British Library Cataloguing in Publication Data*

Couple therapy : a handbook
  1. Couple therapy
  I. Hooper, Douglas    II. Dryden, Windy    III. Series 616.8915

  ISBN 0–335–09893–2
  ISBN 0–335–09892–4 (pbk)

*Library of Congress Cataloging-in-Publication Data*

Couple therapy : a handbook / edited by Douglas Hooper and Windy Dryden.
     p.   cm.—(Psychotherapy handbooks series)
  Includes index.
  ISBN 0–335–09893–2.—ISBN 0–335–09892–4 (pbk.)
  1. Marital psychotherapy—Handbooks, manuals, etc.   I. Hooper,
Douglas.   II. Dryden, Windy.   III. Series.
  RC488.5.C64   1991                                    90–27358
  616.89'156—dc20                                          CIP

Typeset by Colset Private Limited, Singapore
Printed and bound in Great Britain by Biddles Limited, Guildford and King's Lynn

To Mavis and Louise: the other halves of our couples, for their patience, love, and hard work.

# Contents

# The editors and contributors

DAVID BARKLA was formerly Head of Information and Research, Relate National Marriage Guidance, Herbert Gray College, Rugby

IAN BENNUN is a District Clinical Psychologist, with Torbay Health Authority and Department of Psychology, University of Exeter

MICHAEL BUTLER is a Counsellor, with Albany Trust Counselling, Victoria, London

JEREMY CLARKE is a Counsellor, with Albany Trust Counselling, Victoria, London

JEAN COLLARD is Consultant, One-plus-One, Marriage and Partnership Research, Central Middlesex Hospital, London

PATRICIA D'ARDENNE is a Top Grade Clinical Psychologist, Enfield Health Authority, Enfield

WINDY DRYDEN is Professor of Counselling, Goldsmiths' College, University of London

ANDY FARRINGTON is Course Teacher and Senior Behavioural Psychotherapist, North Trent College of Nursing and Midwifery, Sheffield

SARAH GAMMAGE was formerly Education Officer, Relate National Marriage Guidance, Herbert Gray College, Rugby

WAGUIH GUIRGUIS is a Consultant Psychiatrist, Psychosexual Clinic, St Clement's Hospital, Ipswich

BRIDGET HESTER is a Private Therapist and Training Consultant, Crayke, York

MARY HINCHLIFFE is a Consultant Psychiatrist, Bristol and Weston Health Authority, Barrow Hospital, Bristol

DOUGLAS HOOPER is Consultant Psychologist; Visiting Research Professor, School of Applied Social Studies, University of Bristol

BRIGID HULSON is a Research Worker, Maudsley Hospital, Denmark Hill, London

ADRIAN JAMES is Senior Lecturer in Social Work, Department of Social Policy and Professional Studies, University of Hull

PENNY MANSFIELD is Deputy Director, One-plus-One, Marriage and Partner-ship Research, Central Middlesex Hospital, London

LISA PARKINSON is Director, Family Mediators Association, Henbury, Bristol

ROBIN RUSSELL is Lecturer in Psychology, Goldsmiths' College, University of London

THOMAS SCHRÖDER is Consultant Clinical Psychologist, Southern Derbyshire Health Authority, Department of Psychotherapy, Derby

SHOSHANA SIMONS is a Private Therapist, Kilburn, London

EDDY STREET is a Consultant Clinical Psychologist, South Glamorgan Health Authority, Department of Clinical Psychology, Cardiff

ANNI TELFORD is Senior Lecturer, Department of Nursing and Community Health, Birmingham Polytechnic

KATE WILSON is Lecturer in Social Work, Department of Social Policy and Professional Studies, University of Hull

# Preface

In many ways this book has assembled itself because of the obvious need for a non-doctrinaire account by a variety of contributors of the issues which penetrate and surround therapeutic work with couples.

We have deliberately adopted an integrated approach to the work and have not asked a representative of each theoretical or technical group to explain how they carry out couple therapy. No specific approach can be shown by research to be substantially more or less effective than any other, although some specific problem issue may of course yield to one technique rather than another.

What is important to us is to emphasize the importance in all 'caring' spheres of enabling more couples to have their problems and difficulties taken seriously and helpfully. High rates of divorce and of co-habiting have made for a greater range and complexity of problems so that contextual understanding, as well as clinical skill, is an important factor.

The authorship reflects this in that we have assembled counsellors, nurses, psychotherapists, sociologists, psychiatrists, social workers and educators to illuminate various issues for us. They, therefore, write from a variety of both professional and practice settings, which reflects the fact that couples present themselves and their problems (both directly and indirectly) in many ways. If the book contributes to both the availability *and* the expertise of readers choosing to undertake couple therapy, then all of us who have contributed will be amply rewarded.

Douglas Hooper and Windy Dryden

# PART I

# The background

# Why couple therapy?

DOUGLAS HOOPER AND WINDY DRYDEN

This handbook brings together a collection of chapters whose authors describe both practice and work settings in which the problems of couples are assessed and tackled. This is a vigorous activity which provides a considerable literature for both the clinician and the researcher in which the emphasis is on the patterning of the interactions between two individuals who are particularly closely involved with each other.

It may therefore seem strange to pose the title of this preliminary chapter by the joint editors as a question. However, various pressures have been identified which do pose some questions which need to be answered because of very radical shifts in social relationships on the one hand, together with proliferation of complex human relationships on the other hand. We shall begin by discussing the concept of the couple.

Until very recently the concept of the couple was largely included in the concept of marriage which for many societies, both west and east, organized our ideas about a specific form of intimate adult relationship. Because it had obvious utility, the marriage of a man and a woman was given specific legal recognition, as well as the more ancient religious recognition. As a result of intensive social traditions and pressures, most societies expected that when a man and a woman separated out somewhat from their respective families of origin they would 'marry' and thus secure a new union upon which to build a separate family. This was the predominant western, and especially Protestant, mode until very recently. Marriage itself was always part of other cultures as well in the sense of creating a special union of young men and women. But frequently this did not presage a separate family but rather a new unit within a larger 'extended' family group. The conflict between eastern and western social structures is one of the factors leading to current difficulties for young Asian and other couples trying to adapt to both of these social patterns in the contemporary social scene. Yet these conflicts are often still expressed within the concept of eastern and western marriage, rather than between marriage and non-marriage.

It is this latter phenomenon which determined that the appropriate title for this

book was 'couple' and not 'marital' therapy. Since the late 1960s the phenomenon of the committed couple has emerged which is not necessarily a marital
relationship in the old accepted sense and which includes gay and lesbian couples
as well as heterosexual couples. There are many reasons for this but the most
important (for heterosexual couples) are probably the effective control over conception, and the concomitant emergence of the feminist view of the rights and
roles of women. These two factors alone have had a major impact on the relationships formed between men and women although they are not the only ones of
course.

The other major social phenomenon of the 1970s and 1980s related to these
factors has been the sharp rise in divorce. It is perhaps paradoxical that the concept of 'the couple' should be linked to marriage breakdown, but the divorce
phenomenon may have made couples cautious about formal marriage or remarriage. For example there has been a threefold increase in the numbers of couples
cohabiting between 1979 and 1987. It is too early to tell whether these couples
will stay unmarried so that a subsequent breakup will not be represented in the
divorce statistics.

However, the number of people currently involved in divorce is very substantial. In 1961 there were 25,000 divorces which were granted by the courts. By
1988 this figure had risen to 152,000, which represents over one-third of a million
individuals. Provided there are no substantial changes in patterning, then the best
estimates are that 37 per cent of couples currently marrying will seek divorce during the course of their relationship, according to Haskey (1989) on the basis of
data from the Office of Population Census and Survey.

Although this book is *not* about divorce *per se*, these data illustrate that not only
do many marital couples divide but also the potential for non-marital couples is
very considerable. Best estimates of the numbers of 'cohabiting' couples is
somewhere in the region of 650,000–700,000 pairs as compared with a population
of about 20 million married couples of all ages. Couples who are not formally
married are, then, a very substantial subgroup of the population of couples in
our society. And with that subgroup there are further groupings of a particular
kind especially relating to whether this is a union of two people without experience
of divorce as compared with one in which one or both have already experienced
the legal break-up of a previous relationship.

The growth of the very substantial number of people experiencing divorce has
led to interventions of a different kind from the more orthodox approach to resolving marital difficulties. These are dealt with here under the headings of conciliation and mediation (see Chapter 13) and there are arguments about whether or
not these modes of intervention differ from counselling and therapy. The focus
is certainly different because many of the couples involved are already separated
physically yet the socio-emotional problems of the couple are similar. They often
experience great distress, with one partner disproportionately affected by the
breaking relationship. What conciliators and mediators do is to focus on conflict
resolution as the chief mode of practice because it is here that the most painful
problems appear to lie. Yet conflict resolution techniques are also appropriate
at other stages of couple breakdown when high levels of conflict often emerge.

The next important issue which this book needed to be involved with was that of same-sex couples (see Chapters 11 and 12). There are no reliable estimates of the number of sustained same-sex couple relationships, but many agencies have reported dealing increasingly frequently with gay or lesbian couple difficulties. Writers dealing with these couples in this volume draw our attention to the degree to which this has been a 'hidden' area of work because of the blocks which hetero-sexual therapists sometimes experience when same-sex couples come for help.

In some respects, of course, the problems which these couples present *are* dif-ferent because of the psychological structure of same-sex relationships. But they are ultimately intimate personal relationship problems in which all the usual pro-blems (of communication, distorted emotional interchange, role conflict, dif-ferential personal development) of heterosexual couples are very likely to appear. However, there is the additional element of familial and social disapproval which may enhance the tensions which exist.

## Why therapy?

The decision to use the term 'therapy' rather than 'counselling' for the work described in this book is an intriguing one. The likelihood is that these terms will become increasingly interchangeable as techniques and training develop because the modes of action are themselves likely to become increasingly similar to each other.

One of the most helpful discussions of the matter has appeared recently in Dryden, Charles-Edwards and Woolfe's (1989) introduction to what they call the 'nature and range of counselling practice'. They conclude their discussion of the counselling/therapy issue by saying

> In our view, attempts to resolve this issue in terms of some overarching theoretical plan are futile and serve no purpose. Both enterprises lay stress upon the need to value the client as a person, to listen in a non-judgmental and accepting fashion, and to foster the capacity for self-help. If there is a distinction it lies in more mundane and down-to-earth concerns about the nature of the training, the settings in which people work, and the problems and issues with which they are typically confronted.
>
> (Dryden *et al.* 1989: 8)

They see the core concepts for modern practice as being drawn from three areas: the psychodynamic approach, non-directive counselling, and what they call mainstream psychology in its behavioural and social manifestations.

James and Wilson (1986) make a useful contribution by listing what they call 'operational concepts' in both marital counselling and therapy which they distinguish from 'explanatory concepts'. Their major conceptual headings are

1  establishing a working alliance
2  working with communication
3  changing behaviour through agreements
4  creating therapeutic tasks
5  recognition of relationships between mini and maxi problem areas.

for which they draw on a number of areas of theoretical explanation. In fact, of course, they have substituted the concept of *marital work* as a term for either couple therapy or couple counselling. The term fits their target readership (social workers) and illustrates once more the idea that selection of terms in this endeavour is very often a question of deciding upon a particular horse for a given course!

What is particularly interesting is that one of the features which has been said to distinguish counselling from therapy – personal therapy for the therapist – has never been applied to working with couples. As far as we are aware, no training programme in Britain has yet required that the trainee therapist and partner should themselves engage in couple therapy before being deemed fit to practise. Yet in principle at least, this would seem to be quite powerfully indicated by those therapeutic approaches which believe in making explicit the unconscious assumptions of any therapist. Those who argue for such training would probably say that individual therapy is an adequate basis for marital therapy, although a moment's reflection will reveal that this is clearly untrue because of the extensive interactional phenomena which are involved in work with a disturbed couple. To reassure readers, we should add that it is not our intention to propose such 'couple therapy training' but to draw attention to a curious anomaly in the counselling/therapy debate.

A fitting conclusion to this discussion would be to return to Rogers's (1942) classic account of his own early work. He titled the book *Counselling and Psychotherapy*; in the first chapter he says that whatever the individual professional is called, it is the 'approach to the attitudes of his client' which is the concern of the book. He continues

> If in his work he deals with individuals who are maladjusted, or perplexed, or failing . . . and if they leave . . . him . . . facing life more constructively, then his techniques and methods are of interest to us.
>
> (Rogers 1942: 3)

He concludes by making light of the distinctions, saying

> these terms [counselling and psychotherapy] will be used more or less interchangeably in these chapters . . . because they all seem to refer to the same basic method.
>
> (Rogers 1942: 3)

Perhaps Rogers did us all a disservice when he invoked the descriptive term counselling to describe what he clearly saw as one form of psychotherapy – indeed he describes it as the 'new' psychotherapy. The contemporary problem is that a book title has either to use both terms or to choose between them: we have here opted for the latter.

## Couples, individuals and families

So far, then, we have discussed issues arising from our use of the word 'couple' and of 'therapy'. There are also some interesting and important things to be said about the concept of 'couple therapy'. The thrust of this handbook – and many others – is that there is an area of discourse and of intervention which is particular to couples and which is distinct from both the world of the individual on the one hand, and the larger family on the other. Working conjointly with a couple is now widely recognized as being an effective and efficient method for handling the problems arising from the intimate but troubled couple world – and this is amply documented in the research chapter of this handbook (Chapter 16).

Yet there does seem to be a certain tension in therapeutic work with a couple which often seems to take it back into work with each individual – as if the problems 'really' belong to the individual world of each person. But the evidence is now strong that if the core of the problem is in the interactive processes, even though these are conducted inside the heads of the couples, then the interactive sequence is the one which needs examining, exploring, clarifying and changing. This cannot mean that the personal life experience of each person is unimportant. Indeed it is the interaction of the personal experience worlds of both partners which leads to the emergent problems. Sometimes one member of the couple does have some clearly clustered disordered thoughts, feelings or behaviour. For example one may be severely phobic about a particular situation. And this aspect of the disturbance may need particular care or treatment. But the disorder itself will still be part of their *joint* experience which therefore needs a joint approach to the problem. There are traps for the unwary here, and especially for the practitioner who is used to 'individualizing' most problems. If one partner has a particularly clearly expressed problem, the other partner may feel free to be quite disengaged and request (or demand) that the 'sick' partner be treated. This is a very common pattern for men to perceive their woman partner in this way. Yet the critical step may be for the therapist to help the other partner to see how the intrapersonal may be defined and confirmed by the interpersonal.

The other end of this continuum is that many writers in family therapy will include 'marital' (or couple) therapy as part of family therapy, assuming that because it shares some of the same characteristics that it is really only one part of broader family therapeutic approaches.

The interesting historical point is that modern family therapy does trace part of its roots to the early work of Don Jackson in the Marital Research Institute at Palo Alto, California, whose particular interest was in fact work with couples.

Marital therapy has therefore contributed a good deal to family therapy in understanding the process of dyadic interaction, although a family group clearly possesses several more dimensions. Because of the overriding dominance of the adoption of systems theory as the metaphor of choice for understanding families and family troubles, the marital dyad is perceived in this formulation as a *sub*-system of the larger family system, just as the parent–child dyad may be seen as a sub-system. However, it can be argued that the 'marital' pair seen as a sub-system of the family system are in fact separate from the couple seen as a self-contained dyad in its own right. That is to say that the way in which the couple functions or is dysfunctioning may well stand prior to, and separate from, subsequent familial bonds.

The various theories which support couple work are also not all drawn from the systems approach. In particular, those therapists using a framework drawn from object relations theories will use very different language from that used by 'systemic' workers of various hues. This is because the object relations explanations rely upon dyadic interactive processes alone since the partner functions, indeed, as *object* for the other partner – a view which is not reducible to systems language.

In addition the way the couple present their difficulties very frequently indicates that they see the relationship as the prime issue. Here the pioneering study by Brannen and Collard (1982) provides evidence that the production and recognition of the 'couple problem' goes through a series of refinements which sound very different from the creation of a troubled family system.

Significantly the development described by family therapists and others are often group processes, with group dynamics at work: thus the concepts of 'scapegoat', myth, and so on, to describe covert shared experiences. Troubled couples may locate the problems in one partner, but often as part of subtle interaction and negotiation between each person which extends in time.

Human pairing *does* seem to have distinctive characteristics which make the phenomena of continuity or discontinuity a matter of investigation and treatment in their own right. Indeed, common experience suggests that pairs other than the personally committed couple are often troublesome in many other social and work situations. This suggests that the ability and inability to relate effectively to one other person is of fundamental importance, and different from the ability to cope with a larger group.

But it is equally wrong to identify the couple, and conjoint therapy with couples, as divorced from wider familial patterns. It is clear in everyone's experience that wider links may keep in place a poor and unrewarding pair relationship because it serves some broader purpose of the family of origin of one member of the couple. Sometimes indeed, it may make therapeutic sense to examine such bonds *in vivo* as it were, to see if anything can be done to liberate the couple to have a more effective joint life. The problems of doing just this tend to be technical and especially ethical. If, for example, a woman is still overly enmeshed with her family of origin, it is not likely that an antagonistic partner will allow a therapist to request his partner's parent to join in the therapy, even though this may appear crucial to progress. It is more likely that a therapist will help to achieve an appropriate disengagement by judicious individual sessions with the partner involved.

In other words, we are clearly recognizing the importance to the couple of relationships which each has away from their respective partner. The careful and competent therapist will clearly recognize the power of these extra-couple relationships in the conjoint work, but mostly dealing with them in a representational rather than a real context. These issues are developed more broadly by Eddy Street in Chapter 5 but this preliminary analysis is, we hope, helpful in putting forward the case for the distinctiveness of couple therapy.

**Development of the book**

The issues of couple therapy are explored in three parts within this volume, with the largest part being the 'meat' of the sandwich devoted to therapeutic approaches.

This section is preceded by two sharply contrasting chapters from the sociological and psychological viewpoints. Chapter 2 explores ways by which sociologists can help therapists to use sociological concepts more effectively, perhaps, than in the past. Penny Mansfield and Jean Collard tease this out from their own and others' work in an interesting and novel way.

Brigid Hulson and Robin Russell take a more vigorous path in Chapter 3 in that they review the very extensive literature on couple relationships, drawing out the evidence for underlying qualities, patterns and characteristics. Most of the work they quote is on normal as opposed to troubled couples, which may sharpen the difference too much for some therapists. But it is a salutary reminder of the wealth of information and concepts *not* drawn from the necessarily narrower field of the individual practitioner.

The therapeutic approaches part begins with a penetrating study by Thomas Schröder (Chapter 4) in which he draws out from the various approaches used in couple therapy the critical issues. His approach fits well with the increasing number of writers who wish to explore the thematic nature of therapy which is regardless of concept and ensuing technique. Eddy Street (Chapter 5) follows this with a balanced chapter arguing for the place of couple therapy alongside family therapy. The chapters by Ian Bennun (Chapter 6) and Mary Hinchliffe (Chapter 7) which follow then engage with some clear and important therapeutic practice issues. Conjoint therapy has been an important mode for couple therapy but resources and commitment often determine whether both members of a couple can be helped and Ian Bennun's work has clarified these issues.

Mary Hinchliffe reminds us that crises so frequently create opportunities for therapeutic movement but she also comments on the importance of understanding the background to the crisis in order to make most effective use of the opportunity. Waguih Guirguis (Chapter 8) follows with a description of what might almost be called the 'new' sex therapy. Early confidence in the therapeutic efficacy of sex therapy has now been replaced by a more sober understanding of the complex issues involved. Sexual dysfunction is very variable and some aspects are more amenable to treatment than others. In addition Waguih Guirguis details what can be called a 'whole couple' approach so that therapists can feel more confident about realistically assessing and working with the problem.

The next four chapters deal with important new issues in couple therapy. Troubled relationships often arise in a context of power and gender; Anni Telford and Andy Farrington (Chapter 9) bring the issues out in their discussion of the related gender problems for both the couple and therapists. Michael Butler and Jeremy Clarke (Chapter 11) and Shoshana Simons (Chapter 12) deal with the same-sex couple and bring together their own experience and the sparse literature, probably for the first time. This helps the therapist who is not gay or lesbian to appreciate the world of these couples and in particular to identify the many similarities of therapeutic work as well as the important differences.

It seems right that in the same place in the book, Patricia d'Ardenne has written a vigorous essay (Chapter 10) on the needs which couples from the ethnic minority groups in many communities have for therapeutic work. She is able to draw on an increasing amount of source material and presents a challenge to therapists from the dominant society to make more effective service available and to adapt practice to suit another culture. She also emphasizes, however, that good therapeutic technique applies across cultural groups and that with commitment, an experienced therapist can provide what many couples badly need.

The final chapter in this part is by Lisa Parkinson (Chapter 13), who deals with the help which is needed when couples part. Some writers have been at pains to distinguish conciliation or mediation – the terms are used variously – from therapeutic work and the author handles these issues usefully. She also describes an interesting experiment in a more comprehensive approach to encompass the financial, material and psychosocial issues involved in a breakup. As the pro- mised divorce law reforms unfold, couple therapists will no doubt be involved in sharp debate here.

The last part deals with matters which are the penumbra of core therapeutic work. Sarah Gammage (Chapter 14) discusses the problems of using educational methods as a way of pre-empting difficulty and of re-educating people in the wake of major problems. These attempts shade off into many other ways by which peo- ple learn about couple relationships, but the community has difficulty generally in developing this resource. David Barkla (Chapter 15) reviews the major agen- cies working with couples who are obviously influential in helping to develop practice. There is a considerable knowledge gap about the degree to which the statutory agencies in particular offer therapeutic work to couples away from the main teaching and research centres. From his particular position he also has some important comments on how the national agencies function, which point up the difficulty of providing effective service.

Research (Chapter 16) and training (Chapter 17) often occupy a modest place in a practice handbook but these two chapters underscore the effectiveness (or otherwise) of much that has gone before. Kate Wilson and Adrian James's elegant and succinct chapter strikes an optimistic note in terms of the results which can be achieved by working with couples. There is a vigorous and mature literature, which increasingly has significant contributions from British writers and which offers solid ground for practitioners. The book closes with Bridget Hester's account of the training needed by couple therapists, and what is currently available. She draws attention to the frequent inclusion now of specific training on couple work into more general therapy training. Some places will remain important specialist training centres, but the spread of couple therapy training awareness appears to be increasing.

This book testifies that couple counselling and therapy is alive and well – if that is not too great an irony! This should surprise no one, particularly in view of the high demands which couples make of each other for a mutually rewarding and stimulating life experience. This is probably in marked contrast to the expec- tations of many couple relationships in previous generations which were often created with very different assumptions about the social realities, especially between the differing socio-economic groups. But the 'new' partnerships may well be more difficult to maintain in order to produce the personal satisfactions to which many couples aspire. There is not a great deal of evidence that people are better prepared for the current demands of couple relationship than they were for the, perhaps, less demanding tasks of pair relationships in a previous generation, nor that the practice of intimacy has become any easier. Indeed, in some ways it may be that intimate couple relationships are now much more problematic because of the intense social, economic, sexual and psychological demands which this fragile human arrangement is asked to bear.

In a prescient book chapter entitled 'Couple therapy' Ryle (1979) wrote:

> Neither the old nor the new morality has resolved the painful paradoxes inescapably present in that centrally important relationship . . . a relationship at once calling for the most adult and mature behaviours, and calling forth most primitive and childish ones. . . . In this work [of couple therapy] I believe we often witness the emergence, from extreme personal pain, of resource and growth. . . .
>
> The emergence of a more developed consciousness, of the capacity to tolerate more uncertainty, of the acceptance of more individual responsibility, and the letting-go of a comfort-adherence to provided solutions, and of coercive dependency upon the other, represent real human gains.
>
> (Ryle 1979: 149)

We believe that the editors and authors have produced an important contribution to this rewarding field of work.

## References

Brannen, J. and Collard, J. (1982) *Marriages in Trouble: The Process of Seeking Help*, London: Tavistock.

Dryden, W., Charles-Edwards, D. and Woolfe, R. (1989) *Handbook of Counselling in Britain*, London: Tavistock/Routledge.

Haskey, J. (1989) Current prospects for the proportion of marriages ending in divorce, *Population Trends 55*: 34–7

James, A. and Wilson, K. (1986) *Couples, Conflict, and Change*, London: Tavistock.

Rogers, C.R. (1942) *Counselling and Psychotherapy*, Boston, Mass: Houghton Mifflin.

Ryle, A. (1979) Couple therapy, In S. Walrond-Skinner (ed.) *Family and Marital Therapy: A Critical Approach*, London: Routledge & Kegan Paul.

# 2

# The couple: a sociological perspective

JEAN COLLARD AND PENNY MANSFIELD

## The need for a dialogue

Family sociologists and family therapists have a basic focus of interest in common, yet they rarely engage in dialogue at a theoretical or conceptual level. Morgan has outlined several reasons for this:

> Much is due to academic boundaries and the history of the divisions of academic labour. Other reasons may be a result of some quite profound ideological and cultural traditions that pervade many aspects of our daily lives as well as our professional practices; between the individual and society, between methodological individualism and holism, between the private and the public.
>
> (Morgan 1988: 233)

The lack of confluence between practice and scholarship is of central concern to us since we are both sociologists working for a multi-disciplinary organization which seeks to increase the understanding of marriage and partnership through research and through endeavours to put research into practice. The opportunity of working in this way alongside colleagues from different disciplines has provided us with many fresh insights.

As sociologists we have found that therapeutic concepts can illuminate our research, and we are also aware that for therapists, our work can provide a helpful background for their practice. However, despite this acknowledgement of mutual interest and benefit it is rare for there to be any collaborative research between therapists and sociologists.

### A collaborative project

At One-plus-One Marriage and Partnership Research, we have had one example of sociologists and psychiatrists/psychotherapists joining together to design and carry out research in an area of common concern. Since one of us was actively involved in this research, it is useful to comment upon some of the issues it raised. The project was a small in-depth exploratory study of clients with marital problems (forty-eight husbands and wives from twenty-eight marriages) who were currently attending two therapeutic agencies – a hospital out-patient marital unit, and Marriage Guidance (now Relate). The principal focus was the process by which partners in troubled marriages seek help with their difficulties, and it set out to explore how people become aware of their problems, their searches for help among their own social networks, their various attempts to approach agencies, and finally, their having become clients (Brannen and Collard 1982).

Those of us undertaking the research all had, in varying measure, some therapeutic experience and training, a factor which may be of importance when multi-disciplinary ventures into the world of therapy are being considered. We were aware of the need for the clear demarcation of roles, and it was agreed that in the research we were all to behave as investigators and must resist any temptation or pressure to be drawn into the stance of counsellor. At each interview therefore, whether our expertise was psychiatric or sociological, we decided to introduce ourselves simply as 'social researchers'.

Each partner of the marriage was to be interviewed separately at home, with one researcher conducting the interview and another observing it, save in those instances where both partners were to be interviewed at the same time, in which case each partner was interviewed simultaneously but in different rooms, with only one interviewer present at each. To ensure comparability, every interview was always based on a framework of standardized questions, but we allowed ourselves considerable flexibility and latitude in probing and follow-through, for we wanted to offer maximum opportunities for individual response. Such a freedom of approach proved highly beneficial in the amount of spontaneous material it generated: in some instances the interviewer had to return for a second visit in order to complete the questions.

Since all those interviewed were active clients, we had to exercise caution to preclude any possibility of the interview turning into a therapeutic session – from either side. One of the safeguards we adopted was that of always having two interviewers present in the client's home, even if not always in the actual interview. We believe that having a second interviewer 'on site' can provide a steadying context, especially when it comes to ending the overall encounter.

We were also wary of allowing a relationship of too great an intensity to develop between researcher and respondent, especially where it proved impossible to complete the interview in a single visit. We were anxious to avoid any confusion with the process of ongoing therapy, for at times we needed to explore the same problem areas as the therapist.

Since certain questions about difficulties in the marriage were very likely to arouse painful and disturbing feelings, and could (and sometimes did) trigger highly emotional reactions, we sought to minimize the focus on these by asking respondents to talk about them 'in a nutshell', a verbal device which was not always entirely successful. On occasions it was difficult to maintain the balance between 'holding back', yet 'staying with' the person sufficiently in order to 'see through' to a conclusion the discharge of these feelings. At such times we had to re-emphasize the boundaries of our position and try to hold very firmly to our research brief.

This collaborative research shed interesting light both on the sociological interview and the therapy session. One of our questions asked respondents to describe what they considered were the most effective ways in which counsellors might be of help to them. From their replies it was clear that the meanings and prescriptions they held and constructed about the counselling process were not simply determined by what happens in the counselling session itself: they were also considerably influenced by their own prior expectations, which had been shaped by their experiences within their own families and by the responses and reactions they obtained from their social networks. At one point, when respondents were describing their 'ideal' situation for the disclosure of their problems, we were surprised when several, both men and women, cited the research interview itself. That they did so in no way cast discredit on any counselling experience; it simply underlined the importance for them of having an attentive and non-judgemental investigator and listener, a feature we hope that therapy and research hold in common. However, it must be said that a few people valued being interviewed in their home, 'on your own territory', which helped them to feel more at ease; one woman even expressed a wish that her therapist could visit her as we had done.

It is regrettable that to date collaborative research of this nature, between the sociologist and the therapist, has so rarely taken place, since although the professional perspectives differ, there are many commonalities. However, despite our recognition of mutualities, our many dialogues with therapists in a variety of settings have made us aware of the gulf in understanding which can exist between a sociological and a therapeutic view.

## Two views of the same scene

There often seems to be an implicit difference of perception between therapist and sociologist, a division commonly expressed as a contrasting priority of focus. If one presses the analogy further, whereas therapists can be said to zoom in on the inner worlds of individuals, in order to explore the personal and private areas of their lives, sociologists are seen to use a wide-angle lens in order to capture the broader perspective of the outer world of society, its structures and institutions. Perhaps this analogy of the different lens can be extended even further: it is the lens itself which creates and limits the perspective; when pointed at the identical view a zoom lens offers a more detailed image of less of it, and a wide-angled lens a less detailed image but of more of it. Each perspective is equally valid, but neither perspective can on its own be regarded as complete.

The call for a greater dialogue between those holding these different perspectives comes from the growing number of sociologists and therapists, working in the field of marriage and couple relationships, who wish to widen their observations; they recognize that private lives have public significance, and correlatively, that social trends have individual consequences. A genuine dialogue should not blur the differences between the viewpoints, but rather should recognize the value of each, so that an enhanced and more comprehensive view of marriage and the family can be achieved as a result of sharing the perspectives. And how appropriate and how necessary this seems, since the family can be regarded as the unique nexus of the individual and society, combining and reflecting both the structural and the personal at one and the same time. From a temporal dimension also, the family experience is one of constant oscillation and containment, holding within it the impact of the past, the present and the future. For the majority of people, their sense of history and their sense of the future are inextricably bound up with the complex web of relationships which have composed, and which currently compose, their 'family'. To quote Edward Shils

> The first link in the chain which builds past and present and future into the structure of a society is reforged every time an infant is born and survives.
>
> (Shils 1981: 169)

When, as at present, therapist and sociologist stand on either side of marriage and the family, one inside, one outside, we tend to view each other's perspective as predominantly a backdrop to our own observations, a perception that is too limited, since that backdrop is not simply a static context against which experience takes place but is an integral part of the experience. The therapists Christopher Clulow and Janet Mattinson in their recent book *Marriage Inside Out* acknowledge this link:

> Marriage is a social and psychological institution. It is a bridge between public and private worlds. To understand adequately what is happening outside marriage involves taking account of private relationships between men and women. Equally, the private face of marriage has to be understood in the context of the social environment in which couples live their lives out together.
>
> (Clulow and Mattinson 1989: 6)

Therapists who work with couples cover a range of professional orientations. Nevertheless, most programmes of training will have included the psychological development of the individual, and an exploration of dyadic interaction, the latter probably with most of the emphasis on the stresses and disturbance that can occur, since couples who seek help will be doing so because their relationship is in trouble.

In the therapeutic situation itself, the main focus on the couple will fluctuate between the inner worlds and the outer realities of the partners as experienced by each other. But there will in addition always be some evidence and reminders of the world beyond the consulting room for not only the social setting that the couple daily encounter together, but also their very relationship will have been shaped and influenced by it. Therapists are bound to speculate about such external influences, and at times will wish to relate their clients to their wider social context (Chester 1985).

## Therapy and the wider social context

When we look back to the 1960s and early 1970s we can see that, for many therapists at that time, interest in the social environment was dominated by a concern with the effect of social factors; certain components were distinguished which, particularly when clustered together, could be considered to form constellations of social disadvantage and adversity (see, for example, Dominian 1968).

A catalogue of such factors might include: a deprived or disrupted family background; inadequate housing; unemployment and economic poverty. Any combination of these could be regarded as being capable of precipitating or heightening disturbance within a family. As Morgan points out, *Marriage Matters* (1979), the report of a Home Office Working Party on marital problems, having covered the sociological contribution to research in under three pages, links it strongly to epidemiological studies (Morgan 1985). Such an approach was based on the assumption that the presence of certain social characteristics might make it possible to identify individuals likely to be particularly prone to difficulties in marital relationships.

It is more likely that therapists today will be interested in the contemporary social landscape, as a constantly shifting context in which both they and their clients live. There is a general awareness of the considerable extent to which our society has changed, particularly within the past three decades, and therapists will want to keep themselves informed of the magnitude and speed of such changes, as well as wishing to have some understanding of the likely causes. Changes in the patterns of sexual behaviour, and in the expectations held about men's and women's domestic and work roles, for instance, have important implications for contemporary couple relationships. It may therefore be useful for therapists to feel they can position their clients on a current continuum of behaviour and attitudes and experience, and indeed the couple themselves may harbour the wish to discover where they stand in relation to others, a yearning which may indirectly have contributed to their having sought help.

As researchers we encountered this quest for assessment among many couples. When interviewing 130 newly-wed husbands and wives, we noted that the interview was often used by them as an opportunity to test the experience of 'my marriage' against an external definition of marriage. For some, the underlying question was 'Is *my* marriage like most other marriages – is it a proper marriage?', whereas others confidently asserted that they were sure that their marriage was not at all the same as other marriages. In different ways both these groups of newly-weds were making a similar point about marriage; both implied the existence 'out there' of a yardstick by which any marriage could be measured.

Although therapists and social researchers alike would wish to dispel any notion of an external gauge or criterion of marriage, any one of us may unwittingly purvey implicit definitions and assumptions about marriage through the questions we ask – or those we omit. Conformity to a model of marriage may be implied, for example, by a research decision, apparently innocuous, to frame questions for 'husbands' and 'wives' rather than for 'people who are married' (or even 'people sharing a home together').

In our own research we thought we were very aware of such pitfalls, yet we were taken by surprise when a number of newly-wed couples challenged our request to interview each spouse separately yet simultaneously. Our wish to collect data in this way was regarded by these recently married partners as an unwelcome bias on our part toward perceiving them as two separate individuals rather than as a pair: central to their own definition of being a couple was the concept of 'one-ness'. For all these newly-weds, being a couple was thus synonymous with being married, although many of them were extremely unclear as to what might actually constitute 'being a couple'. The definition of a couple is an essential element in any sociological perspective on the contemporary couple, and this is something we address in a later section.

In order that the sociological perspective we develop in the chapter resonates with therapists, it is necessary first to clarify some basic issues. Our own encounters and experience of working with counsellors and therapists have made us aware that, to the non-sociologist, a sociological approach to marriage is generally held to be one in which the structural aspects of marriage and family life are over-emphasized at the expense of the relational. We consider that such a view may stem from the era when sociology had achieved a new popularity (1950s and 1960s) and certain theoretical approaches were dominant, conveying a particular perspective which still represents for many *the* sociological view. The continuing influence of this stereotypical frame of reference has formed a barrier to valid dialogue and restricts our mutual comprehension. We want therefore to catalogue briefly the ways in which the sociological understanding of marriage and the family has developed over the years, to show how far it has extended beyond those earlier confines, and in particular to share the ways in which social researchers like ourselves have tried to grapple with the complex interaction between individuals' experiences and the social structure.

First however, we must define our limits: although we are contributing to a book about couples, we do so from an empirical study of the experiences of marriage and within a theoretical framework of marriage and the family. Such limitations are inevitable because historically 'couples' equal 'marriage', and statistically this is still true – the majority of people living as couples are predominantly heterosexual and most of those are married. However, as we intend to show, by adopting a theoretical perspective which does not assume a set of natural, taken-for-granted meanings, we can begin to develop a new construct for understanding couples.

Our own recent research experience has been an inquiry into marriage: examining the experiences of getting married and the processes through which men and women perceive and construct their lives as married partners. Although each marriage is different, and moreover each partner in a marriage has a unique perception of that marriage, nevertheless all these marriages existed within a common social landscape. We were therefore able to view the marriages we observed within the context of MARRIAGE as a socially recognized partnership, a legal status and an institution. However, although all marriages consist of couples, not all couples are married. So, in substituting couple for marriage, what do we mean?

## Definitions

In the past few decades we have witnessed massive changes in what is called family life. Even to make such a statement as this, is in fact to crystallize the change; whereas once we would have spoken of THE family, we now refer to families or family life.

A parallel shift can be seen in the title of this book: it is dealing with *couple* therapy whereas its predecessor of only six years ago was concerned with *marital* therapy (Dryden 1985). In his preface to the two volumes of *Marital Therapy in Britain* Dryden introduced a definition:

> The term 'marital' therapy is used in both volumes to reflect the current convention whereby therapeutic interventions with couples who are in committed relationships are given the title 'marital'. I am not entirely happy with this term since it may well offend couples seeking therapeutic help who are not married or who are gay. Since in my opinion, no acceptable alternative exists, I have reluctantly acceded to convention.
>
> (Dryden 1985: pp. xi–xii)

In this statement Dryden is acknowledging that for many therapists the defining element of 'marital' is that of commitment. A simple equation is formed – marriage equals commitment; therefore, commitment equals 'marital'. However, for many gay and lesbian couples their close relationships are part of a political statement, a rejection of that system of values upon which marriage is founded – namely permanence and exclusivity.

> Marriage is the focal point of the entire ideology of 'the family' and of supposed 'family values', and moreover, is the site of state intervention in all our lives. It is through the institution of marriage that government governs, and it is in defence of marriage that anti-gay prejudice speaks and legislates with the greatest virulence.[1]

Yet we are also aware that many cohabiting heterosexuals share those 'family values' and expect their unions to be regarded as 'marriage-like' although they do not wish to affirm their personal commitment to each other in a public ceremony. Although many gay and lesbian couples of the type described earlier would be offended to have their relationship defined as 'marital' (and therefore each partner as 'committed'), the 'marriage-like' cohabitees are likely to welcome such a title as external acknowledgement of their committed partnership. The real offence lies in our assuming commonality where there may be little or none: therapists (and sociologists) who do so run the risk of misunderstanding the nature of a particular couple's relationship.

However, the shift from marriage to couples raises interesting questions. Is this change made simply in order to be able to embrace all dyadic variations under one familiar heading, or are we perhaps engaged in a fundamental challenge to hitherto accepted definitions? While the use of the term 'couple' to denote marriage and marriage-like relationships at one level indicates nothing beyond the diminishing relevance of legal status, at another level it would seem to assume that a wide range of cohabiting relationships can be 'just like marriage', thereby implying a false continuity, and disregarding all other aspects of change. However, Schröder considers that the commonalities between dyadic relationships far outweigh any differentiating features (as, say, minorty status for gay couples), a 'fact which is acknowledged in the practice of most agencies offering help to couples' (Schröder 1989).

Definitions must always be considered in relation to social change; when any people behave differently from the social norm we regard them as being in some way different, but when increasing numbers of people start to behave in a new and different way, we begin to reconsider our definitions of their behaviour. In the 1950s and 1960s, when divorce was much less common, homosexuality illegal and cohabitation regarded as either the predicament of an unfortunate minority who were unable to marry or simply bohemian, everyone who could not be positioned in a normal family was considered deviant. And any troubles experienced by individuals from these 'deviant' relationships were regarded as cause and effect of their deviance.

However this interpretation, which had been fired by high moral indignation from those concerned about what they considered was the decaying nature of family life, began to be challenged in the early 1960s. Fletcher's *The Family and Marriage in Britain*, published in 1966, was the forerunner of the later spate of accounts of the changing face of family life and it held an influential position as a standard textbook for over a decade. The book was written as an argument against what he considered was 'the prevailing current of gloom and moral denigration' (Fletcher 1966: 239). For Fletcher and other reassuring optimists who followed him, 'a relatively high divorce rate may be indicative not of *lower*, but of *higher*, standards of marriage in society' (Fletcher 1966: 213).

This reassurance was gradually extended from the family to cohabitation, both heterosexual and same sex. Possibly as an antidote to the moral disapprobation of some earlier commentators, great emphasis was placed on the *advantages* of a pluralistic family scene. The freedom couples now had to choose whether or not to marry, and whether to remain married, was regarded as part of the spirit of individualism which characterized modern western society in the late twentieth century. According to Clark and Haldane, 'it is a position which appears to have had a major influence upon policy makers, as well as on practitioners of marital counselling and therapy' (Clark and Haldane 1990: 20).

Paradoxically a pluralist view of marriage may actually obscure rather than emphasize difference. When an attempt is made to accord equal consideration to different life-styles, a range of alternatives to marriage may all be assumed to be fundamentally no different from it. But to assume this would simply maintain a 'marital' focus. So rather than assume what may turn out to be a false commonality between all couple relationships, it seems preferable to discover those features which even very different couples may hold in common. As an approach to this, it is necessary to review trends in marriage and family life in the 1960s, 1970s and 1980s.

## Recent trends in marriage and family life

Ironically the change in family life with which we are most familiar is that of divorce – the frequently quoted fact that one in three marriages now end in divorce must be the best-known statistic in Britain; it hangs powerfully over our deliberations on contemporary personal relationships, and prefaces a great many articles in the press about families.[2] We live in a divorcing society; indeed England and Wales (with Denmark) are at the top of the league of divorcing nations in the European Community (EC). The divorce rate in Scotland is lower, and lower still in Northern Ireland. Although between 1960 and 1980 the rate of divorce increased fivefold, in the 1980s it has remained fairly constant. As divorce has become more common, so there has been a trend to divorce at an earlier stage of the marriage – over one-third of divorces occur in the first six years. The majority of divorces (60 per cent) involve a child under the age of 16; after the divorce nine out of ten children will live with their mothers. Youthful marriages, where the bride is under 21, are at highest risk; there is also a clear relationship between social class and divorce – 1970 figures for England and Wales show a rate of divorce of seven per thousand in the professional class compared with thirty per thousand among unskilled manual workers (Haskey 1984). Pregnant brides have also been found to be more divorce-prone although the strong association between age at marriage and pre-marital pregnancy makes it difficult to disentangle the effect of age and pregnancy. Analysis of the experiences of women born in 1946 suggests that early childbearing may be a more important predisposing factor to marital breakdown than teenage marriage *per se* (Kiernan 1983).

A variety of explanations for the increasing frequency of divorce have been offered: men, and especially women, have higher expectations of marriage, and expect more personal fulfilment from it than previous generations of husbands and wives; there is easier divorce – successive laws have made divorce more available to those whose marriages have broken down (especially to the less well-off, and to women: more married women are economically active and therefore capable of supporting themselves); and with increased longevity, today's newly-weds, if they stay wed, are likely to celebrate their fiftieth wedding anniversary, whereas in the middle of the nineteenth century the average man or woman could not expect to celebrate their fiftieth *birthday*. The list could be longer – and every proposed explanation can be challenged. Are people today less happy in marriage than previous generations were, or is it that the level of marital unhappiness is more visible because the freedom to escape marriage has increased?

Up until the late 1970s the concern over high levels of divorce was reduced by the apparent popularity of marriage. As long as people continued to get married – and remarry – there was hope that all was well with marriage; after all, divorce allows people to start all over again and about one in three marriages is a remarriage for one of the partners. However, throughout the 1980s we have witnessed a fall in marriage rates. The average age at first marriage was 22 for brides in 1970; in 1988 it was 25. There are several reasons for this. First, the 1960s were the golden age of marriage, with a trend towards earlier marriage and young people marrying over a narrower age range. This rush to marriage of the 1960s contradicts the popular image of the 'swinging sixties' as a period characterized by individual choice – the legalization of homosexuality and abortion, and the liberalization of divorce laws. By 1972 one in three brides marrying for the first time was a teenager. Clark and Haldane comment on the paradox 'that rebellious youth should have sought out the institution of marriage so assiduously' (1990: 16). Our own study of first marriage shows the persistence of young marriage as a *rite de passage*, a way of becoming an adult. The story of the 1960s was probably more about young men and women born in the post-war baby bulge, wanting to have the symbols of adulthood as soon as they could, rather than any mass rejection of traditional values.

Relative to former generations, today's young people are delaying marriage; since the early 1970s the proportion of teenage brides has fallen dramatically from one in three in 1974 to one in nine in 1988. Again, there are a variety of explanations for this delay. For some, there is the facility to avoid marriage. For example a single pregnant woman may now choose to terminate the pregnancy or to become a single mother rather than risk a hasty marriage. The economic recession in the late 1970s presented a much more bleak climate in which to marry and settle down as compared with the expanding economy of the 1960s; several studies show that some young people at that time did not feel able to marry (Mansfield 1985).

There is a wariness about marriage today; marriage is being reappraised in the shadow of divorce. Over half of the couples who married for the first time in 1987 had cohabited before the wedding; cohabitation can now therefore be considered the norm. So far wariness about marriage does not amount to a total rejection of it, since most people marry eventually and most childbearing still takes place within the framework of marriage. However, an increasing number of children are being born outside marriage (a quarter of all live babies are now born outside marriage) and just over one half of those births are jointly registered by the non-married parents, implying some degree of commitment in these relationships. It is predicted that if present trends continue, as many as one in two children may be born outside marriage in the year 2000.[3] This is the kaleidoscope of change within which we have to consider couples.

## Ways of understanding marriage . . . and couples

The classic sociological preoccupation has been the tension between the individual and the group. There are several ways in which sociological theory has tried to relate the personal/interpersonal to the social/structural. This relationship has been variously expressed: between public and private, society and the individual, macro and micro, the institutional and the personal. We shall describe three perspectives: functionalist, conflict and interactionist.

### The functionalist perspective

In order to understand the foundations of the sociology of the family, it is necessary to look first at the traditional version of functionalism, which has played a leading historical role.[4]

The sociology of family, kinship and socialisation has been the bastion of functionalism, framing its analysis against an idea system in which men, women and children all fit nicely in their places.

(Collins 1975: 225)

The kind of sociological analysis which can loosely be termed functionalist, with its emphasis upon the structure of society and the roles individuals play within it, was at the centre of the sociological models of the family emanating from the USA in the 1950s. Within the functionalist perspective, attention is directed to the macro-social context rather than to the interaction between individuals. Emphasis is placed on the functions which marriage fulfils, both for the married couple and for society; it creates stable structures in which children are legitimized and socialized and in which the physical and mental health of the adults can be optimized. All this is achieved through the adoption of marital roles: that is to say, a range of behavioural expectations (roles) related to gender which is relatively fixed; the man has the instrumental role of provider – the anchor of the family in the outside world – while the woman, through the expressive role of housewife, is the anchor of the family within the home. Such roles arise from the institution of marriage itself, which

sets up standards and practices that let people fall neatly into niches giving them roles and rules of conduct.

(Blumstein and Schwarz 1983: 18–19)

This approach prevailed until critiques of it (most notably feminist) appeared in the 1970s: the functionalist models 'originating in the 1950s became the received wisdom in the textbooks of the 1960s, and then in the 1970s served as objects for rebuttal in the critical temper of the time' (Goldthorpe 1987: 56)

The reason why functionalism held sway for so long is related to the fact that the institutions of marriage and the family have historically been inextricably bound to basic biological processes which made these appear natural, inevitable and necessary. However, over the last two decades all manner of changes – social, economic, cultural, technological and ideological, in varying combinations – have challenged the prevailing model. And it gradually became evident that the constraints imposed by functionalism in terms of the set roles and rigid social norms showed it to be an inadequate theory to cover the changes that have taken place in family life. Research findings began to confirm what many already believed: there was considerably more variation in men's and women's perceptions and interpretations of their family roles than the functionalist perspective had ever allowed. And, although attempts were made to incorporate into it some degree of flexibility in terms of the individual re-working family roles, functionalism remains too rigid to be of contemporary use as a paradigm for understanding the complex and often ambiguous processes involved in family life today.

## Conflict perspectives

In themselves theories are in no way eternal verities: they are simply ways of trying to understand society and make sense of the process of living. New theories are generated and existing ones rediscovered in accordance with their suitability for understanding society at different moments in time. Among challenges to the functionalist perspective were the feminist critiques which demanded a way of looking at marriage which would emphasize the inequalities between husbands and wives.

Traditional functionalism is an approach which lays stress on consensus and stability but the second major perspective is in direct opposition to this, since it is founded upon conflict and change.[5] Although there are several different strands within this second approach, they are all based on the same three fundamental concepts: conflict, bargaining and power. In one version of the conflict perspective, marriage is regarded as primarily an *economic* relationship and is viewed as a micro-version of the macro-structural inequality between men and women. The historical dependence of wives upon husbands in marriage, which both creates and sustains women's relative powerlessness in a man's world, is an illustration of this. However, an economic model of man as an individual intent upon retaining as many economic resources as possible is an over-rational one; no account is taken of personal resources, and similarly the costs and benefits in the marital bargaining process are given an objective rather than a subjective value.

Another form of the conflict approach rests on the premise that, since marriage is a relationship of partners who have different and contradictory values, conflict is inevitable; the relationship between the spouses is therefore bound to consist of the avoidance, regulation and resolution of conflict through constant negotiation and bargaining. The partner with most power, that is the one who has greater access to and control over resources, is the one who will hold control in the relationship. Such an approach can be very useful when looking at a couple since it draws our attention to a tension which is always present. All couples consist of two individuals who come from different pasts, who experience the present differently, and who are both therefore making different assumptions about the future. And since all these differences are inextricably linked to their places in society, this can give a further twist to the tension. However, valuable though this approach is, it fails to take into account the co-operation, mutuality and common purpose which, though not neccessarily consistently achieved, are nevertheless present in the relationship of any couple in addition to the tension and conflict. Marriage, like all other close personal relationships, is in a constant state of flux, and the participants perpetually move in and out of conflict, negotiation and agreement. It is of course the case that certain moments in married life may be outstandingly clear as being in one or other dimension, but for most of the time, differences are coexisting rather than being resolved. As soon as one issue has been successfully negotiated, something in the overall situation changes, so that the couple relationship can never be in a state of stasis.

### An interactionist approach

A third important perspective, and one which we would see as seminal to our own work, is the interactionist approach. Fundamental to this perspective are the beliefs that the understanding of any aspect of human behaviour requires knowledge of the definitions and interpretations of the situation by those personally

involved, the recognition that change is continual, and that the state of continual
flux is accompanied by a constant challenge to redefine and reinterpret:

> To a certain extent, sufficient for any practical purposes, I understand their
> (fellow men's) behaviour if I understand their motives, goals, choices and
> plans originating in their biographically determined circumstances.
>
> (Schutz 1962: 496)

In an era of rapid change in family life it is particularly important to discover
how people define and interpret their existence as a couple. The vital statistics
of family life – divorce rates, marriage rates, and cohabitation – tell us nothing
about why people behave as they do or what goals they are seeking to achieve
in their lives.

Looking at how couples construct their lives will help us to make sense of the
changes which are challenging the prevailing paradigm of marriage and the
family. To accept the importance of human agency does not mean that men and
women are able to construct their lives free from constraint. If that were so, as
social researchers we would be mere chroniclers of our times. It is true we collect
other people's narratives, but we then relate those narratives to a range of public
images, definitions and beliefs. Individually created meanings are often shared,
and may indeed have been shaped, by similar experiences, similar pasts and
similar plans for the future.

The interactionist approach, although broad, takes as its starting-point the
view of the individual, and holds that by getting close to that experience we can,
in cognitive and evaluative terms, began to understand how the individual makes
sense of it. The focus therefore is the world of individuals, the sense they make
of it, the definitions they use and the ways in which these are shared. And this
in turn leads to an exploration of how these individuals, when partners, create
between them the world of the 'couple'. The interactionist perspective does not
perceive partners as fitting into 'ordained' roles but instead, looks at them in their
everyday lives as they continually create and recreate their *own* roles and identities
for themselves, and through each other.

### Marriage and the social construction of reality

We cannot consider the interactionist perspective and marriage without reference
to a seminal essay on 'Marriage and the construction of reality' by Peter Berger
and Hans Kellner, which was published in 1964; in it they argue that the
individual validates his or her personal identity through relationships with others,
and that marriage creates for the individual a 'sort of order in which he can
experience his life as making sense'. Getting married is described as a transition
in which 'two strangers come together and redefine themselves'. It is through
their conversation that the partners form a new understanding of the world, which
in turn results in a sharing of future horizons, thus stabilizing for both of them
their sense of 'who they are'. This essay has been tremendously influential. It
was a starting-point for many researchers who were trying to find fresh ways of
looking at marriage in the mid-1960s. From our own point of view, Berger and
Kellner identified four aspects of marriage which we found of critical importance

when formulating our research: the nature of transition; the concept of a relationship in process; the ways in which individuals make sense of present experience
with respect to their past lives; and the assumptions they hold about the future
(Berger and Kellner 1964).

However, the widespread influence of Berger and Kellner has generated some
subsequent criticism. It has been argued that their position fails to recognize 'the
effects which macro-structures have on everyday life, and more specifically, the
ways in which structural factors determine how the expectations and experiences
of men and women will differ in marriage' (Burgoyne and Clark 1984: 10). Additionally Berger and Kellner's portrayal of marriage has been accused of not standing up to empirical scrutiny. In the essay they present a view of marriage which
is male-centred, middle-class, and one oblivious to the dilemma (experienced by
either or both spouses) of finding and maintaining a balance between the constraints on individual freedom imposed by marriage, and the continuing pursuit
of freedom in order to enhance personal identity (Mansfield and Collard 1988;
Askham 1984).

### Marriage: the beginning of the rest of your life?

Perhaps we can best illustrate the interactionist approach from our own research.
In 1979 we initiated an exploratory study of the beginning phase of marriage;
sixty-five young newly-wed couples who had been married for three months were
interviewed in depth about their experiences and reactions, husbands and wives
being interviewed separately and simultaneously (Mansfield and Collard 1988).

A great many previous studies which looked at marriage had been preoccupied
with fixed marital roles; the man as husband, the woman as wife, were investigated in a variety of situations and contexts and at different points of time in their
married lives. Such a research approach seemed to us to be rigid and role-bound,
which we considered too limiting, and we wanted to move beyond this. Our concern was to try to understand why individuals chose to get married, how the transition from being single to being married was experienced, and how each spouse
defined married life. We wanted to be able to link all this to other aspects of their
individual and joint lives, and in turn relate it to their particular cultural and
temporal context. We were also seeking a way of incorporating into our study
the processes through which men and women perceive and construct their lives
as partners. Above all, we were looking for an approach in which the flux, uncertainty and change endemic in all relationships, which in our view is central to
the understanding of human behaviour, could be better explored. We were
therefore greatly drawn to a perspective based on the premise that individuals
largely create their own lives, and make choices such as that to get married, *because
it makes sense to them to do so.*

At a time of rapid change, which both surrounds marriage and is found within
marriage itself, it is essential to discover how those who marry (and couples who
do not) define and interpret their existence as married people and as couple partners. In order to study this effectively, we believed it was necessary for some
research to focus, *not* on marital problems and difficulties, but on 'unremarkable
people doing unremarkable things', while recognizing that in the normal course

of everyday living, conflicts and crises are of course at times bound to occur.

The very familiarity of ordinary domestic life can, however, present problems when anyone sets out to scrutinize it. It is easy to overlook or ignore completely clues which may be vital for an understanding of the couple. When, in a research interview or elsewhere, married people recount the mundane routine activities that make up so much of their daily lives together, they frequently seek confirmation that their 'verbal shorthand' is understood: 'You know what I mean?' And indeed, as researchers or therapists we are often tempted to acquiesce as affirmation and as a sign of our understanding. We often believe we *are* familiar with the meaning of what has been said – and this indeed may be the case. But, by so doing, we may at times prevent the discovery of subtle explanations and nuances. On occasion, it can be very helpful for the researcher to become 'anthropologically strange'; that is deliberately to stand back and ask the seemingly obvious question, or probe further in a way that suggests there are no shared assumptions between the respondent and us. To do this can highlight some of the accepted ambiguities of living as a couple, and can help to illuminate the interface between the social and the personal by revealing more about the social material with which people construct their lives as couples.

Some interpretations of the interactionist perspective have been criticized for stressing relational aspects at the expense of the structural. With this in mind, we were interested to find that the accounts the newly-weds gave us, both of their day-to-day lives and their plans for the future, showed clearly the strong influence that social and economic structures can impose, not only in the way their external worlds were affected, but also by the way these worlds shaped the private relationships between these husbands and wives. We found an example of this when we asked all men and women with jobs the question: 'Do you think there will ever be a time when you cease work for a while?' Although all women answered in terms of the possibility of childbirth/child-care, the majority of men seemed at a loss to understand what the question could mean, and hazarded replies related to their work: 'You mean when I retire?' 'If I get the sack?' 'Perhaps – if I'm made redundant?'

Some men, however, used it as an opportunity to reflect on the economic and social pressures they felt under to remain in work, even at times when they themselves might have preferred to give it up for a period. These men described how their awareness of the financial bread-winning importance of their job conflicted with their wish to share with their partner (or even, in one or two cases, take over) all family responsibilities, including child-care. Some men criticized the social expectations which they believed constrained any possibility of their becoming the 'modern' fathers they ideally wished to be, and felt undermined by the social pressures which prevented them from achieving this full participation in a sharing partnership.

However, although it is evident that for most contemporary couples 'sharing' is a crucial concept and a basic tenet for future life together, this is not easy to achieve and maintain in a social climate of continual change:

> we are people in process . . . an age of transition . . . there is turmoil ahead
> as we struggle . . . to bring our relationships into a better balance of those

things which have only recently become so dear to us: intimacy, companionship, sharing, communication, equality. For the old ways of being die
hard.

(Rubin 1983: 215)

In our research on young married couples we found that there was a common
assumption that modern marriage, and therefore their own marriages, all should
conform to a sharing model, and they tried hard to achieve this. Yet however
much partners may feel they have 'become one' the story of any couple is always
the tale of two people; although they speak of the same everyday life, there will
always be two separate accounts. The experiential reality of the same events may
well be very different for each partner, and may often run counter to the ideology
of 'togetherness' which many couples take for granted in their mutual understanding. Because this sharing of everyday reality forms, for many people, such
a basic part of 'being a couple', it may at times obscure or distort the multiple
realities of the life a couple lead. It is therefore particularly important for
researchers to try to differentiate between the smooth ideal of togetherness which
individuals strive for, and the often ragged and disjointed experiences of their
daily encounter.

'Togetherness', however, was a word which the newly-weds repeatedly returned
to; it seemed to embrace their understanding of what couple relationships should
be – and, in their eyes – were all about. The word appeared to encapsulate for
them all that they found rewarding and satisfying in married life. However, when
we compared each partner's accounts of physical and psychological intimacy, it
was clear that men and women interpreted togetherness very differently. The
majority of the men sought a 'life in common' with their wives: they wanted a
home life, a physical and psychological base, somewhere and someone to set out
from and return to each day. In contrast, almost all the wives described the marriage they wished for as a 'common life', shared with an empathic partner who
was able to provide both material and emotional security. Women wanted a close
exchange of intimacy which would make them feel valued, so that their husbands
would view them not simply as a wife, but as a person in their own right.

## Contemporary couples: new approaches

### *Deconstructing marriage?*

In the last section we reviewed and commented on some very different ways of
looking at and understanding marriage and couples. We want now to return to
the themes of 'definitions' and 'trends in family life', which we introduced earlier.
In particular, we want to examine the flow and interrelationship between the two,
since they can show us the continuities and interactions between individual
experience and the broader context of social structure. We can then see the
strategies and constraints that family members adopt and are subject to in their
dealings with the social structure, and also the ways in which they create or
elaborate personal styles of family living in response to these.

The changes that are currently taking place in family life can be regarded in alternative ways: they can be seen as revealing the *breakdown* of traditional marriage, and viewed rather pejoratively; or they can be considered as evidence of the *dismantling* of the old style, a necessary activity before a reconstruction can be commenced – a more positive point of view. 'Once upon a time' there was *The Family*, composed of a male and a female and their children. The male and female had legally contracted to stay together for the rest of their lives, to be sexually exclusive, and to support each other as spouses and parents by means of their respective roles of bread-winner and home-maker. At first, anyone who departed from this model was considered deviant or abnormal. Later, such 'deviants' were regarded as individuals who were leading a different life-style. Gradually as the number of people living these alternative life-styles multiplied, the situation reversed and it was the norms that were under question, or even rejected by some. The reasons for rejection were evaluated: the traditional model of marriage no longer suited contemporary life; it was a model founded on inequality and therefore did not reflect the ideological challenge made to patriarchy by feminism; it was a model of exclusive heterosexual relations with no place for homosexual relationships; it was an ethnocentric model.

Many of the traditional 'givens' of family life are challenged by recent trends. For some, the present high levels of divorce suggest that *permanence* is now far less reliable, and therefore of diminishing significance as a definition of formal marriage. Others point out that, despite this, the *ideal* of permanence still remains strong and that the current high rates of remarriage bear witness to this. Sexual *exclusivity* is regarded in the same way as permanence, valued as an ideal, yet frequently disregarded in practice. One wonders how great the gap between reality and an ideal have to become before an ideal becomes virtually meaningless.

The legal status of marriage is also in question, and may never become irrelevant if the law subsumes cohabitation into marriage. The Local Government Finance Act 1988 (which created the Community Charge or Poll Tax) in its definitions of marriage surprisingly includes 'not being married'. In Section 16 (9) the Act states

> people are married to each other if they are a man and a woman (a) who are married to each other and are members of the same household or (b) who are not married to each other but are living as husband and wife.

However, despite the apparent contradiction of this, in practice all that it amounts to is a redefinition by inclusion. This being so, if we can clear our minds and look afresh at the partnerships people are currently creating in practice (albeit within the social constraints and traditions that still pertain), we may be able to begin to build up some new concepts and definitions which more accurately reflect the present evolving reality.

We noted earlier the dilemmas that confront us as soon as we attempt to define couples. In the past the term 'marital' has often been used to include, in one definition, a wide variety of couples for whom the only common element was that of commitment to each other. Implicitly to make such a grouping was evidence of a failure to appreciate the real and vital differences that may have existed between them.

Part of the difficulty lies in the fact that, up until now, our construct of marriage has been composed of all-or-nothing elements. Despite the evidence of widespread impermanence and infidelity, we still continue to regard marriage as a partnership of permanence and exclusivity, because these are still publicly declared as absolutes: 'till death us do part, for richer for poorer, in sickness and in health'.

A couple who are not legally married, however, have no such absolutes; increasingly, in practice, married couples also may decide to disregard them, as the incidence of divorce and the evidence of extramarital affairs testify. The old construction no longer holds and is, both in ideology and in practice, being dismantled. We therefore have to search for ways to explore and record some of the attempts couples are making to construct their new partnerships.

We believe the interactionist perspective can provide such a framework within which it is possible to develop a way for understanding the partnership of contemporary couples, since it allows both for *deconstruction* – the taking apart of the process of becoming or being a couple – and it can at the same time provide for the *reconstruction* of definitions and processes.

### Commitment and interdependence

There has of late been a growing interdisciplinary approach to the study of adult relationships, with the aim of distinguishing some general features. The study of personal relationships has so far been dominated by psychology, although it seems that marriage and family have been left to one side rather than subsumed under the rubric of close relationships (Duck and Perlman 1985). Scanzoni and colleagues (1989) have tried to argue for a 'higher order construct known as the sexually bonded close relationship' and in their book *The Sexual Bond* address many of the issues in an attempt to come up with a fresh way of looking at the contemporary scene. They contend that the dimensions once so taken for granted 'as givens', are now accepted as variables, which need to be considered anew when trying to understand 'sexually bonded close relationships'.

There are two features which have always been regarded as fundamental to the issues of becoming and remaining a couple: *commitment* and *interdependence*. Interdependence is a difficult concept to define, but we have found Kelley's definition helpful:

> Two or more persons exercising mutually contingent influence over one another through exchanging valued rewards (and costs) to the extent that persons can be said to be interdependent.
>
> (Kelley *et al.* 1983)

And Brickman gives a useful definition of commitment:

> A force that stabilizes individual behavior under circumstances where the individual would otherwise be tempted to change that behavior.
>
> (Brickman 1987: 2)

However, commitment in his view is not fixed, but is seen as 'something that grows and changes over time'.

Interdependence also may wax and wane, but if two people are to be defined as 'a couple' there needs to be a level of interdependence on at least some of the following dimensions – sexual, economic, emotional, practical and social. To discover more about this, it is necessary to look closely at the couple: do they have a sexual relationship, do they share a household, are they emotionally attached, do they present themselves to others as a couple?

In marriage, it can be argued that interdependence arises out of commitment, although we know that modern courtship may involve varying levels of interdependence in the period before any explicit commitment. In fact pre-marital cohabitation can be said to be the final part of the courtship process. The relationship between commitment and interdependence is most likely to be one where the two are in constant interplay. Just as levels of interdependence will vary at any given time so we should expect the degree of commitment between a couple to fluctuate.

Bernard sums this up neatly in her reference to degrees of being married:

> It seems to me not at all unthinkable that we may one day arrive at the idea not of an all-or-nothing marital status, an either-or-one, but one of degrees of being married. 'How committed are you?' we may ask rather than merely 'What is your marital status?'
>
> (Bernard 1976: 101–2)

## The relationship as a 'project'

One way in which the level of interdependence and degree of commitment in a couple can be examined is in terms of 'the project'. Here the focus is on the partnership, the way in which each partner has to rely on the co-operation of the other in order to realize his or her own future plans.

We first came across this approach when we were trying to clarify our thinking about the importance of the effect of the future on an individual's present choices and actions. For the newly-weds whom we interviewed, settling the future had been a significant motive for getting married. They spoke of wishing to limit their choices and the binding commitment of marriage was regarded as an attraction: marriage provided the framework for creating the rest of their lives. Berger and Kellner (1964) refer to the 'narrowing of future projection of each partner' as helpful in gaining a sense of personal identity. Though as Askham (1984) shows in her study, the pursuit of personal identity may conflict with the search for stability and security within marriage.

Berger and Kellner describe how the rest of life can be perceived as a designed project, with decisions seen as 'a means to an end in terms of the overall life-plan':

> The design includes identity. In other words, in long-range life planning the individual not only plans what he will do but also plans who he will be. In the case of the individuals who are of great personal importance to each other, these projects overlap, both in terms of planned careers and planned identities. One individual is part of another's project and vice versa.
>
> (Berger and Kellner 1964: )

Morgan also has explored interrelationships within families in terms of projects: he takes the concept from Sartre (1957) and discusses the overlapping of projects 'in order to realize my project I need others who are themselves attempting to realize their projects through or with me' (Morgan 1975: 216)

The projects undertaken by the newly-weds were on the whole predictable: husband's career, creating a home, having a family. However, although projects may be shared, this can be either because the project of each partner overlaps, or because the project of one partner takes precedence. The importance of considering projects in this way can allow us to gain insight into the variety of ways in which couples are independent and committed.

### Institution or relationship?

The notion of institution in opposition to relationship can be found across a wide range of writing on marriage and close relationships. In recent years the emphasis has shifted from institution to that of relationship, a change strikingly exemplified in the change of name of the *National Marriage Guidance Council*, relaunched in 1988 as *Relate*.

Some argue that the move away from marriage as an institution has been too total. Green considers the concentration on marriage as a means of personal fulfilment has been overly exclusive, so that

> Marriage as a practical social enterprise seems an almost forgotten topic, so involved have we become in 'relationships'. . . . Is the future likely to be a return to a far more practical and down-to-earth institution with a new balance of roles but more related to the way in which marriage was seen in previous times?
>
> (Green 1984: 302–3)

The apparent shift towards relationship is frequently regarded as simply a rejection of the institution, based on the interpretation of institution as a combination of the formal conscriptions of state, church, and of course law. Such an interpretation is neatly summed up by Scruton:

> persons entering marriage . . . pass together into a condition that is not of their own devising. . . . The obligations are not contracted between the partners but imposed by the institution.
>
> (Scruton 1986: 356)

Additionally it is a rejection of the model of marriage as essentially the performance of roles, of having obligations, duties and correlative rights, all of which have been carefully defined. But, as men and women became increasingly eager to carve out their own individual roles, so the idea of marriage as a social institution came under fire.

It comes as no surprise that when writers on the family talk about the institution of marriage they usually do so in a way that creates a sharp division between the social and the personal, with the institution of marriage presented as some fixed entity which lies outside (or even above) us all. The implication drawn from rising divorce and increasing cohabitation is that the institution (the social) has been rejected in favour of the personal.

However, there are other definitions of institution that recognize the dependence of institutions on human agency. Giddens, for example, rejects the notion that institutions are above us all, by arguing that an institution can exist only if people attach legitimacy to its prescriptions and proscriptions:

> by institutions I mean structured social practices that have broad spatial and temporal extension . . . and which are followed or acknowledged by the majority of members of a society.
>
> (Giddens 1981: 164)

Cultural patterns may persist, but over time they may change; institutions are not handed down as tablets of stone from on high but are created by people who both conform to them and in turn change them.

### A need for social recognition?

The past two decades have commonly been portrayed as the 'me' decades, with great emphasis on the individual. Individualism has been described in terms of 'permanent availability' (Fahrer 1964) and so the degree of individualism significantly influences (both consciously and unconsciously) a person's sense of commitment. The tension in modern couples between their individual identity, and 'being together', has attracted much analysis and has become a central concern for those helping couples in trouble.[6]

However, in putting the major focus on people's individual personal meanings, and their inner worlds, we may be neglecting not only the importance of their interface with the social, but also the possibility that the social recognition of a couple may actually assist them in preserving their identity, at the same time as it is helping them to be become interdependent with, and committed to, each other.

Corbin (1978) makes some useful distinctions when she reviews the declining importance of the institution of marriage:

> Marriage must decline in importance as kinship and the 'social' work required of kinship diminish. Firstly by taking kinship in its strictest sense, to the extent that restrictions on sex and marriage in terms of relatedness disappear so should marriage. Once anyone can marry anyone else, there is no reason to marry at all.
>
> (Corbin 1978: 207)

However, when she considers the future she sees that the deconstruction of marriage will in fact amount to a reconstruction:

> I think people will probably continue to get married for some time to come but also that 'marriage' will gradually imply something quite different. Having no major implications for affinal relations, for descent, for future marriages, for the transmission of social identity from one generation to another, it will be primarily a public affirmation of the couple's identity

and fortification of the fact that two people are a couple. Though not marriage in a kinship sense, it will by no means be meaningless. The state may continue to use it as a legal contract to regulate the claims of one spouse to the property of the other and to decide the priorities of other claimants including children. At a less legal level, it will be a public affirmation of the couple's identity.

(Corbin 1978: 208)

Couples who are outside the present legal status – in particular homosexual couples – frequently find that their personal sense of being a couple is insufficient for them. As Plummer (1978) shows, living as part of a couple without social recognition requires continual conscious construction:

For many heterosexuals liaisons may be routine not rapture, but homosexuals who are challenged at every point must often give fuller consideration to what they are doing. They have to think about their relationships with the community, to work out a relationship with their families, to consider carefully the roles they will play. None of these can be taken for granted, the meanings and rules which govern their relationships must be consciously constructed.

(Plummer 1978: 195)

In 1989 Denmark introduced registered partnerships for homosexual couples;[7] this may be a version of the public affirmation of a couples identity to which Corbin refers.


## Some implications for therapy

The lack of social recognition and fortification for any partnerships outside the law, whether heterosexual or homosexual, can constantly create difficulties for them. However, as we have shown, married couples also are finding the construction of their lives as couples difficult. As Kiely notes

In the field of marital counselling there is a tendency to explain marital problems as if all couples experiencing them were a single group . . . and to locate the problems predominantly, if not exclusively, in the personalities of the individuals who are married.

(Kiely 1984: 92)

Kiely relates this to his own experience of counselling couples:

A striking feature of many couples . . . was the seeming lack of personality disorder. These couples appeared emotionally healthy and mature even if at the time of referral they manifested symptoms of stress.

(Kiely 1984: 93)

He concluded that what we may be witnessing is the impact of social change on contemporary marriage. We can argue then, that part of the shift is from *marital problems* to *marriage as a problem*, and this can apply to all couples whether or not they are legally married. For we are in transition as a society, moving away from marriage in the sense of kinship and obligation, to another form of close relationship which is socially recognized and fortified. But the implication of all this, in terms of every couple's deconstruction and reconstruction of the traditional model of marriage for themselves, may prove for many to be very painful.

The lack of social support and legitimation may lead many couples not in marriage to seek reassurance from therapists. They may want to have their own reality confirmed by another, one who is in a position to locate them in the landscape of all couples. Of course some married couples may also seek help for similar reasons.

The conscious and unconscious construction to which Plummer (1978) refers when discussing homosexual couples holds true for many heterosexual couples who are not married; they may always feel that their relationship is at a point of formation, and that they cannot go on to 'automatic pilot' for even a short time. Since their sense of being a couple has to rely solely on everyday reality, the points at which that breaks down are pre-eminently far more threatening. Transitions which inevitably alter the levels of interdependence within the couple, such as one partner working away from home, may only affect and not totally destroy the partner's degree of commitment; however, outsiders may perceive this change as indicating potential or actual dissolution of the relationship.

The way in which reality has to be continually created is an endless process of deconstruction and reconstruction. Particular flexibility is required in the couple when there are no set roles on which to fall back. Any transition such as the birth of a child, the return to work, or a move to a new area, is bound to affect the nature and level of interdependence, and inevitably thereby, the associated degree of commitment. In an attempt to establish their security and stability, a couple may wish to view their interdependence as a fixed lattice, but the very rigidity of this perception may mean that their relationship is unable to accommodate external and internal change. In such a case the issue has to become the deconstruction of the present reality. However, although the wish for this may be presented to the therapist by one partner (or even both) as a plea for dissolution, which in one way of course it is, it is not necessarily a call to end the partnership. Instead, it may reveal the first awareness of the need and wish for reconstruction.

## Notes

1 *The Pink Paper*, Issue 100, 25 November 1989.
2 Unless otherwise stated all statistics quoted in this section are available from *Marriage and Divorce Statistics 1988, 1980, 1976*, Series FM2 of the Office of Population Censuses and Surveys, London: HMSO.
3 *Marriage and Partnership 1990*, Information Pack, London: ONE-plus-ONE, Marriage and Partnership Research.
4 For a full discussion of varieties of functionalism see Morgan (1975).
5 See J. Bernard (1964) The adjustments of married mates, in H. Chistensen (ed.) *Handbook of Marriage and the Family*, Chicago, SU: Rand McNally; C. Safilios–Rothschild (1976) A macro and micro–examination of family power and love: an exchange model,

*Journal of Marriage and the Family* 38, May: 355–62; J. Scanzoni and L. Scanzoni (1976) *Men, Women and Change: A Sociology of Marriage and the Family*, New York: McGraw-Hill.

6 See for example Askham (1976); Clulow and Mattinson (1989).

7 The Danish Registered Partnership Act, Act no 372 of 7 June 1989.

## References

Askham, J. (1984) *Identity and Stability in Marriage*, London: Cambridge University Press.

Berger, P. and Kellner, H. (1964) Marriage and the construction of reality, *Diogenes*, Summer. 49–72.

Berger, P. and Luckman, T. (1970) in H.P. Dreitzel (ed.) *Recent Sociology No 2: Patterns of Communicative Behaviour*, New York: Macmillan.

Bernard, J. (1976) *The Future of Marriage*, Harmondsworth: Penguin.

Blumstein, P. and Schwartz, P. (1983) *American Couples: Money, Work, Sex*, New York: William Morrow.

Brannen, J. and Collard, J. (1982) *Marriages in Trouble: The Process of Seeking Help*, London: Tavistock.

Brickman, P. (1987) *Commitment, Conflict and Caring*, Englewood Cliffs, NJ: Prentice-Hall.

Burgoyne, J. and Clark, D. (1984) *Making a Go of it*, London: Routledge & Kegan Paul.

Chester, R. (1985) Marriage in Britain: an overview of research. in W. Dryden (ed.) *Marital Therapy in Britain*, 2 vols, London: Harper & Row.

Clark, D, and Haldane, D. (1990) *Wedlocked*, Oxford: Polity Press.

Clulow, C. and Mattinson, J. (1989) *Marriage Inside Out*, Harmondsworth: Penguin.

Collins, R. (1975) *Conflict Sociology*, New York: Academic Press.

Corbin, M. (ed.) (1978) *The Couple*, Harmondsworth: Penguin.

Dominian, J. (1968) *Marital Breakdown*, Harmondsworth: Penguin.

Dryden, W. (ed.) (1985) *Marital Therapy in Britain*, 2 vols, London: Harper & Row.

Duck, S. and Perlman, D. (eds) (1985) *Understanding Personal Relationships: An Interdisciplinary Approach*, London: Sage.

Fletcher, R. (1966) *The Family and Marriage in Britain*, revised edn, Harmondsworth: Penguin.

Giddens, A. (1981) in K. Knorr-Certina and A.V. Cicourel (eds) *Advances in Social Theory and Methodology* London: Routledge & Kegan Paul.

Goldthorpe, J.E. (1987) *Family Life in Western Societies*, London: Cambridge University Press.

Green, M. (1984) *Marriage*, London: Fontana.

Haskey, J. (1984) Social class and socio-economic differentials in divorce in England and Wales, *Population Studies* 38: 419–39.

Kelley, H.H., Berscheid, E., Christenson, A., Harvey, J.H., Huston, T.L., Levinger, G., McClintock, E., Peplau, L.A., and Peterson, D.R. (eds) (1983) *Close Relationships: Perspectives on the Meaning of Intimacy*, New York: Freeman.

Kiely, G.M. (1984) Social change and marital problems: implications for marriage counselling, *British Journal of Guidance and Counselling* 12, 1: 92–100.

Kiernan, K.E. (1983) The structure of families today: continuity or change?, *OPCS Occasional Paper* 31.

Mansfield. P. (1985) Young people and marriage, *SMGC Occasional Paper* 1

Mansfield, P. and Collard, J. (1988) *The Beginning of the Rest of Your Life?*, London: Macmillan.

*Marriage Matters* (1979) A consultative document by the working party on marriage guidance, London: HMSO.

Morgan, D.H.J. (1975) *Social Theory and the Family*, London: Routledge & Kegan Paul.

—— (1985) *The Family, Politics and Social Theory*, London: Routledge & Kegan Paul.

Morgan, D.H.J. (1988) Two faces of the family: the possible contribution of sociology to family therapy, *Journal of Family Therapy* 10: 233–53.

Plummer, K. (1978) Homosexual Couples, in M. Corbin (ed.) *The Couple*, Harmondsworth: Penguin.

Rubin, L.B. (1983) *Intimate Strangers: Men and Women Together*, New York: Harper & Row.

Scanzoni, J., Polonko, K., Teachman, J. and Thompson, L. (1989) *The Sexual Bond*, London: Sage.

Schutz, A. (1962) in M. Natanson (ed.) *Alfred Schutz: Collected Papers*, vol. 1, The Hague: Martinus Nijholt.

Schröder, T. (1989) in W. Dryden, D. Charles-Edwards and R. Woolfe (eds) *Handbook of Counselling in Britain*, London: Tavistock/Routledge.

Scruton, R. (1986) *Sexual Desire: A Moral Philosophy of the Erotic*, New York: Free Press.

# 3

# Psychological foundations of couple relationships

BRIGID HULSON AND ROBIN RUSSELL

The marital relationship is perhaps the most important social and personal bond in the lives of many people. It is also frequently problematic. It is not surprising, therefore, to find that marriage is the subject of a huge number of books and articles (currently about 3,000 a year). Despite this considerable volume of 'research', the number of different theories of marriage which are widely accepted is surprisingly limited. Likewise, the number of general psychological findings which transcend the obvious is small.

During the late 1980s the influential *Journal of Marriage and the Family* contained a series of reviews looking back to the founding of the journal. In one of these reviews, Nye (1988) states

> As we look back over fifty years, we see that much has been done and much is being done. But as we look at current family conflict, divorce and dissolution, family stress, violence, and unmet personal and relationship needs, it appears that family problems are multiplying considerably faster than research and therapy can address them.
>
> (Nye 1988: 316)

In another review Broderick (1988) concludes 'although we have achieved a great deal in the intervening fifty years, many of the burning questions of the 1930s remain unanswered today' (1988: 569).

There are several reasons why we cannot claim to have a theoretical understanding of marriage based on reproducible evidence. One reason is that much empirical research has focused on sociological variables such as religion, social class, education and so on, perhaps because these are easier to assess than psychological qualities. A problem with this strand of research, however competently it is done, is that findings do not necessarily hold from one time period to another, or from one culture to another. For example the significance of religion alters with time; norms about relationships change, the employment of women alters their status radically.

Another reason for the unsettled state of theories about relationships is that psychological studies have largely been seen as the province of the therapist; academic psychologists have tended to avoid the study of this important field. However valuable the insights of the therapist may be, they do not readily lend themselves to the cumulation of generalizable principles. Of course, neither do endless empirical studies necessarily lead to an improvement in our basic understanding of relationships.

Nevertheless, some facts about relationships have become evident. To understand relationships, we must recognize that each has a beginning, a middle and an end. The proper study of the subject requires us to examine these phases separately. Accordingly we shall start by reviewing what is known about the process of choosing a mate, then proceed to examine processes in ongoing relationships, including those that play a part in the breakdown of relationships between two people.

Our intention in this chapter is to review and discuss some of the empirical literature on the psychological foundations of couple relationships. The reader should be aware that we are not deliberately ignoring forms of relationships other than marriages. The problem is that the overwhelming bulk of research on sexual relationships has been conducted on married couples. The only large-scale research of which we are aware which examines male and female homosexual relationships and heterosexual cohabiters on an equal basis with married couples is that of Blumstein and Schwartz (1983).

## Choosing a partner

While there are numerous theories about who chooses whom, in fact these theories fall into two categories: those which invoke the notion of similarity and those which invoke the notion of complementarity. Similarity theories lead to the expectation that couples will tend to resemble each other in at least one respect. Complementarity theories are more ambiguous, but suggest that a person with a particular attribute will gravitate towards someone else either because the other person lacks that attribute or because they possess a different attribute.

For example the principle of complementarity leads one to expect that dominant people will marry people who are submissive, or that people who need to nurture others will be attracted to those who are naturally dependent. Each person has needs which are fitted by or complemented by those of their partner. Similarity theory would predict that dominant people choose other dominant people as partners, and that submissive people choose submissive partners.

The extensive literature on this issue has been reviewed by several authors, including Thiessen and Gregg (1980), Epstein and Guttman (1985), and Tyler (1988). The conclusion to be drawn from the evidence is clear; relationships are based on similarity, not complementarity. In other words, dominant people do, in fact, tend to select dominant partners, just as submissive people choose other submissive people. The belief that opposites attract is generally not the case.

Perhaps we are like our partners because we are attracted to people who remind us of our parents, our siblings, or ourselves. Perhaps we tend to meet others who come from the same place as ourselves ('marrying the girl next door'). We may share attitudes with our partners because we met them at a political rally or in church, or share a world view because we are of the same generation. The explanations abound.

Data also show that couples tend to resemble each other in qualities like age, attractiveness, personality, IQ, education, socio-economic class, politics, religion, and social attitudes generally. However, couples also resemble each other in less fortunate qualities like a tendency to become alcoholic (Rimmer and Winokur 1972), schizophrenic (Kallman and Mickey 1946), or manic depressive (Baron *et al.* 1981). Couples tend to look alike. This is true of their faces (Hinsz 1989) and their bodies (D.F. Roberts 1977). It is also the case that couples tend to match on unobservable physiological characteristics like blood pressure (Suarez *et al.* 1983) or blood type (Rushton 1988). People even show a tendency to get together with other people whose names start with the same letter (Kopelman and Lang 1985)! At this point, let us dispose of one old wives' tale: the idea that couples grow alike. Several investigations into this possibility have shown that young couples resemble each other to the same degree as older couples. The only way in which couples increase in similarity over time is in obviously changeable habits such as alcohol consumption or amount of social activity (Price and Vandenberg 1980).

The weight of evidence points to the simple conclusion that, from the outset, individuals are positively attracted to others who are like them in very many ways. Whether people are aware of it or not, choice of partner is a matter of finding someone else sufficiently like yourself.

What happens to couples who are not particularly similar? A few studies have looked at the extent to which people in stable and unstable marriages exhibit personality similarities, as revealed by paper and pencil personality tests. These tests attempt to assess qualities such as shyness, dominance, nervousness and so on. Results reveal that happily married couples are more alike in these respects than the unhappily married (Cattell and Nesselroade 1967; Barton and Cattell 1972; Meyer and Pepper 1977; Richard *et al.* 1990). It seems, however, that personality is not the only attribute in which it may be important for couples to match on. Heaton (1984), for example, found greater marital satisfaction among couples who shared religious beliefs and practices. Relative attractiveness may also play a role. A review by Feingold (1988) suggests that courtship progress among dating couples is partly predicted by how well they match on physical attractiveness. A less obvious finding emerged in a study by Davidson *et al.* (1983) which looked at how much couples communicated their feelings to their partners. They found that discrepancies between partners in amount of self-disclosure were associated with less satisfactory marriages. From all this evidence it is fair to conclude that a good long-term relationship is founded upon compatibility based on similarity on a wide range of personal qualities.

## Ongoing relationships

When two people decide to settle down together on a long-term basis, they usually do so because they have very strong positive feelings for each other. Over time, these feelings may or may not change. Using data from a questionnaire by Russell and Wells (1986) on a sample of over 1,000 married couples throughout Britain, we find that, on average, mutual regard fades over the course of the marriage. But this average trend overlooks the fact that this happens only to some couples. Others continue to feel a powerful bond, the constituents of which will be examined later.

The 'honeymoon period' seems to last for about three or four years. In Britain, probability of divorce is virtually non-existent at first, it then peaks sharply in the fourth year, after which it slowly declines (Haskey 1982). Fisher (1987), in a paper called 'The four year itch', reviews evidence which suggests that this pattern obtains in many cultures. So why do some relationships stay happy while others deteriorate? The answer must be, in part, that some people choose more compatible mates than others. But a number of other influences impinge on the relationship later on. Let us look at some factors associated with stability.

As long ago as 1939, Burgess and Cottrell found that people's marital satisfaction was related to their occupation. In general, those whose work could be called middle class were more happily married. Gibson (1974) also found that the highest divorce rate in Britain occurred amongst shop assistants, clerical workers and unskilled workers. Many studies have found that, in general, more educated people also have better marital relationships than the less educated. There is one quite obvious interpretation of these findings: the greater the level of education and the more prestigious the occupation, so the greater the chance of a higher income. On the whole, the higher the income the more satisfactory the marriage (Cutright 1971). Low income may affect the marital relationship in a number of areas. There may be an increased likelihood of conflict over the allocation of money and the freedom with which any one individual may spend it (particularly if only one member of the couple is earning). In addition, the less the income the less the freedom there will be to socialize, go on holiday and so on. Couples on lower incomes, then, may be more vulnerable to stress and feel more restricted by their relationships.

On the other hand, it also appears to be important that partners are similar with respect to education, and particularly important that the woman is not more highly educated than the man. This is probably why highly educated women have trouble finding a suitable partner and are more likely to divorce than those with a little less education (Houseknecht and Spanier 1980). At the same time it may be that a more highly educated partner is perceived as a threat to the less educated individual, particularly when it is the woman who is more educated. Educationally discrepant marriages may also be less successful because, in the long term, intellectual needs are not met. Indeed, South and Spitze (1986) found that highly educated women were the most satisfied with their marriages to begin with, yet after a few years, these women were the least satisfied with their marriages.

Several studies have shown that those who marry young are more likely to divorce. Booth and Edwards (1985) attribute this fact to a lack of necessary skills in young people for dealing with a sustained intimate relationship. Sexual infidelity is also a particular problem for those marrying young. This suggests that lack of experience at the time of marriage may result in the feeling later on that they had not really been in the position to make an informed choice. In many different cultures, couples are generally close in age, usually with the man about three years older than the woman (Buss 1989). This makes intuitive sense. They come from the same generation, so share common experiences and are likely to face certain kinds of problems later in life together. However, relationships where one of the partners is relatively old while the other is young do not seem to suffer from a lack of these advantages. Despite conventional wisdom on this subject, Vera *et al.* (1985) found that age-discrepant marriages were just as satisfactory as those where the couple were closely matched.

## Children and marriage

The arrival of children generally causes a deterioration in the quality of the relationship. Argyle and Henderson (1985) combine the results of four studies which show that the presence of children lowers marital satisfaction. The effect is strongest when the children are adolescent presumably because it is usually a time when, among other things, conflict results from attempts to challenge and redefine the child–parent relationship. After the children leave home, the quality of the relationship returns to the high level of satisfaction present before their arrival, which is the same as that of couples who have no children. Belsky *et al.* (1985) have shown that the negative impact of children mainly affects the wife and does so within the first six months of the child's life. Sons may, in addition, have a more detrimental effect on relationships than girls (Abbott and Brody 1985), possibly because boys may make more demands than girls. Schumm and Bugaighis (1986) also found that poor mothers in full-time employment were affected far more than others. It would seem, therefore, that lack of money and time for child-care create especially stressful conditions.

Ruble *et al.* (1988) have presented a slightly different perspective on the impact of the arrival of children, indicating that the effect may be more indirect. They present findings which indicate that wives' negative feelings concerning some aspects of their relationship are connected with violated expectations about who does what at home. After the birth of their first child, women reported doing much more of the housework and child-care than they had expected. The presence of children obviously constitutes an extra strain on a couple. The birth of a child is a time when depression is likely to occur. The couple face a loss of freedom, extra responsibilities and more work. Most of the extra stress appears to fall on the woman. The effect of this may be that she blames her partner for the state of affairs. The outcome can often be a deterioration of their feelings for each other.

## Relationships after marriage

Remarriage is a fairly common occurrence among divorcees. The chances of divorcees remarrying are affected by factors such as the presence of children, age at divorce and social class. Haskey (1987) traced over 1,000 British couples who divorced in 1979 to see whether either or both partners remarried in the following two and a half years. Approximately one-third of both divorced husbands and wives remarried. In addition, about 40 per cent of those husbands and wives who remarried did so within the first three months after their divorce (presumably to the co-respondent!). Generally the older people are when they divorce the less likely they are to remarry early. Divorced husbands from the non-manual social classes are more likely to remarry within two and a half years of their divorce than those from the manual classes. Yet on the other hand, divorced wives from the non-manual classes are *less* likely to remarry. It is hard to resist the conclusion at this point, that only better-off men can afford a second wife, after paying out alimony, and that ex-wives of such husbands do not wish to lose out on substantial maintenance payments by marrying again.

McCarthy (1978) showed that remarriages are more likely to end in divorce than first marriages. They also end in divorce more quickly than do first marriages (Weed 1980). Why might this be so? A study of remarriages by White and Booth (1985) showed that the higher divorce rate of remarried couples was limited to relationships where both spouses had been previously married and there were stepchildren in the household. While remarriages could be just as happy as first marriages, husbands and wives with biological children (regardless of whether they were in a first marriage or a remarriage) reported more satisfaction with family life than those with stepchildren. Having stepchildren appeared to cause tensions for both the natural parent and the step-parent. The authors concluded, therefore, that the unstable nature of remarriages may result from the particular stresses arising from the presence of stepchildren and not from the quality of remarriages *per se* or because of the characteristics of individuals whose marriages had failed.

It is worth stressing that it should not be assumed that there is something inherently 'wrong' with people who have divorced. While it is true that their first marriage has broken down, this suggests a lack of compatability, rather than implying failure on the part of one or both partners. Their chances of successfully remarrying may be good. While therapists hardly need to be reminded of this, clients involved in divorce are likely to need reassurance on this point, as well as a number of others.

## Influence of the family of origin

The belief that events and relationships within the family of origin play a key role in influencing a person's ability to form and maintain intimate relationships is widely held. There is also some evidence to support it. In their classic study, Burgess and Cottrell (1939) found that marital satisfaction depends partly on position within the family. Oldest or middle children enjoy the most satisfying marriages while only children have the least satisfying marriages. Parental divorce may also affect development. Keith and Finlay (1988) showed that it led to lower educational attainment, less likelihood of marrying, earlier marriage, and a greater chance of divorcing. However, the route by which early family life may influence later marital quality was assessed more directly by Kotler and Omodei (1988) in a study of Australian couples. Their findings indicate that emotionally healthy parents produce children who get on well with all members of the family. As a result, they grow up to become emotionally healthy young adults. Their emotional health results in a satisfying start to their subsequent marriage. This relationship benefits their emotional health during marriage, leading to a satisfying marriage in the long term. So good relationships within the family of origin may have a beneficial effect in later life.

Physical attraction is frequently assumed to operate only early on in a relationship, fading away in significance as the couple mature. However, Peterson and Miller (1980) have found that attractiveness still has an impact on relationships among older couples. Our own work, using the Russell and Wells data, has revealed a great deal of idiosyncrasy in judgements of how attractive or unattractive a person is. This means that the outsider may consider individuals unattractive, while their partners find them very sexy. The questionnaire distinguished between people's judgement of how attractive they found their partner and how attractive they thought other people found their partner. Results showed that it was their own judgement of the attractiveness of their partner which made for a good relationship. If anything, other people finding their partner attractive was a drawback. So it is a person's private feelings that contribute positively to a relationship. What outsiders think is largely irrelevant.

The influence of personality, social attitudes, background, sexual attitudes and sexual behaviour on an individual's satisfaction with their relationship was investigated by Eysenck and Wakefield (1981) using a large sample of British couples. Marital satisfaction was found to be predicted best by factors relating to the sexual relationship, moderately by background and personality factors and minimally by social attitudes. Results of this study also indicated that couples selected each other for similar sexual and social attitudes prior to the marriage. That mate choice should be influenced by the extent to which couples share certain sexual attitudes and that factors relating to the sexual relationship should be a primary determinant of marital satisfaction is unlikely to surprise many therapists. Clearly the way the relationship works is barely distinguishable from sexual satisfaction. Indeed, Hawton (1985) cites marital discord as the most frequent single cause of sexual dysfunction. Moreover, certain sexual problems may also provide clues to other associated difficulties in the relationship such as the division or form of power (Crowe 1986).

Another factor which has been found to have a bearing on marriage is religion. For example Filsinger and Wilson (1984) found that, amongst a group of church-going Protestants, the more religious a couple were, the greater their degree of marital adjustment. It is not at all obvious that all religious beliefs have beneficial effects on marriage. In Britain many people are Muslim and their tradition imbues people with definite ideas about appropriate sex roles. Virtually nothing is known about the quality of the relationships they form. Research is urgently needed on this and other groups in the population, in order to inform therapeutic practice (see Chapter 10).

## Characteristics of couple relationships

Whether it is implicit or explicit, in every long-term relationship there is an organizational structure in which each member takes the responsibility for certain tasks, roles (e.g. the bread-winner) or decisions. Responsibilities within the relationship will not necessarily be specialized; they may be shared, divided or even alternated in some way. The success of a relationship may partly depend on how well this organization functions and how satisfactory or fair the members perceive it to be. Schaninger and Buss (1986) found that happily married couples practised more role specialization, with less husband dominance in family finance handling, and greater joint and wife influence in decision-making. In addition, the establishment of equality and equity at an early stage of the relationship was found to be important for the survival of the marriage.

Several studies show that the way a person thinks about their relationship is connected with how satisfactory they find it. For example Madden and Janoff-Bulman (1981) show that wives feel less satisfied with their marriages if they blame their husbands for the problems in their relationship and are happier if they believe that they have some personal control over conflicts. Fincham *et al.* (1987) also found that people in distressed marriages attributed unpleasant behaviour in their spouses to global aspects of their character. People in happier marriages were more likely to blame their spouse's unpleasant behaviour on circumstances. Segraves (1982), among others, has suggested that a consistent misattribution of characteristics and motives to the other spouse is a salient influence in the development of chronic marital discord. The author goes on to explain how easily a couple can become locked in a mutual misperception.

> A husband may be afraid that his wife will leave him if she becomes more independent, and his wife may fear that men will dominate and destroy her autonomy if she is emotionally dependent on them. On one level, such a conflict appears irreconcilable as a power struggle. On another level, the true concerns of each spouse are not in conflict.
>
> (Segraves 1982: 189)

Ability to communicate with each other successfully is a prominent criterion for a good relationship. Successful communication is necessary in nearly all areas of a relationship and involves both verbal and non-verbal elements. Generally unhappy couples have difficulties or conflicts when communicating. Cousins and Vincent (1983) drew data from observations of couples discussing an upsetting incident unrelated to their marriage. Analyses of their data revealed that couples expressing sympathy and approval in their relationship had a greater degree of marital adjustment. Couples who were sarcastic or critical of each other had poorer marital adjustment. On the basis of these findings and others, Cousins and Vincent suggest that 'Interventions that stress the acquisition of supportive and expressive skills for marital enhancement may succeed because of the reduction in aversive behaviours and strategies, rather than because of an increase in empathic or expressive interaction' (1983: 681). A number of therapeutic techniques focus directly on the issue of negativity by attempting to translate the negative to the positive. Crowe (1988), for example, describes how in 'reciprocity negotiation' the therapist takes the role of intermediary or negotiator. When one member of the couple states their complaints about the behaviour of the other partner the therapist suggests that they restate them as constructive requests. Instead of saying 'He's always home late', a wife can ask her husband to telephone home if he is detained at work.

In an interesting study of communication between partners, Birchler *et al.* (1975) arranged for each person to interact with their own spouse, an opposite-sex, non-distressed spouse, and an opposite-sex, distressed spouse. Results indicated that effective communication arose from properties of the dyadic interaction itself rather than from the properties of individuals. That is individuals may learn ineffective communication styles with their spouse while remaining socially competent in their interactions with others. This underlines the point, made earlier, that divorcing people can be reassured that they need not assume responsibility for the breakup. They need not believe that there is something about them that makes future relationships prone to failure.

Before leaving the subject of communication, it may be worth sounding a note of caution. It should not simply be taken for granted that the more communication there is, the better. Davidson *et al.* (1983) found that the best marriages are associated with an intermediate amount of self-disclosure between partners. There can be too much of a good thing. Rofe (1985) studied marriages in Israel, and found that the most satisfying marriages for both partners involved people who were rated as Repressors (as opposed to Sensitizers). It may be that a certain amount of fiction is helpful to relationships. Therapists who believe in complete frankness on the part of their clients should tread warily.

## Marriage and health

There is growing evidence indicating a link between a person's mental and physical health and the quality of their interpersonal relationships. Argyle and Henderson (1985) cite evidence that separation and divorce have adverse consequences on physical and mental health and on feelings of well-being. Indeed, the effect of separation on death-rate is more serious than the death of a spouse (see Argyle and Henderson, 1985; Table 2: 16). The adverse effects of separation on health seem to apply more to men than to women, for reasons which need to be researched. Divorce or separation also have an adverse effect on mental health and general feelings of well-being. Just as a good marriage helps prevent ill-health, so it speeds recovery from medical treatment. While other personal relationships are also important, marriage appears to matter more than friendships or relationships with family or people at work.

Brown and his associates, working in London, have investigated the possibility that a confiding relationship can reduce the chance of depression developing in women following a stressful event (e.g. death of a close relative). In particular they have looked at the support provided by husbands, lovers or people named as very close by women, and defined these potential confidents as 'core ties'. In a study of largely working-class mothers, Brown (1986) found that confiding in a core tie at a time of crisis did not necessarily reduce the risk of depression. Only women who received active emotional support from the confidant were less likely to develop depression. In a further study, Andrews and Brown (1988) found that low self-esteem and lack of support from a core tie at a time of crisis were associated with a considerably increased risk of developing depression. Some women, however, were found to be at particularly high risk of depression. These were women confiding in at least one person at a time of crisis but receiving either emotional support from a non-core tie, or no emotional support at all. This suggests that it is better to keep your troubles to yourself than to confide in the wrong person. These findings point to the importance of close relationships at times of crisis. Moreover, they indicate not only the preventive effect of a supportive relationship on depression, but also the detrimental effect of an unsupportive one.

Renne (1977) in a substantial study found that the physical and mental health of couples with bad marriages (one-fifth of the sample) were worse than that of people who had separated or divorced. The separated or divorced, in turn, had poorer physical and mental health than those who were satisfactorily married. So the important determinant of health seems not so much the fact of being married but having a good close relationship. Kennedy *et al.* (1988) have reported a comparative study of married versus separated or divorced (S/D) individuals and found that S/D individuals had poorer immune system function in several ways. This was particularly true of recently separated women who retained an attachment to their (ex)husband; they were also more distressed and lonelier. S/D men were more distressed than married men. In the group of married women, poorer marital quality, assessed by a standard questionnaire, was related to greater depression and to some extent poorer immune response. Good marriages, then, may protect health via the immune system. Such marriages, also, involve mutual disclosure of problems in other spheres, and lead to the people involved being buffered against the effects of stress from other sources.

Although people on their own are worse off than the average person with a partner, when those in relationships are divided into those who have good versus bad relationships, those in bad relationships are found to be worse off than those on their own. This can be put in simple terms: a good relationship is good for you but it is better to have no relationship at all than to have a bad one. Divorce may be a painful cure for the even more painful condition of being in a bad marriage. It follows that therapists should not necessarily strive to preserve an unsatisfactory relationship. Indeed, it may be their task to facilitate its ending. This point becomes particularly obvious when one contemplates the plight of women who remain with partners who may injure or even kill them.

Strube (1988) explored factors affecting decisions to leave abusive relationships. He suggests that women who stay in such relationships are economically tied to their partners and will tolerate abuse so long as it does not become too severe or involve the children. They are also committed to making their relationship last (e.g. more likely to say they love their assailants, less likely to separate). He goes on to consider several theoretical models which may account for the reasons some women remain in abusive relationships. Embedded within these theories is

> the basic assumption that the decision to leave or remain in an abusive relationship is a 'rational' decision from the perspective of the decision maker. The decision is based on an analysis of available 'data' and follows predictable 'decision rules'. The outcome may be considered abnormal by normative standards (i.e. Who in their right mind would choose to remain in an abusive relationship?), but the process is not pathological.
>
> (Strube 1988: 240)

One particularly relevant theory Strube discusses is the theory of reasoned action. This suggests, for example, that women who choose to stay in abusive relationships may do so because they possess unrealistic beliefs about the consequences of leaving or staying. Intervention strategies should aim to educate and thus alter such beliefs. He further proposes that interventions aimed at removing external barriers to leaving, or directed towards increasing the woman's sense of self-efficacy may also be helpful.

The work of investigators who have studied violent but stable relationships suggests that an assumption which has been implicit in this chapter so far should be made explicit and then rejected. This is the assumption that the quality of the relationship is more or less the same thing as its stability. Throughout the review of factors affecting marriage, it is taken as read that something associated with divorce must be bad for the relationship, and therefore that stable relationships must be good. There is evidently some sense in this assumption. Other things being equal, people in a good relationship can be expected to want to stay together. People who are unhappy with each other may be expected to split up. But there are cases where the relationship is fairly stable, despite the fact that the participants are miserable. No more convincing examples exist than those of long-term violent relationships. We shall turn our attention to factors associated with violence between partners in a moment.

Before doing so, however, let us note another consequence of distinguishing between quality and stability of a relationship. This is that there also exist relationships which mean a very great deal to the participants, but which are transitory. There may be many reasons for the couple to feel uncommitted to each other. One may have extensive travel plans, or be working in a particular place for a limited period, or be young and eager to gain experience before deliberately entering a long-term relationship.

Brief, passionate affairs have received far less scientific scrutiny than other forms of relationships. They are, by definition, short-lived. They may be secret. The people involved will not approach therapists for help, nor will the consequences of their life-style bring them to the attention of the social services or the apparatus of the law. For these reasons, there is very little that can be said about them here. We should, nevertheless, remember that such relationships exist, and that they are a source of great satisfaction to those involved.

## Violent relationships

In contrast to the brief, passionate affair, there is now a wealth of literature on violent relationships. There seems to be a disturbingly high prevalence of violence within marriages. American estimates of the percentage of couples experiencing violence at some time in their marriage vary from 28 per cent (Straus *et al.* 1980) to 60 per cent (Gelles 1974; Walker 1979). What little is known about the prevalence of spouse abuse in Britain indicates a slightly lower level in British marriages (Jones *et al.* 1986; Hammer and Saunders 1984; Andrews and Brown 1988).

It is commonly assumed that men are more aggressive and are more likely to hit their wives than their wives are to hit them. However, the figures drawn from two large surveys show that, if anything, women are more likely to use severe violence (punching, kicking, using a weapon, etc.) against their partners than men are (Straus and Gelles 1986). The reason for the far greater social concern over the battering of women is probably that violent men cause more damage to their partner than violent women do. It is the cases that reach hospital that receive most attention.

One of the most widely studied variables in the field of marital violence has been social class. The idea that marital violence is an exclusively working-class phenomenon has long been refuted. Spouse abuse in fact occurs across all levels of society. However, low-income groups appear to be most prone to couple violence (K. Coleman *et al.* 1980). Straus and colleagues (1980) showed that violence was particularly high for couples subsisting at or below the poverty level. Indeed, there appears to be a strong relationship between marital violence and income level with a consistent decrease as income level goes up. Lack of work may be important in its own right. A.R. Roberts (1987) found surprisingly high rates of unemployment in a group of men charged with violence against their partners. Straus *et al.* (1980) found that part-time employment was a better predictor of marital violence than unemployment.

A low level of education of both husband and wife also appears to be related to violence (Steinmetz 1977). However, Straus *et al.* (1980) found that those in the middle educational range were most likely to be both victims and perpetrators of violence. At the upper end of the range men were more likely to be victims than women. The reason for these findings is far from obvious and should be the subject of future research.

The likelihood of violence occurring in a relationship has also been associated with the marital status of the couple. In Lewis's (1987) group of battered women, 60 per cent were cohabiting with their partners as compared with 22 per cent of the control group. Nearly half of Roberts's (1987) sample of batterers were cohabiting with their partner while only 19 per cent were married (the remainder being made up of former lovers and so on). He suggests that this may be due to the fact that the majority of batterers are young and so are a high proportion of people who choose to live together without marrying.

Roberts (1987) and Schurger and Reigle (1988) have reported an association between alcohol use and marital violence. Van Hasselt and colleagues (1985) found a higher rate of alcohol abuse in physically abusive males compared with non-abusive males in discordant marriages. Two reasons, not mutually exclusive, might explain this finding. First, in conditions where spouse abuse may be likely to occur, for example in conditions of acute stress or at least in conditions where the relationship is very strained, alcohol abuse could simply be another symptom of an unhappy state. That is heavy drinking may be a byproduct of the situation itself. Alternatively alcohol may play a causal role of a type; it may reduce inhibition and increase aggression but it also provides an excuse for the violence and support for the claim that the assailant did not know what they were doing at the time. Gelles (1987) discusses the importance of moving towards making a person responsible for their actions, that is not accepting violent behaviour attributed to drugs, alcohol, or loss of control.

Violence in the family of origin has been strongly associated with spouse abuse. Parker and Schunaker (1977) reported that about 68 per cent of their abused wives had mothers who had been abused, whereas 25 per cent of the non-abused wives had witnessed their mothers being abused. When Lockhart (1987) investigated women's reports of their own and their partner's family background the only significant predictor of abuse of the women was wife abuse by the father of the male partner. Schurger and Reigle (1988) also found that being hit as a boy as well as observing parental violence predicted wife-battering. Similarly Rosenbaum and O'Leary (1981) and O'Leary and Curley (1986) found that seeing parents fighting and receiving abuse from them were critical distinguishing features of men who abused their wives.

The studies reported so far, however, concentrate on wife abuse, ignoring violence directed towards the husband. Data from a large American sample were used by Kalmuss (1984) to investigate the inter-generational transmission of marital aggression in both sexes. Measures were taken of how frequently, as a teenager, subjects observed parents hitting each other and how frequently, during this period, subjects were hit by parents. Observation of parental violence was found to be more strongly related to involvement in subsequent severe marital aggression. In addition, observing one's father hitting one's mother increased the likelihood that sons would be victims as well as perpetrators and that daughters would be perpetrators as well as victims. These findings imply that children growing up in violent families do not simply learn that violence is an acceptable form of behaviour. Rather they may learn about the use of and acceptance of violence in a more role-specific form.

Studies examining the relationship between attitudes towards spouse abuse and the occurrence of violence within marriages also indicate, not surprisingly, a positive association. Straus (1980) found that violent wives as well as violent husbands expressed more approval of violence than did non-violent husbands and wives: 31 per cent of husbands and 25 per cent of wives could see some justification in hitting a spouse. The relationship between approval of violence and tendency to abuse a spouse may operate, at least partly, through learned behaviours and attitudes in the family of origin. However, not all individuals from violent families grow up to be victims or perpetrators of marital violence. Similarly those who come from relatively violence-free families can still be involved in violence in their later relationships. It may well be the case that attitudes towards marital violence are developed as a justification for violence which has already occurred.

The power structure of the relationship is a further predictor of marital violence. This may be reflected by differences in education and income between spouses or by psychological variables such as subjective dependency or decision-making power. Hornung and colleagues (1981) considered both individual status and the comparative status of the husband and wife in relation to marital violence. Here, 'status inconsistency' referred to a discrepancy in an individual's educational and occupational attainment, that is unexpectedly low or high educational qualifications in relation to a person's occupation. 'Status incompatibility' referred to relative attainments, where the husband and wife were of unequal occupational status. Status inconsistency and status incompatibility were both associated with an increased risk of spouse abuse. Certain types of status inconsistency (such as under-achievement in occupation by the husband) and certain types of status incompatability (for example when the woman was high in occupation relative to her husband) were found to involve particularly high risks of spouse abuse.

D.H. Coleman and Straus (1986) also studied the relationship between marital violence and the power structure of the marriage. They examined the degree to which there was consensus about the power relationship and the level of marital conflict. Egalitarian couples were found to have the lowest rates of conflict and violence while male-dominant and female-dominant couples had the highest rates. Although consensus about the legitimacy of a male-dominant or female-dominant power structure reduced conflict and violence in such families, there was still a much higher risk of violence in these than in egalitarian marriages with a similar level of conflict. At high levels of conflict wife-dominant relationships were the most violent.


## Conclusions

In this chapter we have reviewed the empirical literature on various psychological components of couple relationships. We have also suggested, in places, how the findings of such studies can be translated into practical intervention strategies. In other places, we hope that the facts speak for themselves. For example it can be assumed that a couple who are rather different from each other will not get on too well together, whatever the therapist does. There is probably little a therapist can do with a couple who simply do not find each other attractive. In many instances, however, therapists need to use research findings to inform practice rather than direct it. For example we showed that income, education and occupational status are related to the quality of marriage. Although we can postulate why this is so, in actuality it is impossible to say which of these things matter because all of them are liable to occur together. The poor may be more likely to divorce because they have little money and are subject to more stress. Alternatively it might be lower job satisfaction rather than lack of money that creates the stress. It could also be the case that divorce is more common in those from the working class because they marry earlier, when they possess less personal maturity. On the other hand, one could explain the finding that earlier marriages are more likely to dissolve by noting that early marriages are more prevalent among sons and daughters of manual workers.

Consider another example: studies showing that spouse abuse is more likely to occur among working-class couples. It would be easy to jump to the conclusion that working-class couples have more violent natures or an ideology that more readily accepts violence. But it could well be the case that middle-class couples simply have the resources to divorce or move away when conflict escalates, a harder option for those who live in poverty.

Consider, too, the finding that more positive communication occurs between happily paired people. Do they get on well because they verbally reward each other, as researchers have suggested? Or do they approve of each other and say so because they get on well? Such research findings present us with a chicken-and-egg problem which plagues much of the literature we have cited. Take another example. Do bad marriages lead to mutual blame, or does mutual blame lead to a bad marriage?

To ask whether something is causal or consequential may be too simple. For example in examining published studies of the relationship between the quality of marriage and depression, Barnett and Gotlib (1988) find evidence enabling them to argue that depression is *both* a cause *and* a consequence of an unsatisfactory relationship. Until more sophisticated research teases apart the complex network of interacting causes and effects, we can make only informed guesses about this subject. Yet it is vital to do so. Therapists have no option but to develop implicit or explicit theories to guide their attempts to alter unhappy relationships.

If we permit ourselves to speculate about what makes some couples remain together happily while others do not, we would argue as follows. Some children are sensibly brought up by happy parents. Such children either acquire the capacity to be drawn to well-chosen friends and sexual partners, or they inherit that capacity from their parents. Probably both processes operate. Other children experience a more unfortunate upbringing. Their ability and desire to sustain a satisfactory and lasting relationship in adulthood is impaired. They may select a less suitable partner and be less capable of giving and receiving affection and love.

So some individuals are at a disadvantage to start with. It is possible to overcome these disadvantages, just as it is possible to fail to capitalize on them. If we put aside the effect of family background, it seems reasonable to suggest that the primary causal influence on the quality of an ongoing relationship is stress. This may arise as a result of a large number of factors: poverty, bad housing, the death of a parent, pressures from work or children, social isolation resulting from a change of neighbourhood, and so on.

But to talk of relationships in this way is misleading. It carries connotations of something relatively static, on which an occasional external influence impinges. Instead we would argue that a relationship is a process, a continuous interaction in which the main influence on one person is the other.

We have referred to the questionnaire data gathered by Russell and Wells (1986) on a national sample in Britain. Using the kinds of statistical methods that are common in econometric modelling, it is possible to look at, even to quantify, the elements underlying successful and unsuccessful marriages. The results of such analyses have shown that it is inappropriate to talk of quality of marriage as if it is a single entity. Instead it is necessary to recognize that a marriage may be quite good for one of the partners and bad for the other, without either being aware of the discrepancy. To understand the relationship more fully, one must examine the state of mind of the two partners separately. Having said that, it is also important to acknowledge that the love that one feels for the other has a major impact on the love that the second feels for the first. Calculations show that the degree of mutual influence of this type has a causal strength of about 0.7. What does this mean?

Suppose that the husband, say, as the result of some external cause, feels more love for his wife. This external cause may be a promotion at work, resulting in an overspill of good feeling. It may be because, having talked to a friend, he realizes how lucky he is to be married to his wife. Whatever the reason, suppose his positive feelings for his wife increase by one arbitrary unit. This has the effect on his wife of making her positive feelings for him increase by 0.7 of an arbitrary unit. This, in turn, has the effect on him of making his positive feelings for her increase by a further 0.5 (0.7 × 0.7) of a unit, which further raises her positive feelings for him by 0.35 (0.7 × 0.5), and so on.

In other words, external causes operating on either of the partners have a knock-on effect on the other, and the effect of the external cause reverberates through the relationship, having a considerable effect *largely through the effect of each person on the other*. Most people in relationships feel good about the other most of the time. They are in a virtuous circle. If, however, some unfavourable influence perturbs the balance, they can get into a vicious circle and the quality of their relationship can spiral downwards towards mutual dislike, a process which experienced therapists have seen many times.

Finally, let us describe what we mean by a good long-term intimate relationship. This can be characterized as one where each person loves the other. We would argue that all the factors we have been describing – social, familial, educational, financial, etc. – are of minor importance compared to the core feelings that partners have for each other. The reader will be asking what we mean by 'love', and how we can discuss such a controversial topic as though it was simple. The analyses of the Russell and Wells questionnaire data show that a large number of feelings all vary together and relate very strongly to ratings of marital success and failure. It is this complex array of feelings which we define as love.

Some research on relationships strikes us as sterile. Several researchers have claimed that communication is the key to a good relationship; others have claimed that sexual satisfaction is crucial. We regard both as components of a bundle of connected feelings that any open-minded person would label 'love'. Any researcher can extract one of the components and show that it is a very strong predictor of marital satisfaction, where marital satisfaction is defined by some of the other components. What is the point of such research?

Let us be more explicit. The analyses reveal that the following things are all closely interconnected: considering the relationship successful, not wanting to terminate it, feeling fortunate to be with that particular person, claiming to be happy, to love them and to feel loved by them, to respect them and to feel respected by them, to be proud of them and to feel that they are proud of you, wanting to be with them, enjoying your time with them, finding their company pleasant, feeling an urge to discuss problems with them, feeling that you understand them and they understand you, trusting them, wanting to touch and cuddle them, feeling attracted to them, thinking that they are attracted to you, enjoying sex with them, not experiencing conflicting feelings about them, not being irritated by them, feeling there is a romantic side to the relationship, that there is enough give and take, enough kindness, and considering companionship to be important.

People who feel this way towards someone who reciprocates the feelings are fortunate. Helping people who feel otherwise to reach this goal, or, if things are too bad, enabling people to terminate the relationship with minimal upheaval, is a worthy aim and a considerable challenge.

## Acknowledgements

We should like to thank P.A. Wells and the editors for helpful comments on early versions of this chapter.

## References

Abbott, D.A. and Brody, G.H. (1985) The relation of child age, gender, and number of children to the marital adjustment of wives, *Journal of Marriage and the Family* 47: 77–84.

Andrews, B. and Brown, G.W. (1988) Marital violence in the community: a biographical approach, *British Journal of Psychiatry* 153: 305–12.

Argyle, M. and Henderson, M. (1985) *The Anatomy of Relationships*, Harmondsworth: Penguin.

Barnett, P.A. and Gotlib, I.H. (1988) Psychosocial functioning and depression: distinguishing among antecedents, concomitants, and consequences, *Psychological Bulletin* 104: 97–126.

Baron, M., Mendlewicz, J., Gruen, R., Asnis, L. and Fieve, R.R. (1981) Assortative mating in affective disorders, *Journal of Affective Disorders* 3: 167–81.

Barton, K. and Cattell, R.B. (1972) Real and perceived similarities in personality between spouses: tests of 'likeness' versus 'completeness' theories, *Psychological Reports* 31: 15–18.

Belsky, J., Lang, M.E. and Rovine, M. (1985) Stability and change in marriage across the transition to parenthood: a second study, *Journal of Marriage and the Family* 47: 855–65.

Birchler, G.R., Weiss, R.L. and Vincent, J.P. (1975) Multimethod analysis of social reinforcement exchange between maritally distressed and nondistressed spouse and stranger dyads, *Journal of Personality and Social Psychology* 31: 349–60.

Blumstein, P. and Schwartz, P. (1983) *American Couples*, New York: William Morrow.

Booth, A. and Edwards, J.N. (1985) Age at marriage and marital instability, *Journal of Marriage and the Family* 47: 67–75.

Broderick, C.B. (1988) To arrive where we started: the field of family studies in the 1930's, *Journal of Marriage and the Family* 50: 569–84.

Brown, G.W. (1986) Depression, in G.W. Brown and T.O. Harris (eds) *Life Events and Illness: Studies of Psychiatric and Physical Disorder*, New York: Guilford Press.

Burgess, E.W. and Cottrell, L.S. (1939) *Predicting Success or Failure in Marriage*, New York: Prentice-Hall.

Buss, D.M. (1989) Sex differences in human mate preferences: evolutionary hyphotheses tested in 37 cultures, *Behavioral and Brain Sciences* 12: 1–49.

Cattell, R.B. and Nesselroade, J.R. (1967) Likeness and completeness theories examined by sixteen personality factor measures on stably and unstably married couples, *Journal of Personality and Social Psychology* 7: 351–61.

Coleman, D.H. and Straus, M.A. (1986) Marital power, and violence in a nationally representative sample of American couples, *Violence and Victims* 1: 141–57.

Coleman, K., Weinman, M., and Hsi, B. (1980) Factors affecting conjugal violence, *Journal of Psychology* 105: 197–202.

Cousins, P.C. and Vincent, J.P. (1983) Supportive and aversive behavior following spousal complaints, *Journal of Marriage and the Family* 45: 679–82.

Crowe, M. (1986) The negotiated timetable: a new approach to marital conflicts involving male demands and female reluctance for sex, *Sexual and Marital Therapy* 1: 157–73

—— (1988) Indications for family, marital and sexual therapy, in I.R.H. Falloon (ed.) *Handbook of Behavioral Marital Therapy*, New York: Guilford Press.

Cutright, P. (1971) Income and family events: marital stability, *Journal of Marriage and the Family* 33: 291–306.

Davidson, B., Balswick, J. and Halverson, C. (1983) Affective self-disclosure and marital adjustment: a test of equity theory, *Journal of Marriage and the Family* 45: 93–102.

Epstein, E. and Guttman, R. (1985) Mate selection in man: evidence, theory, and outcome, *Social Biology* 31: 243–78.

Eysenck, H.J. and Wakefield, J.A. (1981) Psychological factors as predictors of marital satisfaction, *Advances in Behavior Research and Therapy* 3: 151–92.

Feingold, A. (1988) Matching for attractiveness in romantic partners and same-sex friends: a meta-analysis and theoretical critique, *Psychological Bulletin* 104: 226–35.

Filsinger, E.E. and Wilson, M.R. (1984) Religiosity, socioeconomic rewards, and family development: predictors of marital adjustment, *Journal of Marriage and the Family* 46: 663–70.

Fincham, F.D., Beach, S. and Nelson, G. (1987) Attribution processes in distressed and nondistressed couples: 3. Causal and responsibility attributions for spouse behavior, *Cognitive Therapy and Research* 11: 71–86.

Fisher, H.E. (1987) The four year itch, *Natural History* 96: 22–33.

Gelles, R.J. (1974) *The Violent Home*, Beverly Hills, Calif: Sage.

—— (1987) *Family Violence*, Beverly Hills, Calif: Sage.

Gibson, C. (1974) The association between divorce and social class in England and Wales, *British Journal of Sociology* 25: 79–93.

Hahlweg, K., Schindler, L., Revenstorf, D. and Brengelmann, J.C. (1984) The Munich marital therapy study, in K. Hahlweg and N. Jacobson (eds) *Marital Interaction*, New York: Guilford Press.

Hammer, J. and Saunders, S. (1984) *Well-Founded Fear: A Community Study of Violence to Women*, London: Hutchinson.

Haskey, J. (1982) The proportion of marriages ending in divorce, *Population Trends* 27: 4–8.

—— (1987) Social class differentials in remarriage after divorce: results from a forward linkage study, *Population Trends* 47: 34–42.

Hawton, K. (1985) *Sex Therapy: A Practical Guide*, Oxford: Oxford University Press.

Heaton, T. (1984) Religious homogamy and marital satisfaction reconsidered, *Journal of Marriage and the Family* 46: 729–33.

Hinsz, V.B. (1989) Facial resemblance in engaged and married couples, *Journal of Social and Personal Relationships* 6: 223–9.

Hornung, C.A., McCullough, B.C. and Sugimoto, T. (1981) Status relationships in marriage: risk factors in spouse abuse, *Journal of Marriage and the Family* 43: 675–92.

Houseknecht, S.K. and Spanier, G.B. (1980) Marital disruption and higher education among women in the United States, *Sociological Quarterly* 21: 375–89.

Jones, T., McClean, B. and Young, J. (1986) *The Islington Crime Survey*, Aldershot: Gower.

Kallman, F.J. and Mickey, J.S. (1946) The concept of induced insanity in family units, *Journal of Nervous and Mental Diseases* 104: 303–15.

Kalmuss, D. (1984) The intergenerational transmission of marital aggression, *Journal of Marriage and the Family* 46: 11–19.

Kalmuss, D.S. and Straus, M.A. (1982) Wife's marital dependency and wife abuse, *Journal of Marriage and the Family* 44: 277–86.

Keith, V.M. and Finlay, V. (1988) The impact of parental divorce on children's educational attainment, marital timing and likelihood of divorce, *Journal of Marriage and the Family* 50: 797–809.

Kennedy, S., Kiecolt-Glaser, J.K. and Glaser, R. (1988) Immunological consequences of acute and chronic stressors: mediating role of interpersonal relationships, *British Journal of Medical Psychology* 61: 77–85.

Kopelman, R.E. and Lang, D. (1985) Alliteration in mate selection: does Barbara marry Barry?, *Psychological Reports* 56: 791–6.

Kotler, T. and Omodei, M. (1988) Attachment and emotional health: a life span approach, *Human Relations* 41: 619–40.

Lewis, B.Y. (1987) Psychosocial factors related to wife abuse, *Journal of Family Violence* 2: 1–10.

Locke, H.J. and Wallace, K.M. (1959) Short marital adjustment and prediction tests: their reliability and validity, *Marriage and Family Living* 21: 251–5.

Lockhart, L. (1987) A reexamination of the effects of race and social class on the incidence of marital violence: a search for reliable differences, *Journal of Marriage and the Family* 49: 603–10.

McCarthy, J. (1978) A comparison of the probability of the dissolution of first and second marriages, *Demography* 15: 345–60.

Madden, M.E. and Janoff-Bulman, R. (1981) Blame, control, and marital satisfaction: wives' attributions for conflict in marriage, *Journal of Marriage and the Family* 43: 663–74.

Meyer, J.P. and Pepper, S. (1977) Need compatibility and marital adjustment in young married couples, *Journal of Personality and Social Psychology* 35: 331–42.

Nye, F.I. (1988) Fifty years of family research, 1937–1987, *Journal of Marriage and the Family* 50: 305–16.

O'Leary, K.D. and Curley, A.D (1986) Assertion and family violence: correlates of spouse abuse, *Journal of Marital and Family Therapy* 12: 281–9.

Parker, B. and Schumaker, D. (1977) The battered wife syndrome and violence in the nuclear family of origin: a controlled pilot study, *American Journal of Public Health* 67: 760–1.

Peterson, J.L. and Miller, C. (1980) Physical attractiveness and marriage adjustment among older American couples, *Journal of Psychology* 105: 247–52.

Price, R.A. and Vandenberg, S.G. (1980) Spouse similarity in American and Swedish couples, *Behavior Genetics* 10: 59–71.

Renne, K.S. (1977) Health and marital experience in an urban population, in J.E. De Berger (ed.) *Marriage Today: Problems, Issues and Alternatives*, New York: Wiley.

Richard, L.S., Wakefield, J.A. and Lewak, R. (1990) Similarity of personality variables as predictors of marital satisfaction: a Minnesota Multiphasic Personality Inventory (MMPI) item analysis, *Personality and Individual Differences* 11: 39–43.

Rimmer, J. and Winokur, G. (1972) The spouses of alcoholics: an example of assortative mating, *Diseases of the Nervous System* 33: 509–11.

Roberts, A.R. (1987) Psychosocial characteristics of batterers: a study of 234 men charged with domestic violence offenses, *Journal of Family Violence* 2: 81–93.

Roberts, D.F. (1977) Assortative mating in man: husband/wife correlations in physical characteristics, *Supplement to the Bulletin of the Eugenics Society* 2 (entire issue).

Rofe, Y. (1985) The assessment of marital happiness, in J.N. Butcher and C.D. Spielberger (eds) *Advances in Personality Assessment*, vol. 4, Hillsdale, NJ: Lawrence Erlbaum.

Rosenbaum, A. and O'Leary, K.D. (1981) Marital violence: characteristics of abusive couples, *Journal of Consulting and Clinical Psychology* 49: 63–71.

Ruble, D.N., Fleming, A.S., Hackel, L.S. and Stangor, C. (1988) Changes in the marital relationship during the transition to first time motherhood: effects of violated expectations concerning division of household labour, *Journal of Personality and Social Psychology* 55: 78–87.

Rushton, J.P. (1988) Genetic similarity, mate choice, and fecundity in humans, *Ethology and Sociobiology* 9: 329–35.

Russell, R.J.H. and Wells, P.A. (1986) Marriage Questionnaire, copies available on request.

Schaninger, C.M. and Buss, W.C. (1986) A longitudinal comparison of consumption and finance handling between happily married and divorced couples, *Journal of Marriage and the Family* 48: 129–36.

Schumm, W.R. and Bugaighis, M.A. (1986) Marital quality over the marital career: alternative explanations, *Journal of Marriage and the Family* 48: 165–8.

Schurger, J.M. and Reigle, N. (1988) Personality and biographic data that characterise men who abuse their wives, *Journal of Clinical Psychology* 44: 75–81.

Segraves, R.T. (1982) *A Combined Psychodynamic-Behavioral Approach*, New York: Plenum.

South, S.J. and Spitze, G. (1986) Determinants of divorce over the marital life course, *American Sociological Review* 51: 583–90.

Spanier, G.B. (1976) Measuring dyadic adjustment: new scales for assessing the quality of marriage and similar dyads, *Journal of Marriage and the Family* 38: 15–28.

Steinmetz, S.K. (1977) *The Cycle of Violence: Assertive, Aggressive, and Abusive Family Interaction*, New York: Praeger.

Straus, M.A. (1980) Victims and aggressors in marital violence, *American Behavioural Scientist* 23: 681–704.

Straus, M.A. and Gelles, R.J. (1986) Societal change in family violence from 1975 to 1985 as revealed by two national surveys, *Journal of Marriage and the Family* 48: 465–79.

Straus, M.A., Gelles, R.J. and Steinmetz, S.K. (1980) *Behind Closed Doors: Violence in American Families*, New York: Doubleday.

Strube, M.J. (1988) The decision to leave an abusive relationship: empirical evidence and theoretical issues, *Psychological Bulletin* 104: 236–50.

Suarez, L., Criqui, M.H. and Barrett-Connor, E. (1983) Spouse concordance for systolic diastolic blood pressure, *American Journal of Epidemiology* 118; 345–51.

Thiessen, D. and Gregg, B. (1980) Human assortative mating and genetic equilibrium, *Ethology and Sociobiology* 1: 111–40.

Tyler, P.A. (1988) Assortative mating and human variation, *Scientific Progress* 72: 451–66.

Van Hasselt, V.B., Morrison, R.L. and Bellack, A.S. (1985) Alcohol use in wife abusers and their spouses, *Addictive Behaviours* 10: 127–35.

Vega, W.A., Kolody, B. and Valle, R. (1988) Marital strain, coping, and depression among Mexican-American women, *Journal of Marriage and the Family* 50: 391–403.

Vera, H., Berardo, D.H. and Berardo, F.M. (1985) Age and heterogamy in marriage, *Journal of Marriage and the Family* 47: 553–66.

Walker, L.E. (1979) *The Battered Woman*, New York: Harper & Row.

Weed, J. (1980) *National estimates of marriage dissolution and survivorship: United States, DHSS, Vital and Health Statistics, Series 3*, Washington, DC: United States Government Printing Office.

White, L.K. and Booth, A. (1985) The quality and stability of remarriages: the role of stepchildren, *American Sociological Review* 50: 689–98.

# PART II

# Therapeutic approaches

# 4

# Approaches to couple therapy

## THOMAS SCHRÖDER

### Introduction

Therapy, in my experience, is a circular rather than a linear process: images slide in and out of focus repeatedly; themes emerge, are temporarily set aside, then rediscovered; problems are reworked continuously rather than resolved on first encounter. It follows that thinking and writing about therapy would come closest to its subject when adopting the same circular pattern. However, accounts of therapy are rendered much more accessible by imposing a linear order, presenting events and thoughts as if they seamlessly and logically followed on from one another; rather like memories sum up and simplify past experience, gaining structure at the expense of complexity.

This chapter has elements of both patterns. While discussing the events arising during the course of a couple's therapy in chronological order, many issues will be revisited several times, much in the way that they would occur and reoccur to therapists, of whatever theoretical orientation, in the course of their work. Naturally the opening and closing stages show most similarities, with the unfolding process of the middle part being most diverse and unique (one might say that couple work, like other forms of therapy, has a beginning, a muddle, and an end).[1]

The diversity of couples presenting for therapy is mirrored by the diversity of approaches which therapists can adopt in their efforts to be of help. In fact, so great is the variety of pathways that it may appear as if one could not hope to link them up but only describe them alongside each other. Thus, clearly delineated perspectives are provided by the well-established theoretical schools (such as behavioural, person-centred, cognitive, experiential, psychodynamic, or systemic), extending their particular formulations and interventions to work with couples. One might think of them as different types of maps charting the same landscape, much as for instance a topographical and a geological map will show different features within the same contours. To view the area of couple therapy in these distinct ways is of great value in two respects. For the field as a whole, it serves to sharpen our understanding of therapeutic issues by offering alternative and at times mutually incompatible viewpoints, thereby highlighting the contradictions which could become the focus of further inquiry. For particular therapists, the various theoretical persuasions serve to provide relatively coherent frameworks; useful for the beginner to internalize selectively and gain confidence in, and important for experienced practitioners to draw on in order to challenge and amend their established maps, especially when entering difficult terrain or unfamiliar territory. Of course, this geographical metaphor has its limits. Practitioners will be well aware of the interaction between their psychological maps and the territory. To some extent we not only select but also evoke what we feel familiar with.

Nevertheless, the case for attempting to integrate the different approaches is strong. There are clear areas of convergence between the various theoretical persuasions, though probably more in their practice than in the theoretical accounts of it. Empirical research points to broadly equivalent outcomes of different forms of therapies, though it is the subject of much current debate whether this is due to common factors operating in all approaches, or to the finite potential for change in each client which limits the effects of whatever specific factors are active, or simply to a lack of differentiation in research designs which is compounded by statistical techniques such as meta-analyses. More importantly answers to the questions which therapists have to pose themselves and decisions they make during the course of therapy will only in part be based on their background and rationales, but otherwise depend on the clients and on the setting.

Which theoretical systems will in the end be integrated into a couple therapist's personal approach seems to me less a matter of their conceptual elegance than a function of their value in helping to organize clinical experience. It follows that integration of approaches cannot be achieved in general on paper but has to be struggled for in particular in practice.

How therapists describe themselves will depend in part on their context (for instance whether the agency they work in values a particular theoretical affiliation or favours 'eclecticism') and in part on individual features such as temperament, past learning and life experiences, and current stage of personal and professional individuation. My own development as a couple therapist so far has been one of successively grafting first an interpersonal, then a general psychodynamic, and latterly, a specifically object-relations framework on to a rootstock of person-centred clinical practice and libertarian/egalitarian ideology. This process naturally owed as much to a changing emotional stance as to intellectual exploration and I am curious where it will be leading me. Meanwhile, I hope that all these influences have discernibly contributed to the following observations without obscuring too much of what is of value in other viewpoints and convictions.

Before considering the issues facing the couple therapist in the first session, a few general points and conventions need to be addressed. Most couples seen in therapy are heterosexual; the majority of these are married. However, the approaches discussed here are just as valid for homosexual and for unmarried pairs, and terms like 'spouse' or 'partner' will be interchanged for each other. Special issues, for instance those arising for gay couples, will be taken up elsewhere in this book (see Chapters 11 and 12). Similarly there is no distinction drawn here between 'therapy' and 'counselling' or 'patients' and 'clients'. However, issues of levels of intervention and of setting are discussed later in this chapter. Unless stated otherwise, the mode of therapy referred to is conjoint work with a single therapist. Other, less frequently used modes of therapy are discussed in the relevant section.

The clinical examples used, while derived from real life, are greatly altered and often composite accounts of several couples. Any of my patients who might read this chapter and think that they recognize aspects of themselves in the descriptions, I would like to reassure that I can find aspects of myself in them, too.

## The first session

When meeting a couple for the first time, the therapist's initial reaction may well be one of disorientation, of being faced with pressures and demands which are hard to make sense of, to a degree not usually encountered in other forms of therapy. The reason for this can be understood by referring to the nature of the initial interactions. In conjoint couple therapy the strongest relationship in the room is already well established but so far unknown to the therapist, who experiences only one result of it (i.e. how the couple relate to him or her as a third party). The circumstances are thus markedly different from those in individual work where the development of the therapeutic relationship (and the distorted perceptions of it) can be monitored right from the start by the therapist who, as an 'insider', has privileged access to it. In group therapy, further strong relationships may also develop between group members. Although the therapist is not party to these they can nevertheless be observed in their development from the first meeting onwards.

A further complication, which will be elaborated later in the section on the therapeutic alliance, is presented by the triangular constellation in conjoint couple work, which means that the therapist in relating to one partner will necessarily exclude and isolate the other. This is quite in contrast to family therapy, where the therapist is subject to comparable interactional pressures, but may relate to a subsystem leaving other family members to support each other. Working with a co-therapist does mitigate but does not eliminate the special triangular issue in couple therapy.

Two parallel but interwoven processes which will frame the entire course of therapy are therefore already in evidence: on the one hand a continuous reworking of an understanding of the couple's way of relating to each other (see the later section on the 'Formulation question'); on the other hand the continuous attention which needs to be paid to the state of the relationship between the couple and the therapist (see the section on the 'Process question').

In trying to structure the disparate impressions and in order to simplify their answer to the central question 'How will I attempt to help this couple?', therapists may well want to organize their thinking around a number of subsidiary questions and decisions: 'How did this couple come to be here?' 'Who is my client?' 'Which mode of therapy would be most appropriate?' 'What should the purpose of therapy be?' 'Where should the focus of therapy be?' 'How does this couple have problems?' 'How does this couple make use of me?' While this list is by no means exhaustive it does cover a number of key issues in couple therapy which we shall consider in detail.

### Questions and issues for the therapist: determinants

As already mentioned, there are three major determinants influencing the answer to the various questions outlined above: the contribution of the therapist, the contribution of the client, and the context of the setting. The relationship between these determinants and the questions can be diagrammatically represented as shown in Figure 4.1.

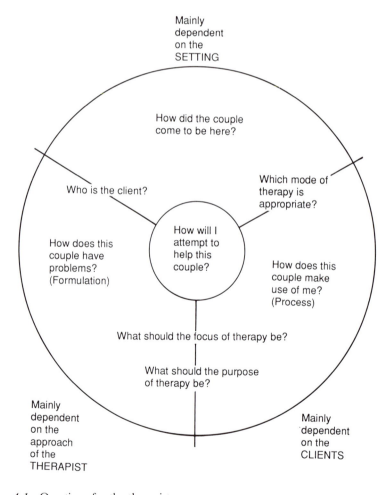

*Figure 4.1*  Questions for the therapist

While all three determinants clearly have some bearing on each of the issues which therapists have to consider, there is a difference in the degree of influence which they exert. This is represented in Figure 4.1 by the position of the questions in relation to the boundaries of the three sectors.

### How did the couple come to be here?

This is one of the first issues to be considered by the therapist, perhaps even before the couple have walked through the door. It is largely determined by the helping setting and the circumstances of the couple's referral. The setting might be a specialist agency (conveying that relationship distress is taken seriously, but perhaps also raising anxieties about the severity of problems), a generalist service (putting couple therapy in the context of other forms of help, but perhaps also increasing doubts about the necessity for work on the relationship), or a service with a primary focus on another task, for instance child-care, offering couple therapy as an adjunct to other forms of intervention (affording couples some distance from their difficulties, but perhaps also conveying that their relationship is attended to almost as an afterthought).

There is still a great deal of stigma attached to seeking 'official' help for such private matters as difficulties in intimate relationships, and before crossing this threshold most couples will have already exhausted their informal resources, such as friends or families. At this point they can refer themselves to a direct service, like 'Relate', or embark on the formal part of a 'help-seeking career' (Brannen and Collard 1982) by contacting a referral agent, for instance their general practitioner (GP).

Referrers, in their turn, shape a couple's expectation of therapy by conveying their own opinions and preferences and by selecting a setting. Indeed, the process of referral may already indicate an aspect of the couple's problem (for an examination of these issues see Clulow 1985). As the clients' expectations have a major bearing on the establishment of the working alliance and the therapeutic contract (see the relevant sections), it is of value for any therapist to enquire about the help-seeking process.

In some instances it may be that only one partner is presenting, either because the referrer thought couple work appropriate but did not manage to convince both spouses of this, or because the referral was occasioned by individual therapeutic work having become 'stuck', and couple therapy is being seen as promising more 'leverage'. This leaves the therapist with the dilemma whether to 'convene' the missing party. From a systemic, particularly a strategic perspective, this might be thought of as commonplace. From other viewpoints practical and ethical problems arise. Practically it may be very difficult to establish and keep a focus on the joint problems if one partner has been brought in because of, and subsidiary to, the problems of the other. Ethically the message conveyed may be that the therapist values the relationship more highly than the individual's concerns. This latter issue is particularly poignant if the initial patient is a married woman, who may find herself in the familiar situation of having her own needs set aside in deference to a marriage which is already likely to afford greater psychological protection to her husband.

The particular issues of working with only one partner from the couple will be addressed in Chapter 6. For our purposes we shall assume that the couple present jointly, and go on to discuss the question of who the client is from a different angle.

### Who is the client?

At first sight this might seem a rhetorical question: after all, there is the couple sitting with the therapist. However, the precise answer as to where the focus of help should be is likely to differentiate therapists according to their understanding of the nature of relationships and hence according to their theoretical approach to couple therapy. Figure 4.2 represents a continuum of views on the relative importance of the couple – compared with individuals (on the left end) and families and wider systems (on the right end) – for the direction of therapeutic effort. Examples of theoretical approaches are given above the line, and therapists will be able to locate themselves somewhere along this spectrum with, or near to, their preferred theoretical framework.

On the left pole we find cognitive approaches, for instance Rational-Emotive Therapy (Dryden 1985), focusing on the individual's thoughts and perceptions about the relationship which may be changed and reconstrued in therapy without necessarily making reference to the partner at all. The Client-Centred Therapy approach (following Rogers 1951) can be located next to it. Here the emphasis is on helping partners to attain individual 'congruence' (consistency between experiences and self-concept), as a result of which they are able to provide better conditions for personal growth for each other.

Further along on the spectrum we find behavioural approaches to marital therapy (for instance Jacobson and Margolin 1979), where therapeutic efforts concentrate on the couple's interaction, emphasizing individual satisfaction as being dependent on the partner's response.

An experiential/interactional approach, such as Emotionally Focused Therapy (Greenberg and Johnson 1988), lying next on the continuum, would construe the couple as a balanced system while maintaining a therapeutic focus on each partner's blocks to experiencing self in relation to the other.

Yet further along the line we would find the psychodynamic approaches to marital therapy (for instance Meissner 1978). In these the couple is understood as a psychic entity in which the partners have chosen each other partly on the basis of the 'fit' of their individual histories, leading them to develop shared phantasies and adaptive styles.

Systemic approaches (for instance Sluzki 1978), which emphasize the couple's role as a subsystem of families and wider social contexts, would be placed at the right pole of the continuum.

### Which mode of therapy is appropriate?

Much of the previous considerations have focused on conjoint work with a single therapist; however, there are several other options available. Even though, by this stage of their help-seeking career, the couple have established themselves

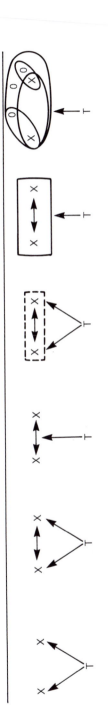

RET

CCT

BT

EFT

PsDT

ST

RET = Rational-Emotive Therapy
CCT = Client-Centred Therapy
BT   = Behavioural Therapy

EFT  = Emotionally Focused Therapy
PsDT = Psychodynamic Therapy
ST    = Systemic Therapy

*Figure 4.2* A spectrum of approaches to couple therapy

as presenting with joint rather than individual difficulties, they could still be seen entirely separately by different therapists for individual therapy. Alternatively they could be worked with in *collaborative mode* – by two different individual therapists who communicate with each other about the couple – or in *concurrent mode* – separately by the same therapist. Moreover, they could be seen together with other couples for *conjoint group* work. While all these possibilities appear in the literature on couple therapy, they do not seem to be widely practised. The relative neglect of couples groups is, to my mind, particularly regrettable.

The setting plays an important part in deciding which mode of therapy is preferred. Especially in agencies where individual therapy is the norm this may well be extended to presenting couples. Furthermore, there may be practical limitations, such as the lack of a like-minded colleague, which preclude collaborative work. There is the option of mixing modes, for instance by alternating conjoint and concurrent therapy, or by contracting some concurrent sessions if partners find difficulties in focusing on the relationship because they have become temporarily overwhelmed with their individual needs. While this expands the therapist's repertoire it brings its own drawbacks, as anyone who has been 'entrusted' with secrets in individual sessions and struggled with the question whether these can be legitimately referred to in joint sessions, will know to their cost. (Personally I find the restrictions placed on my thinking by such an arrangement so disabling that I prefer to tell spouses right from the start that I shall feel free to bring individual material into conjoint sessions.)

The way in which the couple present their difficulties is the other main factor in making decisions about the mode of therapy. Grunebaum and colleagues (1969) offer a theoretical rationale for this by suggesting three consecutive questions to be considered by the therapist in the process of treatment planning. As a first step, the question of the couple's commitment to working on the marital difficulties is explored. If such a commitment cannot be established, individual or collaborative mode is recommended. If, however, the spouses are resolved to tackle their joint problems, the second step consists of an enquiry into the locus of their symptoms. In the case of serious difficulties manifesting themselves *outside* as well as inside the relationship, concurrent therapy is considered to be the best option. For couples whose predominant difficulties arise from within the relationship, the final question concerns duration. Those with acute difficulties of relatively recent onset (often, one might add, understandable in terms of a particular transition point in the couple's life-cycle) are thought to benefit most from conjoint therapy, whereas it is assumed that couples with long-standing, chronic problems are best helped in a group where they have the opportunity of combining work on individual and on relationship problems.

This particular model still awaits empirical support and may well be too specifically prescriptive. It does, however, draw on developmental concepts both from an individual and from a couple perspective and could therefore be of use to therapists as a rough guide for decisions about therapy mode as illustrated by the following brief clinical examples.

*Case example: Mr and Mrs A*

Mr and Mrs A were referred to an NHS psychotherapy unit by their GP, who had repeatedly been consulted by Mrs A complaining of depression and a variety of minor physical symptoms. In the course of these consultations she had deplored what she felt to be a lack of closeness in her marriage. Her husband, having recently been troubled by anxieties about his work, had agreed that all was not well with the relationship, and both presented for the assessment apparently eager to work in couple therapy.

In the first interview it emerged that Mrs A's symptoms had started after the youngest of their three children left home. She had tried to compensate for this loss by taking up a vocational training in evening classes, but she was left with a feeling of emptiness which she attributed to her and her husband having developed very separate lives, his centred around his work and hers concentrating on the family. This was mirrored in their sexual relationship, which had long since been inactive. Mr A seemed quite content with the current situation; while he could recall feeling angry about some aspects of the marriage, this belonged to the distant past and he now held out little hope for changes. Mrs A was at the brink of recognizing that what she was looking to was a return to the very early days of their marriage when they had been united against parental disapproval.

A recommendation of separate individual therapy was made on the basis that a joint commitment to work on the marriage had not been established. Mrs A took up individual therapy within the unit while her husband found a setting which allowed him to attend to his personal growth without defining himself as a patient. The couple decided to separate within months of the assessment.

*Comment* This couple, while overtly maintaining an interest in improving their relationship, showed in the assessment that they had been 'emotionally divorced' for some time. This situation was clarified and reinforced by the offer of separate treatment, which may well have helped to allow a relatively amicable separation.

*Case example: Mr and Mrs B*

The B couple, both in their early 20s, contacted a voluntary counselling agency after nine months of marriage. Their frequent arguments had left both of them emotionally bruised and uncertain if their relationship was viable. Mrs B's main complaint was about her husband's habit of going out at night with his friends or his workmates without telling her, let alone inviting her along. Mr B was particularly aggrieved about his wife's continuing close relationship with her mother, whom she visited almost daily. Their counsellor decided to see both of them concurrently for a limited number of sessions with a view to conjoint work at a later date.

*Comment* This couple clearly showed acute and recent difficulties arising from within their marriage, suggesting eventual conjoint work as a viable option. However, in their development as a couple they had not yet negotiated the phase of mutual adjustment and remained at a pre-marital or 'courtship' stage, behaving as if they were still relatively uncommitted and denying interdependency. On the understanding that they both still had to reach a stage of dedication to working on their marriage, their counsellor opted for initial individual work undertaken, for practical reasons, by herself.

*Case example: Mr and Mrs C*
A psychiatrist referred the C couple to their local Clinical Psychology department with a diagnosis of 'morbid jealousy' on the part of Mr C. Both partners were quite desperate about their current situation, which involved Mrs C's withdrawal from what she experienced as a stifling marriage and her husband's desperate and self-destructive clinging to her. His background was one of early abandonment by his parents, followed by a succession of residential homes and eventually a foster-mother who at last provided stability for several years. Her history was characterized by an emotionally cold stepfather whom her mother had married for convenience after the breakup of an earlier relationship. Their marriage had been initially satisfying for both partners but deteriorated after the birth of their first child some five years ago. During the assessment their therapist felt himself inundated with the painful feelings they were bringing and noticed how each of them seemed to find it difficult to let go of his attention even for a moment and to make room for their partner's concern. It also emerged that Mrs C had trouble in getting on with her work colleagues and often felt ostracized, while Mr C experienced great problems in relating to their children. It was decided to offer the couple separate therapy in collaborative mode with a possible option of meeting as a foursome in conjoint therapy in the future.

*Comment* This couple showed enduring distress arising from within the marriage while both partners also had problems outside the relationship. Furthermore, they were both at a stage in their individual development which made it very difficult for them to tolerate conjoint work; although they wanted it, they did not seem to have the capacity for it as yet. Presumably this match between them had played a major part in their choosing each other in the first place, and in setting up an unspoken 'contract' of looking after each other's neediness which could not survive the arrival of a needy infant. A doubt in the assessor's mind about their ability to share a therapist even in separate sessions prompted the offer of collaborative rather than concurrent work.

*Case example: Mr and Mrs D*
Mr and Mrs D were referred to a specialist agency as a 'last resort' by their social worker, who had been involved with the family for some years. In their initial interview they presented with a history of constant arguments, followed by frequent breakups and reconciliations, dating back for nearly two decades. Coming from different cultural backgrounds, they had married 'against the odds', and now seemed unable to live together peaceably, but equally unable to let go of each other. Both felt individually vulnerable, Mrs D on account of her deprived background and her husband because he had never fully adjusted to living outside his native country. By now the couple felt demoralized by their failure to resolve their differences and shamed by the two oldest of their four children, who would

often adopt a patronizingly indulgent role in the face of their parents' 'childish' tussles. It was agreed that the Ds would join a couples group.

*Comment* This couple showed long-standing difficulties, arising from within the marriage, in the context of an intense emotional involvement. In view of the close involvement of two of the children in the marital conflict and of the role reversal between generations, family therapy would have been an alternative, and possibly preferable, option. This was not considered because the setting did not allow for it. It was thought that a group might give both of them opportunities to work with their individual predicaments as well as providing a setting for comparing their relationship with that of other couples and for beginning to change it.

### Co-therapy

One particular topic related to the mode of therapy concerns the question of whether conjoint work is better undertaken by one or by two therapists. (Given the complexities of couples group work, co-therapy would always appear to be the preferable option.) Although it should ideally be answered from the theoretical standpoint of the therapist, bearing the interests of the clients in mind, in reality practical considerations will play a major part. Given that most agencies offering couple therapy have long waiting lists and given that workers experienced in conjoint work are scarce, it is hardly surprising that the double demand on resources made by co-therapy is sometimes regarded as a luxury which services can ill afford. This situation is compounded by the lack of empirical evidence indicating that foursomes in conjoint therapy are more effective than triadic work (though it has to be said that this may be due to the failure of relevant studies to differentiate between various client groups). Furthermore, co-therapists need time to establish and build their working relationships and the difficulties in creating a stable therapy partnership add to the odds against this mode of therapy. Consequently it is often found only in specialist settings or in those with a commitment to training or research.

However, this begs the question of how prevalent co-therapy would be if the above constraints were not operating. One important consideration might be that the presence of two therapists circumvents the triangular problems mentioned above. Other rationales derive from the theoretical persuasion of the therapist.

The behavioural couple therapist, for instance, being grounded in theories of social learning, would be well aware of the modelling function which working with a co-therapist provides: for better, if the therapists demonstrate how one can co-operate without concealing differences, or for worse, if the co-therapy partnership provides an example of a dysfunctional relationship. Experienced behavioural therapists could therefore be expected to prefer co-working.

From a cognitive viewpoint, on the other hand, the second therapist would introduce an unnecessary complication, as the work of challenging and restructuring maladaptive cognitions can be adequately undertaken by a single worker. Therapists working within a systemic framework could be expected to welcome an additional worker; not as a co-therapist but rather as a live supervisor either in the room or behind the one-way screen.

For the psychodynamic couple therapist, co-therapy would be the preferred mode for conjoint work. It provides the opportunity of gaining insight into and influence on the couple's conflicts by having them reflected and contained in the co-therapy relationship (for an illustration of this process see Skynner 1979). The possible drawback lies in the possibility that co-workers who are unaware of enduring conflicts between themselves may unwittingly work them out through their clients – to the detriment of the latter.

If practically possible, therapists, regardless of their theoretical persuasion, would ideally provide themselves with an opportunity of finding out whether and with what clients they function better in co-therapy.

### What should the main purpose of therapy be?

Here the choice for the therapist is between three broad categories: therapy can aim to be mainly *supportive*, mainly *prescriptive*, or mainly *exploratory*. Purposes may change over the course of treatment, and most therapies will be an admixture of the three categories. However, in asking themselves the question at the beginning of and repeatedly during the treatment, therapists will at least be aware what they are aiming at.

Supportive therapy, which aims to help the clients to build on and strengthen their current ways of coping with problems, is often underrated and therefore warrants some further thought. It is most likely to be useful with couples at either end of a spectrum regarding the severity of their disturbance. At the mild end, therapy is likely to be quite short and the therapist may be required only to provide a 'listening ear'. At the other end of the spectrum, supportive work is likely to be protracted and requires considerable skill and experience. Two examples may serve to illustrate.

*Case example: Mr and Mrs E*
Mr and Mrs E were routinely referred to the social worker in a maternity hospital following a stillbirth. Although presently very distressed, neither of them had a history of early or repeated loss, and they used the five conjoint sessions they had to talk through their grief and to worry about the effect which the bereavement might have on their two other children. Their therapist did not intervene beyond listening, reflecting and commenting positively on their abilities as parents.

*Case example: Mr and Mrs F*
Mrs F and her physically handicapped husband, some twenty years older than her, were seen in the context of a pain clinic which Mrs F had been referred to after repeated unsuccessful surgical interventions for severe back pain. She was bitter about the hospital's failure to find and remedy a physical cause for her pain, but worried about the effect her persistent complaint and complaining would have on her marriage. On assessment she related a long history of losses, including no fewer than six miscarriages with medical complications, without showing any sign of upset. The couple were seen for nearly two years, with sessions often focusing on their achievements together, for instance their raising of two daughters.

Their therapist deliberately stayed away from exploring the many interesting links in the material they presented.

*Prescriptive or exploratory therapy?*

Prescriptive therapy aims to teach clients how to replace maladaptive thoughts or actions with more constructive ones, or directly prescribes actions which enable new learning. In exploratory therapy the aim is to help couples to investigate and understand the feelings, assumptions and motivations through which they cause problems for themselves; enabling them to make conscious choices about their conduct. The choice between these two is often based on the theoretical background of the therapist. For instance cognitive or behavioural couple therapists are more likely to be prescriptive; person-centred or psychodynamic workers are more likely to be exploratory. Occasionally patients or referrers may have clear preferences.

As the purpose of therapy is closely related to therapeutic goals, it has a bearing on the initial formulation and maintenance of a therapeutic contract, an area which will be discussed below.

## Where should the main focus of therapy be?

As with the purpose of therapy, there are again three broad categories available for considering the main focus: *feelings* ('emotions'), *thoughts* ('cognitions') and *actions* ('behaviour'). Often the focus will shift over the course of treatment: typically therapies will cover all three areas. However, by asking themselves the above question at the beginning of and at intervals during the treatment, therapists will at least be aware of what they are focusing on.

It is largely dependent on the theoretical stance of therapists whether they regard feelings as primary or derived phenomena, whether they see cognitive and emotional changes as resulting from changes in behaviour, or whether they regard new actions as indicating changed perceptions. While these and other distinctions are of considerable academic interest, couples coming for therapy will want help with their most pressing problems. The therapist is likely to find no difficulty in pinpointing in which of the three areas the couple shows most problems. Often these are divided between partners, for instance one finding it hard to be in touch with feelings while the other has trouble in thinking clearly or acting decisively. The question then arises whether therapy would ideally focus on the strengths of the partners or concentrate on the area they have most difficulties with. The best indication is likely to come from the patients themselves. If they come to view their inhibitions in one or other area as a problem, they may tolerate or even welcome that area to become the focus for therapy. If not, they are unlikely to agree to a contract which centres around it.

## How does this couple have problems? (The 'Formulation Question')

This is one of two questions (the other being 'How does this couple make use of me?') which runs as a theme throughout the course of therapy. As will be argued below, the initial formulation and the continuous reworking of the answer to it provides one-half of the frame in which work with a couple takes place. If at all, a conclusive summing up of the couple's problem would be possible only after the therapy has ended.

How therapists formulate their patients' problems is largely dependent on their theoretical framework. However, it should not be forgotten that the couple will have their own views about the nature of their difficulties. Inevitably both partners will have different ideas and frequently each will be convinced that the solution to their problems would be simple, if only the other would be sensible enough to adopt those ideas and behave accordingly. Even if taken together, the couple's formulation of their difficulties is bound to be too narrow, otherwise they would have no need for help from a third party. Nevertheless, since it is based on their personal experience, it provides one important perspective on their predicament and the therapist's task is to enhance and amplify it, rather than ignore or repudiate it. While there are clear differences between the explanatory frameworks of the different theoretical schools, there are also a number of commonalities and we shall consider both in turn.

Looking at differences first, these are conditional on the different perceptions of the couple as outlined above in the section 'Who is the client?' Running through the same spectrum, we would see a rational-emotive therapist organize an account of a couple's difficulties around an understanding of how individuals can give themselves problems through their unrealistic expectations of marriage or other committed relationships.

For the person-centred therapist the key to understanding a couple's disharmony lies in the problems each spouse has in becoming a collaborative partner in an enterprise which could enhance growth for both. Approaching couple therapy from a behavioural angle one would conceive of couple problems as maladaptive patterns of interaction which lead both spouses to evaluate the relationship negatively as costing more in effort and discomfort than it offers in satisfactions and rewards.

A therapist operating within the framework of Emotionally Focused Therapy would structure the formulation of a couple's difficulties around the restricted exchange of information about each partner's experience of an emotionally charged issue, resulting from individually acquired protectiveness about the feared risks of such an exchange and leading to a climate of insecurity which in turn makes it harder for both to be authentically aware of their feelings.

For the psychodynamic couple therapist the key to understanding tensions in relationships lies in the changes in the internal balance of the couple which provides both partners with a chance to experience warded off aspects of their own personalities in the other where they can be either admired or persecuted, thus allowing for the reworking or repetition of unresolved conflicts from early relationships. This dynamic is also held to explain why the spouses were unconsciously attracted to each other in the first place.

Adopting a systemic point of view, one would see a couple's difficulties as one facet of the mechanics which regulate a wider order, such as families or extended social networks. To look at distressed relationships separately is therefore thought of as reductionist and probably detrimental to a proper formulation.

Another factor which differentiates theoretical approaches to couple therapy is the extent to which they draw on information from the couple's or the individual partners' history to arrive at their problem formulation. The systemic and the psychodynamic approaches occupy the diametrically opposite positions in this respect. For the systemic therapist, the interaction of the couple is entirely comprehensible from the observation of current circumstances (this is known as the principle of 'equifinality'); consequently references to the past are held to obscure the formulation and to divert the attention of the couple away from the changes they have to make in the future. (This does not mean that intergenerational issues are of no importance: they figure particularly in the structural variant of the systemic approach. However, it is only their manifestation in the here and now which is taken to be of interest.)

The psychodynamic therapist, on the other hand, seeking to understand couple difficulties as an enactment of the partners' individual but corresponding internal conflicts, relies heavily on a reconstruction of early experience – of relationships in general and of the parental couple in particular – in order to make sense of the couple's interaction and reaction to him/herself. (For an integration of the two positions see for instance Scharff and Scharff 1987.)

Descriptions of supposedly stable configurations of couples are equally dependent on differences in theoretical approach. There have been various attempts to devise typologies of couples which would simplify the formulation of specific cases. Some, such as 'male withdrawal vs. female withdrawal vs. withdrawal by both partners', are too broad to be clinically informative (what is mostly the same for all may ultimately be all the same to most); others are more elaborate. Of the more informative descriptions one might cite Willi's (1982) four patterns of collusion (narcissistic, oral/dependent, anal/sadistic, and phallic/oedipal) based on Freudian psychosexual stages of development, and Sluzki and Beavin's (1965) seven types of dyadic interaction, based on the concepts of symmetry, complementarity and competition.

I doubt that general typologies are of great help in the formulation of a particular case, apart from allowing therapists who are faced with difficulties in their work to recognize features of their own couples in the descriptions, reassuring them that they are not alone in their struggles. They can, however, be useful summaries of patterns which couples move in and out of; Mattinson and Sinclair's (1979) four combinations of splitting conscious and unconscious yearning and rejection between partners are another case in point.

Despite the differences outlined above, most theoretical approaches have several aspects of formulating couple problems in common. One of these concerns the recognition of stresses inevitably arising from the various stages of the couple's life-cycle. The idea of delineating psychosocial stages of individual development, each with its inherent tasks and conflicts, and delimited from the next by crisis or transition points which are instances of maximum danger and opportunity, originated from Erikson (1950). In relation to adult life it has been expanded on by Levinson (1978), popularized by Sheehy (1976), and transposed on to family life for instance by Duvall (1977).

While well known to therapists, these concepts are unfamiliar to many couples, who find it far from obvious that ordinary events – such as moving in together, coping with the first baby, supporting ailing parents, having children at the adolescent stage, seeing the last child leave home, or dealing with the changes brought about by retirement – should predictably require adjustments from both partners which may well lead to the emergence of previously contained conflicts. Disruptions of the expected course of events – such as redundancy, the birth of a handicapped child, or an untimely bereavement – are equally stressful, often without this being generally and fully acknowledged. In either case, it may be a great relief for a couple to think about their predicament as being related to the life-cylce, because it normalizes their distress by placing it into a commonplace context and attenuates feelings of shame.

Another concept commonly used to organize an account of couple problems is that of repetitive, self-maintaining interactional sequences which, if they are within the awareness of the spouses, are differently interpreted by both. A clinical vignette might best serve to illustrate this point.

*Case example: Mr and Mrs G*
Mr and Mrs G had been attending for marital therapy for several weeks when they turned their attention to an issue which had been frequently leading to arguments. Mrs G described how the atmosphere at home could be quite harmonious until her husband started to stay late at work. This tended to happen out of the blue, which naturally made her concerned enough to ask him questions when he finally did show up. On being met with what she felt to be his indifference she would repeatedly enquire how long this would be going on for and, confronted with his reluctance to listen to her, she would feel compelled to make her point more vigorously. Instead of paying attention to her feelings, her husband would come home even later until the tension, which was building up all the while, finally erupted into a major row. If only he would be more thoughtful and considerate, none of this needed ever have happened.

Mr G saw the matter somewhat differently. He thought that trouble usually started when his wife had one of her jealous turns, usually over some trivial issue like him having to stay on at his work. This was such a well-worn complaint that by now he was reluctant even to mention that he might be late. When she got like that she would start pestering him with constant questions, making his home life such a misery that he would prefer to stay out, even if he did not need to, to let her calm down. Irritatingly, rather than becoming more reasonable, she seemed almost to enjoy nagging and nagging him, and although he did his best to keep out of her way to avoid a row, it would finally erupt. If only she could be more rational and get a grip on herself, none of this needed ever have happened.

Most couple therapists would probably agree that these disparate accounts represent two different but interdependent perspectives of the same interactional sequence which both partners maintain and escalate by increasingly determined efforts to pursue what they think would resolve the conflict, while perceiving the conduct of their partner as destructive and probably motivated by malice. What distinguishes different theoretical approaches is whether this formulation is thought to be sufficient or is elaborated; for instance in terms of the maladaptive beliefs the partners hold, or of the costs and benefits they see themselves deriving from their relationship, or of the links between the collusive pattern and the partners' experiences in their families of origin.

## How does the couple make use of me? (The 'Process Question')

This is the other question which presents as a leitmotif over the whole span of a couple's treatment. Therapists may at times experience this consciously, like a running commentary on the moment-to-moment fluctuations of the process; or, at other times, be generally but indeterminately aware of the state of the relationship.

One aspect of this theme is the extent to which the couple makes appropriate use of the therapist as a therapist; this will be covered later in the section on the working alliance. Other aspects are provided by the many ways in which spouses can make use of therapists for other purposes; either by involving them directly in their interactions; or by relating to them as if they primarily had other than therapeutic functions; or by manoeuvring them into enacting something important for the couple. We shall consider these possibilities in turn, bearing two points in mind. First, that – while they may all be present in the first session – it may take considerable time for such 'hidden agendas' to become conspicuous and comprehensible; second, that they are different perspectives on the same issue rather than mutually exclusive categories.

The most common form of involving a therapist in the couple's interaction, whatever the theoretical framework for the therapy, are bids by one partner to form a special coalition excluding the other partner. It will be argued later that the handling of this process is the basic problem for the therapist in triadic couple work. The force with which such bids are made in the first session gives the therapist an indication of the difficulties that can be expected for maintaining a working alliance with both partners. Likewise, therapists are frequently employed in the couple's interaction as regulators of the distance between the spouses. A visible sign of distance is the degree to which the partners talk to each other directly or choose to channel their communications through the therapist. In some approaches they would be directed to address each other (for instance Ables and Brandsma 1977), in other approaches alterations in the couple's use of the therapist as a mediator of their exchanges would be monitored as indicating changes in their relationship.

Whether a couple is thought to make use of their therapist for other than therapeutic purposes is of course entirely dependent on how therapeutic tasks are defined in the first place. For instance a couple attempting to use the therapist mainly as an arbiter to their disagreements may be well inside the bounds of a behavioural approach, but would elicit an intervention in psychodynamic couple therapy. Other ways of trying to use therapists as if their primary function was something different (usually discussed in psychodynamic theory under the heading of 'transference'), are more universally held to be outside the therapeutic contract. For example a couple may attempt to relate to their therapist as if his or her main function was to act like a parent towards them. Or, some couples may treat their therapists as if they were opponents in a fight. Such transgressions of the therapeutic boundaries are in some approaches regarded as an impediment to therapy – with the implication that they should be stopped or circumvented. In other approaches, they are seen as a source of information about the couple's predicament, indicating the ways in which the partners create interpersonal difficulties, or in which they elicit a particular emotional reaction (often referred to as 'countertransference') from their therapist.

The process by which therapists are compelled to enact an important aspect of the couple's relationship (a phenomenon which in psychodynamic theory is often discussed under the heading of 'projection' or 'projective indentification'), if acknowledged at all, is also regarded in sharply different ways. In some approaches it is seen as an attempt to dislodge the therapist from a helpful stance into one which colludes with the couple's pattern of difficulties – with the implication that it needs to be avoided. In other approaches it is valued as providing direct access to marital interaction which would otherwise remain outside awareness, and its ramifications are traced beyond the confines of therapy (see Mattinson 1975). In keeping with the literature on individual therapy, the purpose of this process can be understood in two main ways: it can either be used in order to communicate something which cannot be verbalized, or it can be employed to get rid of a painful feeling by evoking it in the therapist who then experiences it 'on behalf' of the couple. In this detail, little attention is paid to it outside the psychodynamic framework. To assess the respective contributions of the therapist and the clients to this process is complicated; it requires as a minimum a consultative/supervisory backup and it is greatly helped by the therapist being aware of his or her own response patterns as a result of having been in personal therapy.

In all approaches it is ultimately the couple's capacity to make constructive use of their therapist which determines success or failure of the therapy. The task of helping them with this has to be accomplished throughout the treatment but its magnitude can be estimated from the first session.

## Therapy unfolding

Once the therapist has begun to answer the various questions outlined in the previous section, and a decision has been made to conduct couple therapy, a process is set in motion which may well be described with the metaphor of the frame and the picture.

The frame, in this context, is meant to consist of first, the establishment of a good enough therapeutic alliance together with the subsequent monitoring and, when necessary, repairing of the working relationship throughout the course of therapy; and second, the agreement of a therapeutic contract together with the attendant formulation and continuous reformulation of the couple's predicament. *Maintaining a stable frame*, in the way outlined below, is fundamental to couple therapy in any theoretical approach. It is in itself the main therapeutic intervention of counsellors and therapists operating at a basic level of competence. It is thus always necessary, and may be sufficient for helping couples whose problems are not too severe and relatively recent.

The picture is meant to consist of the various specific interventions made during the course of therapy. They are divided here into the 'staple' and the 'special'. 'Staple' interventions (for example helping the couple to negotiate disagreements or to communicate better) are those which have high face-validity, and are therefore relatively easily understood – though not necessarily adhered to – by the couple. These can be confidently used by therapists of various theoretical persuasions, and require an intermediate level of sophistication. 'Special' interventions (for example transference interpretations or paradoxical injunctions), by contrast, are not so directly accessible and may not rely on being consciously perceived or intellectually understood by the couple. They are highly specific to a particular school of thought and will mainly be used by therapists with specialist expertise and experience. The relationships between these elements can be represented as shown in Figure 4.3.

The balance between staple and special interventions will in part depend on the therapist's theoretical background. For instance psychodynamic or strategic therapists might mainly move between frame maintenance and special interventions, whereas behavioural therapists might mainly concentrate on staple interventions and on attending to the frame. Marital therapists who are not committed to a particular approach and who can operate at a high level of sophistication might make use of special interventions whenever there appears to be a therapeutic impasse which cannot be accounted for in terms of the frame, and will consequently return to staple interventions as soon as the block is removed.

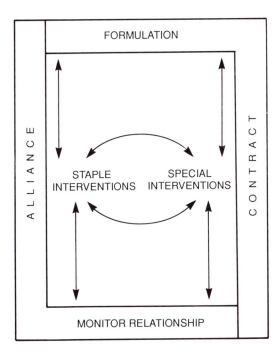

*Figure 4.3* The frame and the picture

Both types of interventions will be considered in detail in the section on the 'picture'. However, difficulties in therapy which can be understood in terms of breakdowns of alliance and contract will have to be dealt with by attending to the frame, and it is to these that we shall turn our attention next.

### The frame: the working alliance

Most therapists would agree that establishing a good working alliance is crucial to the success of any therapeutic endeavour; a view supported by empirical studies (see Beutler *et al.* 1986). However, as there are various definitions of the term, it is important to be clear what is meant by it. The following observations assume that the working alliance consists of an understanding between the therapist and the couple

1  that they have a joint therapeutic task to do
2  that the potential social aspects of their relationship have to be set aside for the benefit of the task
3  that their joint work requires a climate of mutual trust and good will.

Other issues often connected with the alliance, such as establishing joint goals, are dealt with below in the section on contracting.

Much has been written about the need to establish, maintain and repair a working alliance in individual therapy. Its quality in early sessions has been cited by researchers as a predictor of eventual positive outcome. Integrative therapists have regarded it as a unifying concept explaining the specific agency of factors which hitherto had been called 'non-specific'. Indeed, one strand of psycho-analytic thinking (which initially coined the term) has broadened its understanding of the working alliance from regarding it as a necessary precondition for the development and resolution of a transference neurosis, to attributing much of the potential for therapeutic change to the gradual disillusionment and adjustment to reality which is the consequence of repeated manageable breakdowns and repairs of an empathic alliance.

However, the establishment and subsequent monitoring of the working alliance is of particular importance in conjoint couple work (especially when conducted by a single therapist), more so than in any other form of therapy. Indeed, it is in my experience unusual for couple therapy not to be hampered by repeated alliance breakdowns. Why should that be the case? In the first place we have to acknowledge that there can be at least two forms of alliance in operation: one between the therapist and each spouse and another between the therapist and the couple. Where the emphasis is placed will of course depend on the therapist's answer to the question 'Who is the client?' in the way outlined above. However, having an alliance with the couple is dependent on having engaged each partner individually, and it is this form of alliance which is vulnerable to the pressures created by a triangular relationship.

From the couple's point of view, it may well be that an important issue from early individual development is revived in the therapy; namely the transition from two-person to three-person relationships bringing in its wake new challenges, such as feelings of jealousy, rivalry and exclusion, which were previously outside experience. How well these have been coped with in the past by both spouses individually will determine their tolerance of a third party, here the therapist, getting involved in their relationship; an issue which for some couples is first manifested when the birth of their first child leads to relationship problems (see Clulow 1982).

From the therapist's point of view, the difficulty lies in relating to two people individually and as a couple at the same time, and to maintain that stance under the pressures created by the determined efforts of one or both partners to form a dyadic relationship. In my view it is this dynamic which presents the unique challenge, or the special opportunity, in triadic couple therapy.

If stresses on the working alliance leading to its intermittent temporary breakdown are inevitable, the question arises how these lapses are best dealt with. This can either be done indirectly, by attending to the factors which led to the alliance breakdown, or directly, by drawing the couple's attention to the state of the alliance itself. Among the indirect techniques which therapists can use are strategies such as disengaging from the couple (in order to break the developing special alliance with one partner), addressing spouses jointly rather than individually, or switching the focus of attention to the partner who is in danger of being excluded. While these may be helpful, it has to be emphasized that the quality of the alliance is based on subjective experience. To give equal time to both partners may be satisfactory for one of them, but might not feel anything like enough for the other. To address the state of the alliance directly with the couple appeals to the rational and co-operative aspect of the partners, but requires from both of them the capacity to temporarily set aside their own needs in order to make space for those of the other. If couples cannot tolerate the temporary deprivation entailed in triadic work they would be better off with a different mode of therapy.

### The therapeutic contract

Agreeing and maintaining a therapeutic contract provides the other component of the frame in which couple therapy can take place. It is dependent on the establishment and maintenance of a working alliance. If there are impediments to the therapeutic work which cannot be dealt with by specific interventions, the contract will have to be attended to either by restating or by reformulating it. If this proves unsuccessful, the therapeutic alliance will first need to be attended to in the way outlined in the preceding section.

For the purposes of this chapter it is assumed that the contract consists of agreements on three areas: the therapeutic goals; the tasks and responsibilities of the therapist and the couple; and the parameters of therapy, such as frequency or duration. Considering the agreements on goals and tasks first, these follow on directly from the formulation of the couple's problems and are therefore markedly influenced by the therapist's theoretical approach. However, they may need to be revised as therapy unfolds and new material emerges. It would weaken the frame and obstruct the therapeutic work, were the therapist to persist rigidly with the initial formulation.

There are wide variations in the extent to which couple therapists make therapeutic tasks and goals explicit. Some therapists state right at the beginning what they see as the roles and responsibilities of themselves and of their clients; others aim to 'socialize' the couple into their form of therapy in the first few sessions; yet others leave their assumptions largely implicit, trusting that they will clarify and demonstrate them through their conduct in the sessions. While these are matters partly of approach and partly of personal style, it is important to consider their likely impact on the couple. This to my mind is a trade-off between promoting security and fostering independence. Explicit contracts reduce anxieties and create a climate of safety and predictability, but may engender dependency. Implicit agreements underline the couple's competence and autonomy, but may be disorientating and raise anxieties. What matters is that the decision on how far to elucidate the agreement is made knowingly, for if the terms are cloudy in the therapist's mind they are unlikely to be clear to the couple.

As far as the parameters of therapy are concerned, a failure to make these explicit would clearly be unhelpful. Whatever their theoretical approach, it is incumbent on therapists to clarify the length of sessions; mode, frequency and duration of therapy; requirements for and limits of confidentiality; possible obligations to third parties; and – in the case of therapy outside the statutory services – level and mode of payment. Of course, this is not to say that these features are immutable, but rather that initial arrangements and subsequent alterations will have to be spelt out.

Some therapists contract for trial periods, for instance six weeks, before reviewing the agreement. This can be informative and constructive, if it is done purposely, either by viewing the arrangement as an extended assessment, or as a very brief time-limited therapy, and if the rationale for it is conveyed to the couple. However, if the trial period is used because of the therapist's indecision or ambivalence it is likely to weaken the working alliance, destabilize the frame, and thus to impede the therapy.

Having discussed the establishment and maintenance of a stable frame, we can now turn our attention to the picture which it holds, that is to those staple and special therapeutic interventions which go beyond frame maintenance, but depend on it for their effectiveness.

### The picture: staple interventions

Examples of these will be presented roughly in the order in which they might come to the therapist's mind, starting with minimum interventions – in keeping with a therapeutic maxim of doing as little as is necessary and sufficient – and following on with increasing degrees of involvement, often required because the simpler intervention was insufficient or did not have the desired effect. Four examples of staple interventions are described:

1  education
2  reframing
3  assisting negotiation
4  assisting communication.

## Education

This represents the simplest level of intervention and shades into work with couples who are not currently in distress, such as marriage preparation or Marriage Enrichment (see Chapter 14). As already mentioned, knowledge about naturally occurring stresses in the family life-cycle is of use to many couples and may be sufficient intervention for some. Similarly an appreciation of different arousal patterns in men and women may help sexual adjustment, while information about child development could assist adapting to parenthood. By the time couples come for help they are often beyond the stage where education alone would be of benefit, but it can play a role in many therapies, provided the partners are in a state of mind which allows them to listen to and assimilate it.

## Reframing

This represents a somewhat more involved level of intervention. It assumes that a couple possesses the information necessary to resolve their problems but perceives it in a way which prevents them from using it. In altering the context to information, for instance by redefining a perceived liability as an asset, the therapist widens its applicability while at the same time demonstrating the benefits of flexible thinking. Extensively used by cognitive and interactional systemic therapists, it will probably be employed at one time or other in therapies conducted from other theoretical viewpoints.

## Assisting negotiation

It has been said about nations at war, that in the beginning each side hopes it will win, later on both sides hope the other will lose, and in the end each side hopes only to lose less heavily than the other. Much the same seems to hold true in relationship warfare. Couples coming for therapy are often in the middle or last stage of this process; indeed, one might argue that as long as both partners think they will ultimately win overall, neither has an incentive to give up a belligerent attitude in favour of a negotiating stance. It is, however, precisely this shift which would help the couple to deal with future disagreements constructively.

Even if both partners are of a mind to limit the damage they inflict on each other and to start negotiating (regardless of whether this happens in the service of a better relationship or of a less destructive separation), there can be several obstacles to the process. One of these might be an anxiety that, for the benefit of agreeing, the spouses would have to desist from voicing their respective complaints. It may take some time for the couple to realize that, quite to the contrary, it is vitally important that both should become aware of their needs and wants, accept responsibility for them, and express them in specific terms which can be responded to by their partner. This enables them to turn complaints into requests (for instance 'You never care about the garden' becomes 'I would like you to weed the flower-border once a month') which can be heard and acted upon.

Another obstacle might be a backlog of unexpressed past resentments which need to be aired and heard before it becomes possible to focus on the present and the future. This may well be at variance with approaches to therapy which concentrate on the here and now, but, especially with regard to long-standing complaints, neglecting to give them a hearing puts a strain on the alliance which may render therapeutic work impossible.

Successful negotiation in a therapy session is useful in two ways: it demonstrates to the couple that they can reach agreements, and it serves as an example of the process by which this can be accomplished. The resolution of the actual issue is more like a fringe benefit, welcome but secondary. This is because the couple could not possibly address in therapy all current areas of disagreement, let alone future ones. Furthermore, as Haley (1963) has pointed out some time ago, each specific issue which is settled is part of a larger negotiation about who has the right to make decisions about a particular area. This delineation of 'spheres of influence' saves much time and energy for both partners (much like the Congress of Vienna or the Yalta Agreement did for nations), which would otherwise be taken up in constant combat. It is not discontent with the fact of divided decision-making but dissatisfaction with the balance of who determines what, which makes for unhappiness in relationships.

Helping a couple to negotiate better assumes that the partners are by and large able to communicate with each other. If this is not the case they may need help with this area of their relationship first, as outlined in the following section.

*Assisting communication*

As mentioned above, a couple's efforts to negotiate their disagreements often founder because of the partners' difficulties in expressing their needs and wishes to each other. This is but one example of communication failure which is a prominent feature in distressed relationships and which is blamed by many couples when they describe their difficulties. The couple therapist will have little trouble in identifying how partners both suffer from and contribute to their misunderstandings. However, describing miscommunication is one thing, explaining it is quite another. Explanations will vary according to theoretical approaches which in turn determine interventions.

Approaches to couple therapy which are derived from learning theory will conceptualize communication failures in terms of skills deficits. The logical response would be to equip the couple with the competencies they are lacking. This has been elaborated under the heading of 'communication training' (e.g. Bornstein and Bornstein 1986) and represents a sound first line attempt to deal with miscommunication for the therapist who feels comfortable with a prescriptive stance. Techniques include listening exercises, reformulation exercises (for instance changing 'you' to 'I' statements) and reciprocal role-play in which partners are invited to represent the other's point of view. Therapists who prefer an exploratory stance will aim to achieve the same goal by demonstrating attentive listening and accurate communication themselves, for the couple to emulate.

The alternative explanation – either favoured from the outset or adopted when communication training fails – would be to assume that partners have the ability to communicate, but experience blocks in using them. Different approaches would conceptualize this in different ways and use their own special interventions to deal with it (all examples of interventions used here are described in detail later).

Cognitive therapists would concentrate on the dysfunctional beliefs or attributions which the partners associate with successful communication and aim to dispute and restructure these.

Behavioural therapists might attend to the infrequency of rewarding consequences following attempts at communication from each spouse and aim to increase these for instance by monitoring and behavioural contracting.

Systemic therapists might look at the way in which miscommunication serves the maintenance of the equilibrium of a wider system and respond by a structural or strategic intervention.

Experiential therapists might concentrate on the difficulties of either partner genuinely to know about the feelings they wish to communicate and aim to clarify these by a focusing exercise.

Psychodynamic therapists might attend to the reaction of partners to each other as if they represented a relationship from the past or a disavowed aspect of themselves (see Dicks 1967) by offering an interpretation.

None of these interventions is mutually exclusive; all of them are, however, highly specific and in practice few therapists will have a broad enough repertoire to use all or most of them with expertise. Similar alternative explanations to the ones outlined above have also been elaborated for the sexual communication of couples, for instance by Hawton (1985) and Tunnadine (1983) (see also Chapter 8).

### Special interventions

The following examples of special interventions are not presented in any specific order. While the list is by no means exhaustive, at least one example from each of the major approaches has been included. These are

1  interpretation
2  cognitive restructuring
3  focusing
4  contingency contracting
5  structural interventions
6  strategic interventions.

### Interpretation

In the wider sense of the word, interpretations are widely used in various approaches to couple therapy. In so far as they are about sharing parts of the therapist's formulation with the couple, they are linked to the maintenance of the frame. In prescriptive approaches this will take the form of impressing upon the couple an explanatory model of their troubles; in exploratory approaches it will take the form of putting forward explanatory hypotheses which can be confirmed, modified or discarded.

In the narrower sense, however, interpretations are specific to psychodynamic approaches and formulations. Here too they are statements designed to draw the spouses' attention to something they had hitherto been unaware of, but will focus either on the ways in which the couple jointly protect themselves from internal pain or from anxiety arising from unconscious conflicts (interpretations of

defences); or on the ways in which they re-enact, or manoeuvre each other and
the therapist to enact, aspects from conflictual past relationships (transference
interpretations). Again, interpretations function as hypotheses about such
mechanisms, but the therapist will also listen out for 'unconscious communication' (see for instance Malan 1979) in order to validate or refute the proposed
explanations.

Dynamic interpretations will often convey, or seek to clarify, parts of what one
might call a 'complete formulation' (meaning a conclusive understanding of the
couple's problem, an ideal which actual formulations can only approximate)
which would consist of the following elements:

1  an understanding of the way in which partners collude in each expressing for
   the other aspects of their selves which are feared to be unacceptable (for an
   elaboration see Willi 1982)
2  an understanding of the partners' early experience predisposing them for their
   choice of mate and enabling them to be initially attracted to and later repelled
   by the disowned aspects of themselves in the other
3  an understanding of the couple's joint adaptive mechanisms allowing them to
   maintain the initial unconscious 'marriage contract'.

The reference to early experience may also have the effect of reducing the spouses'
shame about their predicament by demonstrating that their current responses are
reasonable reactions, albeit to circumstances which no longer pertain.

Observations about the relationship of the couple to the therapist are distinguished from those which serve the maintenance of the working alliance by concentrating on the repetition of past experience (an issue discussed by Scharff and
Scharff (1987) as the alternation between 'contextual' and 'focused' transference).

*Cognitive restructuring*
Changes in the ways in which partners think about themselves and their relationship would be seen by most couple therapists as a desirable outcome. However,
cognitive and cognitive-behavioural approaches place promoting this aim in the
forefront of the therapeutic endeavour and have consequently developed
specialist interventions going beyond education and reframing which have been
discussed above.

The first step in cognitive restructuring consists of identifying maladaptive
cognitions (according to the theoretical position of the therapist referred to for
instance as irrational beliefs, undifferentiated constructs, or negative automatic
thoughts) together with their antecedents and consequences. Subsequently they
have to be rendered dysfunctional, for example by being disputed, confronted
with contradictory evidence, or prescriptively altered. Finally, they have to be
replaced by more adaptive alternative cognitions. Depending on the stance of the
therapist this can take the form of direct cognitive rehearsal (for instance of coping
statements), or of hypothetical or actual 'experiments' which allow for alternative
cognitions to be confirmed by new evidence. Being able to think differently allows
partners to feel and act differently with regard to their relationship.

*Focusing*

In its elaborated form, this kind of intervention is mainly used in experiential or person-centred approaches to therapy; in its simpler forms it will be used by many therapists of differing theoretical persuasions. Focusing aims to help clients to attend to and deepen aspects of their emotional experience which they had previously been unable to access. Naturally in experiential couple therapy the point of reference is the partners' emotional experience of the relationship. Being able to have new experiences allows both partners to change their emotional responses to each other and to the relationship, and therefore to shift hitherto fixed constricting patterns of interaction.

There is a variety of ways in which therapists can assist emotional focusing, ranging from the empathic response, highlighting a particular feeling, of the person-centred therapist to the active techniques (such as repetition and exaggeration of actions, or empty chair work) of the gestalt therapist. The sequence which is common to all consists of the detection or evocation, subsequent expression and amplification, and ultimate acceptance of previously unelicited emotional experience.

*Contingency contracting*

This refers to the practice of agreeing written contracts with couples, setting out particular behaviours which the partners have identified as desirable in the other, and making the performance of these either directly contingent on each other or introducing a 'currency', such as points or tokens, to ensure the overall balance of rewarding responses. Originating from an operant behavioural paradigm and currently probably not widely used (given that many behavioural couple therapists incorporate cognitive approaches in their work), it nevertheless highlights two features especially elaborated in behavioural couple therapy: a detailed and fine-grained description of actions which partners would find rewarding, and their subsequent monitoring. The necessity of describing what partners want of each other in a specific and feasible form has been discussed above as part of helping couples to negotiate. Monitoring the progress of these interchanges in a structured way (for example by frequency counts or rating scales) and feeding the results back into the therapy, is specific to behavioural couple therapy and is not in this detail attended to in other approaches.

*Structural interventions*

As the name implies, these techniques, which belong to the repertoire of systemic therapy, make use of a structural model of family systems (Minuchin 1974) and are therefore probably most effective in the treatment of families rather than couples. However, interactional concepts like symmetry and complementarity, and notions like boundaries and territory also apply to dyads. Structural interventions rely heavily on recreating interactional patterns within the sessions and changing them actively by instruction or confrontation. By unbalancing the system, its structures can be altered which in turn makes the couple more amenable to the staple interventions described above.

*Strategic interventions*

This type of intervention is directed towards the balance of a system, in our case the marital relationship. It works on the assumption that the couple has an invest-ment in maintaining its difficulties because they are of functional value for them, and that the partners are therefore not amenable to change through other means, such as the 'staple' interventions discussed above. Strategic interventions aim to dislodge this balance by aligning themselves with the resistance to change rather than against it, for instance by highlighting and ritualizing problematic interactions.

A special type of strategic intervention is a paradoxical injunction which informs the couple of the positive value of the predicament they present, and instructs them to persist with it. Some workers (for instance Selvini-Palazzoli *et al.* 1978) regard paradoxical injunctions, which aim at change while professing to preserve the status quo, as the only viable response to the paradox which the couple present by working hard to maintain the status quo while professing their eagerness to change.


## Termination

There are three main ways in which the ending of the therapeutic work with a couple can come about: either as a premature drop-out resulting from an irreparable breakdown of the working alliance, or as happening at a predeter-mined date in time-limited therapy, or as being agreed between the couple and the therapist. While in the latter case termination is a distinct phase of therapy, issues relating to endings are permanently present in time-limited couple therapy.

The literature on the termination of couple therapy is relatively sparse. Endings, with their painful connotations of separation and loss alongside the hope of a new beginning, generally receive short shrift in writings on therapy, but perhaps there is something specific in the parallel between the breaking of the therapeutic bond and the threatened or actual break up of the couple which give the topic its particular charge in marital work.

Therapists vary in the degree to which they regard endings as absolute. At one extreme, the couple is not expected ever to be in contact again. Underlying this position is a 'curative' model of therapy which seeks to eliminate difficulties once and for all. Its advantages lie in the way in which issues of loss and separation cannot be avoided but have to be faced and dealt with here and now. Its disadvan-tages lie in the sense of failure and of arbitrary deprivation which can be engendered if some unresolved problems remain. At the other extreme, the cou-ple is thought likely to consult again, much in the way that they would see their general practitioner from time to time. Underlying this position is a 'health maintenance' model of therapy which favours repeated but less intensive interventions. Its advantages lie in the way it allows therapists and couples to do the minimum necessary at any one time, knowing that there will be opportunities to do more, rather than feeling compelled to strive for a complete resolution of difficulties. Its disadvantages lie in the sense of dependency which can be engendered by the couple never having to decide that they can go it alone. Many therapists will locate themselves in between these poles, for instance by contracting follow-up sessions. The following observations are made from a vantage point nearer the absolute end of the spectrum.

In general, the issues are similar to those in the termination of individual therapy. Thus one might say that from the therapist's point of view the business of termination is one of disengaging from the couple and of gauging the results of therapy.

Disengaging from the couple comprises a practical and an emotional task. The practical task concerns the ending of the contract and the dissolution of the working alliance, that is the handing back to the couple of the previously jointly carried responsibilities for the therapeutic task, leaving them to practise and consolidate their gains on their own. According to the theoretical approach this may be discussed under headings such as 'generalization', 'skills maintenance', 'internalizing the therapy', or 'maintaining a new balance in the system'.

The emotional task is one of breaking an attachment and of handling loss; primarily for the couple, but also for the therapist. Apart from a possible sense of relief that the commitment is about to be over, this is also likely to involve painful feelings, which the partners can aim to avoid in a number of ways detrimental to a constructive ending. The recurrence of couple problems which had previously been resolved, or the emergence of new concerns, hitherto unmentioned, are familiar signals in the run-up to a termination date that the couple wishes to prolong the therapy rather than cope with the ending. Similarly the partners may take a very negative view of the therapy, indicating that they do not need to feel loss as they are not losing anything of value. Alternatively they may take an exaggeratedly positive view, avoiding the need to address their disappointments and unfulfilled hopes. Often these attitudes may be as split between the spouses as their outlook on the future, with one partner holding a 'depressed' view that they will not be able to do anything constructive in their relationship without the therapist's continued help, and the other holding the complementary 'manic' view, expecting no further problems to arise. One might thus summarize the therapist's task as one of helping the couple to retain what was good in the therapy without having to devalue it, to remember what was not good without having to idealize it, and to mourn the passing of the attachment while recognizing the need for an ending.

Gauging the results of couple therapy raises not only all the issues usually discussed under the headings of negative or positive outcome, but also an additional one: what if the couple decide not to stay together. While most therapists would probably intellectually count a considered separation as a positive outcome, there are subtle but strong pressures to feel it as a failure, with the consequent temptation to avoid this issue when reviewing the therapy with the couple. Inevitably the initial formulation of the couple's problem will have a bearing on this evaluation.

As with individual therapy, judgements about outcome may be different from each of the perspectives of patients, therapist, third party (in marital work this frequently means children), and independent observer. While the couple's and the therapist's evaluation will be closely related to the agreed goals, the independent perspective can also rely on 'objective' measures (see Chapter 16 on research) to decide whether therapy was 'for better or for worse'. For my own practice, I cannot conceive of an indifferent result of marital therapy. If the couple derive no benefit from going through a demanding and intensive process, they will have confirmed for themselves that it is no use expending effort on trying to resolve their difficulties and they will be in a worse position than before as a result of this experience.

However, if things have gone well and the outcome on balance is judged as positive, the termination of couple therapy will ultimately enable both parties to cease interrupting each other's existence: couples will be free to get on with their lives, and therapists will be free to get on with their jobs.

## Note

1 Many of the thoughts in this chapter have emerged from discussions with colleagues and friends; in many instances I will have made other people's ideas my own, either directly or in modified form. It is by now impossible to discern what came from whom, so I shall acknowledge my general indebtedness to others for what is written in these pages. To the couples whom I have attempted to help in their struggles I owe all of my practical learning. They have provided me with constant supervision; but more than that, I believe that some of them held a genuine wish to make me better, and all of them helped to rearrange the relations of my internal couple. For this I am grateful. To my family of origin, my current family, and some people on the way from the one to the other, I owe the experience that close relationships are both inherently difficult and fundamentally worth having. For that, too, I am grateful.

## References

Ables, B.S. and Brandsma, M. (1977) *Therapy for Couples*, London: Jossey-Bass.
Beutler, E., Crago, M. and Arizmendi, G. (1986) Research on therapist variables in psychotherapy, in S.L. Garfield and A.E. Bergin (eds) *Handbook of Psychotherapy and Behavior Change*, 3rd edn, New York: Wiley.
Bornstein, P.H. and Bornstein, M.T. (1986) *Marital Therapy*, Oxford: Pergamon.
Brannen, J. and Collard, J. (1982) *Marriages in Trouble: The Process of Seeking Help*, London: Tavistock.
Clulow, C.F. (1982) *To Have and To Hold*, Aberdeen: Aberdeen University Press.
—— (1985) *Marital Therapy: An Inside View*, Aberdeen: Aberdeen University Press.
Dicks, H.V. (1967) *Marital Tensions*, London: Routledge & Kegan Paul.
Dryden, W. (1985) Marital therapy: the rational-emotive approach. in W. Dryden (ed.) *Marital Therapy in Britain*, London: Harper & Row.
Duvall, E. (1977) *Marriage and Family Development*, 5th edn. Philadelphia, Pa: J.B. Lippincott.
Erikson, E.H. (1950) *Childhood and Society*, New York: Norton.
Greenberg, L.S. and Johnson, S.M. (1988) *Emotionally Focussed Therapy for Couples*, New York: Guilford Press.
Grunebaum, H., Christ, J. and Neiberg, N. (1969) Diagnosis and treatment planning for couples, *International Journal of Group Psychotherapy*, 19: 185-202.
Haley, J. (1963) Marriage therapy, *Archives of General Psychiatry* 8: 213-34.
Hawton, K. (1985) *Sex Therapy: A Practical Guide*, Oxford: Oxford University Press.
Jacobson, N.S. and Margolin, G. (1979) *Marital Therapy: Strategies Based on Social Learning and Behavior Exchange Principles*, New York: Brunner/Mazel.

Levinson, D.L., Darrow, C.N., Klein, E.B., Levinson, M.H. and McKee, B. (1978) *The Seasons of a Man's Life*, New York: Ballantine.

Malan, D.H. (1979) *Individual Psychotherapy and the Science of Psychodynamics*, London: Butterworth.

Mattinson, J. (1975) *The Reflection Process in Casework Supervision*, London: Institute of Marital Studies.

Mattinson, J. and Sinclair, I. (1979) *Mate and Stalemate*, London: Tavistock.

Meissner, W.W. (1978) The conceptualisation of marriage and family dynamics from a psychoanalytic perspective, in T.J. Paolino and B.S. McCrady (eds) *Marriage and Marital Therapy*, New York: Brunner/Mazel.

Minuchin, S. (1974) *Families and Family Therapy*, Cambridge, Mass: Harvard University Press.

Rogers, C.R. (1951) *Client-Centred Therapy*, London: Constable.

Scharff, D.E. and Scharff, J.S. (1987) *Object Relations Family Therapy*, London: Jason Aronson.

Selvini-Palazzoli, M., Boscolo, L., Cecchin, G. and Prata, G. (1978) *Paradox and Counter-paradox*, New York: Aronson.

Sheehy, G. (1976) *Passages*, New York: Dutton.

Skynner, R. (1979) 'Postscript to: the family therapist as family scapegoat', *Journal of Family Therapy* 1: 20–2.

Sluzki, C. (1978) Marital therapy from a systems perspective, in T.J. Paolino and B.S. McCrady (eds) *Marriage and Marital Therapy*, New York: Brunner/Mazel.

Sluzki, C. and Beavin, J. (1965) Symmetry and complementarity: an operational definition and a typology of dyads, *Acta psyquiatrica y psicologica de America Latina*, 11: 321–30. English translation in P. Watzlawick and J.H. Weakland (eds) *The Interactional View*, New York: Norton.

Tunnadine, P. (1983) *The Making of Love*, London: Cape.

Willi, J. (1982) *Couples in Collusion*, London: Jason Aronson.

# 5

# Couple therapy in the family context

EDDY STREET

## Introduction

This chapter sets out to discuss the family influences on the behaviour of couples, to look at the ways these influences should be taken into account in the therapeutic process and to pose the question as to whether or not it is possible to engage in couple therapy without touching on family issues. As a first step it is important to decide what is exactly meant by the word 'family' for it can be used in a variety of ways. For example in Britain since the Second World War the majority of our legal, financial and social legislation has been based on the notion of the 'normal' nuclear family. These policies rest on the view that the family is the basic social unit in society and that apart from educational provision, the state should work to uphold the sanctity of the family and should not in normal circumstances intervene in its function. This outlook rests very much on the assumption that the prime function of families is 'child-care', and neglects to a certain extent the care of other family members less able to look after themselves (e.g. infirm, elderly or handicapped people) and it certainly neglects the fact that nearly everybody has a psychological relationship to a social unit which can be termed a 'family'.

The dominance of child-care to family life has meant that in many issues that affect couples, concepts such as 'parental responsibility' and 'the best interests of the child' are used to a considerable extent. For couples with children this can unfortunately lead many to thinking that their own needs have to be totally submerged in order to meet the needs of the child; it seems to imply that adult needs can be suspended and that a balance of everyone's needs is not possible. For couples without children, many feel that the status of being a family is denied them because they do not parent and that in some ways there are things lacking in their life even though they operate as a cohesive social group, supportive to each other in so many different ways.

The importance of the family to us all, however, is that it involves our own past and future with all the implications of that psychologically. It involves recognition by family members that each person has a history and that history affects the ordinary process of living. As a unit the family also has an orientation towards the future which may involve pregnancy, childbirth and care of a baby, but at a more fundamental level this orientation involves the eventual death of the couple. Hence each couple have to deal in a day-to-day way with the fact that each of them is a child of particular parents who have their own unique psychological demands and needs. Each couple has to deal with the ordinary life-cycle events of the future. Families therefore do not necessarily involve the care of children as an ongoing activity, but it does involve the world of the child – because we were all children once and this has an influence on how we are as individuals throughout our life.

Being a part of a couple naturally involves being in a family context. Although the presence of children is undoubtedly an important and central element for the life of many couples, it is not the only way in which family influences are felt. This chapter will, therefore, focus on family influences by paying due regard to children, but not being over-burdened by them – which in itself is a good way of being a parent.

## Families and development

Families are about continuity and change; they are about the generations. We all need to move from what 'was' to what 'is to be' and while doing this we all need a sense of who we are in a way that remains stable and constant. The nature of human development guarantees that the family context is the principal social arena in which this happens. At one time it was thought that human development occurred 'within' a person, that is as time went on the person's development emerged from inside him or herself. However, our understanding of the unfolding of human psychological growth has moved on from this 'internal' conception. It is now seen that the course of development is produced as a result of an interactive process (Lidz 1968).

Research has demonstrated not only the way adult behaviour affects child development (Schaffer 1971), but also how child behaviour affects that of adults (Bell and Harper 1980); how children affect marital interaction (Lerner and Spanier 1978); and how adults naturally affect each other (e.g. Noller 1984). In this way the development of human behaviour has to be seen as a reciprocal process taking place in the social context of the family. It also has to be seen as encompassing the whole life-span. Throughout life we are all required to meet particular tasks and make adaptations so that we deal with living efficiently and effectively. A gradual process of change occurs to allow us to meet the requirements of our lives. The old idea that development is entirely confined to childhood derives in part from the view that adults have of themselves, which involves the notion of 'constancy' at its core. But change does take place in the process of the struggle for 'what is it to be' and such changes occur through our interaction with the people with whom we share our lives. Hence the developmental tasks revolve around the issues of intimacy and autonomy, themes which at different times throughout life present themselves in different ways. These are issues which cannot be avoided for they lie at the heart of our own identity. We all have to come to terms with the extent to which we want to need someone else and be needed by them, and the extent to which we wish to remain as a separate autonomous person. Our development as individuals is therefore intrinsically linked to our development as part of a couple and this in turn is very much related to the developmental tasks that face the whole family. The tasks of each individual meshes in with the tasks for all.

Each stage of life brings with it different problems to solve and it is possible to outline the different tasks through the life-cycle. This is presented in Table 5.1.

This formulation is naturally an 'ideal type' for life itself does not follow straight lines all the time. Individuals die prematurely, couples divorce, remarry and care for someone-else's children, women have children in 'later life' and men may unexpectedly face employment changes. Some families have to care for sick and handicapped people throughout life, some individuals do not leave home and some leave home to live a single life. Whatever the course of a person's destiny each moment brings with it a task to solve, inevitably linked to the activities of another person. This is the case for all of us regardless of whether the 'other' sleeps next to us in bed, is in the next room, is back at the 'old' home or is just an 'object' inside us.

In this way the generations are linked through the developmental tasks as illustrated in the Family Life-Cycle chart (Table 5.1). But the generations are also linked in each person by virtue of their history. A person of 50 for example will quite likely at one and the same time be a grandparent, a parent and a child and the past will have given messages as to how each family role is to be filled. At a particular moment a grandparent talking to the grandchild may very well be giving messages that were originally received from his or her own grandparent. Five generations at work during one interaction! Such messages may be about how men and women 'should' behave both in general and to each other; how success and failure is to be dealt with; who gets angry and why; how close people are to be. These messages can cover any aspect of emotionality, ways of behaving, attitudes, and so on. They may be given in direct ways that are family sayings such as 'Don't try too hard, you'll wear yourself out', 'It's best to be cautious with money'. The stories families tell about themselves – family myths – also contain strong messages, such that tales of an errant uncle may indicate that it is all right for men in this family to be a bit delinquent. Similarly family scripts (Byng-Hall 1985) offer an outline of a set way of behaving. 'Eldest boys do well, but don't stay close to mother', 'You're just like your grandfather, stubborn all the time'. By this means we are witnessing the 'trans-generational process' at work (Boszormenyi-Nagy and Speck 1973) the process by which we receive the information as to how we are expected to function within our family.

The sense we make of this process in ourselves will to a large extent determine the way we select a mate and whom we select. Through this process the family of origin will have passed on messages about gender behaviour, life plan, sexuality and rules of family functioning and what then becomes important is to find somebody whose messages fit in with our own. These messages which affect our sense of identity, our behaviour and hence our relationships are not, however, written on tablets of stone: the usual changes of life mean we constantly have to review them in relation to ourselves and our partner. Such personal explorations are the stuff of adult development in a relationship and these can and do lead to marital difficulties when one partner is needing to explore and the other is not, or when the mutual exploration seemingly leads to diametrically opposed movements. Whatever the nature of these explorations, they originate from the self-image that is linked to family messages and family history.

There is a stage of life therefore when the familial processes are conditioning what would be appropriate mate selection and appropriate couple behaviour – appropriate in terms of the messages that have been given to us by our family. However, we each have the task of separating from our family of origin and this is not just the physical leaving of home. It is the way in which we redefine ourselves by using the family messages without being dominated and constricted by them (Bowen 1976). If we have developed a sense of separation from our family, we also develop a feeling of choice about how we will behave; then it becomes possible to meet another person as he or she truly is and have an intimate relationship with another mature being. However, this does not occur that easily, for all of us retain psychological vestiges of our families of origin. It is found that individuals tend to be attracted to others who have achieved the same degree of separation (Bowen 1976). So an individual who very much follows their family's pattern will tend to pair up with a similar person. A common pattern is that of a woman remaining very close physically and psychologically to her own parents and framing the marriage around this. The chosen male partner is no less unseparated, and even though he may have relatively little physical contact with his parents, the man still complies with the family's psychological instructions and messages. Bowen (1976) has argued that often in such circumstances one partner 'borrows' some ego strength from the other in order to go out and deal with the outside world. The other partner has to remain wedded to family tradition to counteract the depletion of energy necessary to construct mature adult behaviour. In our present culture more often than not it is the man who does the borrowing and the woman the lending.

However, each couple also has the opportunity through their relationship to explore their 'selves' so that they can attain a more mature separation from their family of origin while still maintaining a positive attachment to it. Each individual can test out and experiment with different ways of behaving and being and they can invite their partner to share in what has to be a mutual exploration. This is the way in which being in a relationship provides the conditions for growth and development. It therefore follows that any improvement in couple functioning will develop only through some growth of the self and this in turn is attained only by an increased degree of separation from the family of origin.

The couple will therefore bring to therapy the tasks they have to deal with in terms of life-span development, the myths, messages and scripts of their family of origin and their efforts to separate maturely from their families by establishing an autonomous and intimate relationship. Although each person will be dealing with these related processes, more often than not the couple will present with one complaining how the other does not help in one of the daily tasks that they face. The task of the therapist is therefore to move from personal blaming to placing the problem in its couple and hence family context. The therapist will therefore

**Table 5.1** The family life-cycle

| Phase and tasks for individual | Phase of parents | Parenting tasks | Marital tasks |
|---|---|---|---|
| *1 Babyhood*<br>Discovery of own body. Object constancy. Self-other discrimination. Development of basic trust. | Young adulthood | Considerable constancy of caring needed. Accept extreme dependence. Begin to accept baby's personality. | Maintain links of family, and outside world. Support for carer. Acceptance of third individual. Redefinition of closeness. |
| *2 Toddler phase*<br>Learning to walk and ability to move away from caring adult. Cope with ability to hurt loved ones. Accept pain, shame and doubt. Begin to discover gender identity. Self-identity begins. Limitation of acceptable behaviour explored. | Young adulthood | Careful management of distance. Sensitivity to self-esteem of child. Accept and help define personal characteristics. Accept play. Provide appropriate tasks to develop skills. Begin to negotiate agreed discipline philosophy. | Maintenance of support for carer. |
| *3 Pre-school phase*<br>Learning about three-person relationships. Balancing feelings of belonging and being 'outside'. Begin to learn values and rules. | Young adulthood | Accept child's gender identity. Establish clear generational and role boundaries. Give clear rules and values. | Confirm context of marital relationship within context of clarifying generational boundaries. |
| *4 Early school years*<br>Accept care from adults other than parents. Begin separating from parents. Share caring adult with classmates. Enjoy and use peers. | Early mid-life | Accept ability to separate and allow closeness to peers and to teachers. Encourage interests, even when different from the family. Balance children's and parents' outside interests. | Negotiate end of childbearing phase. Deal with change in maternal role. Renegotiate separateness and togetherness. Redefine commitment to the marriage. |
| *5 Adolescence*<br>Find ways to accept and enjoy sexuality first in fantasy then by identifying potential partners and exploring relationships with them. Exploring and then developing identity characteristics of the self. Differentiate from parents. | Mid-life | Tolerate re-emergence of early tendencies. Accept intense mixture of progressive and regressive trends. Acceptance of impending adulthood of offspring. | Re-establish the couple as an entity separate from the family. Support during periods of crisis and doubt that mid-life brings. |

| | | | |
|---|---|---|---|
| 6 *Young adulthood*<br>Establish separate life-style and domicile. Find adult social roles. Set up enduring relationships and loves. Negotiate with society about capabilities. | Mid-life | Accept distance of young adult offspring. Accept offspring as peers. | Find satisfactory marriage without children. Maintain separate and mutual interests. |
| 7 *Courtship and marriage*<br>Balancing the merging processes of loving with the maintenance of the separate identity. Begin to negotiate life together. | Mid-life | Begin to manage in-law status. | Re-evaluation of marital pair as parents. Review notion of marriage. |
| 8 *Young adulthood parenting phase*<br>Accept dependency of self and others. Accept roles that family life brings. Rely on the help of others including extended family. | Late mid-life | Grandparent phase. Accept new need for offspring to be close as adults. Provide additional adults for children to identify with. | Preparation for closeness that retirement will bring. |
| 9 *Early mid-life phase*<br>Reappraisal of own power and status. Creation of self-roles other than sex and work-roles. Awareness of mortality. | Retirement | Accept ending of parental tasks. | Accept changing nature of dependency and of the sexual relationship. |
| 10 *Late mid-life phase*<br>Acceptance of achievements and plateau of achievements. Continuing development of spiritual and cultural interests. Accept dependency of parents and future loss. | Old age | | Accept future loss of partner. Accept life alone after partner's death. |
| 11 *Retirement*<br>Acceptance of loss of work-roles. Evaluation of life successes and failures. | | | |
| 12 *Old age*<br>Acceptance of dependency. Acceptance of infirmity and death. | | | |

*Source:* After Dare 1979

need to establish the overall life tasks facing the couple and the way these tasks relate to their family of origin. The simplest way to do this is to construct a genogram (McGoldrick and Gerson 1985) which quickly and graphically allows for family composition, life-cycle stage and history to be made clear for all to see. This can be done in a quiet way removed from the tense emotionality that characterizes the early couple sessions and it serves to relax and orientate clients to the family influences on their problem. Then questions should be asked such as 'What would your mother/father do if they faced a similar difficulty?' 'What would your grandparents say about this problem?' Answers to such enquiries make plain the family messages relevant to the presenting problem. By such methods the therapist is then able to construct a model about the nature of the struggle for the individual, the couple and the family; this model can then be slowly shared with the clients. In this way the couple can move their appreciation of the problem from individual hostility or indifference to a task they face jointly, a task embedded in their own particular familial context.

## Marital tasks and parenting

The essential themes of all marital tasks are those which revolve around each person being a separate human being who has his/her own integrity both within, and also outside of, a close, caring relationship with another adult. The couple relationship has to cope with the issues of separation and togetherness that being a parent entails. Similarly the balancing of intimacy and autonomy is another aspect that confronts adults who are parents. These issues manifest themselves through the ordinary daily problems that parenting brings. The manner in which an adult deals with being a parent demonstrates how that person is solving the problems of being an adult to a significant child. It is solving these problems that constitutes the identity of the person being a parent at that particular time. Parenting is therefore a couple issue which is essential to the development of the individual who has embarked on that particular course at that time of his/her life.

As Table 5.1 demonstrates, at different stages of life the needs of children require their parents to behave in different ways. Parents have to deal with complete dependency when the child is an infant while when adolescence is reached parenting involves 'letting go' as well as dealing with the ambivalent dependency of that age. For many years of marriage the parenting needs of children will be the primary practical tasks that have to be faced: the way in which these tasks are dealt with is very revealing as to how a couple relate to each other. The therapist needs to be very interested in this, as daily problems offer an understanding of underlying meanings and processes. Issues of power, responsibility, authority, caring, support, and so on all enter into the parental task; couples will demonstrate their typical interactive style when they deal with the particular tasks that come along. For example a difficulty which nearly all young parents face is that of sleep problems with their infants, since in the early months of life nearly all children encounter disturbed sleep patterns. This may be caused by some very minor neurological immaturity or some minor organic complaint; it could even be that the child sleeps in a bedroom next to a noisy water tank! The precipitating event can be quite small and not necessarily related to emotional issues. However, a problem is posed for the parents to solve.

Some of their attempted solutions may unwittingly reinforce aspects of the problem behaviour even when the original precipitating event is removed. The parents may resort to taking the child into bed with them to offer some comfort and get some sleep themselves. This consequence by simple learning can become an expected outcome for the child of any distress, however minor. By continuing with the same solution to what objectively has become a different situation the parents maintain the difficult sleeping behaviour in their child. If in this case one parent, say the mother, is totally responsible for dealing with night-time behaviour, it could occur that a solution is maintained in which the mother and child sleep in the marital bed and the father sleeps elsewhere. The parents now face the important task of beginning to negotiate the rules of conduct that are to be applied in caring for the child while maintaining an appropriate marital relationship. However, the couple may find it difficult to work out a balanced solution to which they both agree: 'You should learn to let him cry more, then he'll go to to sleep. He'll soon learn to go sleep if we don't go to him.' 'He must be in some pain. He won't go to sleep until we see to him.' The conflict around the sheer task of coping with the dependency of a third person therefore not only serves to create the environment in which the third person can confront their own tasks but also presents issues in which the parents begin to negotiate their joint tasks. Thus minor difficulties with children often lead to situations in which parents have to resolve some couple issue.

If such a problem is presented in therapy, the therapist needs to investigate the different meanings of care that the couple have for each other and for the child. The need would be to establish whether their understanding and past experience of care and support allows them to deal with the care and support required at that particular life-cycle stage. The importance of distinguishing between couple/adults' needs and the needs that flow from the parenting context should be fully explored as the boundary between the couple as parents and as adults should constantly be monitored and maintained throughout marriage.

Children's problems can find their origin in the way in which their parents deal with their marital relationship. In this case, children's problems are contextually related to the parents' attempt to solve their marital tasks. For example a couple may be struggling with the changes in the maternal role at the end of the childbearing phase. For many reasons, several of which could be intergenerationally linked, a parental couple may change the maternal role only minimally. This may indicate that the nature of their intimacy requires that the majority of their time is spent together in parental ways. Facing the parental tasks in such a manner results in only a minimal degree of separation becoming allowable for the child as the parents are unable to encourage effectively their child's interests outside the family. Such an interest would be threatening to their own roles. Consequently the outside world of both parent and child does not develop as fully as it might and the pleasures and satisfactions of life become defined as occurring only 'in and only for the family'. This would primarily protect the couple from having to confront too directly the renegotiations of their own separation and togetherness. The child is therefore placed in an environment where the opportunity of separating from the parent is limited and the chance to share with others outside the family is curtailed.

Should the couple discuss this problem with a therapist, again the theme of the difference between being a couple and being parents would need to be discussed. One would expect that such a problem would be closely related to the separation from the family of origin of both adults and there may well be involved grandparents to be taken into account. The issue of separation is likely to be associated with problems throughout the generations and the therapist should be able to deal with this issue in the present-day marital context, the present-day parenting context and also several historical contexts. Many questions can be asked to allow this to happen. 'How did you deal with this problem when you were as old as your child?' 'How did your parents deal with you?' 'What would have happened if you did it differently?' 'How is it that your brother doesn't do the same thing?' In doing this the therapist will allow the couple to explore their own family influences and look at possible alternatives for how they might tackle things.

This last example introduces the element of the child possibly being able to take independent action with regard to parental behaviour. If through the process of therapy the couple begin to do something for themselves, such as going out without the child, the child may well 'complain' by behaving badly with the baby-sitter (grandmother?), having a stomach ache or throwing a temper tantrum as the parents are leaving. In this situation the therapist will need to help the couple improve their parenting skills (being firm, being clear, being authoritative) so that they can protect the part of themselves that is the adult relationship. It is in fact impossible to enhance the relationship skills of a couple without enhancing their parenting skills. There is a clear link between the two: in any therapeutic process, each of the themes of parenting and being a couple will at different times predominate, but the one cannot be dealt with to the neglect of the other. The therapist needs to be mindful of this for in the hurly-burly of family life one cannot easily separate marital, parental and individual issues from each other.

## Marital intimacy, the family and marital interaction

One of the problems of intimacy itself is that it is threatening. In order to be truly intimate one must be both available and to an extent willing to be vulnerable. The actual amount of intimate interaction in marriage can be very low – even less than a few minutes each day. It is possible to deal with many of the ordinary tasks of living without really speaking to your partner. As the possibility is potentially always present, those couples who wish to avoid it can set up patterns of interaction that serve as distance regulators. In fact it is not the very distressed couple who avoid intimacy: all couples will have their interactive mechanisms for turning down the intensity of their relationship and hence preventing intimacy. Each of us will have our difficult emotional area, determined by our past experience, which is fearful to investigate and which is too threatening for us to truly share with our partners; at these times we each will attempt to move away from the possibility of intimacy. In couple relationships therefore there tends to be a dynamic interaction between solving the ordinary problems of life efficiently and dealing with the intimacy of the relationship.

One of the prime ways in which individuals create some distance in their relationship is to change the subject or more usually talk about someone else! It is very interesting watching how quickly in any dyadic interaction individuals stop talking about 'I' and 'we' and start talking about 'he' or 'she'. This is the process of triangulation at work, for it is more emotionally benign if two people discuss a third rather than talk about themselves and their relationship. This process has its roots well in infancy when the child becomes aware that the principal caregiving adult is in relation not only to the infant but also to another adult. In couple relationships there is a general change over time as to the people with whom the couple predominately triangulate. In the early days of a relationship the couple will triangulate their friends. They will talk about them and argue about them as a means of touching on issues (albeit tangently) that need to be discussed. Primarily at this stage they will be trying to see if it is possible to negotiate without the attendant intimacy. As the relationship proceeds, the next 'target' for triangulation will be the 'parents-in-law'; this is an important stage in any relationship as of necessity it involves parts of the negotiations about what type of 'family' is being created. The third and in fact the easiest individuals who can be triangulated are children. Children are ever present; they have changing needs which have to be met and they can learn very easily how to behave in certain ways that aid the process of triangulation and the avoidance of intimacy. There are a number of patterns which are quite common in terms of the triangulation of children.

1  There are those couples who avoid their intimacy by devoting themselves to the children. Their *raison d'être* is as parents and they even call each other 'Mother' and 'Father'. This type of couple see only the parenting aspect of marriage; marital issues are only parenting ones and consequently the marriage is one of static adults rather than of developing individuals. These couples naturally need their children to remain as children, for after all parents can be parents only if there is a child. Such couples invariably have lost the skills of relating in a growing emotional way and problems often ensue in the family if the children manage to separate. The children often learn behaviour or acquire 'illnesses' that keep them as children.

2  Some couples particularly avoid their marital conflict by arguing about the children. Typically a child will exhibit some behaviour which is defined as difficult and the parents will disagree about the ways to handle it. Their disagreement will continue unresolved and their conflict about themselves will be avoided. In these families the child learns that if the parents look as if they might approach the problematic intimate area then they will exhibit their difficult behaviour; hence by the child's action the parents are 'saved' from the feared consequences of couple intimacy.

3  Some couples deal with their intimacy by having a child emotionally closer to one parent than another; this may even go as far as a son being 'married' to his mother or a daughter to her father. In this situation some adult needs are inappropriately met by a child, which lessens the need for the partner to

be available. Here the child learns to bury some of his/her own needs in the interest of an adult and this may produce difficulties for all as new developmental tasks have to be met.

Children may become emotional barometers for how the marital relationship is progressing (Byng-Hall 1980). Some learn to become a problem when the marital conflict becomes intense. At that moment the parents allow their marital boundary to break and may stop their own conflict and focus on the child in some way. Some children find themselves having particular problems with one parent when the couple relationship is under stress. In this way the focus again moves from the adult problem to another type of problem. As each child learns the rules for intruding into the marital relationship, he or she is naturally learning their own rules about how dyadic intimacy is handled. Those children most involved in their parents' marital interaction will be most triangulated and hence will find it more difficult to separate as adults and create truly intimate relationships of their own.

Some of the natural behaviour of a child may at different stages of a child's life be 'appropriate' and more helpful to the particular triangulation-intimacy needs of the adult. At these times the ordinary everyday activities will provide a solution to the difficulties the parents face as a couple. However, development has to proceed and the child's behaviour will in the normal course of events alter. When it does this will serve only to reinforce the non-resolution of the intimacy difficulty of the parents. It is not surprising therefore that marital problems become uncomfortably apparent at times of developmental transition and these problems may find their replication in the developing self of the child.

The therapist needs to develop a good understanding of the transition point that the couple is facing for this will give a very good indication of the ways in which their interactions may be stuck and the ways in which their interaction could develop. For example couples have to deal differently with each other when their children go to school, which is the first major family separation. With such a change, the couple's adult needs remain the same but they will have to make a transition from meeting those needs in one way to organizing themselves and interacting differently so that they can be met in another way. The therapist needs to be very mindful of the multitude of transitions that can bring a couple along for therapy.

In dealing with couple interaction, the therapist also needs to acquire a good sense of the interactive means by which the couple regulate the intimate distance between themselves and the ways in which triangulation is related to this. In discussing a couple's interaction with them it is therefore essential that the behaviour of others are taken into account so that the full effects of the complete interactional field can be appreciated. With particular couples this may not be possible at all unless the other people (children or parents) are also present in the room. Some couples will complain about the effects of their own attempts to regulate distance, for example their naughty child, their demanding children, an adult relationship of a partner. Other couples, however, have little awareness of these processes and do not consider how they are affected by the behaviour of others or indeed how they affect others' behaviour. Naturally the therapist will be attempting to unravel the fears of intimacy that lead to the need to keep closeness and distance at particular levels. The therapist will also attempt to bring to awareness the way the couple use the triangulation process; the therapist will be attempting to show that triangulation involves the collusive activity of both partners and that the existence of this collusion will prevent their joint action as a couple in dealing effectively with the behaviour of others.

The most effective means of the therapist doing this is to use the intimacy of the therapy session itself to engage the couple in a process of triangulation with the therapist. Each couple will use different means of engaging the therapist that are designed to prevent some intimacy. By virtue of understanding the process of family triangulation for any couple, the therapist is at different times able to accept or reject the triangulation offered and use it for therapeutic means. In one sense the therapist will be attempting to stop the couple's collusion so that they can establish joint action *vis-à-vis* the therapist as a third person. Many couples will expect the therapist to behave in ways reminiscent of someone in their family: it is this that the therapist is trying to prevent and indeed exploit. Such is the force of the triangulation process in some families that the influence of the behaviours of others on the couple is very great. In these circumstances the therapist will have to determine whether or not the issues can be dealt with by merely talking to the couple or whether other family members need to be invited to sessions.

## Families or couples; the therapist's response

Any individual who enters counselling in a sense brings their family with them. Regardless of the relationship status of the individual, the messages from our parents and the family rules for behaviour have an active presence for us all. We are all also struggling with the attempt to be truly our own person, separated from all those influences that have shaped our lives. We are looking for the opportunity to exhibit choice in how we are, by positively choosing to be the same as or different from the way our parents wanted and expected us to be. It is impossible to avoid any of these processes and struggles. When a couple enter the consulting room, not only do they bring along these individual factors and the way in which they interactively relate but also they 'bring' along their children. The obligation to clothe, feed and care for the children will require everyday decisions and problems to be faced and the children themselves will in a variety of ways be interacting with the parents such that they seemingly add to the particular marital difficulties of the couple. The children may indeed be the only vehicle by which the couple feel themselves to be in distress. With the pressure from these actual and ever-present psychological forces, the erstwhile couple therapist will ask, 'Who then should I see, the couple or them and their children?'

In response to this question, Whitaker (1982) would answer that one can see only the family. His view is that to treat just the married couple is to deny the total family system and that it is an inefficient method of treating one subgroup as family scapegoat. He believes that the two-generational unit is the basic unit for any treatment and in fact the three-generational unit is preferable. In this respect he follows Ackerman (1960). Whitaker clearly has the view that the children's presence is essential as it completely alters the perspective from a couple struggling with their pairing relationship to two parents struggling with the problem of their projections and power dynamics of their competition as parents. Children also tend to 'do the dance of their parents' in that they will relate to each other in the same way that their parents relate. Excluding the children and treating only the couple is seen as tending to facilitate emotional divorce between the husband–wife relationship and the children and especially at a time when the issues for this particular generational boundary will be strained. Whitaker presents his view cogently and places it in a life-cycle framework when he states

> therapy of the husband–wife axis tends to make believe that the two are back in adolescence trying to re-choose their mate, trying to re-open their individualisation as though it had never been damaged by the years of marriage. Treatment of the husband–wife axis in the systems framework, which takes the children into account, adds the third dimension of reality, already biologically established, and makes this a fact in the therapy of the twosome.
>
> (Whitaker 1982: 170)

The family therapeutic approach is therefore an effort to develop a wholeness of the family group and individualization concurrently (see Anonymous 1972). Framo (1976) also adopts the view that the family of origin has to be seen as a therapeutic resource and used accordingly.

The position outlined above is very much from the perspective of an approach (followed in the bulk of this chapter) which symbolically recognizes the role of transference in *all* relationships and which is growth orientated for all concerned (Whitaker and Keith 1981). Other therapists, however, do not take such a firm position on the role of family members. Their view is that it is possible to effect change and bring relief to distress by seeing the couple alone; indeed this is the approach of the majority of those who embark on couple therapy or counselling. Many of these approaches in fact have different targets for the process of the therapeutic work, for example, communications (Satir 1964), behavioural exchanges (MacKay 1985), cognitions and beliefs (Dryden 1985) have all figured as the focus for change in couple therapy. Thus the need to take into account the 'family' may for some be diminished and the 'unit' of treatment is clearly that of the couple.

The view taken here is somewhat different from that of Whitaker, but one which nevertheless upholds the primacy of the family. In the 'battle for structure', Whitaker insists on who is to attend and struggles with the family about non-attenders from any generation. However, this may not be possible but one should be able to let the couple know very early on that their parents or their children may be required to attend. This puts the family issue clearly on the agenda: although couples often respond by saying 'They wouldn't want to come. We don't want them to come', they still have to think about it as a theme – an issue which is present in the room with the therapist and the couple.

The therapist may be inclined to insist on the presence of other people when it is clear that the couple's interaction is very much stuck with the behaviour of those other people. So, for example, the couple who repeatedly discuss a parenting issue will be helped to move forward if the children and their behaviour are brought to the session. Similarly the continuation of 'in-law' difficulties may require the older generation to be present; in this case it needs to be recognized that a balanced view of involving both sets of 'in-laws' is required. Even if other family members do not attend, it is still possible to bring them into the consulting room in other ways; family histories, and genograms, make excellent vehicles for establishing couple's expectations of each other and the origin and source of these expectations. Discussions with each spouse about their triangulated position with their in-laws will reveal many typical family interactive patterns. Questions such as 'What would your mother (father, uncle, grandmother, etc.) say about that if they were here?' are also very apposite throughout the therapeutic process. For couples who have children, discussion about the varying parental tasks are not only necessary but also essential. By a variety of means the therapist can bring into play the child's perspective (see O'Reilly and Street 1988). Discussions with the couple about their individual hopes and dreams (projections) for their children, discussions about their fantasy of what family life would be like for their children, and discussions about their own unfulfilled childhood wishes, all make child material relevant. Despite these techniques, those therapists that have actually met and interacted with a couple's parents or children will know what an enlightening difference is produced. It is after all the reality.

## The role of the therapist

The difference between those who view the family and marriage as one unit, and those that concentrate on the couple is not merely one of focus or aim: the core of the difference lies in the way in which the role of the therapist is perceived and taken on. Many therapists will, within terms of the caring aspects of their relationship, offer an experience in which they, from the position of expertise, observe, feedback and offer guidance for change. This is a model which rests on a form of emotional neutrality between clients and therapists as the therapist needs some position of objectivity from which to apply his or her knowledge to the particular problem which the clients bring. Other therapists will see their role as attracting their clients' emotions, so that they may intervene by interpreting the transference induced by the situation. In order to do this a different type of neutrality is needed so that therapists have the space to analyse which emotions belong to the clients and which belong to themselves, so that they can then deal with those that belong to the clients. In the family approach outlined here, the therapist's role is to join the family and willingly adopt a position which implies some generational linking with the family.

The therapist in some sense is attempting to create a 'family' in the consulting room, a family in which the roles change because the therapist behaves differently at different times. By accepting a triangulated position and then by using the feelings produced in themselves, therapists may be able to talk from the perspective of a parent, a child or a grandparent. The therapist therefore initially encourages and fosters the linkages with the couple that are relatively benign and comfortable for them, so that the therapist can then move positions in the 'family' which contain the possible threat and hence hold the key to exploration and growth. Therapists are therefore deliberately seeking to become a part of the family process so that they may then assert their right and ability to separate as individuals. Through this mechanism of the therapist moving in and out of triangles, and then in and out of dyads, individualization occurs; through this experience couples in their family are instructed in and learn the process for themselves.

### Skills of the therapist

The skills the therapist will use in the first instance flow from the obvious needs of the clients. Each member of each couple that attends will have two basic requirements of the therapist: that the therapist listens to his or her version of the story and that the therapist behaves in a way that he or she expects. Each individual comes along with a personal agenda, the majority of items being related to everyday matter of fact issues; the couple will also covertly have negotiated a triangulated position for the therapist (Street 1985). They will have worked out a way in which the therapist can behave that will be involved but not make the slightest degree of difference to their relationship. Some couples 'agree' that one of them will be blamed. Some want the therapist to be judge so that after the judgement they can disagree. Some want a magician miraculously to change the other. Some want a 'friend for husband', others a 'lover for somebody – anybody'. As therapy progresses and the change process occurs, the couple will react by changing the nature of the triangulation that is offered to the therapist; this can be a very rapid event as the couple try to find a position that removes the force of the therapeutic efforts because of their fears of change and intimacy. By making available information from three generations – children, the couple and parents – the opportunity for triangulation is increased tenfold and calls into play the full range of the couple's emotions and hence offers a much wider opportunity for change and development. When such information is not available, the range of emotional expression is constricted and hence the change produced is constricted itself.

The therapist engages with the couple in a process closely akin to 'playing' in the true sense of the word. New roles are taken on, new ways of relating tried, with nothing lost during the process of struggle and experimentation. The therapist therefore initiates the clients to new ways of interacting by engaging in that interaction. The therapist will be very aware of the position of the family in the life-cycle, for this will provide the context for many of the problems that will be facing them and bring to the fore the tasks as yet untried (Carter and McGoldrick 1989). These tasks will in fact form the context for the solutions that are to be attempted. The therapist will be dealing directly with the couple's intimacy by insisting on an intimate interaction with him/herself; this will be done while providing an opportunity to reassess those family messages and traditions that influence the style and direction of interaction.

The therapist can be seen to oscillate between being directly 'in' the intimate relationship of therapy and then 'out' of it by making reference to similar processes in the family. For example a male therapist has the choice of acting as a 'father', of making public his feelings about acting as a father, making links to how the client's father may behave or in commenting on how a child may feel about this act of fathering. New areas for exploration and growth are opened up when such therapeutic interventions are made.

The therapist will therefore be offering the couple an opportunity as a pair to embark further on the journey of separation and individualization. By this means the symbols and metaphors of everyday life become readily apparent. In talking about who cooks the tea, nurturance questions will be dealt with; in discussing sexual appetites, dealing with individuals who want too much is touched on; in focusing on doing things apart, the fears of adolescence will be confronted; and who drives the car is about power and leadership. And so it will go on for family themes are like seamless cloth, with the therapist changing between the warp and the weft.

The skills that are necessary for this approach require that the therapist should have a clear background knowledge of the way individuals are affected by their history. Therapists should have the ability to collect historical and current information from any source and file it away until an appropriate moment. To make use of information and to make use of self, therapists should have the skill of forming whole pictures from only fragmentary knowledge and then be able to communicate this constructed wholeness to the family. It is of course necessary to have the skills of receiving feedback in such a way as to be able to use it, and to be adept at monitoring the self moment to moment. The ability to adapt, adjust and take on skills is another requirement, for it is important in dealing with the complexities of families to be able to use techniques and thoughts that have been developed in other schools of therapy. As in a family, no one has a monopoly on knowledge. Perhaps the most important set of skills are those that involve working with children at some depth and intensity. We need to be able to imagine what life is like for children and to recall how life as a child was for us. Throughout the process, therapists will be developing their own own sense of self, through meeting with the family and extending their own creativity in the ongoing process (Street 1989). This can be achieved only by therapists developing their own style so that their own personality is an integral part of everything that is done (see Minuchin 1989).

*Case example: Mr and Mrs T*
Mrs T went to her GP as she was feeling very miserable and finding it difficult to deal with the running of the house. The doctor soon established that she felt dissatisfied and unsupported in her marriage and he made a referral for some marital work. Mr and Mrs T attended the first session; they had two children aged 17 and 15. Mr T did not work; he received an invalidity pension for the severe arthritis in his neck. As is usual practice, the couple were invited to the first session and for this session and most of the second, Mrs T said that the problem was hers – she was the type of person who often felt insecure and was always dissatisfied; she wished her husband would tell her to go. Mr T agreed with his wife. He offered some self-criticism as to how he was dealing with things, but basically felt his wife should try harder.

Throughout the first two sessions, the therapist considered that the prime task was just to 'hear' what was being said by husband and wife. Both of them seemed to want the therapist to blame the wife, as if in some way that would make things better if somebody actually agreed with them about the 'cause' of the problem. The reason for this became apparent, for a typical interaction was the husband caringly but patronizingly attempting to 'analyse' his wife's problem; they were intimate only when he attempted to be his wife's therapist. As the husband felt in some way that he was failing at this job, then the triangulation offered the therapist to be 'wife's counsellor'. Once the therapist had done his job then obviously he could pass the woman back to the man as if nothing had happened. However, because of the self-blame and mutually agreed criticism, it was not immediately possible to enter effectively into the symbols of this triangulation directly. The therapist therefore undertook to construct a genogram and this did allow for some relaxation in the couple as they moved away from the 'let's blame the woman' position. While doing the genogram, they reported on some difficulties with the older boy, who was not as co-operative around the house as they would like. Mrs T had always had a difficult relationship with her father and there had been some periods of estrangement. She had always felt herself to be 'on her mother's side' against her father. Mr T's family came from another town; his father had died when he was a small boy. Mr T visited his mother regularly, often just to do small jobs around the house: she was quite dependent on him. He also felt responsible for his mentally handicapped brother, who was institutionalized quite a distance away. Again he would visit regularly. He felt that it was his role to keep the family going – his wife in a typically complementary way felt that he did little to keep their 'own' family going. Mrs T felt cut off from her family of origin. She believed that her father saw no good in her and that her mother was so burdened with her own difficulties that she had now little time for her. Roles in their family of origin and related messages hence served to form the context in which Mr and Mrs T were attempting to be intimate with each other. Clearly this couple were struggling with the transitional stage of life, when the children were psychologically leaving, when their own parents were becoming elderly and they were finding a great deal of difficulty in renegotiating their intimacy. In the past, Mr T with his illness had simply been of one of the children in terms of how Mrs T cared for him. She feared that if she had some 'independence', everyone would forget her. He feared that if he did not remain a child, his disabilities would become more of a problem. She helped him in this by keeping him as a child and making believe that he was a good 'therapist' for her. In fact they were both dissatisfied with their relationship.

After the genogram work, the principal focus of the next session was on the theme of who is a 'father'. Mr T was father in his family of origin but not much in his family of marriage. Mrs T thought 'fathers' to be hypercritical and felt that she also did some fathering in the family. The therapist wondered if *he* should be a father to everyone. 'No, you're much nicer as a wise cousin', he was told by Mrs T. At this point the problem of the adolescent boy came to the fore. He was behaving in a typical way – coming home late for meals, being untidy, not helping around the house – and clearly the issue of fathering had raised the theme of discipline. So from a metaphorical discussion of being a father, the couple and therapist had passed to an actual problem of parenting. The topic of discussion became the way in which the couple dealt or actually did not deal with their son. In going through some possible actions they could take, both husband and wife put up objections because their son 'wouldn't do that' or 'he wouldn't let that happen'. From here it became relatively easy to secure their agreement to bring their children to the next session. When this happened the therapist began by joining with the boys and encouraging their adolescent criticism of their parents. This was done in a good-humoured way which allowed the parents to see adolescent thoughts and action as being less noxious than they had imagined. It proved simple to ask the children about their parents' relationship with their grandparents. Both boys knew of the difficulties and both commented on how strange they found it that their parents did not visit their grandparents together as a couple. The bothersome lad said 'If I get married, I'll only visit home with my wife – for protection!'

The theme of joint action of the couple naturally led on to joint parenting with regard to discipline. The session finished with the therapist and parents planning on how the rules of their house would be applied; while this went on the therapist modelled how to shut up a 15-year-old complaining youth!

At the next session the focus was very much on the discipline issue. Some new things had been tried, some had failed and seemingly not much had been achieved. In typical fashion the marital see-saw had moved: now Mr T felt the problem was his fault and his wife agreed with him. The therapist used this as a springboard to talk about how each felt undervalued. Both rapidly associated these feelings to their family of origin: he to his mother and she to her father. Before the therapist could move on to how these feelings might affect their expectations of each other, with one of those leaps that is often produced by the everyday symbols of living, the topic of discussion suddenly changed to how both felt undervalued in their sexual relationships with each other. Such was the rapid movement that the therapist had jokingly to ask them to slow down because he was 'not that good a therapist'. The crux of therapy was now developing, for issues relevant to them as individuals, as parents, as children and as a couple all seemed to converge on one theme. As Mr T said, 'I suppose if you get used to it [being undervalued] it happens everywhere for you.' Having arrived at this point, the therapist decided with the couple that the most appropriate place to start was with their (joint) relationship with their respective parents. This was done as it would prove a helpful link to the separation of their boys, which in turn would have implications for their intimacy when left without children. As a couple they were therefore encouraged to visit both family homes; through the next sessions, the problems, feelings and difficulties of this were discussed. During this time both made efforts to triangulate the therapist by placing him in the role of critical parent to which one of his usual responses was to become a 'complaining youth'. In this apparently confusing but funny interaction, the couple were required to stop being children and to behave like grown-ups. Some new ways of dealing with Mr T's mother's demands were found and a more reasonable contact between Mrs T and her family was established. Both had begun to deal with their families of origin in more mature ways. Matters improved generally and the family as a whole moved on to themes of separation, appropriate to their stage of the life-cycle. Mrs T felt more content and now enjoyed time out with her friends. Mr T felt that he did not have to look after everybody and he began to enjoy his own company; together, as a couple, they began to spend more leisure time together. At the close of treatment, the metaphor that seemed most relevant was the one of seeds being blown off a flower so that it may bloom again elsewhere: this was relevant to all concerned.

From a beginning in which an individual is the focus, this couple's difficulty moved in such a way that a much wider context for their problem was seen. The therapist was able to set the 'problem' within the areas of a couple as a couple, the couple as parents and the couple as children from their own families. The themes of therapy interplayed between these contexts as well as the 'here and now' context of the consulting room. At all times the therapist aimed to focus on issues in one area in such a way that problems could also be highlighted and solutions found in another. To achieve this, specific techniques were used, but all within the framework of the personal interactive style and experience of the therapist himself.

## Conclusion

The view that has been put forward here stresses the engagement of the couple in the group we call the family. From this view a particular way of working follows which stresses both the continuity and discontinuity of family relationships (Keith and Whitaker 1987). It would, however, be incorrect to assume that this is an all-or-none approach, for even if a counsellor or therapist does not wish or does not feel able to embark on such a family approach, there is a value in the concepts and vision of the perspective outlined here. It is impossible for someone not to be related to a family, just as much as it is impossible not to communicate. The working of family history, with their message transmissions, their 'invisible loyalties' and their set roles have an impact on us all. We all attempt to construct intimate relationships so that we may discover who we really are and we all struggle with the developmental tasks that are set for us as we travel life's journey. None of us can avoid the process of being triangulated and triangulating. All of us find some aspects of imtimacy threatening. We are after all just human and the role of the therapist is to be just human in a helpful way. As these things are 'given' regardless of the style, model or theory that one practises as a couple therapist, there will often be blocks and barriers to progress. The appeal of this family approach is that it offers us a creative way of leaving the fixity of 'marital habits' and entering into a wider albeit more complicated world. The ideas of this approach therefore of necessity provide the important background and context for any type of therapeutic and counselling endeavour. For those with the courage and desire to pursue it themselves, it offers an exciting way of working that brings both the pains and pleasures of living.

## References

Ackerman, N. (1960) *Treating the Troubled Family*, New York: Basic Books.

Anonymous (1972) Towards the differentation of a self in one's own family, in J. Framo (ed.) *Family Interaction: A Dialogue between Family Researcher and Family Therapists*, New York: Springer.

Bell, R.Q. and Harper, L.J. (1980) *Child Effects on Adult Behaviour*, Lincoln, Nebr: University of Nebraska Press.

Boszormenyi-Nagy, N.I. and Speck, G. (1973) *Invisible Loyalties*, New York: Harper & Row.

Bowen, M. (1976) *Family Therapy in Clinical Practice*, New York: Aronson.

Byng-Hall, J. (1980) Symptom-bearer as marital distance regulator: clinical implications, *Family Process* 19: 355–65.

—— (1985) The family script: a bridge between theory and practice, *Journal of Family Therapy* 7: 301–5.

Carter, E. and McGoldrick, M. (1989) *The Family Life Cycle: A Framework for Family Therapy*, 2nd edn, New York: Aronson.

Dare, C. (1979) Psychoanalysis and systems in family therapy, *Journal of Family Therapy* 1: 137–52.

Dryden, W. (1985) Marital therapy: the rational-emotive approach, in W. Dryden (ed.) *Marital Therapy in Britain*, vol. 1, *Context and Therapeutic Approaches*, London: Harper & Row.

Framo, J.L. (1976) Family of origin as a therapeutic resource for adults in marital and family therapy: you can and should go home again, *Family Process* 15: 193–210.

Keith, D.V. and Whitaker, C. (1987) The presence of the past: continuity and change in the symbolic structures of families, in C. Falicou (ed.) *Family Transitions: Continuity and Change over the Life Cycle*, New York: Aronson.

Lerner, R.M. and Spanier, G.B. (1978) *Child Influences on Marital and Family Interaction: A Life Span Perspective*, New York: Academic Press.

Lidz, T. (1968) *The Person: Development throughout the Life Cycle*, New York: Basic Books.

McGoldrick, M. and Gerson, R. (1985) *Genograms in Family Assessment*, New York: Norton.

MacKay, D. (1985) Marital therapy: the behaviour approach, in W. Dryden (ed.) *Marital Therapy in Britain* vol. 1, *Context and Therapeutic Approaches*, London: Harper & Row.

Minuchin, S. (1989) My voices: an historical perspective, *Journal of Family Therapy* 11: 69–80.

Noller, P. (1984) *Non-Verbal Communication and Marital Interaction*, Oxford: Pergamon.

O'Reilly, P. and Street, E. (1988) Experiencing the past in the present: a historical approach to family therapy, in E. Street and W. Dryden (eds) *Family Therapy in Britain*, Milton Keynes: Open University Press.

Satir, V. (1964) *Conjoint Family Therapy*, Palo Alto, Calif: Science and Behavior Books.

Schafer, H.R. (1971) *The Growth of Sociality*, Harmondsworth: Penguin.

Street, E. (1985) From child focussed problems to marital issues, in W. Dryden (ed.) *Marital Therapy in Britain*, vol. 2, *Special Areas*, London: Harper & Row.

—— (1989) Challenging the White Knight, in W. Dryden and L. Spurling (eds) *On Becoming a Psychotherapist*, London: Tavistock/Routledge.

Whitaker, C. (1982) A family therapist looks at marital therapy, in A.S. Gurman and D. Rice (eds) *Couples in Conflict*, New York: Aronson.

Whitaker, C. and Keith, D.V. (1981) Symbolic – experiential family therapy, in A.S. Gurman and D.P. Kniskern (eds) *Handbook of Family Therapy*, New York: Brunner/Mazel.

# 6

# Working with the individual from the couple

IAN BENNUN

## Introduction

A distinctive feature of contemporary couple therapy is the conjoint interview. Both partners attend together and are seen by either one or two therapists. Conjoint work can take other additional forms such as a conjoint group, where groups of couples meet together, or concurrent conjoint–individual sessions. In this form of treatment, conjoint sessions are interspersed with individual sessions for each partner. In this chapter I shall address how it may be possible to work with one partner or family member within a broad systemic framework.

Despite the controversies surrounding individual treatment for relationship problems, it has always been recognized as one form of couple therapy. Sometimes couples request this form of intervention (Fibush 1957), but the therapist may also suggest individual rather than conjoint sessions. Partners who find sessions competitive or who are too immature to tolerate the stress of conjoint sessions are often more appropriately seen individually (Blanck 1965; Nadelson 1978). Nadelson (1978) in fact recommends individual sessions when previous unresolved conflicts residing in one partner are deemed to interfere with and threaten the couple relationship. There are other presenting problems which may respond better to individual rather than conjoint sessions including dependence–independence difficulties, problems in sustaining two-person relationships, couples presenting aggressive or violent behaviour and where one partner has exceedingly low self-esteem while the other seemingly appears confident and competent (Bennun 1984).

Those contemporary authors who have attempted to resolve the question of the individual-conjoint interview debate by looking to the empirical data do not seem to be any clearer on directives for clinical choice (Gurman and Kniskern 1986: Wells and Gianetti 1986a; 1986b). As is often the case, the debate has resorted to questions of methodology rather than clinical interpretations of outcome. The ideas repeatedly put forward by Gurman and his colleagues are that individually oriented couple therapy sessions are the least effective of all the forms of couple therapy and that it indeed produces negative/deterioration effects (Gurman *et al.* 1986).

The controversy has not been helped by the confusion surrounding the focus of treatment. There is a clear difference between conjoint sessions for presenting dyadic-interactional problems and conjoint sessions as a way of relieving individual psychopathology such as depression or anxiety. Similarly it remains unclear whether the sceptics have considered, as a basis for their view, the effects of individual psychotherapy on marital functioning (Hurwitz 1967) or on the untreated partner (Kohl 1962). Systemic therapists would not be surprised that changes in the treated partner have implications for spouses. Systems theory posits that a change in any one element of a system would have an effect on all the elements that comprise the system. So if one partner presents with agoraphobic difficulties and improves during the course of individual treatment, the spouse may well have to adjust to a more competent, effective and possibly more independent partner. It is not surprising, then, that individual therapy has been seen as a precursor to later conjoint sessions.

The description offered by Watters (1982) unfortunately may be the most accurate. He describes the arbitrary decisions that are sometimes taken when couple discord emerges during psychiatric and psychological consultations. If relationship issues are identified, then couples are referred for conjoint treatment; if the underlying relationship issues are not uncovered, the individual is treated alone.

## Rediscovering the individual

One of the consequences of the rapid enthusiasm that has emerged from the couple/family/systems movement is the apparent loss of the individual within the systemic morass. A brief account of systems theory may help in understanding why this has occurred in contemporary psychological treatments. The majority of couple and family therapists base their clinical approach within a broad systems theory framework. The ideas behind systems theory, as formulated within the biological sciences imply a relationship between mutually independent units. Systems are defined as a set of objects together, the relationship between them and their attributes. The couple therefore represents a functioning operational system who together combine to determine its total functioning (for simplicity, I refer to just couple and not other generations within the family). Each element (partner) is in a functional relationship with the other and hence is dependent on that relationship for determining its health and well-being. Intervening then with either element (e.g. individual therapy) will precipitate changes in both and in their combined functioning. A change in one partner will lead to the system having to recalibrate or reorganize itself to deal with change, be it positive or negative. (For a more detailed account, see Bennun 1988.)

This view illustrates how couples are interrelated and interdependent and also emphasizes the dependence that each partner/member has on the other, an already known precipitant of relationship distress. One therefore needs to temper the theory to take account of important psychological processes that enhance the individual without ignoring their position within the system.

Systemic couple and family therapy needs to be seen as part of a gamut of treatment orientations rather than *the* established approach. Walter (1989) describes systemic therapies as needing to be mature enough to integrate with other approaches without fear of losing their identity. He further sees as one of the major implications the need to resurrect individually orientated therapies. In making this case, decisions obviously need to be made as to when or why individual therapy is chosen in preference to family or couple treatment and vice versa. The two approaches to therapy have different rules and norms; while both are effective, splitting them arbitrarily may perpetuate the idea that they developed from conflicting realities rather than from different ones. Historically the distinction has been between the intrapsychic and the interactional without any deliberate attempt to place each in a related context, especially when clinical need prevails.

Those who have written on the family life-cycle (Carter and McGoldrick 1988; Falicov 1988) have described how viewing the family as negotiating successive developmental steps can help clinicians understand the complexity of family life; however, it tends to neglect the essence of individuality in its analysis. The life-cycle is a dynamic medium illustrating the simultaneous changes for both individuals and systems, yet it is the latter that usually attracts our attention and provides a framework for systemic therapy. A review of the current literature suggests that there are methods of working with just one member of the partnership/family which can address both systemic and individual areas of change.

## Working with the individual: systemic options

Before examining two models of working unilaterally, that is with just one partner or family member, it is worth considering how this unilateral approach can be used more generally in clinical practice. Indeed it is appropriate to ask whether there is a case to be made for singling out one member in preference to seeing both partners or all family members.

Within the couple context, treating just one partner should always remain an option. Frequently when psychological problems are viewed as part of a marital dynamic, both partners are routinely invited to attend. In a previous section it was suggested that intrapsychic and interaction processes should be seen as coexisting and that systemic enthusiasm should be tempered by remaining cognizant of individual dynamics and how they interact with dyadic processes. As a general statement, it should be accepted that systemic change can come about through working with one partner alone. There are data to support this (Szapocznik *et al.* 1983; 1986; Bennun 1985b) and clearly there are clinical instances when this approach is deemed to be appropriate. It was also noted previously that certain clinical problems may respond more favourably to individual treatment. Individual sessions can also be used as a way of preparing the person to tolerate the stress of conjoint interviews which may best be achieved through developing a positive therapeutic relationship and reducing the risk of the individual feeling exposed and vulnerable when their partner attends. Beck (1989) suggests that therapists should respond to a partner's request to be seen alone, and if acceded to, the nature and meaning of the request should be explored. The individual session may clarify the partner's position *vis-à-vis* the future of the relationship and it may help the partner to explore his or her commitment to the relationship or to distinguish between individual versus relationship concerns.

Clinicians need to be acutely aware of timing and not introduce or reintroduce the partner into conjoint sessions too soon. Often the material of the individual sessions includes the expression of fear that clients' experience of their difficulties will be belittled or negated, that the conjoint session will be too threatening or that individuals need time to consider whether they would like their partner to attend.

More importantly perhaps, the case for this form of therapy can be seen theoretically where particular family systems have stripped people of their individual resources. The role of mother or father, husband or wife implies a dualism but it also implies that there needs to be another person to validate that role, for example a mother needs a child to be a mother. Years of performing that role in relation to another may leave the person without a sense of self or a clear identity; including others in treatment may repeat that experience. While rediscovering the individual may prove to be a valued treatment focus, the sessions may need to take the form of helping the individual redefine rather than rediscover who they are and then adjust to their present circumstances. The clinical literature tends to suggest that this occurs only when someone loses a partner; similarly people can lose a sense of self-worth or a role and mourn the loss of the identity they were forced to relinquish in order for the system to function. In essence the person in the role needs to be extracted from it and be validated. We hear too often 'I am just a housewife' without taking enough care to understand what is behind this sort of statement.

Working with one partner alone can also be used to bring about changes in repetitive sequential interactions. In these interactions, the sequences and outcomes can, more or less, be predicted by the couple or family given previous experience. Structural therapists (e.g. Minuchin 1974) may wish to witness these interactions in order to bring about change, thereby opting for conjoint sessions. It is of course an empirical question whether the interactions that occur outside would be reliably transferred to the conjoint session. Structural therapists would encourage the couple to enact the dysfunctional sequences, and then provide them with some alternatives. However, the degree of generalization from the session remains an assumption, so the value of new learning will always remain uncertain. An alternative approach, more similar to strategic methods (e.g. Madanes 1981), would be to help one partner develop strategies that interrupt dysfunctional recurring patterns while not making these explicit to their partner. Repetitive sequences strengthen systems, so the act of surprise or unpredictability could unbalance the system and necessitate a change in the usual pattern of interaction. Strategic therapists aim to develop 'tactics of change' but some are more appropriately not shared within the couple so as to impact on the system in a more dramatic way. In its most simplistic form, the therapist may advise one person to act differently in a given situation and monitor the outcome to see how it differs from the usual pattern of events. A case where this worked successfully was with a couple where the wife presented with anorexia. Instead of the husband encouraging his wife to eat, which always ended in a row, he was advised to cook for himself alone.

The essential distinction between these two approaches is the extent to which *both* partners are aware of the therapeutic intervention. The element of surprise or unpredictability, as illustrated in this case, can be accomplished only in a one-to-one session. If both partners attend, then this intervention would be shared, so the wife would *know* that the husband was going to do things differently in the future.

A third consideration for unilateral therapy is in cases where one partner has an identifiable problem that is both systemic and intrapsychic in nature. Here the case is being made for individual therapy with two foci, one individually orientated and one exploring how the system maintains it. Jealousy provides a useful illustration because it can be formulated in individual and systemic terms. Jealousy, experienced as an individual problem, can be understood as a loss of self-esteem, rejection, feeling under threat and, at its most extreme, part of a paranoid psychosis. A partner experiencing morbid jealousy (Im *et al.* 1983; Teismann 1979) will characteristically express personal and interpersonal concerns and will inevitably have interactional experiences that confirm their beliefs and which exacerbate the distress. The clinician has the choice to treat conjointly or not, although it may be preferable to work with both individual and interactional aspects in a concurrent way. If the therapist explores early personal conflicts as hypothesized precursors to the current distress with the partner present, then the individual may find it difficult to participate for fear of appearing foolish in front of their spouse. Most people presenting with jealousy periodically admit to its irrational nature and are more likely to do so within conjoint sessions, in a self-defeating manner. In instances such as these, developing a trusting one-to-one relationship in order to explore the possible determinants of the difficulty seems to be indicated. Where jealousy does present, therapists need to be cautious not to collude by establishing a counter-jealous relationship which can be used outside of the session with disastrous escalating consequences.

A related consideration is where the system interacts in a way that maintains individual problems. In the case of jealousy, there is always the question of 'How rational am I being?' whereas in other instances this may not be so. Agoraphobia is such a case in point where an interpersonal formulation of agoraphobia has been presented highlighting how it could be considered as an interpersonal problem, providing the dependent individual with a solution to threat or perceived lack of safety (Bennun 1986). Traditional views of agoraphobia see it as a fear of leaving home or of public/open places, literally as a fear of the market-place. It is seen primarily as an individual problem although conjoint treatments have been used. The interpersonal formulation suggests that while fulfilling a function, agoraphobia maintains a particular dyadic pattern. It may fulfil the husband's need for a weak, dependent wife or alternatively provide the means to avoid challenging the husband's power base within the relationship. Although these systemic formulations may be correct, pacing dyadic interventions is crucial and individual work with both a systemic and individual focus may prove to be more effective. The usual individual behavioural-cognitive treatments tend to ignore interpersonal environments by focusing on presenting symptoms, which may be resistant to change or which promote relapse soon after improvement.

All of these factors need to be considered before deciding on whether to use a unilateral approach. Conjoint sessions can have the same treatment foci as unilateral sessions, but the dangers of joining partners prematurely or not exploring individual issues seems to outweigh adopting a systemic approach to the conjoint session before the therapist has gained an adequate understanding of the presenting problem. Interpersonal factors are usually more obvious within conjoint modes of treatment, whereas the individual-intrapsychic conflicts tend to remain masked until tactfully uncovered. It then may be possible to proceed conjointly once the individual, through individual sessions, has established their place and role in the system within which they function.

## One-person family therapy (OPFT)

Over the last few years Szapocznik and colleagues have developed and evaluated their one-person method of family therapy (Szapocznik *et al.* 1983; 1984; 1986). Although most of this work has involved two-generation families, many of the principles guiding their treatments are useful within the present discussion. The theoretical orientation directing their work has a number of bases. Both strategic and structural family therapy principles inform many of their therapeutic interventions and the approach itself is brief, generally averaging ten sessions. The population with which the method was developed were families with one drug-abusing member, but their methods can certainly be applied and expanded to other clinical presentations.

The goal of OPFT is to bring about changes in repetitive dysfunctional sequences of interactions. In order to achieve this, the entire family is invited for the initial session to assess its structure and choose the one person who, by virtue of his or her position in the family, is central to the most significant repetitive and complementary dysfunctional behaviours. Having identified the one person, most often though not exclusively the member presenting symptomatically, the therapist joins with this one member in following and tracking the family's interactional structure and so is in a position to direct appropriate changes within the family. The final step is to restructure the family interactions by altering the one person's complementary participation. The restructuring in OPFT, unlike in conjoint therapy, incorporates both interpersonal and intrapersonal factors (Szapocznik *et al.* 1984).

The clinical researchers who developed this approach believe it is necessary to convene the whole family initially: whether OPFT can be conducted without this initial conjoint session has not been examined. One would assume that therapists would prefer to meet all family members and gain a picture of general family interactions and relationships as a way of assessing the family, thereby remaining reality oriented in their work. The conjoint interview is clearly an assessment interview so that the therapist can observe, at first hand, the interactions within the family.

The choice of the one person depends on three factors: centrality in family interactions, power, and availability; together these three combine to determine who has most control over family interactions. A positive therapeutic relationship with the one person is emphasized in order that the therapist can direct change and track the family's interaction pattern through the perception of the engaged family member. Because just one member is present, only *analogue enactment* is possible which refers to exploring how the individual has internalized his or her complementary role in the family's interactions. The analogue, by definition, implies a construction of reality as perceived by the individual. There is no one present to confirm or refute this reality, so the therapist needs to maintain a reality-orientated position within the treatment. The engaged person therefore describes his or her representation of interactional patterns instead of an actual enactment which would enable the therapist to observe directly couple/family interaction. What remains important in conducting the enactment analogue is the role the individual adopts within the reported interaction patterns. This needs to be clearly identified so that the complementary roles that occur within interactions can be identified.

The notion of complementarity is important and is based on the premiss of systems theory outlined earlier, that in order for the system to maintain itself, the one person must complement the behaviour of the others. The complementary interactions can thus be divided in two, those of the one person and those of the rest of the family. When these are combined, the therapist then constructs a map of the total family functioning and intervenes through changing the one person's reported behaviour or perceptions. When these two parts of the interaction network are brought together to form the whole, the therapist can use the map to ascertain the relationship between the engaged person and their family/partner and their internalized complementary behaviours within the whole.

A case example will illustrate how complementarity is used within OPFT. A family were referred following several delinquent and anti-social episodes by one of the children. The family comprised both parents and three sons, the oldest son Charles having been the reason for the referral. At the conjoint session it became clear that one source of family tension was the strained relationship between Charles and his younger twin siblings. In examining Charles's behaviour during the first one-person session, he described feeling isolated in the family, seemingly competing for recognition with what he perceived to be a close foursome (parents and twins). He was able to give examples and details which supported *his* view of his exclusion and also gave an account of his anti-social behaviour. These two components – Charles's description of his behaviour and his perception of the rest of the family – were combined by the therapist, who was then able to construct a symbolic representation of the family by bringing together the two complements. By establishing a positive therapeutic alliance with Charles, the therapist identified the complementary behaviours maintaining the problem and began directing changes through Charles. In this case it was important to formulate the interaction of the two complementary aspects: the anti-social behaviour and Charles's perception of being excluded from the family.

Several techniques can be used with the analogue enactments, such as role-playing with the therapist, the one person playing the family's complementary roles, using the empty chair technique from Gestalt therapy, sketching structural relationships and, of course, exploring intrapersonal restructuring (for detail see Szapocznik *et al.* 1984). Clearly this method can be applied to dyadic relationships and it bears many of the hallmarks outlined in the previous discussion of unilateral therapy principles, particularly the interface between the personal and interpersonal. Partners within dyadic interactions also internalize roles/behaviour that support repetitive couple interactions, and this method illustrates how, through one person, changes at both levels can be achieved. The therapist would have to have an initial conjoint session and then continue to work with the identified partner. The way the engaged partner is identified will usually be through presenting symptoms or by exclusion, that is the partner being unwilling to attend. Therapists often exert much energy in attempting to convince the non-attending partner to participate in treatment and waste valuable therapeutic time. Failing to engage the reluctant partner and admitting to this failure after a few sessions may reflect the experience of the engaged member and further exacerbate their possible feelings of helplessness and impotence. As with most forms of one-partner couple therapy, inadvertently repeating with the therapist those interaction patterns that occur within the dyad may undermine motivation to attend and optimism about the future.

### Individual couple therapy

In Britain the percentage of individual partners being seen in couple counselling agencies is increasing (Tyndall 1985) and the usual conjoint procedures have, of necessity, been reformulated to accommodate individual consultations or referrals. Some therapists insist on convening conjoint sessions and are reluctant to see just one partner. Some of the reservations that have been expressed include gaining a biased account of the existing problem, becoming embroiled in couple secrets, the therapeutic relationship being used as a competing relationship and doubting whether dyadic change can be achieved through individual sessions.

A model that goes some way in addressing these reservations has recently been developed (Bennun 1984; 1985a). The model has been used without convening an initial conjoint session, but it is preferable to try and see both partners at the outset. It illustrates that seeing one partner is a viable option in attempting to resolve couple distress; empirically it has been shown to be clinically effective with a range of presenting difficulties (Bennun 1985b). The approach was specifically developed to treat individual partners requesting couple therapy and should not be used if this is unclear at the outset. Individuals are often reluctant to admit to relationship difficulties, preferring to individualize the problem, and complain about individual symptoms.

The dyadic focus, giving attention to the non-attending partner, and exploring contributions to conflict are the three guiding principles that need to be applied within the approach. They are considered simultaneously during the sessions and, unlike the previous model, it is less sequential in its delivery, relying on the therapist maintaining a particular position in relation to the attending and non-attending partner.

## The dyadic focus

Throughout the treatment, a balance needs to be maintained between an individual and dyadic focus. Relationships fulfil a range of psychological and physical needs both for the individual and the couple. When these needs remain unfulfilled or are thwarted, the ensuing distress affects the individual, their partner and the relationship. This triad can be ignored if the focus is purely orientated towards the individual. Similarly if the focus is predominantly on the relationship, the needs of the two persons that comprise the relationship may go unrecognized.

The model maintains the distinction between the intrapersonal and interpersonal that has already been noted and also attempts to maintain a balance between what could be seen as two competing foci. By way of setting a treatment agenda, the dual focus needs to be made explicit: at the initial assessment the couple need to be informed of this. In a way, this can be seen as not letting the eventual non-attender 'off the hook' by subscribing to the view of 'fixing her/him up will improve our marriage'. Just as the OPFT approach requires a conjoint assessment, the approach here too encourages both partners to attend for the first session. If the referral indicates that one partner may be reluctant to attend, the way that the couple is invited initially should acknowledge this reluctance. It is therefore advisable to communicate the need to see the couple conjointly first, indicating that it may not be necessary for the couple to attend together for subsequent sessions. Obviously if there is a willingness to participate fully, then the usual practice of conjoint therapy can proceed if appropriate. However, therapists need to be cautious when faced with the non-symptomatic partner willingly agreeing to attend. While their motives may well be honest, there is always the chance that they wish to attend as a gate-keeper, ensuring that certain information or detail is not included or exposed during the sessions.

Irrespective of whether both attend, the therapist needs to inform the individual or couple of the need to maintain the dual focus and orientate them to this as soon as possible. When partners who are unwilling to attend declare their intention, it is important to convey that, although they would not be there in person, they will be a part of the treatment in their absence. By accepting their resistance, it may increase the possibility that they participate in any therapeutic directives or tasks as they emerge. Indeed, clinical experience has shown that when attending partners repeatedly share the details of the sessions with their partner at home, the latter sometimes has a change of mind and attitude and then agrees to attend. It should be noted that the approach is not an attempt subtly to coax attendance, but rather to use, as productively as possible, their reluctance to attend.

An essential principle of the dyadic focus is the way problems are defined and formulated. Clinically the dyadic focus guides both the therapist and the attending partner in looking at the relationship issues primarily, rather than at psychological problems or processes. Should these arise from the relationship issues, then they are obviously explored in an appropriate way. If the therapist is working towards the resolution of a specific problem, the treatment goal needs to be formulated in terms that include both partners. For example in the case of a woman with panic attacks, the dyadic position that the therapist needs to adopt is one that necessitates the presenting problem being understood as both panic and her partner's inability to help her relax.

It is inevitable that the partner will spend time during the sessions discussing personal difficulties and defocus the relationship; it is equally likely that the relationship will predominate to the exclusion of the individual. Although just one partner attends, both should be the foci of treatment.

### The non-attending partner

Gaining the confidence of both partners is essential to the success of this approach to therapy: it is therefore important to consider the role of the non-attending partner. The initial conjoint session is the most appropriate opportunity to be specific about the non-attending partner's participation in treatment. During the conjoint session, the rationale of the treatment should be explained to both and the therapist's expectations about each partner's contribution to the process of therapy should be made explicit. It may be the only occasion that the couple are seen together so, in addition to observing how they interact, the parameters of therapy can be explained and negotiated. It should also be used to discuss presenting problems, develop therapeutic targets and consider the possible difficulties that may arise (e.g. reactance, relapse).

In order to maintain the collaborative set where both partners acknowledge the difficulties and see the need for change, the following aspects need to be stated. The attending partner should give the non-attending partner an account of the session, preferably on the same day that it takes place. It is useful to negotiate this as a 'ritual' early on so as to assess both partners' motivation. Second, if specific home assignments are indicated that are joint tasks, the non-attending partner must express his or her willingness to co-operate. A related third aspect is that the therapist should receive feedback from the non-treated partner about the task or any other topic that he or she may wish to share. The attending partner should not adopt the 'messenger' role, as this places him or her in an inferior position to the non-attending 'caretaker'. Both have a shared responsibility for creating change and the power relationships should not be reinforced through these artificial roles.

### Contributions to conflict

It is not unusual for therapists to step out of their neutral role and (emotionally) join with one partner in a treatment coalition. While efforts to withstand this are usually successful, a pivotal factor in working with one partner is adherence to the systemic notion that conflict is the result of an interaction and feedback and that one partner is not solely to blame. A fundamental premise in the individual couple therapy paradigm is to acknowledge that both partners contribute to the conflict, and that both are responsible for its resolution. While couple therapy sessions often enable partners to express and discharge emotion, blame is never far behind. In the treatment with one partner, the blaming and scapegoating processes are usually more intense because the other partner is not usually present to defend him/herself or offer a different point of view. In dyadic sessions, the opposing views often escalate the intensity of the sessions and the same is likely to occur in individual sessions. The neutral position that the therapist adopts is to counteract the blaming and scapegoating and to maintain the view that both partners contribute to the genesis and maintenance of marital distress. Therapists should not be side-tracked into deciding what proportion each individual is responsible for; rather they should be clear in communicating an understanding of the problem by presenting a systemic formulation that helps both partners identify their contribution to the conflict.

In keeping with the dyadic focus, both partners' relative contribution to the presenting distress can be made explicit through the reformulation of problems with a specific two-person focus. A distressed couple, complicated by the woman's agoraphobia, should be seen in a context that goes beyond the fear of open spaces. The reformulation could include the fear of going out and the accompanying dependency, *as well as* the man's supposedly strong protective self-perception which he is reluctant to relinquish. Hafner (1986) sees one of the origins of agoraphobia as being in the choice of partner, where the particular choice enables the couple to hold this view as their undeclared (unconscious) basis for their relationship. The man will undermine his partner's attempts toward greater autonomy and she will not challenge his strength and autonomy. It would not be surprising to find the man, in this type of relationship, being unwilling to attend, so it would be necessary to counteract the woman's possible perception that she is responsible for causing the distress. The agoraphobic symptoms will often be strengthened by its apparent capacity to reduce interpersonal conflict. Processes such as these need to be uncovered through careful questioning and developing dyadic hypotheses that account for both partners' involvement.

*Case example: Tony and June*
The case of Tony and June, who were referred to a marital and family therapy clinic, provides some good clinical material. June was originally referred to a mental health centre presenting with anxiety and agoraphobia. Tony was reluctant to attend but the therapist managed to speak to him on the telephone. He felt that the problems had nothing to do with him, that their marriage was satisfactory and that his wife's symptoms were the result of her 'change of life'. When asked if he had discussed this with her, he replied that he had tried but had not been particularly successful. June's account during the initial session was quite different. She felt that her husband did not care about her and always refused to discuss her difficulties and their effects on the marriage.

In this case it was not difficult to establish the dyadic focus because June clearly started with intrapersonal and interpersonal concerns. She felt that with will-power she could go out alone more often and overcome her agoraphobia, but was not sure how this would affect their relationship. The therapist had taken the opportunity when speaking to Tony to state that while he may be reluctant to attend, he should enquire about the session each week and respond to requests made to him through June.

During the individual sessions, she became aware of her dependency on others for support, particularly her need for Tony to be strong and decisive. The more he fulfilled these needs, the more dependent she became, and the more severe were her symptoms. Both these two contributions were included in the formulation of the problem which then had a specific two-person focus. The source of June's dependency was explored and she was later encouraged to take more responsibility for herself while suggesting that Tony relinquish some of his need to control her and their affairs. As she became more competent and confident, she was able to insist on Tony changing his behaviour. Following these changes, the power balance in their relationship altered, and she reported being much happier in her relationship.

## Accepting the challenge of working individually within a systemic framework

The reservations about one person or individual couple therapy outlined above have been incorporated to a large extent in these two individual models. Seeing just one partner will provide an opportunity for the attending partner to present a biased account of the couple relationship and the distress. By insisting on a dyadic focus and encouraging the attending partner to acknowledge that both contribute to the problem, the therapist has the opportunity of checking the validity of the information received as well as using the session as a means of providing and receiving feedback. Although clinical experience tends to suggest that both partners will attend at least the initial session, it can be used as an arena to explain the conditions of therapy. The partner who will not attend future sessions should be given ample opportunity to express opinions about how he or she sees the situation and should be encouraged to communicate with the therapist through the attending partner.

Having the initial conjoint session also enables the triad to convene so that the therapist and non-attending partner can meet and dispel any fantasies about the kind of person the other may be. Of course, any therapeutic relationship can compete with the couple relationship, and attempts to discourage this are valuable. Transference processes are inevitable in any one-to-one therapeutic relationship, but all three participants need to be cognizant of the three sets of two-person relationships: therapist–attender; therapist–non-attender, couple relationship.

All couple and family therapists have had occasions where they have received information about the family or couple by means other than through the therapy sessions. Private telephone calls and correspondence or chance meetings with the therapist are the usual avenues that can be exploited to convey secret information. Individual couple therapy is an easy arena for attending partners to reveal information that they do not want their partner to know and most often this places the therapist in the dilemma of not knowing how to deal with this material. The therapist should make it explicit at the outset that while the content of the session is confidential, the boundary of confidentiality can extend to all those involved; further it must be made clear that all material is available for sharing between the three participants. A possible exception should be instances where the proposed intervention demands that the non-attending partner remains unaware of its content, for example if a strategic or paradoxical intervention is being proposed.

The two-person therapeutic relationship is undeniably a power relationship, but this can be undermined by the therapist colluding with secrets. The secret-holder acquires more power by virtue of his or her direct involvement in the therapeutic relationship, yet the therapist loses power since he or she then loses control of the flow of information. The decision to maintain confidence and thereby participate in the secret may elicit rich clinical material, but it invariably reduces the therapist's clinical options. Naturally therapists will use their discretion and not insist that all material is shared with the non-attending partner: where the attending partner uses the session to come to some resolution about separation, commitment or such like are cases in point.

The final reservation levelled at this approach is doubt about whether dyadic change can come about from individual sessions. Dyadic change is not always the goal of the individual model and the sessions can be a way of achieving individual change. However, the empirical data certainly support the view that dyadic change is possible (Bennun 1985b; Szapocznik *et al.* 1983; 1986) and given the general principles of systemic therapy, a change in one element of the system, will require a consonant change in all of the others. The system will have to accommodate any changes that are achieved through the individual sessions, be they symptomatic relief or gaining a fresh understanding of the dynamics of the relationship. If an agoraphobic wife is able to master her symptoms and become independent and autonomous, then her husband naturally will have to alter his view of her and possibly much of his own behaviour. Similarly if the conflict is maintained by interpersonal misperceptions and distorted cognitive schemata, their alteration through individual sessions could have a favourable impact on the relationship. The balance between conjoint and individual change mirrors the principle of the personal versus interpersonal focus of treatment.

## The way forward

The development of couple therapy approaches that involve seeing just one partner is a shift within its development. In some respects, it illustrates that couple therapy generally has come the full circle again acknowledging that there is place for the non-conjoint perspective. The early psychoanalytic methods saw the conjoint session as interfering with the development of the transference relationship and argued against seeing both partners together. The next stage was characterized by the emergence of the various forms of conjoint and conjoint-group aproaches and the application of systemic methods. Now again, the role of individual couple therapy is being considered as a viable treatment option. This 'second generation' of individual approaches has incorporated systemic principles (as opposed to psychodynamics) which makes it distinctive, albeit in need of constant refining and development. Major issues – including non-compliance, resistance, drop-out and engaging men as active non-attending participants – continue to require special attention.

Related to this point is the need to ask questions of individual models that address which interventions are appropriate with particular couples at specific moments within a treatment contract. Further, the need for more research on the efficacy of one person approaches is necessary: its use and techniques can then be made more convincing and the sceptics may be more willing to reconsider their reservations.

The impact of the individual therapy on the untreated partner is an unexplored area although there are some accounts in the literature suggesting that it is a negative one (Kohl 1962; Hurwitz 1967). The exact nature of the consequences is unclear and this warrants further investigation.

It is not possible to overcome all interpersonal and relationship difficulties within a conjoint approach and it is unlikely that all individual problems will necessarily respond to one-to-one therapy. Working with the individual from the couple allows for an integrated and flexible approach, if both interpersonal and intrapsychic factors can be seen as the basis for the treatment. In this chapter two notions of the individual within the system have been identified as treatment options. One is to identify individual processes that contribute to personal distress and conduct a systemic treatment taking into account personal and interpersonal factors. The second approach identifies working with one partner as a way of reorganizing a system. Each has a different emphasis, yet they support the idea of individuals within systems. The individual within the system needs to be recognized and a flexible individual therapy is a welcomed inclusion within the field of couple therapy.

## References

Beck, R. (1989) The individual interview in couples treatment, *Journal of Family Therapy* 11: 231–41.

Bennun, I. (1984) Marital therapy with one spouse, in K. Hahlweg and N. Jacobson (eds) *Marital Interaction: Analysis and Modification*, New York: Guilford.

—— (1985a) Unilateral marital therapy, in W. Dryden (ed.) *Marital Therapy in Britain*, vol. 2, London: Harper & Row.

—— (1985b) Prediction and responsiveness in marital therapy, *Behavioural Psychotherapy* 13: 186–201.

—— (1986) A composite formulation of agoraphobia, *American Journal of Psychotherapy* 44: 177–88.

—— (1988) Systems theory and family therapy, in E. Street and W. Dryden (eds) *Family Therapy in Britain*, Milton Keynes: Open University Press.

Blanck, R. (1965) The case for individual treatment, *Social Casework* 46: 70–4.

Carter, E. and McGoldrick, M. (1988) *The Family Life Cycle: A Framework for Family Therapy*, New York: Guilford.

Falicov, C. (1988) *Family Transitions*, New York: Guilford.

Fibush, E. (1957) The evaluation of marital interaction in the treatment of one partner, *Social Casework* 38: 303–7.

Gurman, A. and Kniskern, D. (1986) Commentary: individual marital therapy – have reports of your death been somewhat exaggerated?, *Family Process* 25: 51–62.

Gurman, A., Kniskern, D. and Pinsof, W. (1986) Research on the process and outcome of marital and family therapy, in S. Garfield and A. Bergin (eds) *Handbook of Psychotherapy and Behaviour Change*, New York: Wiley.

Hafner, R.J. (1986) Marital therapy for agoraphobia, in N. Jacobson and A. Gurman (eds) *Clinical Handbook of Marital Therapy*, New York: Guilford.

Hurwitz, N. (1967) Marital problems following psychotherapy with one spouse, *Journal of Consulting Psychology* 31: 38–47.

Im, W., Wilner, R. and Breit, M. (1983) Jealousy: interventions in couples therapy, *Family Process* 22: 211–19.

Kohl, R. (1962) Pathological reactions of marital partners to improvement of patients, *American Journal of Psychiatry* 118: 1,036–41.

Madanes, C. (1981) *Strategic Family Therapy*, London: Jossey-Bass.

Minuchin, S. (1974) *Families and Family Therapy*, Cambridge, Mass: Harvard University Press.

Nedelson, C. (1978) Marital therapy from a psychoanalytic perspective, in T. Paolino and B. McCrady (eds) *Marriage and Marital Therapy*, New York: Brunner/Mazel.

Szapocznik, J., Kurtines, W., Foote, F., Peres-Vidal, A. and Hervis, O. (1983) Conjoint versus one-person family therapy: some evidence for the effectiveness of conducting family therapy through one person, *Journal of Consulting and Clinical Psychology* 51: 889–99.

Szapocznik, J., Kurtines, W. and Spencer, F. (1984) One-person family therapy, in W. O'Conner and B. Lubin (eds) *Ecological Approaches to Clinical and Community Psychology*, New York: Wiley.

Szapocznik, J., Kurtines, W., Foote, F., Peres-Vidal, A. and Hervis, O. (1986) Conjoint versus one-person family therapy: some further evidence for the effectiveness of conducting family therapy through one person with drug-abusing adolescents, *Journal of Consulting and Clinical Psychology* 54: 395–7.

Teismann, M. (1979) Jealousy: systemic problem-solving therapy with couples, *Family Process* 18: 151–60.

Tyndall, N. (1985) The work and impact of the National Marriage Guidance Council, in W. Dryden (ed.) *Marital Therapy in Britain*, vol. 1, London: Harper & Row.

Walter, J. (1989) Not individual, not family, *Journal of Strategic and Systemic Therapies* 8: 70–7.

Watters, W. (1982) Conjoint couple therapy, *Canadian Journal of Psychiatry* 27: 91.

Wells, R. and Gianetti, V. (1986a) Individual marital therapy: a critical appraisal, *Family Process* 25: 43–51.

—— (1986b) Rejoiner: whither marital therapy, *Family Process* 25: 62–5.

# 7

# Working with couples in crisis

MARY HINCHLIFFE

This chapter aims to examine the dynamics of vulnerable couples who have reached a point of crisis and to look at the approaches which the therapist can use in order both to support the couple during their pain and suffering, and later to intervene in their moves towards re-establishing greater stability either within the relationship or for themselves.

## Introduction

'Crisis' is defined by the *Concise Oxford Dictionary* as a turning-point especially in relation to disease or it can be construed as a time of danger or suspense. Its derivation is from the Greek 'krisis', which means decision.

In couple terms it is a time when underlying emotional conflicts and problems are made explicit: this may occur after years of implicit behaviour which hints at the difficulties and yet may be ignored by one or both of the partners concerned. It may be a pivotal turning-point where the rules of the relationship are abruptly changed, new roles are defined and a new level of relationship imposed. It is at this particular turning-point that crisis therapy may offer its most beneficial effects in order to establish appropriate resolution and a constructive change. The crisis in itself is only an indicator of the need for understanding and self-expression in dyadic communication. For some couples or individuals this time of challenge and confrontation can become overwhelming and the fear of loss and lack of readiness for change can be paramount. The rules of the relationship no longer regulate its stability or homeostasis and tensions rise associated with major mood disturbances. This may lead to acting out behaviour which demands attention and may take various forms. There may be depressive self-injuring or illness behaviour or there may be anti-social and deviant acts which occur within the context of alcohol or drug abuse. Both couples and therapist may be thrown into insecure and demanding roles in the face of uncontrolled expressiveness.

## The experience of crisis

Several authors have written accounts of crisis intervention (Golan 1978; Smith 1981; Puryear 1981). They understand crisis as a time when balancing processes begin to fail and equilibrium is disrupted. The normal problem-solving mechanisms falter and the individual is thrown into disequilibrium. Anxiety and tension are generated until the problem is resolved and there is a return to equilibrium. Puryear (1981) emphasizes our personal needs for security and understands that they are based on

1  our social support system
2  our relatedness to others within the family or community
3  our own sense of individuality or self
4  our personal self-esteem or sense of value.

Murgatroyd (1985) has applied these ideas to marital crisis in volume 2 of the handbook *Marital Therapy in Britain*. He draws from the ideas of Puryear, which I shall also summarize. The state of crisis is characterized by the following.

1  *Symptoms of stress*   these may be expressed as physical tensions such as chest pain, headaches or abdominal discomfort, or as psychological symptoms which may include fear, anxiety and misery.
2  *Attitudes of panic or defeat*   which may be expressed as agitation associated with acting out in order to discharge tension, or a passivity through a sense of total defeat exemplified by total helplessness or an intoxicated state.
3  *Focus on relief of pain and stress*   the individual searches frantically for support and empathic understanding rather than for a solution to the presenting problem.
4  *Lowered efficiency*   the individual continues to function normally but at a low key level.
5  *Limited duration*   since it is intolerable to remain in crisis indefinitely the effects are necessarily time-limited and usually do not last beyond six weeks. They are improved by 'resolution' or by taking up a 'new role'.

Murgatroyd (1985) emphasizes the dual suffering of partners in crisis both mentally and physically. The fear of physical harm or the actual experience of it heightens and colours the total event. The demoralized individual becomes vague and indecisive and seeks repetitively for reassurance and support from a range of individuals which include friends and professionals alike.

I shall now illustrate some of the above points by describing a middle-aged couple whose marriage had reached crisis point when the wife declared her need for a divorce.

*Case example: Muriel and Tom*
Muriel and Tom have been together for twelve years and are both in a second marriage. Muriel is five years older than Tom and has always understood that he required her to be a mothering figure who ran the home and provided for his material and emotional needs. He had always been a mean man where money

was concerned and rarely showed her any tokens of his affection. However, he was much loved by her grandchildren from her first marriage and, in spite of his problems in expressing true affection, was a conscientious and hard-working man.

Tom for his part enjoyed the instant family and home which Muriel had provided for him but he disliked the time and energy which she put into her grandchildren and social activities.

Their life changed when Muriel took early retirement from a job which had offered her considerable support and opportunities for friendship. Soon after Tom found that he was under threat of redundancy and became extremely anxious for his future. He expressed this by demanding more of Muriel's time and company and she became intolerant of his dependent ways. He responded by taking up an injured and resentful position and began to complain of chest pain and greater irritability. He especially criticized her physical appearance and the effects of ageing and discounted the performance of her grandchildren.

Her intolerance increased and was accompanied by a determination to end the marriage. She accused him of being mentally sick and in need of psychiatric treatment. As Tom's security became increasingly threatened he developed a restless inner agitation which caused insomnia and weight loss and he began to think in depressive terms. He took a small overdose and was admitted to hospital. Here he found symptomatic relief through the use of medication and the support of the staff but continued to deny the possible breakdown of his marriage.

His wife had been overwhelmed by feelings of guilt and continued to express concern through regular visits to the ward. However, she remained determined to end the marriage and accepted the offer of an extended holiday with her family.

Tom became increasingly preoccupied with his chest pain and feared a possible heart attack. He began to slow down and treated himself like an invalid. This involved extended periods of inactivity when he remained rooted to his chair. He returned to his home with appropriate support but did not change. His wife became increasingly anxious about him and returned from her holiday early. She found him a less demanding man in his new role and found that she was able to relate to him as his carer more comfortably. She finally agreed to stay with him until he had gained in strength and stopped the divorce proceedings.

In this example both husband and wife demonstrated symptoms of stress and worked through attitudes of panic and defeat. Both sought for support and understanding in different ways and resolved the crisis by taking up new roles which redressed the balance in their relationship.

### Crisis intervention theory

Smith (1981) elaborates three phases to the crisis through his understandings of crisis intervention theory. These ideas can be applied to crisis in couples and assist us in gaining greater awareness of the emotional processes involved.

1 An initial or beginning phase when a rise in tension occurs as habitual coping strategies fail. Powerful and uncontrolled feelings of anger and despair take over which are projected on to the partner as blame, hostility, rage and

resentment. The individual needs to express his or her own misery and help-lessness but at the same time tries to re-establish the relationship through angry guilt inducing outbursts of verbal abuse or aggressive behaviour.

The level of acting out depends on the nature of the crisis and the fury which is being experienced. It may become extremely hostile and include damage to the partner's person or property. If this is the case then behaviour is fre-quently further disinhibited by the use of alcohol or drugs. Physical battering associated with alcohol abuse has been considered in detail by Murgatroyd (1985).

2  A middle phase begins when emergency coping strategies take over and there may be a rapid retreat into a defensive position which may proceed in the direction of total denial or avoidance.

If solutions have not been found in phase 1 the individual has to begin to apply defensive coping strategies in order to rationalize their experiences and to make sense of events. This may involve a defensive retreat associated with total denial and avoidance of the partner. This position may assume a magical quality of safety associated with the false belief that by avoiding the problem it will disappear. It is not uncommon for hysterical dissociative behaviour to assert itself at this juncture and this total emotional switch off may be expressed as temporary amnesia or confusion or even a hysterical aphonia or loss of voice.

As time passes tensions reduce and the need for retreat or denial begin to cease.

3  The final phase occurs when the problem is opened up, confronted and redefined. At this point the individual is able to move into a more operational or object-focused mode. It is at this juncture that crisis intervention can be most critical in terms of change and growth promotion within the relationship. If, however, the intervention fails because the couple continue to collude in a defensive denial, then this may become their solution until a further break-down in the relationship occurs. Alternatively this may be the stage at which a couple decide to separate and move out of the relationship. It then becomes equally important to use crisis intervention to help the individual.

## Male–female differences in the expression of couple grievances

It is worth commenting at this point on the reported gender differences in the expression of relationship grievances. Interest has been shown in interaction patterns by a number of authors in recent years (Fitzpatrick 1988; Noller and Fitzpatrick 1988; Gottman and Levenson 1988). Their studies show that men's grievances are centred on their partners' complaints and that men react to this by withdrawing emotionally, withholding affection and may not disclose their feelings at all. In comparison they have found that women cope more competently with strong emotions and are able to be more coercive and conflict engaging than their partners. On the other hand men's responses have been shown to be more positive, more reconciling and more pacifying and may appear to be more rational in their presentation. It is difficult to generalize from these findings which do seem to support some of the original gender role differences for the expressive-instrumental dimension as described by Parsons and Bales (1955). Some of these observations are borne out by one's clinical experiences in couple work where the woman appears to be much more closely in tune with her emotional world and the man more frequently attempts to take a problem-solving approach to their difficulties and is less accessible to the therapeutic situation.

Gottman and Levenson (1988) propose a physiological difference between men and women and consider that men are physiologically aroused more easily during confrontations than are their partners and are slower to calm down afterwards. They believe this effect is stronger for unhappily married men. They propose that the level of physiological arousal is punishing to the man and causes him to withdraw from the relationship. Women do not experience the same level of arousal and respond differently. These ideas may have considerable significance for crisis in relationships since this is the point at which physiological arousal reaches a pitch and individual control is temporarily lost. These findings therefore might have application in the understanding of wife-battering during marital conflict and may influence the presentation of individual partners at a time of crisis.

## Dimensions of marital dynamics

Berman and Lief (1975) described three principal dimensions to couple dynamics which are continually changing in the search for homeostasis.

1  *Power within the relationship*   for example the woman may find a new power position within a blaming resentful role which then becomes perpetuated and the relationship adjusts around it.
2  *Intimacy or closeness*   for example there may have been an extramarital affair which has been damaging to the relationship and the couple may distance each other as a form of protection.
3  *Boundary setting*   for example the couple boundaries may change as a result of a child being born and new roles as parents become established.

How does a crisis event effect the principal dynamics of couple relationships? The crisis totally shatters the previous relationship structure and opens the way for new patterns to emerge as the couple seek for peace and order. If they have an investment in preserving their relationship they will be motivated to negotiate change at any cost and will actively seek a new position of homeostasis. In the process they must work through the three major dimensions of the dynamics as described above. However, the crisis may be the pivot which redirects long-term disharmony and becomes the reason for the end of the relationship. The crisis itself may have been sought for subconsciously as an excuse for a total change in the relationship.

Crises can also be characterized more generally and Pittman (1987) gives a useful categorization.

1  *External events*   Major disasters from sudden death in the family to the loss of the bread-winner's job may come into this category. The couple move into

problem-solving roles in order to absorb and cope with the event. Inevitably there is a search for blame and the finger is pointed at possible blameworthy individuals. The well-adjusted couple can cope with this level of probing and analysis but for the less stable couple this behaviour may lead straight into the old routines of attack and counter-attack which then reopen the previous relationship problems and heighten the effect of the crisis.

2 *Structural crises*   These crises occur in couples who have established a stable-unstable pattern of relationship which involves repetitive patterns of instability in a long-standing relationship. External events may feature as a trigger for crisis but the internal dynamics are the overriding reason for its occurrence. The crisis represents opportunities for change in a couple who have previously chosen to avoid it. At one level this type of relationship survives on the peaks and troughs which bind it together and their life-style may also become part of their mutual expressiveness. (An example of this might be the stormy relationship of an alcoholic couple who move from one crisis to another as a result of the drinking partner's behaviour.) At another level the repetitive crises become destructive over time and lead through a process of attrition to the eventual downfall of the relationship.

3 *Developmental crises*   Psychosocial transitions occur at different times in life when developmental tasks have to be negotiated and new roles evolved. They have a special significance in marriage where a relationship also needs to change and new rules and boundaries defined. Vines (1979) describes transitional tasks as 'adult unfolding' and sees them as individual tasks which we all experience in our personal growth into adult life; such tasks include dealing with parental relationships on leaving home, adult self-individuation, mid-life crisis, and retirement. Our capacity to 'unfold' and grow at these times depends on our successful renegotiation of earlier intrapsychic conflicts which in turn relate to pre-existing childhood expectations and scripts. Vines links this experience with external or 'marker event' which coincide temporarily with the developmental unfolding. These are events which have a notable impact and require rapid adaptation and change in an individual's life situation. These 'marker events' therefore have the quality of crisis as we have defined it. Inevitably there is an interaction between developmental and the 'marker event' and in combination they can become the turning-point in the life of the couple or individual.

## Case example: Margaret and Tony

The following case history may illustrate some of the above points in terms of developmental tasks, marker events and marital negotiations. This middle-aged couple married in their early 20s. Margaret had little experience of other boyfriends before marriage and was a shy girl very dominated by her father. She met Tony as a teenager and they established a long-standing courtship before their marriage in their early 20s. He proved to be an emotionally and sexually undemanding figure and gave Margaret considerable freedom to remain closely involved with her parents and her father in particular. During the early years of her marriage when her two children were born, her husband remained a peripheral figure in emotional terms and their sexual closeness was very limited.

She began to get depressed and this depressive pattern developed a chronicity over the succeeding years as their children were growing up. During this time her husband had become more successful in his job achieving higher status and greater responsibilities. Margaret, however, retained a key role in the domestic setting and also carried out a part-time job.

When they reached their early 40s their relationship changed abruptly as Margaret's father died suddenly and she withdrew into an extended period of grief. Tony found her a confusing partner since she began to make new emotional demands on him for his support and interest. He became wary of her and had a brief affair at work. They became increasingly estranged at an intimate level and her depressive symptoms increased. In the mean time Tony developed a number of hypochondriacal symptoms and began to seek advice from doctors. He increasingly avoided confrontations with Margaret since he feared her powerful criticism and blame which disturbed him. The marriage had now reached a point of crisis and Margaret made her distress clear by taking an overdose and being admitted to hospital. At this juncture the wife befriended a male neighbour and then was overwhelmed with a sense of guilt when her husband's abdominal symptoms increased and he was found to be in need of surgery. This gave her a new role within their relationship and opened the way to crisis therapy.

This case demonstrates the effects of the interaction of the developmental tasks associated with mid-life and the death of her parent with the marker event caused by the wife's overdose and the husband's affair. These events brought long-standing marital disharmony to a crisis point. The wife assumed a power position through her overdose in order to achieve greater intimacy with her husband. Her ambivalence about the relationship persisted and she withdrew into a new position by involving her neighbour. The power position changed again as the husband became ill and this facilitated the opportunity for greater intimacy to occur and at the same time new roles were established. The longitudinal aspect of this case history demonstrates the importance of revealing the changes which have occurred throughout the length of the marriage and which govern the couple's level of intimacy.

## The therapist's roles

The descriptions so far have given the impression that therapists may be confronted by a high level of emotional turmoil and uncontrolled anger. This can be an emotionally taxing and demanding experience which requires therapists to take charge and reduce their own anxiety levels in a situation which feels perilously out of control. These issues were well expressed in *Marriage Matters* (1979) in which the authors say 'A practitioner needs to be emotionally secure to help the client in areas where he may be asked to be a guide where there is no map and only an uncertain destination.' The trainee therapist therefore requires support from a supervisor or co-therapist in discovering his or her own capacity to cope with this level of personal challenge in crisis situations. Every therapist needs ground rules for working with couples in crisis and for containing the destructive elements of crisis responses. Some of these guiding principles for therapy are as follows.

1 *Communication*  In order to achieve an empathic relationship with the couple it is important to engage with them both and to provide a sympathetic listener. It is useful to ask permission to use first names and to enter into the couple's own use of language and description of events.
2 *Applying safe limits to expressiveness*  This means that the therapist must be prepared to orchestrate and control the process which is being enacted in the consulting room. Individual partners should have equal amounts of time to speak and to express their sense of hurt and injustice.
3 *Focusing on the present and its problems*  It is also important to stop the couple from hurling insults and recriminations from the past and they should be encouraged to discuss their present feeling state using the 'here and now' experience.
4 *'No fighting' during therapy*  It is crucial to make it clear to the couple that you are not prepared to work with them if verbal or physical abuse ensues during the interview. It may be useful to offer them a model for a distraction technique which they can take home to use in similar situations as a substitute for angry outbursts. One can use simple ideas such as counting to ten before speaking or seeking an alternative activity.
5 On occasions it may be preferable either to defer the interview until a later date or to recommend that one partner leaves the room for five minutes and returns if she or he feels able to participate more rationally. Whatever the technique, the therapist must be seen to be setting clear boundaries to the therapeutic working environment.

As these ground rules are laid down the therapist will begin to demonstrate greater awareness of the couple's difficulties and will begin to communicate in a mode which is congruent with the crisis. Gradually empathy and trust will develop between the couple and the therapist; tensions will reduce as the couple feel able to disengage from the disturbing and violent emotions that were torturing them as they entered the room.

## Understanding and working with anger, bitterness and blame

We shall now consider the underlying causes of some of the most powerful emotions which are expressed during crisis. At times the therapist may be taken unawares by the explosive quality of their expression.

L'Abate and McHenry (1983) discuss the derivation of anger from underlying feelings of hurt and fear of being hurt, which lead to unresolved and unexpressed pain. They conclude that the hurt feelings and fears that underlie anger arise from unresolved grief issues associated with past frustrations and failures in personal relationships. This may have set the scene for feelings of personal inadequacy, low self-esteem and an underlying fear of loneliness and abandonment. This background fear can generate profound feelings of despair and depression which leads on to suicidal thoughts, preoccupations and acts. Alternatively one may see angry acting out and violent behaviour such as Pizzey (1974) describes in her discussion of domestic violence. She says that any threat in a relationship has potential for violent behaviour and this is especially true if there has been a role model for violence in a childhood background. This fear of loss of control may colour the crisis scene by producing high levels of agitation in the potentially violent partner who fears his capacity to batter. Equally the potential victim will become fearful and alarmed and make greater moves towards help seeking.

It is also important in crisis to understand the background derivation for powerful feelings of bitterness and blame which are being expressed. Guerin *et al.* (1987) used the term 'bitterbank' to describe the process of collecting bitter currency over time which is stored and then expressed at times of crisis. In Transactional Analysis terms (Klein 1980) the 'mutual blaming' or 'blemish' can lead over time to the 'racket' of bitterness and this is a process of collecting enough negative strokes to reach the point of clinging to the ego state of anger and hurt until the moment is passed and the emotional energy discharged. These two interpretations support the idea of 'storing' bitterness and identifying the effect it has on emotional distance within the relationship. Again individuals have invariably had childhood experiences of being neglected or discounted in emotional terms and rapidly move into the old childhood positions when their current relationship is in trouble.

## Crisis interventions

### Time out

When tensions are arising and concerns are being expressed about the safety of the couple in terms of potential violence or self-destructive acts, then it may be useful to take control by instructing the couple to avoid confrontations and to limit their time together. The suggestion being made here is that they need to 'cool off' before being ready to carry on with therapeutic engagement. On occasions the time out may be achieved by physical separation; in psychiatric practice the most common procedure is to take the most at-risk partner into hospital for a few days and initiate the first stage of couple therapy from the in-patient setting. Very often couples suggest their own time out and physically remove themselves to their own places of safety in the homes of relatives or friends. This intervention can help the couple to see the therapist as a caring and involved person who is prepared to take a parental role at a time when they are most scarred and hurt and in need of 'licking their wounds'. However, it is equally important not to extend this separation more than a few days and to bring the couple together in order to channel the emotional energies which are being expressed into a more constructive behaviour.

### Interviewing couples as individuals

This is another useful intervention which gives the individual the opportunity to talk freely and uninhibitedly about guilts and anxieties associated with extramarital relationships or behaviour which has not been revealed to the partner. This form of intervention should occur on only one or two occasions and preferably the therapist should interview both individuals, giving each of them equal time and attention. The risk is otherwise that a coalition will be established with the selected partner and this will damage any later attempts to re-establish a conjoint approach.

## Reframing

This is an important intervention which was originally described by Haley (1978). The theoretical basis to this intervention is based on the notion that couples exist through rule-governed behaviour which they continue to use at times of crisis. However, underlying their marital conflict is a mutual protectiveness that keeps the problem going. In other words there are positive attributes to their behaviour which need to be made explicit. The therapist's intervention is directed towards changing the rule of the relationship in such a way that they are unable to continue with their behaviour. An example of this might be to reframe the angry man as caring a great deal about his relationship and the bitter resentful woman as being concerned to protect her partner from her underlying feelings in order to preserve the security of the relationship. At the same time as giving a positive understanding to the disharmony, one also gives a message that it is important for them to continue their dispute as a way of confronting their problems and difficulties.

## Clarifying issues and confronting the couple

The therapist may make a very powerful intervention by directly confronting the individual or the couple when implicit patterns of behaviour are understood during the course of the interview. It may be useful, for example, to reveal that one person is discounting any comments about sexual difficulties which the other is introducing, and then to help them to look at the level of hurt which this involves. At a more practical level it may be very confronting to the couple to refuse to continue the interview if one of them is intoxicated from the effects of drugs or alcohol.

## Identifying and clarifying triangles

During marital conflict a point is reached where the marital system is unable to contain the pressures which are being generated. Emotional needs are expressed by one partner and energies are directed outside the relationship into closer relationships with other family members or into an extramarital affair. At any rate the couple's relationship becomes triangulated and assumes another position of equilibrium or homeostasis. The other partner's energies may become directed into self-protective and emotionally neutral outlets, such as hobbies or work or problems within the family group.

It is, therefore, important to identify the triangle which has been established and then to work with means to reduce the attachment involved and refocus the problems back into the marriage (see Guerin *et al.* 1987). If children are being used as 'scapegoats' in order to triangulate marital conflict, then it is important to assist the parents by giving them permission to free the child from this very responsible role by taking their own responsibility for their problems.

Sometimes the triangulation occurs in over-involved relationships with parents who continue to infantilize the partner concerned and reduce their opportunity to differentiate and disengage from their early roles. Young women who remain 'daddy's little girl' may be psychosexually immature and have major problems in coping with their own sex lives and the sexual development of their children. Equally young men who remain 'mummy's boy' tend to be non-assertive emotionally and sexually and have problems in establishing relationship boundaries and in disciplining their children.

Triangulation may take the form of an extramarital affair which not only expresses the underlying marital difficulties but also serves the purpose of stabilizing the relationship. The crisis may occur because the affair is revealed or for some other reason ceases to stabilize the relationship. In working with such a couple it is important to clarify and crystallize the issues which are being offered to the therapist. If the individual chooses not to reveal the nature of an affair and yet wishes to continue the marriage, then a commitment must be made to ending the extramarital relationship before couple therapy can be offered. Alternatively this may be a reason for ending the relationship and the therapist may play a part in assisting the couple to understand the dynamics associated with the affair and thereby to show responsibilities for the marital problems involved. The following case history may illustrate some points that have been raised.

*Case example: Jennifer and John*
Jennifer aged 40 made a second marriage after the tragic death of her first husband in a drowning accident. She needed a father for her four children and was fortunate in meeting a widower in a similar position to herself. Their marital relationship had always been poor but she focused her energies on the family and found her emotional needs gratified for a number of years until the children left home. She tried to replace them by taking on a business which involved her in considerable activity outside the home and avoided any confrontation with her husband about the problems of their intimacy. Their marriage reached crisis point when John lost his job and turned to her for support and encouragement. This exposed the emotional distance which had become established between them and she became aware of underlying feelings of resentment about re-engagement. She became depressed and preoccupied with suicidal thoughts and feelings. Her initial response was to avoid the marriage and she moved out and took up residence with her eldest son and his girlfriend. In the mean time her husband felt powerless and lost in his overtures to communicate with her. The tensions mounted and she became profoundly depressed and it became necessary for her to be admitted to hospital. This created a useful opportunity to interview her and her husband on separate occasions. It also offered a time out experience and a contract was set up to limit her husband's visits to the hospital and regular conjoint interviews were offered.

Initially Jennifer worked through profound feelings of despair which related to the frustrations of the marriage and her own guilt feelings of intolerance when her husband attempted to increase their intimacy. Their shared perception of the problem was one of confusion and stalemate. John's tolerance became brittle and he threatened to terminate the marriage and resorted to physical and verbal abuse. His self-esteem began to return as he felt himself understood and supported within the crisis intervention. Gradually with time and persistence the couple began to re-engage with positive feelings of goodwill and affection. They began to redefine their problem and achieved greater openness and intimacy.

## Results of working with couples in crisis

The successful couple who have negotiated crisis therapy and emerged with an intact marriage may be tentative and vulnerable at this stage in their therapy. Their need to fight has been defused and the emotional charge that may have sustained the relationship in the past has been lost. They are looking towards each other in bruised and tentative terms, fearful of emotional isolation and emptiness. It becomes important therefore to offer them tasks and goals which begin to redefine their relationship in positive terms, thus offering new roles for caring and its associated rewards. It is important to ask them to make demands on each other for new roles and boundaries within their relationship in order to set up a more comfortable intimacy with each other. The therapist can assist this process by setting goals between sessions which relate to shared activity and mutual caring. If the couple are motivated to preserve their relationship and goodwill exists then they will begin rapidly to find their own new level of more effective homeostasis.

For other couples the personal exposure involved may be too much and the feelings of disloyalty, guilt and shame too painful. There is therefore necessarily a significant drop-out rate either before or after the first interview; Beck (1966) mentions in her study that 50 per cent of clients did not reattend.

The therapist may have to concede limited goals since some couple conflicts may be deep-seated and immutable to change. In other cases modest change may occur and it may take a further marker event to precipitate the couple into greater mutual awareness and demands for change. Other couples remain stuck in a chronic stalemate and prefer to continue the ritual games which protect them against exposure of their own individual vulnerabilities. The crisis, however, may be the prelude to separation and the therapist can play a major part in supporting their decision and reducing the fears of abandonment, blame and background hurt which can then profoundly influence their capacity to resolve the division of their finances and the shared care of their children.

## Conclusion

The crisis can be a critical time for both clients and therapist alike. Mutual sensitivities and vulnerabilities are being expressed in a turbulent and uncontrolled fashion and the therapist's caring, open and receptive stance can offer the way to an empathic and supportive relationship. However, rules have to be laid down and boundaries set for the individual partner's behaviour. These rules can offer a sense of safety and security which opens the way to greater communication and trust. Sometimes the content of underlying resentments and bitterness may be too great for the couple to continue, in which case there may be decisions to give up the relationship. However, the therapist's skill in handling the crisis situation and making appropriate interventions is crucial to the later personal success of the individuals concerned and also their future relationship to each other.

## References

Beck, D.F. (1966) Marital conflict: its course and treatment as seen by caseworkers, *Social Casework* 47: 211–21

Berman, E.M. and Lief, H.I. (1975) Marital therapy from psychiatric perspective: an overview, *American Journal of Psychiatry* 132, 6: 583–91.

Fitzpatrick, M.A. (1988) *Between Husbands and Wives*, Newbury Park, London and New Delhi: Sage.

Golan, N. (1978) *Treatment of Crisis*, New York: Free Press.

Gottman, J. and Levenson, R. (1988) The social psychology of marriage, in P. Noller and M.A. Fitzpatrick (eds) *Perspectives on Marital Interaction*, Philadelphia, Pa: Multilingual Matters.

Guerin, P.J., Fay, L.F., Burden, S.L. and Kautto, J.G. (1987) *The Evaluation of Marital Conflict and Treatment: A Four Stage Approach*, New York: Basic Books.

Haley, J. (1978) *Problem Solving Therapy*, San Francisco, Washington and London: Jossey-Bass.

Klein, M. (1980) *Lives People Live*, Chichester, New York, Brisbane and Toronto: Wiley.

L'Abate, L. and McHenry, S. (1983) *Handbook of Marital Interventions*, New York: Grune & Stratton.

*Marriage Matters* (1979) A consultative document by the working party on marriage guidance, London: HMSO.

Murgatroyd, S. (1985) in W. Dryden (ed.) *Marital therapy in Britain*, vol. 2, Dealing with an acute crisis in marital relationships, London: Harper & Row.

Noller, P. and Fitzpatrick, M.A. (eds) (1988) *Perspectives on Marital Interaction*, Philadelphia, Pa: Multilingual Matters.

Parsons, T. and Bales, R.F. (1955) (eds) *Family, Socialisation and Interaction Process*, Glencoe, Ill: Free Press.

Pittman, F.S. (1987) *Turning Points: Treating Families in Transition and Crisis*, New York and London: W.W. Norton.

Pizzey, E. (1974) *Domestic Violence: Scream Quietly*, Harmondsworth: Penguin.

Puryear, D. (1981) *Helping People in Crisis*, San Francisco: Jossey-Bass.

Smith, L. (1981) *Crisis Intervention Theory and Practice: A Source Book*, Utah: University Press of America.

Vines, N.R. (1979) Adult unfolding and marital conflict, *Journal of Marital and Family Therapy* 5, 2: 5–14.

# 8

# Sex therapy with couples

WAGUIH GUIRGUIS

## Historical background

Sex therapy is one of the oldest professions. Prostitution was the early version of the modern, more respectable, surrogate therapy. The emphasis in the early forms of 'therapy' was on the 'doing', rather than just 'talking'. This emphasis on behavioural change as the main therapeutic element of sex therapy was rediscovered by behaviourists only as late as the second half of this century. The first half of the century was dominated by 'talking' therapy, based on the influential psychoanalytic movement. Psychotherapy for sexual problems was based, during that period, on the assumption that sexual problems were caused by deep-rooted conflicts which could be resolved only by intensive and lengthy courses of psychoanalysis. Unfortunately these intensive and expensive courses gave patients a very good insight into 'why' they had a problem but did nothing to resolve it. Disillusion with psychoanalysis as a viable therapy for sexual problems paved the way for the 'new' sex therapy.

Sex therapy as we know it now is often dated back to the year when Masters and Johnson published their landmark book *Human Sexual Inadequacy* (1970). The book put together, for the first time, fragments of clinical methods which were discovered many years before by ingenious clinicians. The roots of their programme could be traced as far back as two hundred years previously. The British physician Sir John Hunter described in 1786 an effective method of treating erectile impotence by advising the patient to abstain from sex and to try to lose his erection rather than enhancing it (cited in Hunter and MacAlpine 1963: 492). However, the original Masters and Johnson's technique of sex therapy introduced various new concepts and techniques.

1  Sexual problems were joint problems in which 'there is no such thing as an uninvolved partner' (Masters and Johnson 1970: 2). The patient in this model was the relationship and not the dysfunctional partner.
2  A co-therapy team of both sexes was used, so that each partner had individual

sessions with the same-sex therapist as well as the 'round table' meetings in which both partners met both therapists.

3  The main therapeutic agent was a series of behavioural tasks. The couple were encouraged to experience and feed back their experience to the co-therapy team. Transference and counter-transference were discouraged and mini-mized to avoid their interference in the progress of therapy. Some authorities questioned the possibility of eliminating transference issues completely from any form of therapy, no matter how brief or structured it is.

4  The performance aspects of the sexual relationship, like intercourse, orgasms or erections, were banned and so were the demanding forms of touch. The emphasis was transferred to the non-demanding touch and to learning about one's own and the partner's body.

5  In addition to these basic therapeutic techniques, which were used in all sexual dysfunctions, Masters and Johnson recommended specific techniques for specific problems. They used the 'squeeze technique' for premature ejacula-tion, inserting vaginal dilators of graduated size for treatment of vaginismus and 'surrogate therapy' for treating the single man who has no sexual partner.

6  The therapy programme was an intensive daily one and it lasted for two to three weeks. It needed a very high degree of motivation. Apart from the high cost of the course, the couple were asked to leave home, work, family and friends, to reside within the vicinity of the clinic and to have no preoccupation other than working on their sexual problem. Some critics think that these highly selective conditions for entering the therapy programme were the main reason for its high success rate.

The approach as described above appears too simple and could be implemented by anyone who reads about it, or follows some detailed instruction sheets about 'how to do it'. In practice it is far more complicated than that, and it demands a great deal of psychotherapeutic skills. Many authorities believe that Masters and Johnson were unfair to their method when they insisted that their approach was behavioural and denied any psychotherapeutic elements in their work. However, Masters and Johnson's work stands out as a landmark because of four main features.

1  It put fragments of clinical experience and isolated therapeutic measures into a comprehensive programme of treatment, which made a great deal of thera-peutic sense.

2  It was based on an extensive physiological study of human sexual response and a large sample of 510 couples treated over a period of ten years between 1959 and 1969.

3  Masters and Johnson published the first serious outcome and long-term follow-up study in the literature. The results were very impressive with an almost 100 per cent success rate in some cases, like vaginismus and premature ejacula-tion. The results were maintained on follow-up five years later, with a relapse rate of a mere 5.1 per cent. There have, however been critiques of these results, notably by Zilbergeld and Evans (1980).

4  In spite of the many variations, additions and modifications to the original

Masters and Johnson techniques, none of these produced any major breakthrough of equal importance.

## Recent modifications of the original model

Masters and Johnson's work impressed so many clinicians that sex therapy clinics sprang up all over the world. Two decades of experience in applying the original model produced a number of modifications which influenced the current practice of sex therapy.

### *Appreciating the psychotherapeutic component of sex therapy*

Clinicians who tried to stick to the sex therapy technique as described, but not necessarily as practised, by their originators, discovered that the therapy often ended up in a block. To overcome these therapeutic blocks, the therapist had to use other therapeutic skills. Kaplan (1974) tried to integrate, for the first time, the two opposing schools of psychological treatment: psychoanalysis and behaviour therapy. She saw sexual problems as operating at two different levels: the superficial or 'immediate' level which is amenable to behavioural and educational measures and the deep or 'remote' level which can be dealt with only by directing the therapy to a deeper level. This can be done, according to Kaplan, only by using psychoanalytic techniques. The aim is either to tackle the resistance or to get around it (circumvention). The cognitive aspect of sexual dysfunction was also appreciated. Techniques like cognitive restructuring, rational–emotive therapy and teaching communication skills are now an integral part of sex therapy (Guirguis 1988b).

### *Eclecticism*

The blind adherence to rigid therapeutic dogma has given way to a positive eclecticism. Sexual dysfunctions are such a heterogenous group of dysfunctions that it is absurd to assume that there is one approach which helps every couple with a sexual problem. There are, however, two types of eclecticism: the negative and the positive. Negative eclecticism is not a choice, it is a product of helplessness, loss of direction and lack of experience in any one therapeutic approach. Positive eclecticism, on the other hand, is an active choice based on an established experience in one of the schools of psychotherapy, but with enough confidence and flexibility to deviate from the original approach and use other more appropriate approaches. Eclectic therapists are like technicians with a set of tools: the more tools they have in their bag and the more experience they have in using them the more effective therapists they become. Cooper (1986) asked sex therapists in Britain to indicate the main approach they use in their practice. Of the 144 respondents only 33 (fewer than 23 per cent) stated that they used only one approach in their practice, while 111 (more than 77 per cent) of them were using a modified version which incorporated two or more approaches.

## Integration

Like all new methods, sex therapy started by being on the defensive and setting rigid limits, mostly to protect itself. Now that sex therapy is coming of age it is more confident and does not need protection. The split between psychological and physical approaches to sexual dysfunction is disappearing and the divide between 'couple' and 'sex' therapy is almost removed.

The modern sex therapist recognizes that there is no such thing as a purely physical or a purely psychological sexual problem. The most obviously organic conditions, like post-traumatic or post-operative dysfunctions, often have a psychological element. Also, the most obviously psychogenic dysfunctions, like those precipitated by stress or relationship problems, could have a physical component. A modern sexual dysfunction clinic usually has on its staff a medically qualified sex therapist, or an easy access to one. Such a clinic should be able to assess the needs of every couple and structure an individually adjusted programme to meet their needs, whether they are physical, psychological or both. The split approach of either 'physical' or 'psychological' has gradually been replaced by 'how much of each' or the relative risk approach (for more detail see Guirguis 1988a).

The modern sex therapist does not refer partners elsewhere for couple therapy, even if the relationship was identified as the main cause of the sexual dysfunction. Sex therapy has the 'relationship' as its focus, and it should be able to deal with both sexual and non-sexual aspects of the relationship. 'Sensate focus' exercises, which were the main therapeutic tool in the original Masters and Johnson's model, were found to be as effective as couple therapy in couples with relationship problems without any sexual difficulties (Guirguis 1988c; Mobarak *et al.* 1986).

The modern sex therapist should also be able to take one of the partners out of couple therapy to deal, in individual therapy, with any personal difficulty. Examples of this difficulty are a history of being abused as a child, specific sexual phobias, body image problems and severe anxiety. Once the personal problem is dealt with couple therapy can be resumed.

## New techniques

Some sexual dysfunctions were not mentioned by Masters and Johnson, like lack of desire. Some others were recognized only recently, like lack of desire in men; the aftermath of sexual abuse during childhood; and problems related to AIDS or the fear of it. With the AIDS scare, promiscuity is now becoming a life-threatening activity. Couples who are dissatisfied with their sex life are thinking twice before they seek sexual satisfaction outside a stable relationship. The need to improve sexual satisfaction within existing relationships is steadily increasing. To meet the diverse and changing needs of couples, sex therapists had to develop new techniques. To enhance sexual arousal and sexual response, new techniques were devised by LoPiccolo and Lobitz (1972) and by Kaplan (1979). Specific programmes were developed to help women who were sexually abused during childhood (Guirguis 1987a; Hazzard *et al.* 1986; Guirguis 1987c). The use of erotica to stimulate sexual appetite was advocated by Gillan (1977), although not widely used because of legal and ethical issues. Techniques to improve communication skills had to be incorporated in couple sex therapy programmes (Stanley 1981a). Faulty concepts, in the form of unrealistic expectations and myths about sexuality, had to be corrected by cognitive restructuring techniques (Zilbergeld 1980; Kowalski 1985) and by rational-emotive therapy (Ellis 1975; Dryden 1982).

## The diagnostic value of the 'sensate focus' experience

Although the 'sensate focus' exercises were identified as the main *therapeutic* tool in Masters and Johnson's therapy, it is realized now that these simple exercises have an important *diagnostic* value (Guirguis 1988a). They can uncover problems both in the relationship and in the individual partner (Kaplan 1974). Most clinics now spend less time on initial assessment, as more relevant information, undisclosed attitudes and deep-seated problems usually unfold when the couple attempt the intimate 'sensate focus' exercises (Bancroft 1989).

## Organizational change

Sex therapists, particularly those practising in National Health Service clinics in Britain, soon realized that the original model was not applicable to their work setting. They had to modify it to suit the different cultural, social, financial and practical circumstances. The couple therapist team was replaced by a single therapist of either sex. The semi-residential course was replaced by outpatient courses, and the daily sessions were replaced by weekly or fortnightly sessions. These modifications were encouraged by studies which did not detect any significant advantage in using two therapists or daily sessions (Crowe *et al.* 1981; Hogan 1978). Surrogate therapy was either abandoned or never attempted by many therapists in Britain, because of the ethical, legal and psychological risks involved. The couple sex therapy model is now becoming so flexible as to be used with individual partners, single men and women and with gay or lesbian couples. It could also be used in groups of couples or groups of single people and even with trans-sexual couples.

## Stringent outcome and follow-up studies

The euphoria and false sense of security which accompanied the startling success rate of the original Masters and Johnson's work gave way gradually to a more sombre mood. Well-controlled outcome studies produced far more modest but realistic success rates at the end of therapy, which became even more modest on long-term follow-up (Hawton *et al.* 1986; Bancroft 1989).

Although these recent changes did not bring any major deviation from the original sex therapy model, they transformed it from a highly selective and impractical therapy into a comprehensive, flexible, eclectic and very practical therapy. In Britain sexual dysfunction clinics, particularly in NHS facilities, are fairly consistent with very few differences. The differences are due mainly to the set-up and professional background of the staff of these clinics. Discussing the work of one of these clinics will give the reader an idea about couple sex therapy as practised in Britain in the 1990s.

## The Ipswich model

The reason for selecting the Ipswich Clinic as a model, apart from the fact that it is the one the author knows best, is that it is in the mainstream of sex therapy and represents couple sex therapy in Britain today. The changes in approach, philosophy and practice of the Ipswich Clinic mirror the changes in other clinics and reflects the present 'state of the art' in sex therapy.

The Ipswich Psychosexual Clinic was first founded by the author in 1979. The clinic is based at the Outpatient Department of St Clement's Hospital, a psychiatric hospital in a busy part of Ipswich and very close to the new General Hospital, with all its modern medical facilities. The head of the clinic is a consultant psychiatrist with special interest in psychotherapy; the rest of the staff are of various professional backgrounds. Nurses, occupational therapists, social workers, trainee psychotherapists, general practice trainees and psychiatric registrars are amongst the different disciplines involved. Training is achieved mainly by dyadic teaching, by sitting in with an experienced therapist, and by taking cases for therapy under close supervision. More formal teaching takes place in twice weekly teaching and supervision seminars and twice yearly workshops.

The clinic accepts referrals from medical and non-medical agencies. Self-referrals are accepted only in exceptional circumstances and the GP is always informed. Therapy is offered free under the NHS. Both partners are always invited irrespective of who is referred, whether they are married or not, and whether they are heterosexual or homosexual. We do, however, see and treat whoever turns up. We used to insist on seeing both partners for couple therapy but discovered that couple therapy with one partner works much better than with both partners if one of them is disruptive, hostile or detached.

All initial assessments are made by one of the medically qualified members of the staff, with or without a non-medical colleague. This is mainly to exclude any medical or psychiatric condition, even if the referral was from a medical colleague, as we like to make our own assessment using our integrated model (as explained below). Any physical or psychological investigations are usually made at this early stage, but not routinely. Physical examination is offered to every couple but not insisted on, except in cases of erectile failure in men and vaginismus in women. Couples are usually assessed within a few weeks of referral but may have to wait for up to six months before they start their therapy.

Couple sex therapy is done by one therapist of either sex, but a therapist in training may sit in as an observer, with the couple's permission. The sessions last between forty-five minutes and one hour and are held every two to three weeks. The average number of sessions is six to eight: progress by the third or fourth session determines the course and the outcome of therapy. It is our experience that couples who do not make progress by the tenth to twelfth session will not progress any further however many more sessions we give them. All couples are followed-up six weeks after they complete their therapy but there is no routine long-term follow-up.

## The model of causation

In order to have a sense of direction, communicate effectively with professional colleagues and facilitate training, a model of causation and of treatment is needed. The model presented here has developed gradually as our approach to couple sex therapy has changed over the years. It is a working model, which proved to be simple to apply; most couples thought that 'it made a great deal of sense'. There are four main features of the Ipswich model.

1 It puts together fragments from other models, notably those of Stanley (1981b), Kaplan (1974), Bancroft (1989) and Fisch *et al.* (1982). Any similarity between the Ipswich model and any of these models is not, therefore, a chance similarity but reflects the depth of influence these workers have had on the clinic's practice.
2 It is an integrated model which takes account of both the physical and psychological factors.
3 It is a dynamic model which sees sexual dysfunctions not as a static condition but as a constantly changing situation, which develops over time.
4 It emphasizes the role of maladaptive solutions in the initiation *and* maintenance of dysfunctions. Trying too hard, not communicating or criticizing are examples of maladaptive solutions, which can convert a difficulty into a dysfunction. These attempted solutions can also maintain a dysfunction, even after the original cause is removed.

A model of causation has to give some indication as to how to resolve the problem. Our model of therapy, described in the next section, is based on this model of causation. The model identifies the areas which have to be tackled in therapy and points out to the best way of tackling them. Outcome of therapy is also assessed by measuring the improvements in these areas. The model is summarized in Figure 8.1 and is detailed here. This account is based on more extensive descriptions by the author (Guirguis 1984; 1988a; 1988b).

### *Predisposing factors*

These are the factors which make some people more susceptible to react to personal stress, or to stress in the relationship, by becoming sexually dysfunctional. There are four main predisposing factors:

1 false beliefs and concepts
2 unrealistic expectations
3 poor communication skills
4 physical vulnerability.

#### *False beliefs and concepts*
These are strongly held beliefs which are respected and honoured without their validity ever being questioned. They are usually passed on from one generation to the next, almost unchanged, and communicated either verbally or, more often, by example. They are so ingrained in people's minds that they can influence

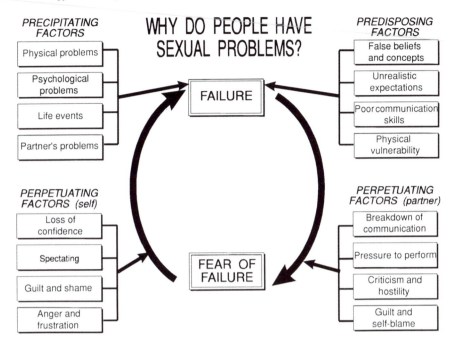

*Figure 8.1*   The vicious circle of failure

feelings and behaviour irrespective of social class, education or repeated life experiences. These false beliefs may take one of two forms: prohibitions and misconceptions.

Sexual and emotional *prohibitions* are surprisingly universal across cultures. These are some examples:

> Nice girls should not do IT, and if they do they should not enjoy it.
> Men should not have feelings, and if they do they should not show them: it is a sign of weakness.
> You should not ask your partner for what you want: if he really loves you, he should know what you want.
> It is wrong to touch yourself, particularly if you are married.
> Sex is only for the young and healthy; if you are old or ill you do not need sex.
> Sex is only to be done and not talked about.
> If you allow yourself to enjoy sex or have an orgasm, you will want it all the time and become a whore.

*Misconceptions* about sexuality are propagated by office gossips, pub or golf-club chats, coffee-morning discussions and by the mass media. These are some examples:

> A man should be able to ''give'' his wife an orgasm, and if he does not he is letting her down.

If a man really loves his wife he should be able to produce an erection every
   time.
The man should always initiate sex and do all the work; a woman should
   be passive, preferably reluctant, receiver of what he "gives" her.
The hardness of a man's erection is a measure of how much he loves his
   partner.
If a man loses an erection he loses everything.

Prohibitions and misconceptions predispose people to sexual dysfunctions by
inhibiting the free expression of their emotional and sexual feeling. It also
enforces a set of rules about the 'right' and 'wrong' ways of feeling and behaving,
which are based not on what is best for the couple but on what society feels most
comfortable with.

*Unrealistic expectations*
Unrealistic expectations are a natural product of ignorance. Ignorance about sex
is widespread, not only at the public level but also amongst professionals. Being
such a taboo subject, our knowledge about sex was, until recently, the product
of bedroom research. It is not surprising that sex is the most poorly understood
function of the human body and is, therefore, an area where expectations are
very unrealistic. These are some examples:

The size of the penis and the tightness of the vagina determine the amount
   of pleasure the couple derive from sex.
The ultimate goal which every couple should aim for is mutual, simultaneous and earth-moving orgasm.
Vaginal orgasm is better than clitoral orgasm and multiple orgasms are
   better than a single orgasm.
Men can have an erection any time if they want to or if they try hard
   enough.
A man cannot possibly be in love with a woman and fail to get an erection
   with her.
A real man should go to bed with an erection and not need any manual
   assistance to get one.
A woman must always respond sexually if touched in the right spot i.e. the
   clitoris.

Unrealistic expectations predispose to sexual dysfunction by putting an enormous
pressure on men and women to perform beyond their physical capability. If they
do not live up to these unrealistic expectations, they experience failure. They also
panic if the slightest little thing deviates from what they think is 'normal'.

*Poor communication skills*
Sex is a form of communication. A couple who cannot talk easily to each other
should not wonder why they cannot enjoy sex together. To communicate effectively the couple need to tell each other what they want, like and dislike about
sex. They should also be able to express their own feelings, particularly negative
ones like guilt, anger, hostility and frustration. If anger and hostility are not freely

expressed at the time they may be pushed aside only to be expressed later in a disguised form. Holding back erections, orgasms or sexual desire is one of the most powerful expressions of anger in a sexual relationship. Placid, timid and overtly quiet men, who are frightened of their own anger, tend to use erections as a weapon in couple conflicts. Women who feel resentful, misused and unappreciated by their husbands will naturally find it difficult to feel loving and sexual towards them unless these negative feelings are expressed and dealt with. Families who pride themselves on the fact that they 'never have rows' are particularly vulnerable.

*Physical vulnerability*
Sexual dysfunctions have a definite physical component. They are psychosomatic conditions caused by an interaction between stress and a particularly vulnerable part of the body. As people who have peptic ulcers have a vulnerable stomach and those who have asthma have a vulnerable chest, people who have sexual problems may have vulnerable sex organs which respond to stress by becoming dysfunctional. The vulnerability could be constitutional, that is the person is born with it, or it could be acquired later in life, as a result of ageing, illness, trauma, drugs or surgical operations.

*Precipitating factors*

These are factors, or stresses, which may not be enough in themselves to produce a sexual problem, unless they are very severe or very prolonged. They are non-specific factors which can produce any psychosomatic condition depending on which part of the body is most vulnerable. If individuals are predisposed to have sexual dysfunctions as a result of one or more of the predisposing factors mentioned above, they stand a high risk of developing a sexual problem if subjected to one of the precipitating factors listed in Table 8.1.

The interaction between one or more of these precipitating factors and a particularly vulnerable couple may produce the first few failures. This may cause only a sexual 'difficulty', from which most couples can recover. A difficulty becomes a problem or a dysfunction if the couple get caught up in the vicious circle of failure (see Figure 8.1).

*The vicious circle of failure*

The vicious circle of failure starts by failing to achieve one of the sexual responses, like having an erection, an orgasm, a controlled ejaculation, or failing to enjoy sex. Because they failed on a few occasions the couple start to anticipate more failures. Fear of failure, or anticipating it, is a sure way of producing more failures. The more the couple fail the more they expect failure, until failure becomes a self-fulfilling prophecy. Once the vicious circle is established it can go on indefinitely, driven partly by its own momentum, but largely by the maladaptive ways in which the couple try and break it. These maladaptive methods act as perpetuating factors which make the vicious circle go faster and deeper. Being caught in a vicious circle is a frustrating situation which is described by some

**Table 8.1**  Precipitating factors

| *Physical problems* | |
|---|---|
| Illness | e.g. diabetes, hypertension, heart disease |
| Pain | due to scars or to osteoarthritis |
| Venereal diseases | or the fear of catching them |
| *Psychological problems* | |
| Depression | spontaneous, post-partum or as a reaction to stress |
| Anxiety | about health, finance or relationships |
| Insecurity | about self, future or about the relationship |
| Fear of pregnancy | or ambivalance about it |
| *Life events* | |
| Loss of spouse | by death or divorce |
| Loss of status | by redundancy or early retirement |
| Death or illness in the family | |
| Extramarital affairs | |
| Loss of children | by leaving home or starting school |
| *Partner's problems* | |
| Medical | mastectomy, hysterectomy, prostatectomy, heart attacks or sterilization |
| Pregnancy | or childbirth |
| Loss of libido | |
| Anorgasmia | |
| Painful intercourse | due to menopause or vaginismus |
| Premature ejaculation | |

couples as 'like being caught in quick-sand: the more we struggle the more we sink'.

For example if a man fails to obtain or maintain an erection the couple's first reaction is silence. They both realize that something is wrong, but neither of them dares breaking the silence taboo. The man loses confidence, starts to doubt his manhood, thinks he is getting old, starts to watch his erections, tries very hard to enhance them or concentrates too much on maintaining them. These reactions can only lead to further failure. When he fails repeatedly he feels guilty for letting his partner down, ashamed of himself for being such a failure, feels angry with himself, with his partner for not helping him or with his penis for letting him down so badly. He finally gives up and starts avoiding any sexual contact. The female partner reacts first by pretending that, as far as she is concerned, there is no problem. She may even declare that it will not bother her if he never gets an erection ever again. This makes the man feel even worse because it feels as if his partner is giving up on him. When she realizes how badly her partner feels about his failure, or when she admits to herself that there is a problem, she may try to help. She may say 'come on, you can do better, if only you try harder'; she may try to build up his 'powers' by exotic food, healthy diet, good drink or even aphrodisiacs; she may try to stimulate him by putting on sexy underwear, wearing expensive perfumes or working hard on stimulating him.

Although under normal circumstances these efforts may help, when the vicious circle is well established they only increase the pressure on the man to perform and make him feel even more guilty for failing her after all the trouble she has taken to help him. When these good efforts fail, as they are bound to, the female partner starts to feel despondent, frustrated, bitter or even hostile. She may become critical. 'You are not trying hard enough'; suspicious. 'You must be having an affair, there is nothing left for me'; rejecting. 'Leave me alone, there is no point in getting all worked up only to be left high and dry'; or she may make cutting remarks like: 'Living like a brother and sister', or 'As if we are two women sleeping together'. Most of these comments may be given with good intention 'to shock him into action' or 'so that he pulls himself together and tries harder', but they unfortunately make things worse. The woman may finally start to feel guilty and blame herself for her partner's failure: 'I am not as young or as attractive as I used to be'; 'It is all my fault, I don't turn him on'; 'He does not love me any more'; 'If I was a good wife he would not have this problem'. Some women even ask their husbands to have an affair or to try with a younger or more attractive woman. Some women may feel so demoralized that they may seek casual sex just to reassure themselves that they are still sexually attractive and can still turn a man on.

A similar reaction, but with a different scenario, may happen in any other sexual problem like premature ejaculation, inhibited ejaculation, anorgasmia, vaginismus or lack of sexual desire. Although these reactions are meant to solve the problem they serve only to complicate it: the longer or more vigorously they are used, the more difficult the original problem gets. That is why couples with sexual problems usually have a more or less similar presentation and respond to the same broad line approach, irrespective of the original dysfunction. What brings a couple to therapy is not usually the original problem but the added complications created by the vicious circle of failure and the unsuccessful attempts to break it. They come not just because the man cannot get an erection, but because since he lost erections he lost confidence, he felt like a failure and his partner felt rejected and unattractive. Similarly a couple who stopped having sex because the female partner lost desire come to therapy only when she feels pressurized and guilty and her partner feels deprived and cheated. Couples come to therapy, therefore, when they realize that their attempt to resolve the problem is not solving it, but making it worse.

## The model of therapy

The focus of therapy is the 'here and now' or what couples are doing to themselves and to each other which is maintaining their dysfunction. Its aim is to break through the vicious circle of failure. Although a vicious circle, by definition, should need to be broken at only one site in order to stop, we found that in most cases we needed to go over the contributing factors and to deal with all of them (Figure 8.2). This not only breaks the vicious circle but also gives protection against further difficulties, teaches the couple new skills and improves the non-sexual aspects of the relationship.

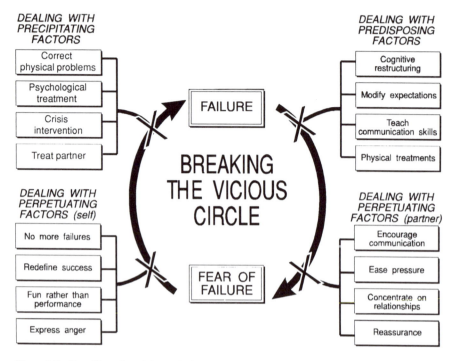

*Figure 8.2*  Breaking the vicious circle

### Dealing with predisposing factors

*Cognitive restructuring*
To deal with unhelpful false concepts and with inhibitions about sexuality, we use two cognitive methods: challenging and correcting faulty concepts, and giving permission.

*Challenging and correcting faulty concepts*  the main strength of faulty concepts comes from the fact that they seem logical – 'That is *surely* what everyone else feels, or says, or does' – or because they seem so undisputably right – 'Decent men or women *must* feel or say or do so and so'. In sex therapy all these 'sacred cows' are examined, challenged and changed. These are some examples:

Give me one single reason why touching yourself is wrong.
What is wrong with looking after yourself; if you cannot look after yourself, how can you look after someone else?
Have you ever asked yourself why you should not initiate sex or ask for what you want?
Unless your partner is a mind reader, do you think he can *really* tell what you want, no matter how much he loves you?

By examining, challenging and questioning the validity of this system of false concepts, the whole system collapses.

*Giving permission* to adopt a more realistic and positive system of beliefs. Couples need an authority figure, like a therapist, to act as the permissive parent most of them have never had. For people to enjoy sex they need to give themselves or be given the permission, to feel or act as follows:

*To enjoy sex*: It is all right to feel sexual: you are not hurting anyone.

*To have feelings*: It is all right to feel angry: it does not mean that you are a bad person.

*To fail*: There is nothing wrong in trying and failing, people will still love you: they may even love you more because you are more human.

*To not enjoy sex*: There is nothing wrong in *not* enjoying sex sometimes: if you don't feel bad about it, you may enjoy it next time.

*To be selfish*: It is more sensible to be selfish and enjoy yourself than to neglect your feelings and worry about your partner's feelings: this way neither of you will enjoy it.

*To be vulnerable*: It is OK to feel weak, tired, fed-up or frightened: it only proves that you are human.

The best permission-giving tool is undoubtedly the ease with which the therapist talks about sexual matters.

### Modifying expectations

Unrealistic expectations can be modified by providing facts and correct information. Reading books is useful in so far as it tells the couple what other couples are like, but it does not tell them what *they* are like. It does not also reassure them if they are different from the people described in the books. The joint physical examination is one of the most effective educational tools. Each partner is examined by the therapist (who should be medically qualified) in front of the other partner. An important part of the examination is to ask couples if they have any questions about sizes, sites or about presence or absence of any part of their anatomy, particularly if they thought the question was 'silly'. These questions, or doubts, should be taken seriously and looked into carefully. The couple should be reassured about their normality, or given an explanation if they deviated from the 'normal'. Hand drawings, photographs, three-dimensional models and illustrated books can all be useful, but nothing rivals holding a hand mirror and exploring one's own body, with the help of the therapist first and the partner later. Stanley calls that the 'guided tour' (Stanley 1981a).

Success and failure depend very much on the criteria for success. Accepting what the body can and cannot do and making allowances for physiological changes due to age, hormonal changes or physical illness, can modify expectations and increase the chances of success. To succeed, the couple need to stop rejecting what is actually possible because they prefer the impossible, and also to accept what 'works' rather than what is 'perfect' even if it does not work.

### Teaching communication skills

Breakdown of communication is not only a strong predisposing factor to having a sexual problem but also a common consequence of having one. As a result of not communicating, the time which used to be spent in talking is now taken up by other pursuits, like work, social activities, charity, church, children, politics or relatives and friends. The most important, and undoubtedly the most difficult, requirement for resuming communication is to reclaim this time back. The other requirement is safety. Communicating real feelings involves taking two risks: the risk of being put down or taken advantage of and the risk of committing oneself by declaring a position. It is much safer to say nothing or say something vague which could always be contradicted later if necessary. There are five main tools for improving communication:

1  spending more time together
2  making it safe to express real feelings
3  developing a common language
4  clearing the air from distorting emotions
5  learning the art of compromise.

*Spending more time together*   communication needs time. To improve communication the couple need to make the time for it. This may involve a number of practical steps, like putting the children to bed early, switching the television off three nights a week or giving up some less important commitments. The couple may have to educate relatives, friends and children to respect their need for this time to spend on their own. The couple may have to learn how to say 'No' more often, particularly to people who have been leaning on them to do more and more. Some very busy couples may have to 'date' each other every Sunday or for two or three periods of one to two hours in the following week.

*Making it safe to express real feelings*   this can be achieved by getting the couple to respect a number of ground rules.

1  Start by talking about neutral subjects on which you are not likely to disagree, like remembering 'happy times'.
2  If you start to misunderstand each other, or to have a row, stop and try again another time when feelings cool down.
3  Take more responsibility for your own feelings: do not look for someone else to blame for them. No one can make you feel angry, guilty or inadequate unless you let them.
4  Say what you mean and mean what you say. If you give a vague or contradictory message, don't be surprised if you are misunderstood.
5  Stop mind-reading and stop expecting your partner to read your mind. If you are not sure, don't guess, ask for clarification.
6  Humans are more likely to pay attention to non-verbal messages, even if they contradict the verbal one. This can be a fertile source of misunderstanding because non-verbal messages are open for misinterpretation. The most effective means of communication is the *verbal* message. Non-verbal messages should be ignored, particularly if they contradict the verbal one. If you look angry but *say* that you are happy, your partner has to assume that you are happy and act accordingly.
7  It is important to ask for what you want and not to expect to be given it without

asking. You should also check, before you offer 'help', that this is the help your partner needs. 'I would like to help you tonight: do you want me to put the children to bed or would you rather I did something else?'

8 No one should be put down or made to feel silly for having a feeling, simply because they cannot explain the feeling in a rational way. Always ask 'how' or 'what' you feel and avoid the question 'why' do you feel like that. No one has the right to dismiss or pass moral or intellectual judgement on someone else's feelings.

9 The fact that two people feel differently about an issue does not mean that one of them is 'right' and the other one is 'wrong': it only means that they are 'different'. You have to respect your partner's feeling even (or especially) if you disagree with it.

*Developing a common language* communication is not the same as talking. Some couples talk a great deal but never communicate because they do not speak the same language. There are two main languages for communication: the emotional, 'heart' or gut language and the intellectual, 'head' or practical language. If two people try to communicate and one of them uses the 'heart' language, such as 'I feel inadequate, as if I let my family down', and the other uses the 'head' language, like 'Don't be so silly, why should you feel like that?', they will both end up feeling completely misunderstood and frustrated. The reason is that they are speaking two different languages, although they both speak in English. A heart message could be understood only by tuning in to the heart level of communication and a head message could be understood only by tuning in to that level.

*Clearing the air from distorting emotions* another reason for misunderstanding is the presence of strong unresolved feelings. These can distort messages and give words a different meaning from the one originally intended. Trying to communicate while the medium through which messages have to pass is clouded by an unresolved emotional charge, like anger, resentment or mistrust, will end up in confusion, misunderstanding and breakdown of communication. Before trying to discuss an important or a sensitive subject the couple are advised to 'clear the air' first, by dispelling any unresolved or bottled-up feelings.

*Learning the art of compromise* any two people with different needs, who come from different backgrounds and have two different minds, are bound to feel differently about many things. To resolve these differences couples need to communicate them, make sure that their feelings are recognized and understood, and then they can try to reach a compromise. Some couples waste their time and energy in the futile attempt to attract each other to their respective points of view. *Accepting* that they feel differently about an issue is the first step towards reaching a compromise which takes into account the opposed feelings of the couple. The compromise may not satisfy either of them completely but it gives some and takes some. This is an art which couples need to learn in couple sex therapy.

*Physical treatment*

Couple sex therapy cannot ignore the remarkable advances in physical methods of treatment (Guirguis 1987b) and should not feel threatened, or be hostile to them. There is nothing more frustrating to the couple, and indeed to the therapist, than not having any symptomatic relief despite doing everything the therapist suggested. The lack of response may, in some cases, be due to a physical cause which could be resolved by physical means. However, physical treatment should be a part of the sex therapy and not a replacement for it, because in many cases the simple measure of removing the physical cause is not enough to remove the dysfunction. We shall consider some examples: vaginismus, erectile problems and menopausal women.

*Vaginismus* is a dysfunction with two components: the emotional in the form of fear of penetration, and the physical in the form of spontaneous involuntary spasm of muscles at the lower third of the vagina. The talking part of sex therapy without the physical component in the form of inserting a vaginal trainer, or a finger, is not likely to resolve the problem or lead to the consummation of marriage. Equally giving the couple a set of dilators without any form of therapy will not resolve it either. The couple need both.

*Erectile problems* have an underlying physical cause in between 40 and 60 per cent of cases (Bancroft 1989). Sex therapy by the most competent therapist and with the highest motivated couple will not restore potency if the man is diabetic and suffers from diabetic neuropathy which is damaging the nerve supply to his erectile tissue. Giving him intracavernous injections or fitting him with a penile prosthesis may give him a rigid penis but will not resolve problems in the relationship, improve communications or remove hostility. A combined approach is more effective (Guirguis 1989).

*Menopausal women* who find intercourse painful and unpleasant will continue to feel the same despite sex therapy. Hormone replacement therapy alone may cure the atrophic changes in the vagina but will not stop the vicious circle or resolve relationship or communication problems. The combined approach will help both problems.

Physical methods of treatment are therefore an integral part of a sex therapy and should not be used as an alternative. They are just one of the tools in the kit of a sex therapist. Non-medically qualified sex therapists should not, however, be discouraged or feel hostile to this integrated approach, as long as they have access to medical advice and recognize when and where such an advice is needed.

### Dealing with precipitating factors

Most sexual problems develop very gradually over a period of time and cannot be traced back to a specific event. If a clear precipitating factor is identified and is still operating, the therapist should attempt to deal with it. However, removing the original precipitating factor does not always cure the dysfunction: by the time the couple seek help the vicious circle of failure has already been established. These are some of the precipitating factors which are worth dealing with during couple sex therapy: drugs, bereavement and sexual trauma.

## Drugs

Doing sex therapy under the harmful effect of drugs can be very frustrating. Antihypertensive drugs can affect both erection and ejaculation. Reducing the dose or changing from one brand to another are always worth considering. Antidepressants can affect orgasmic ability in both men and women and affect ejaculation in men. Reducing the dose or changing to a different group of antidepressants is always advisable.

Alcohol and nicotine are the most commonly used drugs. Contrary to the often-quoted Shakespearian assertion, alcohol takes away not only the performance but also the desire. Alcohol is a depressant of the central nervous system: in small doses it depresses the critical qualities of the mind and releases the socially unacceptable sexual behaviours, which is why most sexual offences are committed under the influence of alcohol. In large doses alcohol suppresses sexual desire and reduces erectile and orgasmic abilities. The effect of smoking on sexual ability has only recently been appreciated (Virag *et al.* 1985). Smoking two cigarettes two hours before making love can reduce erectile ability drastically (Forsberg *et al.* 1979): that is why some clinics, very justifiably, refuse to take couples for therapy if one of them drinks or smokes excessively.

Drugs of abuse are often thought of as stimulants of sexual response. There is no evidence to support that. Apart from the suggestive effect of expectation, drugs of abuse are suppressants of sexual response and the drug-seeking behaviour can disrupt both the sexual and non-sexual aspects of the relationship. Removing the harmful effects of both prescribed and non-prescribed drugs can facilitate sex therapy.

## Bereavement

Couples who started to have problems after experiencing a major loss need help like any other case of bereavement. Loss of a spouse, loss of status, loss of children and loss of job, all need, and respond to, grief work. Some women feel that they have lost their femininity if they lose parts of their body which have a sexual significance, like their breasts, ovaries or uterus, or if they lose the ability to conceive after menopause or sterilization. This makes them lose interest in sex and they may need help to grieve over their loss before they can engage effectively in sex therapy. Some men react to retirement or redundancy by losing their erectile ability, as if potency is dependent on feeling productive, needed and powerful. Some women feel redundant when they reach menopause and often react to it by losing interest in sex. Both groups need help to adjust to their new roles, as a part of their sex therapy programme.

## Sexual trauma

Some women start to experience sexual problems after being subjected to a traumatic sexual experience, like attempted rape or sexual assault. Difficult labour, some gynaecological procedures and radical pelvic surgery can be as traumatic to sexuality as any other forms of sexual assault. Some women feel mutilated, that their body was invaded, and they need a great deal of help to express their anger, guilt and sense of loss. They are encouraged to relive the traumatic experience, get in touch with their unresolved feelings about it and to express these feelings in a non-damaging way (Guirguis 1987a).

### Breaking the vicious circle

To break the vicious circle of failure the couple are advised not only to abandon the previously attempted, and repeatedly unsuccessful, solutions but also to adopt a diametrically opposite approach. Instead of trying to enhance the failing erections, they are advised to try and lose them. Instead of trying to turn each other on, they concentrate on their own pleasure. Rather than trying hard to reach orgasm, they try to stop it. The idea is to ease the performance pressure, as pressure is incompatible with pleasure, and it is the main force which perpetuates the vicious circle. To ease the pressure to perform the therapist has to set up some basic principles and use some basic techniques which apply to any sexual problem. There are also some specific techniques which are used for specific problems.

### Basic principles

These principles have to be discussed fully with the couple and they should be given the chance to express their feelings or reservations about them. Some of these principles may be contrary to what one, or both of them, have always thought to be the 'right' way of solving their problem.

*Sexual dysfunctions are joint problems*   even if one of the partners seems perfectly 'normal' and the other one is experiencing all the problems. Trying to find whose fault it is, or to apportion blame, is not only unhelpful but also in most cases impossible. Accepting joint responsibility can relieve guilt, shame and the feeling of letting the partner down. It also emphasizes the need to work together and for both partners to make the necessary changes rather than waiting for each other to make all the changes.

*Don't try too hard*   as sexual responses are spontaneous reactions which work best when left to happen without interferences from the active mind. Trying to force a spontaneous reaction is paradoxical and logically impossible. The harder one tries to produce a spontaneous reaction like getting off to sleep, having an erection, reaching an orgasm or passing urine the less likely that any of these responses will happen. Most couples find it very difficult to accept that to improve their sex life they have to try *less*, as they are used in all other areas of their life to try harder in order to achieve more. We advise couples to stop, if they found themselves trying too hard: 'It means that you are stuck: trying harder will make you more stuck'. Sex therapy need not be hard work: it should be fun. If it becomes 'hard work', this means that it is not working.

*Be selfish*   sex can work only if it is for you: sex should not be a charity, a favour or a sacrifice. We deliberately use the word 'selfish', in spite of being such an emotive word, because we believe that far more sexual problems are caused by not being selfish enough, than by being selfish. For sex to work individuals should find out about what they want, make sure that they get it, and always take responsibility for their own pleasure. It is unfair for one to make his or her pleasure dependent on the other person's pleasure.

For example if a man says to his partner, 'Unless you enjoy it I can't enjoy it', she will not only feel a failure in not enjoying sex but also feel guilty for spoiling it for him. If he continues to enjoy sex, irrespective of what happens to her, this may seem selfish, but it will make it easier for her to join in the fun, as she will have only her own feelings to cope with.

Blaming oneself for the other person's lack of reactions are equally unhelpful. For example if a man blames himself because he 'cannot give his wife an orgasm', this will not help her to 'give herself' one. The only three possible reasons for not reaching an orgasm are first, that she doesn't know what she wants, second, that she knows what she wants but does not ask for it, or third, that her body is simply not capable of responding with an orgasm on this particular occasion. In any case by blaming himself for the lack of her orgasm he is not making it any easier for her to respond differently.

If couples respect what their body can enjoy and stop forcing pleasure on each other, they would both end up having a much more relaxed and enjoyable time.

*Concentrate on fun and not performance* as fun is usually under your control but performance is often not. Repeated failures are one of the driving forces behind the vicious circle of failure. People fail because they set out to achieve a goal. If there is no goal there is no failure. To avoid failure the couple should start their lovemaking with an open mind and without any specific targets to hit. If they make their criterion for success just 'having fun', they could hardly fail to achieve that.

*General techniques*
To put the above-mentioned principles into practice we suggest to the couple using two techniques: sensate focus exercises and climbing up and down the ladder.

*Sensate focus exercises* these are usually introduced to the couple after discussing with them the principles detailed above. We suggest that the couple put aside two or three periods of unpressurized time a week, in which they do together something physical in which they could not possibly fail. To minimize the chances of failure, we ban the achievement side of lovemaking like sexual intercourse and touching genital areas. This ban eases pressures considerably and makes the dysfunctional partner sigh with relief as he or she no longer has to pretend, look for excuses or try too hard. It also makes the partner without the dysfunction feel relieved as he or she does not have to pressurize, encourage or keep building up hopes only to be dashed later on. We then recommend that the couple take turns in organizing these sessions so that the responsibility for the treatment is shared between them. On the designated night they try to come home early, or put the children to bed in good time, so that they are both fresh and not tired or exhausted.

They start by doing something non-physical, in which they cannot ignore each other, like having a bath together, playing a game or having a small drink. They then proceed from that into a touching session in which they take turns in 'getting' pleasure. We deliberately avoid using the word 'giving' as we expect the couple from then onwards to take responsibility for their own pleasure and stop waiting for their partner to 'give' it to them. The person whose turn it is to get pleasure should ensure therefore that he gets pleasure by concentrating on what happens to his body, exploring different feelings from different parts, experimenting with varieties of pressures or directions and he must give feedback to his partner about what her touch is doing to him so that she can modify her touch accordingly. When he has had his turn she starts having hers and she follows the same rules. We emphasize that these exercises are not meant to turn them on, make them feel sexual or produce erections or orgasms.

We even suggest that if they start having any of these reactions that they should stop. When the couple feel comfortable with non-genital touch we gradually introduce genital touch but still follow the same principles and keep the ban on erections, orgasms and intercourse. When these forbidden reactions start to happen in spite of trying to stop them we feel then that the couple are ready to go on to experimenting with sexual intercourse but with the same principles in mind. But before we lift the ban on intercourse we introduce the second pressure-easing technique.

*Climbing up and down the ladder*    this is based on the 'ladder concept' as described by (Stanley 1981b). We start by drawing two ladders (see Figure 8.3) and assign one of them to each partner. The immediate message which the couple will pick up from that is that we are talking about two different ladders belonging to two different bodies. This means that no matter how hard they try or how much they love each other the fact will remain that they are two different people having two different bodies. It would be futile therefore to try and climb the same ladder or to climb up at the same rate. We start then to go with the couple through the seven different rungs of the ladder pointing out the different reactions they both get at different levels of sexual arousal. We then ask the couple to try and identify with their own ladder and to observe their emotional and bodily reactions against it. We then start having a discussion about the ladder with special emphasis on these points:

1  Every rung of the ladder is enjoyable in its own right. Rung seven is not more superior than one or two, it is only different. Anyone can enjoy the feelings on the higher rungs, but to enjoy the lower rungs people have to train their bodies to appreciate the gentle but enjoyable feelings on the lower rungs of the ladder. We try to persuade couples to stay deliberately on the lower rungs and explore the enjoyment they can get from them.
2  The rate at which bodies climb the ladder vary according to sex, with men being faster climbers than women. It also varies between different people of the same sex and in the same person from one day to the next. The couple should therefore respect their rate of climbing the ladder and respect that of their partners.

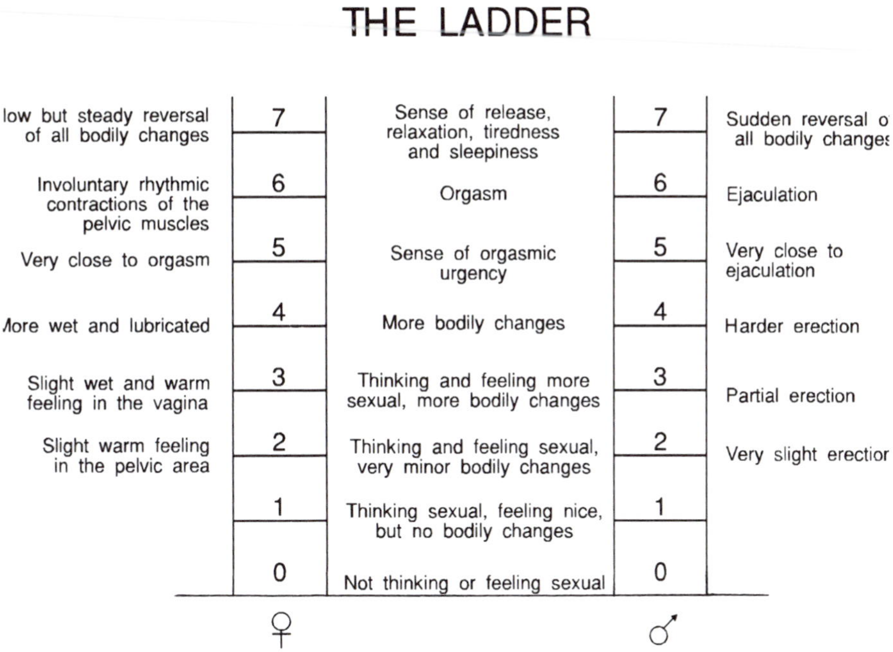

# THE LADDER

| | | | | | |
|---|---|---|---|---|---|
| low but steady reversal of all bodily changes | 7 | Sense of release, relaxation, tiredness and sleepiness | 7 | Sudden reversal o all bodily change: |
| Involuntary rhythmic contractions of the pelvic muscles | 6 | Orgasm | 6 | Ejaculation |
| Very close to orgasm | 5 | Sense of orgasmic urgency | 5 | Very close to ejaculation |
| More wet and lubricated | 4 | More bodily changes | 4 | Harder erection |
| Slight wet and warm feeling in the vagina | 3 | Thinking and feeling more sexual, more bodily changes | 3 | Partial erection |
| Slight warm feeling in the pelvic area | 2 | Thinking and feeling sexual, very minor bodily changes | 2 | Very slight erectior |
| | 1 | Thinking sexual, feeling nice, but no bodily changes | 1 | |
| | 0 | Not thinking or feeling sexual | 0 | |
| | ♀ | | ♂ | |

*Figure 8.3*  Climbing up and down the ladder

3  Climbing does not have to be in only one direction. Couples should try to enjoy climbing down as well as up. No one should feel committed to go up to rung seven every time he finds himself on rung one. He could stay there and go no further.
4  The best way of moving up and down the ladder is not by making a special effort to do so but by relaxing enough to allow yourself to be carried up and down the ladder. If you try too hard you will most probably fall off and find yourself on the ground.

Couples are encouraged to use the ladder in their communication and could for example say something like 'I am enjoying myself on rung two tonight, but if you want to go up to seven you carry on, I am staying here tonight'. Once pressure is eased, communication is flowing freely and fun is replacing performance, the vicious circle of failure will stop and the couple will start to feel more confident in themselves and in each other.

### Specific techniques
Apart from the general techniques discussed above, which are used in all sexual dysfunctions, there are some specific techniques to deal with specific problems: the stop-start technique, becoming orgasmic, vaginal training and intracavernous injection of vasoactive drugs. These techniques are usually introduced at the genital touching stage of the sensate focus exercises.

*The stop-start technique* is used in premature ejaculation and is based on the assumption that premature ejaculation is due to 'a lack of sexual sensory awareness' (Kaplan 1989). Although to the premature ejaculator, ejaculation feels like one big explosion, it is in fact a two-phase process: the phase of emission and the phase of ejaculation. The two phases are separated by a brief, but very distinct, period of one to two seconds during which the ejaculation phase can be stopped and the emission phase reversed. Once the second, ejaculation, phase starts it is a point of no return. To control the ejaculatory reflex and delay ejaculation the man needs to heighten his awareness of these two phases, make use of the brief gap between the two phases and to learn how to lower his level of arousal before the point of ejaculatory inevitability starts. The stop-start technique is devised to help the man to push his level of arousal up to a point very close to the ejaculatory phase, then stop, allowing his level of arousal to drop, then start again until he reaches the critical point, then stop, and so on. With more practice with this technique the man starts off by delaying his ejaculation up to only a few seconds and ends up delaying it for thirty minutes or more. Once he builds up enough confidence on his own he tries the same technique with his partner using her dry hand first, then her wet hand (by using a lubricant) and finally during intercourse. This phase of the stop-start technique needs patience and co-operation from the partner. The man should give a clear and early signal when he feels the urge coming, and his partner needs to stop in good time and without any sudden movement. This simple technique, which most couples can learn, is effective in over 90 per cent of cases (Kaplan 1989).

*Becoming orgasmic* is a gradual programme of sexual exploration and self-stimulation which is used effectively with pre-orgasmic women. It is based on the assumption that anorgasmia is due to sexual inhibition and inability to 'let go' enough for the orgasmic reflex to happen (Lo Piccolo and Lobitz 1972). The programme is a nine-step masturbation and desensitization one, starting by nude bath self-examination, then genital touching, manual masturbation ending up by reaching orgasm on own first and with partner later (Heiman *et al.* 1976). A success rate of 100 per cent, maintained on six months follow-up on this programme, is claimed (Lo Piccolo and Lobitz 1978). However, the shift from reaching orgasm during masturbation to coital orgasm is not always easy, with 20–80 per cent of women remaining anorgasmic during intercourse (Zeiss *et al.* 1978).

*Vaginal training* is used in cases of vaginismus to train the vaginal muscles to react to being approached by an object, like the erect penis, by dilation instead of spasm. It is based on the assumption that vaginismus is an involuntary spasm of the smooth muscles of the lower third of the vagina as a reflex reaction to fear of penetration. Previous attempts to penetrate resulted in pain and reinforced the fear of pain on penetration. If the vagina could be penetrated by smaller objects without tension, spasm or pain, this will associate penetration with being relaxed and free of pain. Vaginal trainers are plastic rods, as long as the average-size erect penis, but of four different circumferences starting from size I, as thick as a finger, to size IV, which is larger than the average-size erect penis. The trainers are inserted in gradual steps, starting with the smallest size, inserted by the therapist first, then by the woman and later by her partner. If inserted under relaxed and reassuring conditions the woman will not experience any pain or discomfort. Repeated insertions of the vaginal trainers in various sizes, both at the clinic and at home, will train the vaginal muscles to relax when approached. This will allow vaginal intercourse to happen without pain and the relationship could be consummated for the first time (Stanley 1981c).

*Intracavernous injection of vasoactive drugs* is a major advance in the treatment of erectile failure. It gave hope to many patients who were beyond any hope of ever achieving an erection again. Patients with severe diabetes, atherosclerosis, severe multiple sclerosis, complete paraplegia and even those with complete destruction of peripheral pelvic nerves can now enjoy having reliable and lasting erections. Injecting a smooth muscle relaxant, of the appropriate dose, inside the cavernous body can give, in most patients with erectile problems of any aetiology, an immediate and reliable erection which starts in one to four minutes, reaches a peak in eight to ten minutes and lasts for one to three hours. (Guirguis 1987b). These injections could be used in cases of psychogenic erectile failure, and some cases of severe premature ejaculation, if there is strong suspicion of an organic factor contributing to it or if the performance anxiety is so high as to make the couple unable to benefit from the classical course of sex therapy. What most impotent men, and their partners, need most is the reassurance that having an erection is still possible, and the hope that one day the erection will last long enough for the sexual act to be completed. An intracavernous injection will, if it works, give all this reassurance in two to four minutes. It is an effective means of breaking the vicious circle of failure, for reducing performance anxiety and regaining confidence. The intracavernous injection is not, however, a panacea and should not be used as a substitute for couple therapy but as an integral part of it. Sticking needles in dysfunctional penises without adequate counselling for both partners is not only ineffective but also an abuse of this effective therapeutic tool (Guirguis 1989).

## Does sex therapy work?

Outcome studies and long-term follow-up studies are very difficult in psychotherapy in general and in sex therapy in particular; the reasons for this difficulty are discussed by Cole and Dryden (1988). Amongst these reasons are the eclectic nature of sex therapy, the lack of clear definitions of the various dysfunctions, the presence of many uncontrollable factors and the absence of an objective measure of therapeutic changes. Comparison of the various published outcome studies gives a considerable variation in the reported success rates. However, most studies give an average success rate of 60 per cent and a failure or drop-out rate of 30 to 40 per cent (Kaplan 1979).

Follow-up studies, including that of Masters and Johnson, were repeatedly criticized for their methodological problems. The most important criticisms are biased or small sample, the low response rate to calls for follow-up, the use of retrospective measures, failing to follow-up treatment failures, using postal questionnaires instead of face-to-face interview, applying dubious statistical methods and for not using 'no treatment' control groups. Two recent long-term follow-up studies tried to avoid some of these criticisms. The studies by Hawton *et al.* (1986) and by De Amicis *et al.* (1985), in Britain and the USA respectively, were critically reviewed by Guirguis (1988c). Although both studies had their own problems they had remarkably similar findings.

Both studies found recurrence of sexual difficulties relatively common on long-term follow-up, with the post-therapy improvement in function regressing three years later to near or below pre-therapy levels. They both found, however, that general improvement in the level of satisfaction with the couple's sexual and marital relationship was maintained on follow-up. They did find, however, a vast difference in long-term outcome for the various types of sexual problems. Lack of desire in both men and women had the poorest long-term outcome; premature ejaculation was also very disappointing. The best long-term outcome was in vaginismus and in erectile difficulties, provided that organic cases were detected and excluded.

Hawton's study came up with a number of interesting findings. The most surprising was that couples who split up and started new relationships had all resolved their original sexual problems with their new partners. The study also found that some couples managed to recover from minor recurrence of their sexual problems by using again the coping strategies they learned during therapy, communicating about the problem, using the original home-work assignments and by accepting that further difficulties were to be expected.

Both studies found that the post-treatment improvement in self-acceptance and in the relationship in general were maintained at follow-up irrespective of the outcome of the target symptom. The US study makes the apparent conclusion that 'sex therapy may be more effective in improving the way clients feel about their sexuality than in reversing specific presenting problems' (De Amicis *et al.* 1985).


## Conclusion

Couple sex therapy has come a long way. The last twenty years witnessed a number of developments. The psychotherapeutic component of sex therapy is now well established and the narrow behaviourist approach is replaced by positive eclecticism. The split approach of either 'physical' or 'psychological' has given way to an integrated approach which takes account of one without losing sight of the other. New techniques to deal with the changeable, complicated and diverse needs of modern couples have developed. Complacency and the false sense of security have gradually been replaced by a more critical and realistic attitude which questions what we are doing, assesses its therapeutic values and looks out for better ways of doing it. The model of causation and therapy presented here is a practical, common-sense model, which reflects these important changes and represents the work of similar clinics in Britain. Although physical factors and physical methods of treatment are an integral part of this model, non-medical sex therapists can use the model as long as they know when and where to refer couples for physical assessment or therapy.

Couple sex therapy has an exciting time ahead of it, but has also many challenges. The introduction of the intracavernous injections increased the effectiveness of sex therapy in cases of erectile impotence and premature ejaculation. Anorgasmia, premature ejaculation and vaginismus are responding to current therapy by an almost 100 per cent success rate. Helping women and men to overcome the damaging effect of being sexually abused as children is developing fast and is helping more couples to enjoy their relationship in spite of it. However, cases of lack of sexual desire in women are still giving very poor response to current methods of therapy. Lack of desire in men responds even less well and delayed ejaculation is still very resistant to present treatment programmes. The high level of first time non-attendance and high drop-out rate, reported by most clinics at a consistent rate of 30 per cent, are two other problems which couple sex therapy has yet to address.

## *Acknowledgements*

The Medical Illustration Department, Ipswich General Hospital, kindly produced the three figures in this chapter.

## References

Bancroft, J. (1989) *Human Sexuality and its Problems*, 2nd edn, Edinburgh: Churchill-Livingstone.

Cole, M. and Dryden, W. (1988) *Sex Therapy in Britain*, Milton Keynes: Open University Press.

Cooper, G.F. (1986) *Survey of Sex Therapists in Britain*, Birmingham: Training and Consultancy Services.

Crowe, M.J., Gillan, P. and Golombok, S. (1981) Form and content in the conjoint treatment of sexual dysfunction: a controlled study, *Behaviour Research and Therapy* 19: 47–54.

De Amicis, L.A., Goldberg, D.C., Lo Piccolo, J., Freidman, J. and Davis, L. (1985) Clinical follow up of couples after treatment for sexual dysfunction, *Archives of Sexual Behaviour* 14: 467–89.

Dryden, W. (1982) *The Effective Practice of Rational-Emotive Therapy*, London: Institute for RET (UK).

Ellis, A. (1975) The rational-emotive approach to sex therapy, *Counselling Psychologist* 5: 14–22.

Fisch, R., Weakland, J.H. and Segal, L. (1982) *The Tactics of Change*, San Francisco: Jossey-Bass.

Forsberg, L., Gustavii, B., Hajerbaek, T. and Olsson, A. (1979) Impotence, smoking and β. blocking drugs, *Fertility and Sterility* 31: 589–91.

Gillan, P.W. (1977) Stimulation therapy for sexual dysfunction, in R. Gemme and C.C. Wheeler (eds) *Progress in Sexology*, New York: Plenum.

Guirguis, W.R. (1984) Erectile failure: psychological aspects, *Postgraduate Doctor* (Middle East) 7: 393–8.

—— (1987a) Helping women who were sexually abused as children, *British Journal of Sexual Medicine* 3: 61–2.

—— (1987b) Recent advances in treatment of erectile failure, *Postgraduate Doctor* (Middle East) 10: 601–10.

—— (1987c) Literature up-date, *Sexual and Marital Therapy* 2: 101–5.

Guirguis, W.R. (1988a) Erectile inadequacy: a guide to diagnosis, *British Journal of Sexual Medicine* 15: 8–11.

—— (1988b) Erectile inadequacy: a guide to treatment, *British Journal of Sexual Medicine* 15: 12–18.

—— (1988c) Literature up-date: a critical review, *Sexual and Marital Therapy* 3: 125–8.

—— (1989) The use and abuse of intracavernous injection of vasoactive drugs, *British Journal of Sexual Medicine* 1: 9–11.

Hawton, K., Catalan, J., Martin, P. and Fagg, J. (1986) Long-term outcome of sex therapy, *Behaviour Research and Therapy* 24: 665–75.

Hazzard, A., King, H.E. and Webb, C. (1986) Group therapy with sexually abused adolescent girls, *American Journal of Psychotherapy* 11: 213–23.

Heiman, J., Lo Piccolo, L. and Lo Piccolo, J. (1976) *Becoming Orgasmic: A Sexual Growth Programme for Women*, Englewood Cliffs, NJ: Prentice-Hall.

Hogan, D.R. (1978) The effectiveness of sex therapy: a review of the literature, in J. Lo Piccolo and L. Lo Piccolo (eds) *Handbook of Sex Therapy*, New York: Plenum.

Hunter, R. and MacAlpine, I. (1963) *Three Hundred Years of Psychiatry 1535–1835*, London: Oxford University Press.

Kaplan, H.S. (1974) *The New Sex Therapy*, New York: Brunner/Mazel.

—— (1979) *Disorders of Sexual Desire*, London: Ballière Tindall.

—— (1989) *PE: How to Overcome Premature Ejaculation*, New York: Brunner/Mazel.

Kowalski, R. (1985) Cognitive therapy for sexual problems, *British Journal of Sexual Medicine* 12: 64–6, 90–3, 131–5.

Lo Piccolo, J. and Lobitz, W.C. (1972) Behaviour therapy of sexual dysfunction, in L.A. Hammerlynch, L.C. Handy and E.J. Mash (eds) *Behaviour Change: Methodology, Concepts and Practice*, Champaign, Ill: Research Press.

—— (1978) The role of masturbation in the treatment of orgasmic dysfunction, in J. Lo Piccolo and L. Lo Piccolo (eds) *Handbook of Sex Therapy*, New York: Plenum.

Masters, W.H. and Johnson, V.E. (1970) *Human Sexual Inadequacy*, London: Churchill.

Mobarak, A., Tamerin, J.S. and Tamerin, N.G. (1986) Sex therapy: an adjunct in the treatment of marital discord, *Journal of Sex and Marital Therapy* 12: 229–38.

Stanley, E. (1981a) Principles of managing sexual problems, *British Medical Journal* 28: 1,200–5.

—— (1981b) Dealing with fear of failure, *British Medical Journal* 282: 1,281–3.

—— (1981c) Vaginismus, *British Medical Journal* 282: 1,435–7.

Virag, R., Bouilly, P. and Frydman, D. (1985) Is impotence an arterial disorder?, *Lancet* 8,422: 181–4.

Zeiss, A.M., Rosen, G.M. and Zeiss, R.A. (1978) Orgasm during intercourse: a treatment strategy for women, in J. Lo Piccolo and L. Lo Piccolo (eds) *Handbook of Sex Therapy*, New York: Plenum.

Zilbergeld, B. (1980) *Men and Sex*, Glasgow: Collins.

Zilbergeld, B. and Evans, M. (1980) The inadequacy of Masters and Johnson, *Psychology Today* August: 29–43.

# 9

# Gender issues in couple therapy

## ANNI TELFORD AND ANDY FARRINGTON

## Introduction

In addressing gender issues we hope to demonstrate that, while linked to sexuality, gender is more the creation of our society and culture rather than any genetic predetermination. As therapists are also a part of the culture it follows that they too are influenced by its values and mores, and this in turn will influence the form therapy takes. By examining the role society has played in the formation of their own and their clients' gender perceptions, therapists can reach a fuller understanding of their clients' problems and their own reactions to them, thus hopefully increasing the chances of a satisfactory therapeutic outcome.

## Gender roles and child-rearing

From the very moment they are born, female and male babies are treated differently. One need only observe the clothing bought by the parents (pink for girls, blue for boys and lemon or pale green if the infants' gender is undetermined) and the gifts given at christenings (silver mugs for boys and bracelets for girls) to perceive the basis of what amounts to a lifelong process of social direction and control.

Hartley (1966) identified four processes which, she suggests, are central to the social development of gender orientation: socialization by manipulation, canalization, verbal appellation, and activity direction. These processes, which are described in greater detail below, start at birth and continue throughout our development.

### Manipulation

This describes the touching and fussing with hair and clothing which characterizes adults' interactions with female babies and children. These indirect indicators of femininity and prettiness are absorbed by the female child into her concept of self.

## Canalization

This describes how children's attention is directed towards specific categories of objects, and the reinforcement they receive when they show interest in them. Thus boys are directed towards building bricks, tools, guns and cars while girls are directed towards such things as soft cuddly toys, dolls, clothes and toy versions of the paraphernalia of domesticity – irons, kitchens and vacuum cleaners. Early exposure to and the resulting familiarity in using and manipulating objects has been shown to have a direct effect on later choices of behaviours (Raban 1950).

## Verbal appellation

In this process the language used to and about children goes towards building their self-concept and future acceptance of the socially defined gender roles, for example 'Big boys don't cry', and 'Where's Daddy's little poppet?' The first example encourages male children to suppress the free expression of their emotions, especially those which involve traditionally 'feminine' tears, while the second example encourages female children to view themselves in terms of their attractiveness for men, as male playthings. One is unlikely to hear the phrase 'Where's Daddy's little poppet?' used towards a boy; 'Where's Daddy's little man?' is much more likely. By the same token 'Where's Daddy's little woman?' is equally unlikely, as womanhood is not something which is viewed or valued in the same way as manhood within western societies.

## Activity direction

The processes of activity direction, as the name implies, involves the direction of the child's activities into what are perceived by the parents as being appropriate gender activities. Therefore, while female children may be encouraged to help their mother around the home with domestic chores, traditionally female labour, male children are more likely to be allocated tasks which are considered to be male, such as fetching and carrying or helping their father in garden or garage.

These processes are not carried out by parents in any systematic or deliberate fashion, rather they should be viewed as the reproduction of the cultural patterns they themselves experienced in childhood. Even with parents who are aware of the processes, it is difficult to resist reproducing – albeit in a very slightly modified form – the same gender orientations. An example can be found in a close friend of one of the authors, who believed in equality for both sexes and was well versed in the theories described. However, she found it impossible to buy her 8-year-old son a doll for his birthday, even though this was what the child requested on frequent occasions. Indeed so insidiuous are these processes that Rabban (1950) found that all children were able to identify their own sex and were able, in many cases, to choose only toys which were considered sex appropriate from a given selection, by the age of 4.

During the pre-puberty stage, ages around 6–12, the emphasis shifts somewhat away from the feminine role. At this age it is much more acceptable, especially amongst the middle classes, for girls to be 'tomboys', play football, ride bicycles or ponies, than it is for boys to be 'cissies' and take an interest in cooking or go to ballet classes. Should a boy show interest in these traditionally female activities he will be seen as a 'softy' or 'tied to his mother's apron strings'. However, this freedom of the female to indulge in what is perceived as cross-gender behaviours will quickly disappear as puberty and sexual function arrives.

## Gender roles during puberty and adolescence

At this stage the female is expected to take a greater interest in clothes, make-up, hairstyles and other trappings of perceived sexual attractiveness, while at the same time she is actively discouraged, through a whole series of familial and societal sanctions, from experimenting with that sexuality. Her leisure activities become extremely curtailed and begin to centre around the home, where she is encouraged to bring female friends. The male, on the other hand, is expected to expand his interest in external leisure activities with such things as sports and going out to clubs, for example, with groups of other males of similar age, and is permitted, indeed encouraged, to experiment and explore his sexuality.

The dichotomy here for the female lies in walking the tightrope between two, both extremely abusive, forms of labelling. Should she experiment sexually with more than one partner she will be termed a 'slag'; yet once she has had a boyfriend for some time, if she does not have sexual intercourse with him she will be termed a 'drag'. As Lees (1986) points out

> The term slag functions as a form of control by boys over girls, a form of control which steers girls into 'acceptable' forms of sexuality and social behaviour. It forces them into a relationship of dependence on a boy, leading as we shall see invariably to marriage. It is the unattached girl who mixes with boys but does not have a regular boyfriend who is most likely to be termed a 'slag'.
>
> (Lees 1986: 45)

To return for a moment to Hartley's (1966) work, the manipulation of clothes and hair may now come not from the girl's mother but from other girls as they try out make-up and hairstyles in the bedroom, which is their only private social arena. Canalization can be seen in gifts, toiletries, fluffy toys and clothes for females and sports equipment and so forth for males. Verbal appellation can be observed in comments such as 'Nice girls don't do that', and 'He's one of the lads'; the first comment places restrictions on girls' behaviours, the second reinforces and encourages very similar sets of behaviours in boys. Activity direction can also be seen in the home, where females are expected to become more involved in domestic chores, often waiting on their brothers or other male relatives, while males are permitted more rather than less personal leisure time.

Activity direction can also be seen in the school. Despite the Sex Discrimination Act 1975, which attempted to legislate against sex bias, Stanworth (1981) discovered within education that it is still more likely that girls will be directed towards languages and the arts while boys are directed towards the technologies and sciences. Stanworth (1981) also found that teachers, both male and female, are slower to identify girls as individuals and remember their first names. She states that although girls may be very capable academically, they are unlikely to be steered towards occupations other than nursing, teaching or secretarial work (all traditionally female) while boys, even those likely to fail examinations, are often pushed to achieve academically to gain entry to higher education and careers which are well beyond the limits of their own capabilities. This educational bias, which pushes one sex's abilities and devalues and negates those of the other sex, can only cause problems in later life for both groups, and result in men feeling that they have failed to live up to their aspirations, and women feeling that they have not achieved their potential level of ability.

## Gender roles and adult life

As we enter adult life the barrage of gender representations continues, through the vehicle of our culture, to inform us of the boundaries of our gender roles. In the same way as child-rearing patterns are not conscious processes, the affirmation of gender roles in adult life is not some far-reaching and deliberate plot. Rather, the gender roles of our society are created insidiously by our own absorption and subsequent reproduction of the everyday cultural stereotypes that we see and hear all around us. We shall consider a few of these cultural representations before moving on to examine the role of gender issues in couple therapy.

In humour there is a preponderance of jokes about females or parts of the female anatomy. Consider for a moment the number of mother-in-law as opposed to father-in-law jokes, or the fact that the majority of comedians who make it on to television are male.

In many films and television the images of women are usually the conventional representations of either mother and housewife or slut. There are very few grey areas in the images presented. This is continued in advertising, where the macho man delivers the chocolates to the mysterious woman, and the mother tricks her teenage son from bed to wash his sheets. No one can live up to the imagery of countless women making their homes or clothes cleaner, brighter, somehow better, while all the time appearing as the perfect symbol of sexuality.

The projection of perfect body and face is continued in documentaries and news, with female news readers requiring 'glamour' as well as journalistic skills and a good reading voice. This quality of sexual attractiveness does not, however, appear to be necessary for men. On the whole, women who appear on television or film are not the physical norm, in either shape, height or appearance, yet these images are sold to women as the norm; throughout western culture women strive to reach these unrealistic ideals of body and face, feeling dissatisfied with their own reality.

*Cosmopolitan*, a supposedly liberated women's magazine, will run articles on how to be assertive beside those on how to apply make-up or the latest fashions. Thus, they suggest, it is all right to be assertive, but only within the confines of the accepted gender role. It is not only that the images presented of women are of housewife, etc. but also that the achievements of women are often marginalized in science, history, music, literature and sport. Thus strong images are suppressed and the role models which might portray a different reality for women rarely appear.

It is important to remember, however, that it is not just women's gender experiences that are controlled and directed: men too are constantly reminded of the traditional masculine role by the emphasis given to power and control. The male as sportsman, soldier, stud, cowboy and, more recently, city dealer are common icons represented in many films.

The traditional images, however, are juxtapositioned with the images of the New Man and the New Fatherhood. This New Fatherhood is not only about providing materially, but also about caring and loving, being present at the birth and providing active child care. Consider the films *Kramer vs Kramer* and *Rainman* in comparison to various Vietnam films which, while vilifying the war, celebrated the 'maleness' of the combatants. The problem here for men is that as traditional industries decline and change and a more female-orientated economy of part-time and service work replaces it, so their traditional images fall apart and they, like women, are faced with a dilemma which centres on their own sexuality. How then can a man reconcile Rambo with the New Fatherhood any more than a woman can reconcile Barbara Cartland's heroines with feminism. The reality for both must lie in a middle path.

## Gender issues and medicine

We have tried to show through a brief examination of child-rearing and culture how our gender perceptions and attitudes are shaped and controlled, but before moving on to discuss specific gender issues in couple therapy it may be of use to consider, albeit briefly, the medical control of women, as this has some bearing on both women's and men's perceptions and expectations of therapists and therapy.

Barrett and Roberts's (1975) study suggested that women's illnesses are much more likely to be perceived as psychosomatic than men's and that general practitioners, because of the nature of their training and the preponderance of males in medicine, are prone to making assumptions about the 'nature' of men and women that are not based on any factual evidence.

> Men, it was clear had a primary natural 'drive' to work to support their wife and family. Women had a similar 'drive' to nourish and cherish their husband and family.
>
> (Barrett and Roberts 1975: 44)

They also found that GPs were, at times, influenced by the attitudes of the husbands of the women under their 'care', even when these same attitudes were at the core of the women's problems. Perhaps most damaging for couples in relationship crisis, when marital problems arose, they were perceived by the GPs as being problematic for the woman only, as she was seen as the dependent partner within the relationship. Thus they suggest that

> In this respect the institution of medicine legitimates and endorses the status quo in relation to the position of women, and in so doing fulfils an ideological function as an agency of disguised social control.
>
> (Barrett and Roberts 1975: 42)

In light of this work it would seem probable that, in their search for help with their relationship, the couple will already have encountered biased gender perception from the medical profession, and, as therapy is often viewed by the lay person as lying within the medical domain, it is likely that the expectations of the client about therapy will already have been coloured by these experiences. Thus the man may perceive the problem not as 'theirs', but rather as 'hers' or expect the therapist to hold his views and attitudes in more esteem than his partner's. The man may see the therapist as already aligned with his partner or the woman may expect her desires for a life outside the home and family to be seen as 'neurotic' by the therapist.

If one is to overcome these preconceptions by the client the therapist had better be aware of gender issues and attempt to ensure that their attitude towards the client is free of any sex bias. As our gender attitudes are culturally constructed this is not always as easy to do as it is to write about, and it is to the specific pitfalls in addressing this problem in therapy that we now turn.

## Gender issues and couple therapy

In this section we hope to demonstrate the links between the theories previously mentioned and couple therapy, showing how the culturally defined gender ideas held by the therapist can adversely affect their relationship with the clients. Five main areas will be considered:

1  therapist language use
2  client language use
3  therapist attitude
4  client attitude
5  expressing emotion.

The examples used to illustrate this section are drawn from our joint experiences of training and supervising therapists, and in all cases the names of both therapists and clients have been disguised.

### Therapist language use

Verbal appellation is a strong force in moulding the ideas and beliefs of children about their own and other's sexuality. It works, as we have seen, through the different types of language used towards boys and girls. As language is the main tool of the therapist it therefore seems to be an appropriate starting-point for this section. There are obvious words which marginalize women by the simple act of non-inclusion. The words 'mankind, chairman and manpower' readily spring to mind, however with practice these can easily be avoided or altered. Thus one may use 'people, chairperson and personnel'.

The English language, however, has particularly subtle nuances of meaning and inference, which can convey more insiduous, but equally damaging, concepts and attitudes. Consider for a moment the following real-life exchange which occurred between a male therapist and a couple who had come for help with a relationship problem.

*Case example: Sarah and George*

    T: Well, Sarah, George has said he was really angry on Wednesday when you went out. Can you tell me what you think happened?

    S: I'd arranged to meet some friends . . . women from the college . . . for a drink . . . we wanted to discuss the shelter for battered wives and how . . . em . . . how we could maybe help out.

    T: So you went out with the girls?

At this point Sarah appeared angry and resentful towards the therapist, and when asked later about the incident stated the she resented the term 'girl'. By using the diminutive term 'girls' for women the therapist had minimized Sarah's meeting to the realms of immaturity and aligned himself, in her eyes, with George her partner.

We would not use the term 'boys' talk', the phrase is 'men's talk', and to use the diminutive to men is an insult; however, the phrases 'girls' talk' or 'girls' night out' is frequently used. Many women find labels such as 'girls' and 'ladies' insulting in the extreme, the first implying immaturity, the second a form of refined dependence. It is therefore preferable for the therapist to avoid using diminutive terms regardless of what interpretation they personally may put on them. It is clients' interpretations which are the most relevant, as they may interpret the therapist's language as insulting, which can result in damage to the therapeutic relationship.

It is also preferable for therapists to avoid using terms which have obvious gender connotations attached, such as gossip, nag, dear, bag, and 'her indoors', regardless of whether the client uses such terms. By the same token, regional variations in terms of female endearment, such as lass, maid, chucky, hen, pet, duck and hinny, should also be avoided, for the same reason. It is interesting that these terms, which either refer to the diminutive or some form of pet animal, are rarely used towards men.

### Client language use

Clients, as much as the therapist, hold concepts of sexuality which are socially constructed, and are as prone to the use of sexist language and labelling. High valuation of sexual stereotypes may cause disharmony within a relationship. If therapists are aware of the implications behind gender-laden language they may use this gently to aid the clients to a deeper understanding of their problems.

Consider the following interchange between another male therapist and a couple we have named Jan and Sam. The therapist is attempting to understand the reason for an argument which occurred the preceding weekend.

*Case example: Jan and Sam*

J: We were out in the pub . . . together . . . like you suggested . . . but . . . well he's a real dick-head and I get angry and . . .

S: And then she started nagging away at me . . . nag, nag, nag.

T: I'm not too sure what you both mean . . . Jan . . . can you tell me what you mean by a dick-head?

J: He's like all men . . . just thinks with his dick . . . this woman went past and I saw immediately he was attracted to her . . . you know . . . his eyes were all over her.

T: And Sam . . . what did you mean by a nag?

S: She goes on and on about things . . . never stops . . . once women get a hold of something they don't let up . . . do they?

T: I'm not saying the argument didn't happen . . . but it seems to me that what you're doing is making it worse by putting gender labels on each other . . . rather than really looking at what's happening between the two of you. Sam, were you attracted to the woman?

S: Well, sex just isn't happening and I . . . well, I was just looking around the shops . . . sort of . . . I wouldn't have done anything . . . just looking.

T: Jan, why did you ask Sam about it?

J: I felt . . . he was more interested in her than me . . . and when I asked him he wouldn't talk about it. . . . I wanted an answer and he wouldn't give me one.

T: So . . . what you're saying is that you feel that you're not having enough sex at the moment, and you, Jan, felt insecure when Sam looked at the other woman. Can you see how, when we analyse it on an individual basis instead of just using those labels, we can make more sense of the situation and it becomes less charged with emotion.

The therapist, by questioning the gender-laden terms, enabled the couple to reach a better understanding of their interactions. He went on to discuss with the couple at some length the concepts of 'femininity' and 'masculinity' as social constructions rather than truths, and attempted to show them that, by thinking of each other in those terms, they had forgotten the unique individual which was their partner. This was followed up by some simple bibliotherapy to help the clients further and a series of communications exercises to attempt to move the couple away from their stereotypical way of talking and thinking about each other.

### Therapist attitude

In this section we would like to move away from language and examine how the therapists' culturally created attitudes and beliefs about men and women may unintentionally colour their position towards their clients.

The socially acceptable behaviours for men and women still lie within fairly rigidly defined patterns; for example it remains fairly unusual within western society for women to work in heavy industry, or for men to function as the prime carers for children or elderly relatives. Thus we see in the activities of adult life the effects of canalization and activity direction. Nor are therapists immune from the effects of the culture in which they live; they too carry on the work of ensuring that our society reinforces the accepted roles of 'feminine' and 'masculine'.

Examples of this may be seen when the therapist, who may be of either sex, advises a woman to lose weight while ignoring the obesity of the male member of the partnership, reinforcing in the woman the idea that her appearance is of more importance than her partner's. It may also be seen when the therapist, helping to draw up a relationship contract, directs the woman towards traditionally female tasks and the man towards traditionally male ones.

Ideally it is preferable for the therapist to take a neutral role, neither presuming that women wish to be 'feminine' nor men 'masculine'. In this way clients are allowed to discover their own gender identities.

Less traditional concepts of the roles of women and men within society can also prove problematic when enforced on to clients. One female therapist, who held firm beliefs about the equality of women, had great difficulty in accepting the therapeutic targets of her more traditional women clients. The couple she is dealing with below are called Sharon and John and they are attempting to draw up a contract.

*Case example: Sharon and John*

> T: John . . . Sharon said she would like you to wash up and take the children out on Sundays to give her a break. How do you feel about that?
>
> J: Okay . . . I'll do that . . . in return I'd like Sharon to pay more attention to her appearance . . . she's let herself go since the kids were born. You know . . . get her hair done and wear make-up when we're out.
>
> S: I have let myself go. . . . you're right.
>
> T: But you should be free to look the way you want. . . . I don't see how getting dressed up to please him will help you.

The therapist had a feminist orientation and had read widely in this area, had considered gender issues in some depth and was skilled in helping men and women in expressing their emotions and becoming more assertive. The stance taken here, however, is one of imposing the therapist's personal viewpoints on the woman; regardless of how therapists may feel about such issues it is preferable that they do not do this. In this example both clients have stated they are willing to move their positions, John has agreed to Sharon's requests and Sharon to John's.

In cases where clients request support in exploring their gender identities it is acceptable for the therapist to provide this. It is also acceptable for the therapist to point out, to either partner, gender attitudes which are jeopardizing their relationship or causing their partner distress. However, it is unethical for the therapist to impose his or her own views on the client. The example described previously is as problematic as a more traditionally orientated therapist encouraging a woman to view herself solely in terms of personal attractiveness to her partner, while saying nothing about appearance to the man. A more balanced view may be that it is important for both partners to consider their sexual attractiveness in an equal way.

There are other ways in which the therapist may bring their gender concepts into therapy. One male therapist had trouble appreciating the problems which many women face in attempting to become assertive. He had great difficulty in understanding the massive cultural influences which are aligned against women becoming assertive as he, as a man, had never experienced the problem. Another male therapist openly smiled at a woman client's attempts to get her two teenage sons to do housework. Female therapists may also have difficulty in understanding male clients, one example being the female therapist who presumed that all men were more sexually active than women and failed to assess the problems within a couple's sexual relationship because of this.

Problems with attitudes may also arise when a heterosexual therapist has to deal with two partners of the same sex, when they allow their own attitudes towards sexuality and gender influence their perceptions of the clients. In the example which follows, the female therapist has problems recognizing the anxieties expressed by one partner within a gay couple. Her socially constructed belief was that men, unlike women, do not desire single-partner relationships, that they had difficulties in being monogamous and had somehow to be taught by women to be so. Thus when she encounters a man expressing anxiety at being left alone she reacts in an unempathic manner and cannot understand the problem. The clients are called Dave and Peter.

*Case example: Dave and Peter*

> D:  I know it's stupid . . . his job takes him out late socializing with clients . . . but I keep thinking that he's going to go with another bloke . . . then where will I be?
> T:  From what you've both told me of your past you've both had plenty of relationships. . . . I don't really understand the problem, Dave.

It is unlikely that the therapist would have had problems understanding the issues if this were a heterosexual couple and the female partner was expressing the same anxiety.

*Case example: Judy and Christina*

A similar problem occurred with a male therapist dealing with a lesbian couple called Judy and Christina. In this case the therapist held the belief that women were houseproud and tidy, and he was therefore unable to grasp the importance of Judy's complaints of untidiness against Christina. His nonverbal and verbal behaviours when presented with the problem make this apparent.

J: I get so fed up. . . . she [Christina] always leaves the house in a tip . . .
that's when the arguments start . . . that's the main issue for me anyway.

T: (The therapist is now unable to maintain eye contact with either
woman.) I . . . er . . . yes . . . I see . . . so . . . what you're saying . . .
Judy . . . is that . . . your . . . er . . . partner (clears throat) . . . er . . .
Christina . . . just doesn't help in your . . . er . . . home (clears throat,
adjusts tie and asks Christina in a puzzled voice) . . . is that true?

These therapists were not being uncaring or deliberately hurtful in any way. They
simply had not addressed their own attitudes towards gender and therefore unwittingly caused problems. Careful self-examination, reading and discussion with
their supervisors helped them overcome and resolve these problems.

### Client attitude

A different set of problems may occur when clients identify too strongly with the
same-sex therapist or if clients of the other sex assume that the therapist sym-
bolizes all of the things they dislike about that sex. While each case is different
and there are no textbook solutions, by examining their own gender attitudes,
being scrupulously unbiased in their language and responses, and pointing out
to clients the mistakes and assumptions they are making, therapists may be able
to minimize this problem. The following interaction occurred at the beginning
of a recent first assessment session and demonstrates how the therapist, a woman,
attempts to tackle the problem from the outset. The female member of the client
pair, Carol, is talking.

### Case example: Carol and Matthew

C: Oh I'm so pleased you're a woman . . . that psychiatrist we saw . . . he
just didn't understand my side of things . . . how can a man understand
the way we women feel?

T: I'm sorry you felt Dr Jamieson wasn't able to understand you . . .
however . . . as you said it is sometimes difficult for a member of a different sex to understand the other's point of view. . . . I hope you'll both
. . . (smiles at man and woman) . . . find me unbiased and able to help
you both equally with your difficulties . . . (turns to male client) . . .
How do you feel about having a woman as a therapist?

Remembering Barrett and Roberts's (1975) work on the medical control of
women, it is possible that the woman has experienced difficulty in relating to the
male doctor. However, by colluding with the woman, the therapist may only
alienate the male client. Therefore the therapist attempts to empathize with the
woman and steers a middle course, finishing by consulting the man on his
feelings.

### Expressing emotion

Within western society from an early age, men are encouraged to express anger,
competitiveness, assertion and the other more 'aggressive' emotions and actively

discouraged from expressions of 'openness', love, pain, and so on. Female therapists, whose experiences of life may differ greatly from this, may be oblivious to the cultural taboos which prevent many men from expressing their gentler emotions in an open and honest way.

*Case example: Liz and Mick*

In the case example used here a female therapist is working with Liz and her partner, Mick. They have a 12-year-old daughter, Susan, who is not present at the interview. Liz has expressed her concern that Mick does not show his affection enough for either herself or Susan.

> T: Well, Mick, it seems that Liz is saying you never show her . . . but more especially Susan . . . that you care about them, how do you feel about that?
> M: I work hard . . . give my wages up every week . . . we've got a nice house.
> T: But Liz is saying that you never tell them you love them.
> M: I always find it difficult . . . I don't count how often . . . but I'm sure I tell them.
> T: How about showing your affection . . . how do you do that?
> M: It's hard. . . . You don't often see men . . . well . . . kissing or cuddling their children.
> T: If you could be more expressive, perhaps Liz and Susan would be happier . . . can you do that?

After this exchange Mick became reticent and reluctant to discuss the matter further for the rest of the session and it was not until several weeks later that Mick was able to reveal his fear and concern about being accused of child abuse should he show emotion towards his daughter. The therapist had failed to understand Mick's problem fully. She had grasped the basic idea that he had difficulty in expressing his emotions, but failed to understand his concern about openly expressing his love to a nearly pubescent daughter. Male expressions of love, within western society, are seen as being closely linked with their sexuality and outside of this they are expected to be undemonstrative.

Male therapists may also experience problems with the difficulties women may have in expressing the more traditionally male emotions of anger, competitiveness or aggression. These are not totally acceptable emotions for women to express and are often seen as 'unfeminine'. Thus many women may suppress these emotions or experience guilt when they feel them or express them in public. The male therapist may have problems understanding the woman's guilty reaction to these emotions. He may misinterpret silence or passivity as the woman not feeling an emotion or alternatively feel shocked when they are expressed in a forceful way by women. All of these reactions will place barriers in the way of successful therapy.

## Conclusion

While we may strive and struggle to overcome our gender biases and be totally fair in our dealings with couples needing help, the very nature of our perceptions of gender, embedded as they are deep in our culture, and our own human fallibility guarantee that we are bound to fail in totally achieving this neutrality. Therefore we must take further steps to minimize this occurring.

One step which can be extremely useful is for therapists to work in mixed-sex pairs, for this may give balance to the therapy in a variety of ways. However, costs, work situation and time constraints may not often make this possible. When it is possible mixed-sex pairing allows the therapists to point out to each other during their debriefing sessions any gender-biased language or actions which are being used. It facilitates the immediate identification and resolution of any therapist attitudinal problems which may occur; this is also the case if either client identifies too strongly with the therapist of the same sex. From a client's point of view the mixed-sex pairing of therapists may initially be viewed more favourably than any single-sex therapist, no matter how unbiased that therapist may be. However, care should be taken when working in the mixed-sex pair format that the therapists do not get drawn into colluding with the couple, each identifying with the same-sex client. To avoid this it is preferable that regular supervision of some kind is sought.

If it is not possible to work in mixed-sex pairs, which it frequently is not, then it is preferable for the therapist to seek supervision from another therapist who will be more able to distance him/herself from the therapy under consideration. It would also be preferable for the supervising therapist to be of the other sex from the therapist actively involved with the clients, as this may facilitate a balance against any gender-laden language, interventions or attitudinal problems.

We have attempted to show that gender is not a predetermined genetic entity, but rather a culturally transmitted phenomenon which we learn in our childhood and which is constantly reinforced and reproduced throughout our adult lives. We hope that we have given a balanced view of how these gender issues affect clients and therapists of both sexes. The work has been written in what we hope is non-sexist language, avoiding the use of sex-specific personal pronouns such as 'he' to mean both sexes, and such terms as the 'opposite' sex, which suggests two factions of some kind. Finally, we hope that we have illustrated that, with forethought and consideration of gender issues, therapists of both sexes can overcome, to a great extent, the potential difficulties of gender bias in couple therapy, reduce client drop-out rate and be more effective in their clinical work.

## References

Barrett, M. and Roberts, H. (1975) 'Doctors and their patients: the social control of women in general practice', in C. Smart and B. Smart (eds) *Women, Sexuality and Social Control*, London: Routledge & Kegan Paul.

Hartley, R.E. (1966) 'A developmental view of female sex-role identification', in B.J. Riddle and E.J. Thomas (eds) *Role Theory*, London: Wiley.

Lees, S. (1986) *Losing Out: Sexuality and Adolescent Girls*, London: Century Hutchinson.

Rabban, M. (1950) 'Sex-role identification in young children in two diverse social groups', *Genetic Psychology Monographs* 42: 81–148.

Stanworth, M. (1981) *Gender and Schooling: A Study of Sexual Divisions in the Classroom*, London: Century Hutchinson.

# 10

# Transcultural issues in couple therapy

PATRICIA D'ARDENNE

## Introduction and overview

Britain in the 1990s proclaims itself to be a multi-racial, multi-cultural society. The ideal of equal opportunities and equal access to services has now gained enough credibility for most of the dominant culture in Britain to believe – despite the occasional reports in the media of racist attacks – that this is a reality. The invitation to write this chapter, indeed, stemmed from a laudable and understandable notion that all couple therapists working in Britain today should understand transcultural issues in order to help them work as effectively as possible with their ethnic clients.

Yet in our appraisal of transcultural issues in couple therapy, there is lamentably little research to inform practitioners what these areas might be. For example most of the research in this country on marriage has given scant attention either to transcultural or inter-racial marriages. Studies on the differing ethnic communities in Britain have examined family and kinship patterns between generations, but not those between couples, including spouses (Chester 1982). On the clinical side, couple therapists would find there are equally few studies on psychiatry across cultures (Cochrane 1979; Fernando 1988), and even less to consider on psychotherapy or counselling clients outside a therapist's own culture (Pederson 1985).

In order to make sense of these contradictions, it is necessary to understand therapy itself as very much an expression of white, western culture. There are limited research methods, and philosophical difficulties that limit the ways we can examine the ethnocentric base of therapy, or compare therapy outcome within and across other cultures (Segall *et al.* 1990).

Deeper reasons, however, for this dearth of information lie in the institutionalized beliefs within our own educational, medical and social structures. It has, perhaps, been more expedient for therapists from the dominant culture to make assumptions about couples needing help across cultures. One of these, according to Dominelli (1988), is that by a process of *assimilation* into the British way of life, clients from ethnic communities will begin to absorb many of the values and perceptions of the dominant culture, which will somehow ameliorate problems related to alienation. Such a position, argues Dominelli (1988), places no value on what black people might have to offer British culture, and renders invisible their day-to-day struggle with racism.

Another position adopted by white agencies is that ethnic groups themselves will offer specialized input, both in establishing and implementing therapeutic need. In this way, MIND (1986) argues, the majority culture is not obliged to examine its own role in alienating ethnic families, nor in providing genuine access to a full range of professional therapeutic services. Many community centres that were initially established to offer advocacy, liaison and advice about statutory services, have ended up offering counselling and therapy services themselves. These centres, argues MIND (1986), are not specialist or appropriate, and are often under-resourced, with only a minimal level of professional input or support, and hugely over-subscribed. Their clients, often from a wide range of cultural backgrounds, thus receive a poorer service than they need or deserve.

Perhaps the least desirable outcome of this limited knowledge has been that the many couple therapists (ASMT 1988) sincerely believe transcultural work to be beyond their skills and range of experience, and turn down transcultural work. Despite their good intentions, therapists thus deprive a substantial proportion of the population who not only need professional help with their relationships, but also may be suffering racism, economic hardship, language difficulties, immigration controls and delays, and separation from their families of origin.

In this chapter I shall briefly refer to some of the historical and organizational barriers to transcultural work with couples as well as review issues that other therapists have already considered in this past decade. There have been some small attempts in Britain to tackle ethnic issues in the context of specific sex therapy, and these will be reviewed, with the implications for practice. There is no evidence to show that therapists are better suited to work only within their own culture, though there is some evidence (NAFSIYAT 1985) that therapists who can work outside their own culture can work more easily within any culture. Transcultural skills are non-specific (d'Ardenne and Mahtani 1989) and transfer not only to other cultural groups, but also may significantly enhance all counselling and therapeutic work.

Next, I shall explore a very specific idea, namely that all therapists have transcultural skills and knowledge. Readers will be offered a more detailed assessment of the skills that are common to all good therapists and demonstrate that it is possible to identify and develop transcultural skills and apply them more effectively and appropriately. If therapy is about empowering our clients, it should also be about empowering therapists too. Couple therapists have both the responsibility for transcultural work, and many of the resources with which to develop it. What is required now is for it to be kept firmly on the agenda for all training, clinical and resource allocation purposes.

Finally, I shall briefly describe those UK agencies that are already involved in transcultural work, and are offering couple therapy for ethnic clients.

## History and research

The Registration of Marriage (Marriage Act 1949) was legislated at a time when Britain was more culturally homogeneous. The details of name and occupation were meant to identify persons getting married, and to bring order to the institution. There has never been any addition to that document that identifies a person's cultural or racial background. Public records, including the 1981 Census, are equally bereft, thus removing a potential prime source of information on inter-racial and minority group marriages (Chester 1982). In brief, there are no figures on what happens to ethnic marriages. Paradoxically it was believed that such monitoring would be construed as distasteful and possibly racist to those completing the census. The 1991 Census will allow individuals to classify themselves culturally, but it may be another two decades before we have any reliable data about trends in marriages of ethnic communities in the UK. It may be even longer before we can gain an overall picture of what it is happening to these couples in terms of marital breakdown, and specifically what kinds of resources they have or have not had access to when help has been sought.

Some research has been carried out on the basis of the 1981 Labour Force Survey. Coleman (1985), for example, looked at ethnic intermarriage in Britain – an interesting topic, since theory would predict this to be a vulnerable group. He found that about 1 per cent of all marriages in Britain were from partners of different ethnic groups. Of these, the main proportion (87 per cent) were between white and black. He found that Afro-Caribbean people (22 per cent of men and 10 per cent of women) were nearly three times as likely to marry a white person as were people from any of the South Asian cultures (Indian, Pakistani and Bangladeshi). Young black men between 15 and 44 years, however, were under-represented in this survey and the true number of inter-ethnic unions may not be known. Interestingly the other ethnic groups were not under-represented, and a more reliable picture emerges. South Asian communities are the least likely to marry outside race and culture (8 per cent men and 4 per cent women). Pakistani and Bangladeshi communities had an even smaller mix. It is interesting to note that the sex ratio with Chinese people was reversed: Chinese women were nearly twice as likely to have white partners than the men (25 per cent women and 15 per cent men). Coleman is able to assess trends between ethnic groups born outside and within Britain and concludes that Afro-Caribbean families are continuing to intermarry, but that no such trend exists with the other ethnic communities studied.

Haskey (1989) has examined the families and households of ethnic and white populations in Britain between 1985 and 1987, and concludes that four out of every ten Afro-Caribbean families are 'lone-parent' families, whereas the figure for what he describes as 'Arab' families is one in every hundred, and one in nine for white families.

The difficulty about this kind of research is that it defines married couples only as those who were living together within one household. The study did not consider any kind of less formal or visiting relationship, however long term, affectionate, supportive or committed. Relationships between men and women were being assessed by the British convention of what constitutes a marriage and a family. It just so happens, according to Littlewood and Lipsedge (1989), that the Asian (i.e. Indian, Pakistani or Bangladeshi) family contains something that British researchers would recognize as being akin to our nuclear family, and that it is therefore less often described as problematic in the literature. Black case-workers argue with good reason that British people can and do put a negative and prejudicial interpretation on differences between conventional Anglo-Saxon family life and others. Researchers may then, as a consequence, construe Afro-Caribbean families as less stable.

Research carries its own cultural assumptions: although these two studies cited are looking at important issues, the methodological barriers are still very great. People from ethnic groups who have experienced racism in Britain may be less willing to give information about their relationships to researchers who are seen as coming from the dominant culture. For their part, researchers can inform themselves about what these barriers are, and establish a method that provides more valid and reliable data.

## Progress in practice

Transcultural issues in medicine were made respectable by the meticulous work of Alex Henley (1979), which was aimed at health care professionals who were in contact with ethnic patients, predominantly from the Indian subcontinent. She set an important standard for carers by placing patient needs within their cultural and religious contexts. She demonstrated that it was possible to provide a vastly improved service to ethnic communities through those in the majority culture increasing their awareness of their power and ethnocentricity (being centred on one's own ethnic area), changing some of their practices, and developing an attitude that strives for full access to health care for all members of the community.

More precisely, Henley (1979) described family customs; religious beliefs; naming systems; diet; attitudes to illness; birth; marriage; old age and death; comparing these practices with the British system, and showing the extraordinary efforts Asian citizens already make to adapt to British habits and institutions. She provided practical guidelines for all health workers about how to ensure that Asian patients can get the care they need with full respect paid to their habits and customs. Her work gave detailed descriptions of family and married life, including the traditional gender roles in the major Indian cultures. More usefully she outlined where some of these roles have changed in a transcultural setting. The relationships between men and women in Britain are necessarily affected by migration and contact with the majority culture, and these changing boundaries are outlined in her work. In particular she referred to the increased choice and contact young couples are being given when their parents arrange their marriages, and Asian women's changing role in work outside the home.

In the field of mental health, the work of Transcultural Psychiatry (UK) has been significant. Despite its title, it is a multi-disciplinary, multi-racial campaigning organization that has promoted debate and discussion on racial matters in mental health. The organization has moved from a position of promoting cultural understanding to challenging many racist assumptions in research, practice and training in mental health in Britain today. Two of its members, Littlewood and Lipsedge (1989), have made a systematic analysis of how white British psychiatry and the institutional racism within it can actually contribute to mental disorder. These authors also place responsibility for the provision of good transcultural practice upon those practitioners in the dominant culture who have in the past regarded the culturally different as exotic and problematic. They argue forcibly that people from black and ethnic communities in Britain today are in fact very resourceful and have to overcome many political and social disadvantages as well as cope with culture shock, with language difficulties, with economic hardship, as well as their own personal and interpersonal problems.

Social case-work in Britain has produced many models of good anti-racist practice (Cheetham 1972; 1982; Dominelli 1988), and has posed the issues differently. Rather than ask what are the problems of the ethnic groups in Britain, and how might we deal with them, why not ask what transcultural skills ethnic clients have to cope with as well as they do, and how might these resources be mobilized in therapy? Triseliotis (1986) reminds us that clients from differing cultural backgrounds respond quite differently to differing approaches in counselling. He suggests, for example, that people from certain Asian cultures prefer a defined, problem-solving approach to a reflective, exploratory one, and that a client-centred, more ambiguous approach will only generate anxiety in cultures which actively structure social relationships. Social workers too have done much to dispel myths about the black family, about sexual stereotypes, and about the relationships between men and women in differing ethnic groups in Britain.

Relate (previously the National Marriage Guidance Council) has addressed itself in recent times to working with couples across cultures (Short 1986) and sees the issues connected to training and education as well as specifically clinical issues. Relate recognizes, for example, that members of differing Asian communities in Britain would prefer to see members of their own culture to a white counsellor. Furthermore, seeing anybody at all outside the family about marital or sexual difficulties requires overcoming enormous hurdles, not least the idea that seeking outside help is itself an expression of failure. Short (1986) proposes several possible ways forward. One is to recruit more black and ethnic counsellors to the service, and have a multi-cultural service within Relate itself. Another is to provide advice and support to those agencies currently offering transcultural therapy with couples. Still another is to encourage local advisory groups who work with members of different cultural groups to set up a number of different services according to expressed need.

In addition Short makes specific recommendations. First, Relate needs to give itself permission to be open about its fears and difficulties in working transculturally. Relate could make a public policy statement committing it to working more multi-culturally. She cites the British Association of Counselling (1986) as a national organization that has already done this.

Second, Relate needs to achieve a proper model of communication with black people whose interests it is claiming to serve. Such an enterprise would require research and additional resourcing to find the best service. Less costly options considered have been using consultants at local levels, buying additional

literature dealing with cross-cultural issues, and upgrading training on transcultural work for its counsellors.

## Specific sex therapy with ethnic clients in Britain

In the sphere of specific sex therapy, several studies (Ghosh *et al.* 1985;
Christopher 1984; Bhugra and Cordle 1988; d'Ardenne and Crown 1986) have
all carried out brief, retrospective studies of western treatment methods applied
to a variety of clients from ethnic communities, and compared their outcome with
clients from the majority culture.

A detailed account of these studies can be found elsewhere (Cole and Dryden
1988), but there are some general points that can be made about these and subsequent studies in the context of couple therapy. First, with the exception of male
Bangladeshi clients in d'Ardenne and Crown's (1986) sample, the ethnic groups
did not fare as well as their white counterparts. Second, the source of referral
for the ethnic clients was much more often medical, than social or psychological.
Ghosh *et al.* (1985) asked their clients about preferred methods of treatment, and
found that many more Asian patients (89 per cent) preferred medical and surgical
methods in contrast to their white controls (6 per cent). The assumption that these
and other authors make is that Asian clients (we are not always told *which* Asian
culture) somatize their sexual difficulties more than white clients. What is not
explained is what kinds of expectations Asian clients have of therapists if they
do not have physical symptoms. Could it be the case that ethnic clients believe
physical explanations of sexual dysfunction to be a more credible port of entry
to western professionals *regardless* of how clients see their difficulty? What is more,
what kind of language can people from two differing cultures use to exchange
psychological issues? Perhaps a physical presentation is easier for both parties
to deal with?

The next finding is that Asian men in these studies almost always respond better
to behavioural and cognitive treatments than their wives or female counterparts.
This finding is regardless of the gender or cultural background of the therapist.
Various explanations abound. Asian men are generally more acculturized, less
isolated, and more fluent in English. It may also be the case that men's dysfunctions are caused more by personal anxiety and intrapsychic conflict than the
women's, which reflect more complex and less accessible social and interpersonal
difficulties. None of these studies was satisfactory from a methodological standpoint; controls were established either on the basis of age or diagnosis, with little
emphasis on social, familial or economic factors. Most importantly, therapists
themselves seem to have made very little adaptation to their clients' needs or expectations. The therapists' expectations may also have influenced outcome. Lorion
and Parron (1985) quote several studies showing that counsellors who were rated
by all their clients as warm retain significantly more low-income and ethnic clients
than those who were rated as cold or distant. Similarly they cite work that demonstrates that when therapists' attitudes to low-income and ethnic clients are modified
more positively through direct supervision and education, that their ability to keep
these clients from dropping out of therapy is improved.

It has in fact been argued (d'Ardenne 1988) that the new sex therapies can be offered successfully to ethnic clients precisely because this therapy is symptomatic, because it does not require much verbal mediation, and because couples themselves can decide their therapeutic goals within the context of their personal and cultural needs. All that is needed are some modifications to therapy style and presentation.

In the case of Bangladeshi clients, for example, other members of the family may need to be involved both during assessment and intervention. The couple is not seen by the therapist as isolated from its family setting, and relatives may be needed to ensure support, give access to time and privacy, and provide a framework for any discussion of problems at home. During sessions, the man was allowed to speak for himself and his wife, and emphasis was placed on performance indicators rather than experiental change. Medical terminology was avoided, and an educational model was explicitly employed. Home assignments were called 'exercises', and instructions given were authoritative, didactic and unambiguous.

All these adaptations to methodology were superficial. They nevertheless allowed new learning to take place between a couple, where couples selected for themselves a carefully graded programme and where they monitored and evaluated change for themselves. Interpreters were used when necessary, and written instructions were translated in Bengla (Bengali), though not frequently. Perhaps the biggest change that occurred was that the therapists in the clinic gained more confidence in treating Bangladeshi clients, and were thus more motivated to develop their transcultural skills.

## Barriers in therapy

Perhaps the most difficult and painful issue facing therapists in Britain wanting to work with couples from other cultures is that the set of practices they have inherited contains inherent barriers for their ethnic clients. Counsellors may accept that their therapy is inappropriate to certain cultures, but nobody wants to be told that he or she is actively placing barriers between themselves and their clients. Nevertheless, therapists, however well intentioned, cannot hope to reach and learn about another cultural group, unless they consider critically their own cultural traditions and are able to respond with some flexibility in their approach.

A transcultural approach may challenge us to be more critical and curious about ourselves, and make us better therapists for all our couples. These barriers include the following.

1 *The primacy of the individual over the family in its many presentations*   There is consequently a lack of attention placed on the social and economic status of the couple and the obligations placed upon it within these contexts.

2 *The stress on the importance of historicity, and the impact of early (and not so early) individual experiences on problems in the couple's life*   In many cultures, the 'here and now' is the proper place for locating difficulties, and history-taking may prove to be not only difficult for the therapist, but also irrelevant to the couple.

3 *The great value placed on clients' abilities to decide for themselves what changes are required for growth* This applies whether it be attitudes (cognitive therapy) or behaviour (contractual and behavioural therapies) or insight (psychodynamic and all therapies) that is the point of concern. Clients from other cultures may seek advice about what their duties are, and seek directive and authoritative guidance.

4 *The use of language – always standard, educated English* Therapy in Britain not only poses barriers to ethnic groups whose first language is not English, but also creates difficulties for anyone speaking alternative forms of English, e.g. Cockney or Creole patois.

5 *The professionalism of the therapist which entails minimal self-disclosure, and a position of power over the clients within the therapeutic relationship* This is especially true when the therapist is from the dominant culture, and one or both of the couple is not. Added to these are the disabling effects of racism and cultural alienation that the couple may also be facing as part of their external reality.

6 *The adherence to strict time-keeping, and fixed location, often the therapists' choice* This is another aspect of working literally, on therapists' own territory and which may continue to aggravate the perceived power imbalance between therapists and their ethnic clients. Therapists argue pragmatically for fixed times and places, but when this is a barrier, there are ways of overcoming it.

A case example here may illustrate these barriers more clearly.

*Case example: Mark and Marie*
Mark is a 32-year-old Jamaican-born garage mechanic married to Marie, a black British-born 30-year-old of Ghanaian heritage. They are referred at their own request for counselling by their general practitioner, following complaints that both of them were wanting to terminate their six-year marriage, and each citing Mark's infidelities as the reason for the rift. They have a daughter aged 5 and a son aged 3 and live in a large, five-bedroomed house in east London with Marie's mother, who owns the family home. Neither Mark nor Marie has sought help before, but they now describe home life as being at breaking-point on the first occasion they attended therapy, accompanied by their children.

The institution they come to is a predominantly white one, where only clients, clerical and cleaning staff are black. They have not reckoned on the waiting-room being small and unaccommodating to small children. They arrive late for their appointment because the bus service to the therapy centre is unreliable. They are told at reception that no additional time can be allocated to them because of the appointments made for other clients that day.

During the interview, Mark is constantly asked to repeat himself, as his Caribbean accent is pronounced, and becomes more so as his anxiety increases with each misunderstanding. Marie ends up interpreting for Mark – a role which she admits later in therapy leaves her feeling that she has received less time for herself than she would have liked, and also angry because she feels Mark had been patronized by the white therapist, who spoke, like her, with a 'BBC' accent.

For his part, Mark expresses a desperate wish to make some concrete plans for his family's future, and appears bewildered when the therapist asks them to talk about their courtship and early relationship. This is compounded when the therapist then starts to pose questions about their very early lives. Mark replies: 'What's that to do with me problems now? I'm settled in England now', and refuses to answer questions which he sees as not only irrelevant, but also sinister. He is later able to say in therapy that he thinks the therapist is blaming his marital problems on the fact that he was born and raised in Jamaica, and that he has problems with British culture!

Throughout the entire first interview, the therapist makes no reference either to both Mark and Marie being black and seeing a white therapist, nor to the fact that Mark and Marie are in fact themselves from very different cultural traditions. The subject of race and culture remain unspoken and to some extent taboo until Mark fails to arrive at the third session, and Marie has once again to interpret for her therapist what some of these barriers have been.

With this couple, therapeutic practice and therapist provide very real but by no means inevitable barriers to effective transcultural work. For example the therapist thinks not only that the issues of race and culture are irrelevant, but also that if she raises the topic, she will be deemed racist by her clients for so doing. She will need to correct this very quickly if she is to be able to negotiate the other barriers of language, historicity, and formal time-keeping. Just as Mark and Marie have had to make adjustments, so the therapist makes a *cultural transition* and meets her clients a little along the way. She will be freed up to ask questions about anything she does not understand because she has acknowledged that there are differences. She will be able to offer a more flexible timetable for their needs, and so help this couple through their immediate crisis.

*Case example: Asha and Arun*
Asha, a 23-year-old law graduate from London, presents with her husband Arun, aged 30, also a lawyer, because of non-consummation of their marriage. Their problem came to light after they had both attended an infertility clinic, and they were referred by that clinic. They are articulate, verbal, and very anxious to please. They are both from well-to-do professional families. Asha is British-born; her parents are from Ahmadabad, India, and moved to Britain in the early 1960s. Arun was born and brought up in East Africa, though his parents were originally from Ahmadabad. The marriage was arranged and both families are very keen indeed for them to begin a family. The longed-for baby is the primary focus of this couple's motivation.

In the first interview, Asha asks the therapist what it is she must do to be sure to conceive a child. The therapist replies that she is unable to answer that directly, and attempts to redirect the interview to any sexual difficulties between Asha and Arun. Both of the couple express difficulty and embarrassment at discussion of so delicate a subject, and Arun asks whether it would be appropriate to invite his older brother to the next session. When the therapist asks what she could learn from Arun's brother, he points out that the whole history of this problem has been discussed in the family, and that it might be easier all round for a member of the family to put the therapist in the picture. The therapist tries unsuccessfully to discourage Arun from this plan, and his brother arrives at the second session.

He is seen together and separately from the couple and gives a history to the therapist, again requesting some practical advice for them.

At the third session the following encounter takes place.

ARUN: Now that we've given you all this information, could you please help us?
THERAPIST: You don't feel you're getting any help at the moment?
ASHA: Well, when are you going to stop my mother-in-law from bullying me?
THERAPIST: The problem is between the two of you. You can deal with this problem together.
ARUN: Nonsense! Asha is very unhappy with my mother, and you just don't seem to be taking that into account!

In this situation, the therapist is faced with the challenge of diverse views about first, the exact nature of the problem, and second, the *boundaries* within which a couple therapist might reasonably be expected to work. She will need to understand that in this culture to be a spouse is also to be a member of an extended family, whose duties and expectations will need to remain firmly on the agenda.

In transcultural therapy, the two metaphors of transition and boundaries have their literal parallels for clients as much as therapists. In our two case examples, at least one of the couple will be going through a process of cultural adaptation. British-born black clients like Marie and Asha will have had to adjust to British racism and cultural prejudice, and those not UK-born like Mark and Arun will have been involved in travel and settlement. During these experiences, clients draw on their inner resources and acquire a wide repertoire of skills that enable them to make constant adjustments to a changing and often hostile environment. These transcultural skills enable clients to maintain an intact cultural identity and it is these skills that can be tapped and used creatively by therapists when helping couples deal with boundaries in their marital and interpersonal relationships.

The barriers for the clinician, therefore, are the difficulties of being accessible to ethnic clients in the community who might be considering couple therapy, of recognizing any specific needs they may have in therapy, and of providing the most appropriate access to it.

## Towards good transcultural practice in couple therapy

Burke (1986) notes that culture is placed on the therapy agenda only when black or ethnic clients are mentioned; it is never an issue within the dominant white culture alone. There is, however, every reason to suppose that *all* therapists and their clients, from whatever culture, operate from their own cultural base, with knowledge specific to their culture, which can be employed and developed once it has been identified. Client couples are always in one sense beyond their therapists' culture. They may differ from therapists in terms of class, age, gender, occupation, religion, life-style, and politics, and a transcultural approach will enrich any therapeutic practice.

More therapists from all racial and/or ethnic groups in Britain need to be recruited and trained, but the case for racial and/or ethnic matching of therapists to clients is neither proven nor, at this stage, practical. In addition, what do you do, for example, with an Irish man married to a Chinese woman?

Cultural knowledge begins with how much *experience and information* the therapists have about other cultures, and in particular, that of their clients. Experience and information can be acquired actively, for example through travel, reading, or working with an ethnic community, or passively, through being educated and reared in a particular community. Some information is acquired directly, through personal contact, and some indirectly, by seeing a film or reading a novel about a culture. All these experiences are of value, and will necessarily be influenced by the opportunities and motivation of the therapists concerned.

Similarly therapists' *personal and institutional* resources also represent a source of cultural knowledge, and may be much more extensive than at first appreciated. Therapists may like to consider which of their own family members have contacts, affiliations and activities, either abroad or with ethnic communities in Britain. In addition, therapists' social networks, including friends, neighbourhoods and local community groups, may be able to provide additional information.

Therapists' own political and/or religious beliefs may provide some interface with other cultures, and offer a model of tolerance and intercultural understanding not present in previous professional training. Similarly experiences with alternative life-styles, health care, education and equal opportunity employers can all assist therapists in their cultural knowledge.

*Case example: James and Takie*

James is a 38-year-old Canadian journalist married to Takie, a 35-year-old Japanese artist, both living in London. The therapist who assesses their relationship problem has visited neither of these countries, but is not daunted by this. He asks questions in the first interview about how long ago and under what circumstances this couple met. He takes the trouble to look up Canada and Japan in the atlas and borrows a book on Japanese culture and behaviour. He talks to a neighbour brought up in the same Canadian province as James about life there. The therapist's own interest in Zen Bhuddism may be of some value in understanding an Oriental perspective, but he does not assume this. Takie comes from a very traditional family, still living in a small village in the northern tip of Hokkaido, but is herself very westernized in her appearance and manners. The therapist listens and is not afraid to say to Takie or James, 'Try and tell me what it's like to be married and living here, and having your family live so far away'.

Therapists' *attitudes and expectations* have a critical bearing on how effective their work with ethnic couples is likely to be. Reference has already been made to therapists' low expectations of success. Such is the power relationship in therapy, however, that black and ethnic clients blame themselves for the lack of success. Most therapists do not regard themselves as racist or culturally prejudiced, and think that all clients are treated equally. Such a position whereby therapists claim that they treat all their black and ethnic clients exactly the *same* as their white clients is called 'colour blindness'. It belies the clients' experience of the dominant

culture, and may make it impossible for couples to bring those experiences to
the counselling agenda. The question of prejudice and the discomfort that this
evokes needs to be tackled explicitly and sensitively within the therapeutic relationship. Just as therapists can and must explore difficult and intimate areas such
as sexuality or bereavement, so they will need to examine alienation and prejudice
between the couple and the outside world, and within the couple's relationship.

In general, good therapists are sensitive listeners and effective communicators.
Additionally the specific cultural skills needed by therapists must include a common language to achieve what Shackman (1985) calls the Right to be Understood.
There may be specific language requirement – if only to make simple communication in your clients' first language, but language skills go far beyond this.
Knowing how and when to use an interpreter embodies a wide repertoire of
abilities, for example. Shackman (1985) describes not only how to use interpreters, but also pitfalls, and these transcultural skills could well be adapted to
work with couples. The dangers of using one partner as an interpreter for the
other are illustrated in the following case example.

*Case example: Fatima and Syed*
Fatima and Syed are a Bangladeshi couple in their late 30s referred to a psychologist because of Fatima's increasing fearfulness of leaving the home, and
increased dependency on her husband for all domestic duties. They have five
children, all of whom speak English, like their father. The therapist visits the
home and is greeted by Syed at the door. He sits between the therapist and his
wife and insists that he will be able to speak for both himself and his wife, as his
wife accepts that he is the spokesman. The therapist asks Syed to ask his wife
if she understands and accepts this.

Syed looks astonished. Fatima is his wife, and will accept what he says. The
therapist insists. He complies. Fatima looks down at the ground and says very
little. Syed says that she does. During the next three or four exchanges, it becomes
clear that Syed is saying much more than the therapist is asking, and he appears
to be showing irritation with Fatima. Both of the couple are now fully engaged
with each other, but have lost all eye contact with the therapist!

At the next session, the therapist has made contact with a Bengali interpreter
who has had mental health training, and who has worked before with the
therapist. She is introduced to the couple, who have agreed to have an interpreter.
The interpreter sits behind the couple, having only eye contact with the therapist.
This time the therapist sits opposite Syed and Fatima, who are side by side,
and speaks to each in turn. The interpreter leans forward to Fatima's ear and
interprets simultaneously all the proceedings, but takes no other part during
therapy. The therapist is thus able to monitor all three people, and will watch
Fatima's face very carefully while the interpreter speaks her words or that of her
husband.

This therapist knows how to signal to the interpreter to slow down, or repeat
phrases, as each is finely tuned to the other with non-verbal as well as verbal skills.
Non-verbal skills are essential to good transcultural work, and therapists are quite
able to inform themselves about eye contact, greetings, gestures, expressions of
strong emotion, and physical space, both from their clients and from other

resources. Therapists are open to the possible changes that could occur, even if they are not exactly sure of what they might be.

Cultural skills also entail knowing how and when to use family and community resources with couples. Networking with other agencies is an unfamiliar activity for some couple therapists, but is essential if the couple themselves are already in contact with other groups. Opportunities for privacy and intimacy may also be difficult, and culturally skilled therapists have to be more flexible with their couples accordingly. It is wise never to assume that a couple has their own bedroom with a door that can be closed if not locked. It is wise to ask if there is a marital bed and whether or not it is shared with others.

We saw earlier with the case of Mark and Marie that strict time-keeping and the making of child-care provision may be beyond the resources of the couple. Sensitive therapists can anticipate this and adapt some of their practices. For example clients can be seen at the end of the day; children's activities and toys can be provided; clients can be seen in their own homes occasionally.

All therapists have some power over their clients, but the situation between clients from a minority culture and a therapist from the majority culture compounds this power imbalance further. The clients' perception of your age, social class, professional background and cultural skills will also affect your *status*, and how your clients see it. With couples, gender may also have a crucial bearing on how you are perceived. In some cultures, it is inappropriate for a person from outside the family, let alone the culture, to discuss personal, especially sexual matters, with someone of the other sex. The fact that this person is professionally qualified to do so may not carry much weight. It is prudent to check with the clients themselves, their families, or those that referred them, if this is acceptable, and to reassure clients about detachment and confidentiality.

Finally, therapists working with couples across cultures are able to choose how much they want to develop their cultural knowledge and skills. It is still by and large the case that white therapists eschew other cultural groups, and may at best find local community organizations to handle their cases. In this way black therapists often feel 'dumped' (Sue 1981) with all black or ethnic clients, with fewer choices for *them* to work transculturally. If couples in trouble are to be given the proper range of choices from professional services in Britain, it is essential that all therapists, but especially those of the dominant culture, make choices on their behalf. At a weekend on counselling across cultures (NAFSIYAT 1986), one white English therapist expressed what she felt to be her appropriate fears about working with Afro-Caribbean couples because she did not understand their culture. To which, one of the black workers replied, 'Why don't you just try? Why don't you listen to them and learn from them and become a better therapist for it?'

## Transcultural agencies

There are specialist agencies offering couple therapy for ethnic couples, but these are still rare. *Exploring Parenthood* is a national advice and counselling service for parents which serves families from many different economic and cultural backgrounds, with offices in London and Leicester. The team aims to help stressed families, and they have a Multi-cultural Families Project, which started in 1990. It runs training workshops and seminars for parents, doctors, teachers, psychotherapists and child-carers. The organization is supported by a group of fifty key contacts, who promote its work on a local, voluntary basis throughout the country. In its Annual Review, Exploring Parenthood (1988–9) says

> Those people who are willing to move out of their familiar surroundings and enter a partnership with someone from a radically different background, often in a new country and with all the problems of learning a new language and combating racism, are the true explorers of our society. And, in an increasingly multi-cultural world, the lessons that such couples and their children have to offer, as they seek to establish their own place and identity, can be helpful to us all in our efforts to inter-relate more successfully.

Inter-ethnic marriages, especially those involving partners who are still resident in another country, or may be about to leave Britain, are seen by *International Social Service* (ISS), an international, non-governmental agency that aims

1  to help individuals deal with difficulties as a direct result of migration, and where co-ordinated actions of several countries, including the country of residence, may be required
2  to study the international conditions and consequences of migration on family life, and to make recommendations accordingly.

This organization has sixteen national offices and correspondents in over a hundred countries. Many of the inter-country cases are the results of the breakdown of transcultural marriages. ISS has carried out research into marriages that cross national, cultural and religious boundaries, and offers initial counselling to couples of different backgrounds wishing to get married. Referrals often come from Registrars who may realize, just before a wedding, that a couple is not informed of the technical or legal implications of a transcultural marriage. ISS has a long-established Foreign Marriage Advisory Service for British nationals intending to marry foreigners. The organization does not involve itself in long-term counselling, but is sufficiently well networked to locate local case-workers for one or both of the couple. In addition, the organization helps with family reunion, and tracing, with child abduction by a parent, with return migration, with foster placements, and with inter-country adoption.

There are a number of cultural organizations that offer specialist help to couples in Britain, including the Asian Women's Centre, the National Asian Marriage Guidance Council, the Jewish Marriage Council, and the Catholic Marriage Advisory Council. These agencies are geared to offer services within their own culture, and suited to their own requirements (Darnbrough and Kinrade 1988). Some of these organizations offer out-group help, and all offer help for culturally mixed couples. Many ethnic groups in London (MIND 1986) are used by the groups as a mental health and therapy resource, and a significant but unmonitored proportion of these cases deal with couples in crisis. Most of these groups are untrained, though there is evidence (MIND 1986) that the type of help that they offer is more sought after and more for couples than services within the dominant culture. There is little evidence available about the quality of service that these groups offer, and a danger exists of creating a two-tier structure in society that disenfranchises ethnic couples from getting professional help. NAFSIYAT (1985), an inter-cultural therapy centre in North London, points out that transcultural issues must not dominate case-work to the point where it is forgotten what ethnic clients have in common with their English counterparts. Good transcultural work ensures that once cultural barriers are faced and dealt with, that access can then be made to deeper interpersonal and intrapsychic conflicts in the couple. This organization opposes ethnic matching for its clients, unless language makes this unavoidable, but trains and provides culturally skilled workers for its black and ethnic clients, which include couples.

## Conclusion

We have little research material about the relationship or psychosexual needs of black and ethnic couples in Britain today. There is no reason to think that the range of problems couples face in a transcultural setting is not as great as those in the dominant culture; indeed they may well be aggravated by alienation, hardship and prejudice. But these couples also have transcultural resources and skills which may be of value to therapy, and which need to be fully utilized by culturally skilled therapists.

What is needed for the future is an organized and integrated assessment of cultural and transcultural needs in the community. Additionally we need a positive and courageous commitment by couple therapists to assess their transcultural skills, to develop them, and to be willing to work with couples of any race, colour or creed in Britain today.

### *Acknowledgements*

I would like to thank the following for their help in the preparation of this chapter:

Robert Chester, Senior Lecturer, Department of Social Administration, University of Hull.

Duncan Dormer, Information Officer, and Penny Mansfield, Deputy Director, Marriage Research Centre (now One-plus-One), Central Middlesex Hospital, Acton Lane, London NW10.

Carolyn Douglas, Director, Exploring Parenthood, 41 North Road, London N7.

Mrs E. Grives, International Social Service of Great Britain, 39 Brixton Road, London SW9.

Mrs Alison Clegg, Senior Tutor, Relate, and all those brave counsellors who undertook the study day on transcultural issues at Relate, Rugby, May 1990.

## References

ASMT (Association of Sexual and Marital Therapists) (1988) *Conference Proceedings*, *ASMT Bulletin*, Abingdon, Carfax.

Bhugra, D. and Cordle, C. (1988) A case study of sexual dysfunction in Asian and non-Asian couples, 1981–1985, *Sexual and Marital Therapy* 3, 1: 111–12

British Association of Counselling (1986) *Tenth Annual Report*, Sheep Lane, Rugby.

Burke, A. (1986) Racism, prejudice and mental illness, in J. Cox (ed.) *Transcultural Psychiatry*, London: Croom Helm.

Cheetham, J. (1972) *Social Work with Immigrants*, London: Routledge & Kegan Paul.

—— (1982) Client groups: some priorities, in J. Cheetham (ed.) *Social Work and Ethnicity*, London: Allen & Unwin.

Chester, R. (1982) A summary of recent UK literature on marital problems: a report for the Home Office Research Unit, unpublished paper, University of Hull, Department of Social Policy and Professional Studies.

Christopher, E. (1984) Experiences of working with people from different cultural backgrounds, unpublished paper presented to the Association of Sexual and Marital Therapists Conference, London, 1984.

Cochrane, R. (1979) Psychological behaviour disturbance in West Indians, Indians and Pakistanis in Britain: a comparison of rates, *British Journal of Psychiatry* 134: 201–10.

Cole, M. and Dryden, W. (eds) (1988) *Sex Therapy in Britain*, Milton Keynes: Open University Press.

Coleman, D. (1985) Ethnic intermarriage in Great Britain, *Population Trends* 40: 4–10, London: HMSO.

d'Ardenne, P. (1988) Sexual dysfunction in a transcultural setting, in M. Cole and W. Dryden (eds) *Sex Therapy in Britain*, Milton Keynes: Open University Press.

d'Ardenne, P. and Crown, S. (1986) Sexual dysfunction in Asian couples, British Medical Journal 292 (19 April): 1,078–9.

d'Ardenne, P. and Mahtani, A. (1989) *Transcultural Counselling in Action*, London: Sage.

Darnbrough, A. and Kinrade, D. (1988) *The Sex Directory: A Guide to Sexual Problems and Where to Go for Help*, Cambridge: Woodhead-Faulkner.

Dominelli, L. (1988) *Anti-Racist Social Work*, London: Macmillan Education.

Exploring Parenthood (1988–9) *Annual Review*, 41 North Road, London, N7 9DP.

Fernando, S. (1988) *Race and Culture in Psychiatry*, London: Croom Helm.

Ghosh, G., Duddle, M. and Ingram, A. (1985) Treating patients of Asian Origin presenting in the UK with sexual dysfunction, paper presented to the Seventh World Congress of Sexology, New Delhi, 1985.

Haskey, J. (1989) Families and households of the ethnic minority and white populations of Great Britain, *Population Trends* 57: 8–19.

Henley, A. (1979) *Asian Patients in Hospitals and at Home*, London: King Edward's Hospital Fund.

International Social Services (1984) *Sixty Years of Service to People*, Cranmer House, 39 Brixton Road, London SW9 6DD.

Littlewood, R. and Lipsedge, M. (1989) *Aliens and Alienist: Ethnic Minorities and Psychiatry*, 2nd edn, London: Unwin Hyman.

Lorion, R. and Parron, D. (1985) 'Countering the countertransference: a strategy for treating the untreatable', in P. Pederson (ed.) *Handbook of Cross-Cultural Counseling and Therapy*, Westport Conn: Greenwood Press.

MIND (1986) *Directory of Black and Ethnic Community Mental Health Services in London*, Voluntary Sector, London, MIND South East.

NAFSIYAT (1985) *Annual Report*, 278 Seven Sisters Road, London N4 2HY.

—— (1986) *January Conference Proceedings*, 278 Seven Sisters Road, London N4 2HY.

Pederson, P. (ed.) (1985) *Handbook of Cross-Cultural Counseling and Therapy*, Westport, Conn: Greenwood Press.

Segall, M., Dasen, P., Berry, J. and Poortinga, Y. (1990) *Human Behavior in Global Perspective; An Introduction to Cross-Cultural Psychology*, New York: Pergamon.

Shackman, J. (1985) *A Handbook on Working with, Employing and Training Interpreters*, Cambridge: National Extension College.

Short, I. (1986) Is MG meeting client needs in a multi-cultural society?, *Marriage Guidance* 22, 4: 3–8.

Sue, D. (1981) *Counseling the Culturally Different: Theory and Practice*, New York: Wiley.

Triseliotis, J. (1986) Transcultural social work, in J. Cox (ed.) *Transcultural Psychiatry*, London: Croom Helm.

# 11

# Couple therapy with homosexual men

MICHAEL BUTLER AND JEREMY CLARKE

## Introduction

In the United Kingdom there is no such thing as a legally defined gay marriage. It takes courage for two men to declare themselves openly as a gay couple. 'The teaching in any maintained school of the acceptability of homosexuality as a pretended family relationship is forbidden according to recent government legislation.'[1] This apparently necessary piece of legislation against the promotion of homosexuality (whatever that means) was largely in response to the furore around a book *Jenny Lives with Eric and Martin*. The proposition that two gay men might live together in a family unit and bring up a child seems unthinkable.

Gay relationships are met by lack of social acceptance, denial of legal and financial definitions (how do a gay couple set about obtaining a mortgage, or draw up a contract about their joint property, or make a will?) and absence of moral, religious, or familial support. Undergirding these minuses are the highly negative images of themselves (queer, faggot, poofter) accumulated over the years, and the received wisdom that gay relationships are doomed to failure. Yet couples where the partners are of the same sex do exist and are much more common than is supposed. In the era of AIDS gay couples are committed to making their relationships work; they come for help and support not only to *gay* counselling organizations but also to marriage guidance centres.

This chapter will try to identify some of the principal differences between working with gay and non-gay couples. Four common areas of difficulties will be highlighted, drawing on the limited research available (mostly American) and the clinical experience of the Albany Trust.[2] These difficulties include the all-pervasive phenomenon of homophobia: the diverse expectations of the couples themselves about their relationship; the sexual contract between the couple in the context of the prevalence of the HIV virus and AIDS; and the adjustments required of males towards their own masculinity in a pair-bonding *gay* relationship.

Our starting-point has to be the response of the counsellor or therapist towards homosexuality and the homosexuals. How receptive is the counsellor to the idea of two people of the same sex embarking upon what they hope will be a long-term relationship? What understanding is there of the emotional stresses and the stumbling blocks which have to be faced? Homosexuality is still in some psycho-analytical circles regarded as an arrest in normal development, sociopathic, narcissistic, paranoid or even a masochistic mental disorder (see for example Bieber 1965; Socarides 1979; van den Aardweg 1984). To replace this with a gay affirmative therapeutic approach may well go against the grain. Sadly gay couples hoping to improve their relationship are still likely to find themselves in therapy which exacerbates their problems rather than resolves them. 'The sexual side of our relationship, or lack of it, was not mentioned, it was skated over' is an example of the comments which not infrequently come our way at the Albany Trust. When discussion of safer-sex techniques is surely a necessary part of all couple therapy, this omission or avoidance on the counsellor's part is beyond belief.

How do we define a homosexual (gay) couple? Are there certain criteria such as time together, shared home, finances and a sexually monogamous commitment? Research into the dynamics of a gay couple relationship is meagre. However, the most comprehensive study to date from the USA is worth mentioning. *The Male Couple* (McWhirter and Mattison 1984) is a study based on interviews with 156 gay couples (not in therapy) living in California. The participants were aged between 20 and 69 years; their relationships together ranging between one and thirty-seven years (the mean age of the individuals was 37.4, and the mean time for a relationship eight to nine years – the median slightly over five-years); the interviews were conducted over a five year period. The most striking finding was that a pattern of developmental stages could be identified within these relationships, which has proved enormously useful in its therapeutic application. Some of the principal characteristics relevant to therapists working with gay couples were as follows.

1  expectations of sexual exclusivity were not necessarily assumed
2  during the first few years most gay couples maintained strict separation of moneys and properties
3  internalized homophobia – ranging from ignorance to deeply rooted prejudice – was often present in gay couple relationships with harmful, often invidious effects
4  gay couples were faced both individually and as a unit with 'coming out' issues: consequently their degree of acceptance and openness of their sexuality was often a source of tension
5  gay couples' expectations derive often from previous family upbringing and heterosexual relationships rarely offered adequate or appropriate role-models, as it were for their own relationships – nor were there obvious gay couple role-models to follow
6  gay couples sometimes over-communicated the stressful or problematic areas of their relationships with each other.

It is difficult to assess how representative such generalizations are and how far they assist therapeutic approaches in Britain. Therapists who choose to work with gay couples ought at least to familiarize themselves with the context in which gay relationships work if they are to offer effective help.

Where does one gay man meet another? There is the chance encounter at work or an advertisement followed through in the personal column of magazines. There is also the commercialized gay scene which has emerged during the 1970s and 1980s as an alternative to straight socializing. But this imposes its own constraints on the potentiality of gay couple relationships. The largely urban disco-culture which the scene revolves around is a highly commercialized and often impersonal environment; while clubs and gay bars have been successful cruising venues they are not equally conducive to initiating longer-term relationships; the current prevalence of HIV infection is not only altering gay men's approaches to sexual satisfaction but also pointing to a need for a 'safer' environment in which to pursue gay relationships.

Many gay couples deliberately cut themselves off from the scene – they may perceive it as threatening to their own sexual monogomy or stability, or simply as incapable of offering a diversity of recreational pursuits. Their success as a gay couple might depend upon avoiding both heterosexual society and disapproval and the pressures of a highly mobile gay scene – hence their invisibility, their relative isolation, and the lack of role models. British gay couples are often discreet (if not closeted) with a fairly narrow social circle and a closed domestic environment; these would seem to be somewhat different from their American counterparts. Outside of fairly elite social circles (the arts, academia, etc) there is even less support and tolerance for gay couples to live openly. Our sexually repressive culture does not allow for the establishing and integration of gay couples within 'mainstream' life-styles.

One such example of this context of homophobia is a recently bereaved gay-partner we met. He had been unable to tell his colleagues at work that his lover was dying of an AIDS-related illness. The hostility and prejudice he anticipated would have been too much to risk in addition to the strain of caring for his lover. Compare this with the situation of heterosexuals whose partners are dying – say – of cancer. One of sympathy and support? It is certainly not uncommon for gay men to face appalling prejudice and discrimination, including loss of employment, housing, social ostracism and verbal and physical violence, as a consequence of living openly as gay.[3]

## Some therapeutic strategies

It will not be possible here to offer detailed and thorough descriptions of gay-orientated couple therapies. Besides, there has been no sustained attempt to appropriate psychoanalytic theory for gay-positive ends compared with the achievement of feminist therapy for example. Such a project is overdue at a time when the psychosexual problems raised by AIDS require an entirely different discourse of sexuality if we are to move beyond the repressive notions of *natural* heterosexuality or *sick* homosexuality (see two useful essays: Watney 1989; Fletcher 1989). The realities of HIV transmission will not respect such boundaries. Nevertheless we can provide here an outline of three different strategies which we consider useful in dealing with the commonest problems encountered working with gay couples:

1  a developmental model of gay relationships
2  sex therapy techniques for gay couples
3  a psychodynamic approach to masculinity for gay men.

With each strategy we shall also suggest some specific interventions to be used.

## A developmental model of gay relationships

The conceptualization of developmental stages in gay relationships addresses many of the difficulties engendered by the absence of social structures, definitions and tolerance discussed above. Gay relationships are here explored within a positively defining structure. The couple's own relationship history, their development, their stages and patterns are set alongside models which have been observed to work, empirically. Difficulties between two individuals – their behaviour and feelings which cause distress – can be seen less as reflecting individual inadequacies (there must be something wrong with you/me) and more in terms of the characteristic hurdles within an overall picture of relationship growth (at this stage that is normal after all). The insecurities in a gay couple which may be due both to internal stresses and an internalization of the myth that gay relationships do not work become less threatening when the concept of developmental stages is used as a therapeutic tool. What follows is based on McWhirter and Mattison's (1984) work in particular.

### Stage One: first year

*Blending*  This stage in gay couple relationships is often experienced as an intensity of togetherness, excluding others, overlooking mutual differences, enjoying intense 'limerance'[4] and shared responsibilities with an attitude of equality (in financial arrangements and day-to-day chores). Generally sexual activity involves several weekly encounters. Loss of limerance, minor ruptures and consequent withdrawal, together with fears of intimacy generated by their process of blending, are the common difficulties at this stage of the relationship.

### Stage Two: one to three years

*Nesting*  Both individuals now begin to pay attention to their living environment, and to enhancing their compatibility – to recognizing shortcomings as well as complementary differences. A decline in limerance creates some ambivalence also at Stage Two. The difficulties are often to do with annoyance, a familiarity which induces bitchiness about each other's different values, tastes, etc. and worries about the sexual side of the relationship – does he still love me? Will he run off with someone else?

*Stage Three: three to five years*

*Maintaining*   The relationship at this stage involves a balance between individualism and togetherness. The ability to resolve conflicts, allow for autonomy and not dependency, and to clear up misunderstandings all encourage trust between the couple to build up and sustain their partnership. Some recognition and support of the couple as a definite 'thing' by friends or family also occurs after this span of time. Problems are provoked by the risks involved in either partner discovering outside sexual interests, or their needs to be separate. The necessity of confronting these issues, with their potential implications of loss, invariably causes tensions.

*Stage Four: five to ten years*

*Collaborating*   Mutual collaboration over these years leads to a sense of productivity – often actualized in material or professional success. This is possible when each partner has a secure independence within a relationship which provides support, guidance and affirmation. Distancing, boredom and taking each other for granted can creep in at this stage, with a decline in the fulfilment gained from being in the relationship, as well as the possibility that one partner gets 'left behind' – especially in terms of establishing a separate and successful identity.

*Stage Five: ten to twenty years*

*Trusting*   This denotes a lack of possessiveness and mutual positive regard, usually symbolized by the merger of money and possessions. For gay couples this seems to occur at Stage Five. The associated problems may well be due as much to the ages of the couples as to their relationship dynamics: rigid attitudes, lack of communication and withdrawal into monotonous routines – often shown by inattention to personal needs and isolation from each other, as well as friends, can crop up if the relationship is taken for granted.

*Stage Six: twenty years*

*Repartnering*   This and discovering a new commitment to each other seems to occur at the milestone of twenty years and when the couple have realized their financial security. There is an assumption that the relationship is also stable until one partner dies. However, restlessness and aimlessness – sometimes brought on by health concerns and fears of loneliness or death, as well as a continuation of earlier unresolved problems – can prevent a couple celebrating their longevity at the same time as challenging and broadening their relationship into new areas.

*Therapeutic interventions*
Simply clarifying the couple's individual expectations and assumptions about their relationship may be the most effective therapeutic intervention when working with

this 'relationship stages' strategy. It is also important for therapists to have clear ideas on positive gay life-styles, and to offer knowledgeable advice on where and how couples might seek to create a support system from within the lesbian and gay community for their relationship. Some gay couples are beginning to consider the positive effects bringing up a family might have for their relationship – the developmental model outlined here is not meant to be prescriptive or universal. It does seem to be the case, however, that such a model allows a gay couple to identify and relate their problems constructively and within a reassuring cognitive framework. In addition, by utilizing a concept of 'stage discrepancy', previously intractable differences can be redefined as opportunities for adjustment and individual change and growth. Couples are very often at different stages individually (stage discrepant). When this is identified by the therapist, it seems to allow for mutual recognition of their partners as well as their own needs.

### Sex therapy techniques for gay couples

Safer sex needs to be a prerequisite of gay relationships and counselling skills in this area, as well as knowledge of HIV transmission, needs to be a prerequisite for all therapists (see Gordon and Mitchell 1988; Green and McCreaner 1989). Gay couples have reported that therapists are often reluctant to discuss the sexual side of their relationship – a failure to do that will quite possibly be fatal to their clients. Many gay couples still find it difficult to discuss sex openly or to negotiate a safer sexual contract together.

Sodomy or buggery is historically associated with gay sex (having been a capital offence until 1861) and it still excites pejorative judgements whenever homosexuality is discussed by self-righteous heterosexuals. (Psychologists will know that 'hysterical' condemnation of a certain act is probably due to suppressed sexual desires associated with that act). In fact, fewer than 50 per cent of gay men regularly practise anal sex according to a recent survey (McManus and McEvoy 1987). An important aim of sex therapy is to cut through some of the misinformation about sexual behaviour and desires. Ignorance and myth is in itself counter-therapeutic and it plays an important part in perpetuating prejudices against gay couples, leading to internalized homophobia.[5]

Masturbation and mutual masturbation are the commonest forms of sexual activity for gay men, with oral sex still popular (thought to be relatively safe in terms of HIV, less so in terms of Hepatitis B). A therapist needs to consider what options are available in working with gay clients. The 'Masters and Johnson' type process can be adapted. This would include proper screening, sex history taking, sensate-focus and self-pleasuring exercises, communication and assertiveness skills in sex, and the impact of these activities on the dynamics of the relationship: all worked out within a programme of regular weekly reporting-back sessions (see Masters and Johnson 1970; 1979; Kaplan 1974; 1979; 1983; Gordon 1988; Reece 1988). Sex therapy can be a stressful experience, however liberating when successful, and gay couples as well as therapists need to consider carefully their level of commitment to making it work: in particular, newly formed gay couples might benefit more from individual work, or from couple counselling around their expectations of the relationship, rather than sex therapy, which assumes levels of long-term commitment, and can raise hidden conflicts and demands for mutual intimacy, all of which a newly formed gay couple might still be exploring.

The most common sexual dysfunction for men (gay or non-gay) is erectile failure. Just as so much of female sexuality is invested in not being fat – with the consequence that the vast majority of women feel inadequate in that regard – so male sexuality centres on being 'two feet long, hard as steel, and able to go all night' (Zilbergeld 1978). No wonder men's penises won't do what they're supposed to do a lot of the time – look out, especially, for those men who spend much time and money on big fast cars instead. The most interesting difference between gay couples and non-gay couples is the frequency of inhibited orgasm problems among gay men as opposed to premature ejaculatory problems among their non-gay counterparts. Performance anxiety and fears of being intimate may well be the common factors to both complaints – pointing to men's fear of being vulnerable in general. What this suggests is that men's sexual inhibitions in relationships generally are probably to do with their being 'men' more than their being gay men or heterosexual. Where there are differences there is a need to explore gay men's negative feelings about sex. Homophobic conditioning often leads to a lack of sexual confidence.

Gay men sometimes attempt to compensate for lack of social and self-acceptance by over-investing sex with other needs – to prove themselves as 'men', to receive warmth and affection. Perhaps like 'women who love too much' some gay men develop hang-ups in sexual relationships from inheriting a legacy of social stigmatization towards their desires.[6] Until quite recently some form of aversion therapy was often the only suggestion for gay men who presented with sexual problems. Therapists need to be clear and positive about their own homosexual desires, as well as knowledgeable in sex therapy techniques, if they aim to help gay couples improve their sexual relationships.

### A psychodynamic approach to masculinity for gay men

We have already noticed how 'masculine sexual psyches' formed in opposition to 'feminine sexual psyches' can inhibit the sexual functioning of long-term relationships, and that is equally true in other areas of gay couple relationships. Men are brought up to be competitive, defensive and emotionally inexpressive in order to get what they want, rather than yielding, vulnerable and open with their feelings. On the face of it, therefore, a gay male couple has a poor prognosis to begin with; in reality (and sometimes even in therapy) gay couples have unique opportunities to resolve their conflicts of masculinity through an enduring and loving relationship.

Gay couples, in addition to their socialization as men, will bring other developmental wounds to their relationship. Commonly these are associated most acutely with gender non-conformity and sexual identity conflicts during the pre-pubertal period and throughout adolescence. The extreme psychological violence inflicted on most gay men while growing up often needs to be worked through in the safety of a supportive intimate relationship later in life. Such are the extent of internalized fears, however, and memories of the traumatic anxieties most gay men experience when first realizing an awareness of their sexuality, that it often takes some form of crisis to motivate couples to address these issues. Gay couples also face added external pressures such as interference from families and weighing up whether or not to risk rejection by disclosing the relationship. Similarly dilemmas in telling friends or work colleagues also create problems for gay couples in negotiating how best to integrate their own relationship-style with the rest of their lives. A characteristic sign of masculine identity disorder in relationships is avoidance. Some of its typical symptoms appear when rather than face the intimacy dysfunction one or both partners begin to depend on external agents for a positive sense of self – such as alcohol, food, work, sex, gambling or bodybuilding for example. The coping mechanisms within the relationship are often forms of over-separation or of over-dependency behaviour. Gay couples seem to face two fears: first, emotional disclosures of vulnerability in an intimate relationship will be exploited as a sign of weakness, or punished as a failing in itself, and second, anxieties about lack of self-worth will be taken as proof of sexual and masculine inadequacy which becoming a couple was meant to resolve. Our approach with gay couples experiencing masculine identity disorders follows the following psychodynamic process.

1 Both partners need to be encouraged to share their own sexual and emotional histories *before* they met – including their conflicts and adaptations – as a way of promoting trust and mutual support.
2 The partners are then given permission to explore their own relationship conflicts in the context of these earlier disclosures. The aim here is for blocking transferences and projections to come to the surface, which, with the aid of the therapist, can be used to identify relationship defence-mechanisms which stem from earlier homophobic conditioning as well as the fear of losing the partner. The empathic context of reworking these conflicts out with a gay-affirmative therapist encourages affective expression and abreactive release which will enable the couple to move beyond their defence patterns.
3 Each partner is then asked to reaffirm the other's positive self-worth as a gay man. This precedes dealing with the intimacy-fears due to masculine conditioning and repression of erotic attachments to men in general. Exploring the context and structure of the couple's own sexual relationship at this stage can help elicit this process. In effect the goal is to consolidate their identity as a couple with gay-orientated feelings of intimacy.
4 The final phase of therapy will involve looking at issues of independence and togetherness with the aim of agreeing upon some mutually defined goals *vis-à-vis* families, friends, work, etc. Having worked through the conflicts generated by their own fears of intimacy, men in gay couples are uniquely placed to respond to the challenges of negative societal attitudes towards male–male relationships.

## Implications for therapists

There has been virtually no research which addresses the question of the sexual orientation of therapists who work with gay couples. It has been suggested elsewhere that positive role-modelling and greater familiarity with the gay world are amongst the benefits of gay couples choosing a homosexual therapist (Rochlin 1981/2). There continues to be a risk of iatrogenic damage being inflicted on gay couples by homophobic therapists. In Britain homosexuality is still pathologized by the psychiatric and therapeutic professions, as evidenced by their refusal to admit openly lesbian or gay therapists. This in itself is a warning to lesbian and gay men seeking help to assess the attitudes of therapists towards their sexual orientation (good advice can be found in Hall 1985). Therapists who are able to talk about either their own or their clients' sexuality non-defensively will probably provide the best setting in which to work with gay couples. For the moment, therapists of whatever sexual orientation who choose to work with gay couples need to accept changes *they* must work towards as well as their clients. These include

1  being clear about positive models for gay relationships
2  offering empathic responses based on acceptance of their own homosexual desires (if not life-style)
3  responding with appropriate strategies and genuine affirmation to clients' willingness to develop and grow beyond their current limitations: therapists who can relate to their own gay-positive experiences will be able to reflect that in their approach
4  being confident enough to explore the conflicts within gay couple relationships, and to challenge destructive patterns with positive alternatives.

Experience of gay support-groups, gay-affirmative supervision, and co-therapy with gay-identified colleagues are all worth-while investments for developing the above-mentioned qualities.

## Conclusion

Until more gay-affirmative training is offered on therapy courses, and until the normative and homophobic consensus within traditional psychoanalysis is replaced by more positive theories of homosexual identities and relationships, therapists will find it difficult to adopt a more integrative approach towards working with gay couples. How long will it be before such a chapter as this is included in a textbook on family therapies?

In our experience there are considerable rewards to be gained from therapeutic work with gay couples. First, the myth that homosexuality and intimacy are mutually exclusive is exploded by those couples themselves who have the courage and commitment to seek therapy. Second, the quality of the work with gay couples is high, due to a combination of their motivation, and sometimes acute, if not debilitating presenting problems. This is perhaps connected to the health crisis caused by AIDS, as well as the general social climate, which is undoubtedly hostile. Third, the psychodynamics of gay couple relationships are relatively new and challenging territories for therapists to help chart. Deep-seated prejudices are often confronted and conventional patterns of gender and sexual orientation are open to question. The therapeutic relationship itself may mirror these processes.

Hopefully the results of this work might contribute to breaking down the 'invisibility' in which most gay couple relationships exist at present.

## Notes

1 Section 28, Local Government Act 1988. It is also worth noting that gay couples pay a large part of their poll taxes towards an education system which deliberately stigmatizes them.
   'There is no place in any school in any circumstance for teaching which advocates homosexual behaviour, which presents it as the *norm*, or which encourages homosexual experimentation by pupils' (DES Circular 11/87).
2 The Albany Trust was set up in 1958 and was instrumental in lobbying for law reforms relating to homosexuals. It has provided a counselling, training and psychotherapy service since 1959, specializing in psychosexual issues across the whole range of human sexualities.
3 There has been very little sociological research done on male couples in this country – a reflection on society's unwillingness to accept their existence. See Westwood (1960) for a pioneering study, written under a pseudonym (real name Michael Schofield)!
4 Limerance is a term which describes falling or being in love, including

   1 intrusive thinking about the desired person
   2 acute longing for reciprocation of feelings and thoughts
   3 buoyancy (walking on air) when reciprocation occurs
   4 intensity of feelings which leaves other concerns seeming insignificant
   5 seeing positive attributes, and reducing negative ones irrelevant or emotionally complementary (thus positive).

   Sexual attraction is a *sine qua non* of limerance but not the sole component. See Tennot (1979).
5 We lack empirical and comparative data for the heterosexual population in this country. A recently planned large-scale survey was cancelled for obscure reasons on the intervention of the Thatcher government. Some people seem neurotically attached to a concept of 'normality' which denies the diversity of pleasurable sexual activities. The Hite Reports on Male and Female Sexuality provide a useful corrective.
6 'Women who love too much' is the title of a book by Robin Norwood (1986). See also Dickson (1985).

## References

Bieber, I. (1965) Clinical aspects of male homosexuality, in J. Marmor (ed.) *Sexual Inversion*, New York: Basic Books.

Bosch, S. (1983) *Jenny lives with Eric and Martin*, London: Gay Mens Press.

DES (1987) *Sex Education at School*. Circular 11/87, London: HMSO.

Dickson, A. (1985) *The Mirror Within: A New Look at Sexuality*, London: Quartet.

Fletcher, J. (1989) Freud and his uses: psychoanalysis and gay theory, in S. Shepherd and M. Wallis (eds) *Coming on Strong: Gay Politics and Culture*, London: Unwin Hyman.

Gordon, P. (1988) Sex therapy with gay men, in M. Cole and W. Dryden (eds) *Sex Therapy in Britain*, Milton Keynes: Open University Press.

Gordon, P. and Mitchell, L. (1988) *Safer Sex: A New Look at Sexual Pleasure*, London: Faber.

Green, J. and McCreaner, A. (eds) (1989) *Counselling in HIV Infection and AIDS*, Oxford: Basil Blackwell.

Hall, M. (1985) *The Lavender Couch: A Consumer's Guide to Psychotherapy for Lesbians and Gay Men*, Boston, Mass: Alyson.

Hite, S. (1976) *The Hite Report. A Nationwide Study of Female Sexuality*. New York: Dell.
—— (1982) *The Hite Report on Male Sexuality*. New York: Ballantine Books.
Kaplan, H.S. (1974) *The New Sex Therapy*, New York: Brunner/Mazel.
—— (1979) *Disorders of Sexual Behaviour*, New York: Brunner/Mazel.
—— (1983) *The Evaluation of Sexual Disorders*, New York: Brunner/Mazel.
McManus, T.J. and McEvoy, M.B. (1987) Some aspects of male homosexual behaviour in the United Kingdom, *British Journal of Sexual Medicine* April: 110–20.
McWhirter, D.P. and Mattison, A.M. (1984) *The Male Couple: How Relationships Develop*, Englewood Cliffs, NJ: Prentice-Hall.
Masters, W.H. and Johnson, V.E. (1970) *Human Sexual Inadequacy*, Boston, Mass: Little, Brown.
—— (1979) *Homosexuality in Perspective*, Boston, Mass: Little, Brown.
Norwood, R. (1986) *Women Who Love Too Much*. London: Arrow Books.
Reece, R. (1988) Causes and treatments of sexual desire discrepancies in male couples, in E. Coleman (ed.) *Integrated Identity for Gay Men and Lesbians*, New York: Harrington, Cork.
Rochlin, M. (1981/2) Sexual orientation of the therapist and therapeutic effectiveness with gay clients, *Journal of Homosexuality* 7, 2/3: 21–9.
Socarides, C. (1979) The psychoanalytic theory of homosexuals, in I. Rosen (ed.) *Sexual Deviation*, Oxford: Oxford University Press.
Tennot, D. (1979) *Love and Limerance: The Experience of Being in Love*, New York: Stein & Day.
van den Aardweg, G.J.M. (1984) Parents of homosexuality – not guilty? Interpretation of childhood psychological data, *American Journal of Psychotherapy* 38: 180–9.
Watney, S. (1989) Psychoanalysis, sexuality and AIDS, in S. Shepherd and M. Wallis (eds) *Coming on Strong: Gay Politics and Culture*, London: Unwin Hyman.
Westwood, G. (1960) *A Minority: A Report on the Life of the Male Homosexual in Britain*, London: Longman.
Zilbergeld, B. (1978) *Male Sexuality: A Guide to Sexual Fulfilment*, Boston, Mass: Little, Brown.

# 12

# Couple therapy with lesbians

## SHOSHANA SIMONS

### Introduction: the wider social context

There is hardly any information available in Britain on the subject of therapeutic work with lesbians which is non-pathological. As a result of misinformation, prejudice and institutionalized homophobia, the specific needs of lesbians for support in their intimate relationships is largely ignored. In view of this fact, my primary area of concern here is to explore the notion of a therapeutic setting in which lesbians may be enabled to reveal difficulties in their intimate relationships without fear that their sexuality will be considered as the problem itself.

To this end, the key issue relevant to the effective counselling of lesbian couples is the eradication of homophobia in the counselling setting. If the therapist is able to be aware of the effects of homophobia on her or himself, on the clients and on the clients' relationships, the areas of interpersonal and individual emotional difficulties will be easier to address.

George Weinberg (1972) first coined the term *homophobia*. It refers to fear of closeness with members of the same sex and more broadly to the irrational hatred and intolerance of lesbians and gay men which accompanies that fear. Weinberg suggests six potential underlying factors which may contribute to manifestations of homophobia in individuals.

1  inculcated fear of closeness with a member of the same sex in childhood
2  taboos instituted by religious injunction
3  secret fears of one's own homosexual feelings
4  repressed envy of the apparent choice lesbians and gay men have to 'be themselves'
5  fear of undermining societal norms and values which define acceptable sex-role stereotyped behaviour for men and women
6  concern about not existing vicariously through reproducing the next generation.

Popular myths see lesbians as pseudo men. Lesbians are classified pathologically as a subheading beneath homosexual men. In reality, the therapeutic issues which arise between two women relate largely to the wider therapeutic issues in working with women in general. For example women's psychosocial development seems to be constructed around the development of a finely tuned empathy for others and the subsuming of personal needs to the needs of partners, children, and so on (Gilligan 1982; Baker Miller 1976; Turner 1987; Surrey 1984). This evidently has enormous implications when looking at the dynamics in intimate relationships between two women (Vargo 1987). Additionally cultural injunctions against assertive female behaviour can have a profound impact on lesbian relationships. For example many women express difficulties in asserting sexual needs. Between two women, the likelihood is greater that both partners will experience difficulties in similar areas.

However, invisibility, lack of external recognition, lack of definition of relationship and social discrimination can seriously damage the development of healthy and intimate connections between women. This point will be illustrated with a case example from my clinical practice later in this chapter.

## Homophobia in the mental health profession

Hite (1988) established in 1987 that as many as one woman in eleven in the USA defined herself as a lesbian and that 24 per cent of lesbians over 40 in her study were having relationships with women for the first time. The majority of them had been previously heterosexually married, suggesting that sexuality is not a 'fixed' phenomenon but is fluid throughout the life-cycle (Kinsey *et al.* 1953).

Despite facts such as these, very little attention has been paid in the world of psychotherapy and counselling to the needs of lesbians, both as individuals and in their relationships. Furthermore, despite the abolition of homosexuality as a separate category of mental illness by the American Psychiatric Association in 1973 (although no similar public declaration has been made in Britain), lesbians continue to report the pathologizing of their sexuality by counsellors and therapists who, even if they purport to be supportive of lesbians, still use theories which seek to find the 'cause' of their lesbianism (Richardson 1987).

In a study of the attitudes of forty male and forty female psychotherapists in Berkeley and San Francisco, California (areas known for their large lesbian and gay populations and more liberal attitudes towards their communities) it was found that lesbians and gay men were perceived to be less psychologically healthy than heterosexual men and women. Garfinkle and Morin (1978) discovered that

> Therapists were found to rate the same hypothetical psychotherapy client somewhat differently when the client was homosexual than when the client was heterosexual. Homosexual clients were seen as significantly less healthy than heterosexual clients on a measure of female sex role stereotyped characteristics.
>
> (Garfinkle and Morin 1978: 109)

In fact some evidence suggests that, despite the pervasiveness of homophobia, lesbians do not differ significantly from heterosexual women in terms of mental health problems (Duffy and Rusblut 1985; Rothblum 1988).

Furthermore, in terms of relationship satisfaction, various studies have pointed to a great sense of satisfaction for women both emotionally and sexually in lesbian relationships (Masters and Johnson 1979; Peplau *et al.* 1978; Kinsey *et al.* 1953). Hite's (1988) study indicated that 96 per cent of lesbians felt loved in a satisfying way and treated as an equal by their partners whereas 93 per cent of heterosexual women believed that they were trying harder than their male partners to make the relationship work.

What *is* significantly different as a factor affecting lesbian relationships is the pressure and stresses associated with the damaging effects of homophobia which the lesbian has to contend with. These include the internalization of negative stereotypes of lesbians by lesbians themselves as well as the effects of sexism and female socialization, an experience shared by all women. An exercise which I do in lesbian relationships groups is for the participants to imagine how their lives might be if there were no homophobia. Because *invisibility* is central to the way homophobia functions, the idea of imagining its *absence* enables participants to see the extent to which homophobia saturates everyday life, often without their knowing. Such an exercise also serves to put relationship problems into a wider social context. Recurring examples of comments by lesbians in these groups include the following.

> I wouldn't have to be cautious about being affectionate with my partner in public.
> We would be able to chit chat with the neighbours about everyday things.
> Our children wouldn't have a "skeleton in the cupboard".
> My parents would allow my partner to come home with me during the holidays.
> I would be able to be honest with my workmates about my home life.

## The role of the therapist working with lesbian couples

In a society which renders lesbian relationships invisible, the therapist may be the only witness to the relationship. Prior to such therapeutic work, lesbian couples generally have to be witnesses for their own coupling, witnesses for themselves as individuals and witnesses for each other. Hall (1988) stresses that this overloads a relationship; she also suggests that lesbian couples can feel that they are entitled to attention for their relationships only when there are problems.

This crucial lack of external witnesses confers upon the therapist a different set of roles in relation to the lesbian couple than to the heterosexual couple. The counsellor of lesbian couples may be the only person to affirm that the relationship does, in fact, exist. This involves a willingness on the part of the therapist to take the relationship seriously, even when the internalized homophobia of the clients may prevent one or both of them from doing so.

Reflective of the fact that lesbians *themselves* also internalize negative feelings about themselves as a result of homophobia, couples seeking relationship counselling can feel that any problems they are experiencing are confirmation of an inherent 'problem' in being a lesbian. For the heterosexual, the popular culture mirrors the 'naturalness' of relationship difficulties. A plethora of images and information are available to affirm the heterosexual relationship and the likelihood of problems arising between two closely involved human beings. From radio phone-ins to problem pages in magazines, the culture affirms and confirms the normality of problems in heterosexual relationships. Lesbians have no external images to turn to for affirmation, save those which are created by the lesbian communities themselves.

However, despite the odds, some therapists are developing ways of counteracting homophobia in the counselling setting. For example Riddle and Sang (1978) explore the ways that therapeutic bias towards heterosexuality can affect therapeutic work with lesbians. They state that it is important that the therapist is able to separate out those concerns associated with homophobia from those associated with individual intrapsychic issues.

*Case example: Lynette and Andrea*
Lynette and Andrea came to me eighteen months into their relationship. Their presenting problem was based around the fact that they had difficulties communicating with each other, particularly around sex, and they had begun to row with each other a lot. Despite a previously satisfying sexual relationship, Andrea had 'pulled away' sexually from Lynette. Both women were from Jewish families and neither had had previous lesbian relationships. They had met through a Jewish Youth movement in which they were both very involved. Each woman expressed a fear of 'disappointing' her family by not seeking out men to marry. They presented themselves to their respective parents as 'flatmates'.

Sessions were spent exploring what each woman enjoyed about the relationship. Not only joy at the intensity and intimacy of connection but also fear of such closeness were expressed. Andrea expressed ambivalence about their mutual love, fearing that if she 'gave in' to her feelings for Lynette she would have to accept that she was a lesbian. In exploring the implications of the fact that they *were* already involved in a lesbian relationship, it became clear that a lot of grieving would have to be done. Andrea said that she would have to let go of the fantasy that 'Prince Charming' would some day come along and look after her. Being a lesbian meant having to 'look after yourself' financially, for the rest of your life; psychologically risk feeling an outsider from the wider Jewish community as well as the family. She expressed that what had enabled her to remain in the relationship was a belief that the relationship was temporary and that she wasn't *really* a lesbian. However, the longer she and Lynette remained together, the more the pressure was building up inside the relationship.

Rather than deal with the real loss of heterosexual privilege the women were experiencing, both women were manifesting their negative feelings about being lesbian via forms of withdrawal from each other. Both women shared an underlying, unspoken belief that if the sex stopped, maybe they would not have to deal with the reality of their 'unacceptable' relationship. However, Andrea carried these feelings for both of them, Lynette appearing as the 'wronged' partner, though in reality it seemed that either of them could have manifested the sexual withdrawal or sexual interest in order to counterbalance the other.

Work on the area of internalized homophobia proved crucial to Andrea and

Lynette being able not only to resume their sexual relationship, but also to develop strategies for coming out to their families. Enabling each woman to put into words the unacceptable feelings she had towards her partner was crucial to this work. For example during one of the sessions I encouraged Andrea to say out loud to Lynette 'Thank God it's *you* who's the lesbian in this relationship!' Both women laughed, seeing the ridiculousness of this rationalization. However, unarticulated rationalizations such as these can act as defences against the pain of claiming one's right to love another woman. The counsellor's willingness to communicate both verbally and non-verbally their *own* comfort with lesbian sexuality is pivotal to the creation of a safe environment within which lesbians can express negative feelings about their sexuality including the pain surrounding experiences of rejection by society.

## The lesbian couple in the context of lesbian cultures

There is no ascribed, taken-for-granted role for a lesbian to play out in a relationship, such as wife or husband. This is often one of the most enjoyable aspects of lesbian relationships, expressing a freedom from the constraints of sex-role-defined behaviour which can bedevil heterosexual relationships. However, it means that lesbians often get caught up in how to define their relationships in the absence of any externally recognized boundaries. Identities are often worked out in relation to friendship networks and social groupings within the wider lesbian communities and beyond. These can include support groups such as lesbian mothers' groups, black lesbian groups, political activities and general community activities.

Relationships between lesbians are frequently multi-layered and often initially based in friendship (Oberstone and Sukoneck 1976; Vetere 1982). This in itself is reflective of the general tendency towards strong friendship bonds between women. However, coupled with the absence of external markers to delineate the beginnings and endings of relationships, many lesbians can experience a sense of confusion as to the status of their relationships if the sexual side diminishes. The question of whether a couple who are non-sexual are still a couple remains the single most recurring presenting problem of women who come for counselling. Additionally the fear of loss of the primary friendship can be an important factor for lesbians when either partner meets a new potential lover.

### Case example: Lena and Mara

Lena and Mara had been together for three years before their initial consultation. Mara was the mother of a 6-month-old son. The couple had ceased being sexual two years previously yet still spent most of their leisure time together. Lena had been present at the birth of Mara's son and had played an active role as a co-parent. The sexual side of the relationship ended as Lena had 'lost interest'. Lena subsequently had an affair with another woman which she considered to be based more on sex than emotional involvement. As such, Mara had not experienced it as a threat. Now, however, Lena had met another woman whom she felt emotionally as well as sexually involved with. Mara now felt in dread of 'losing' Lena and in so doing losing not only her best friend but also a physical and intimate if non-sexual relationship. Both women described their non-sexual closeness as having all the attributes of a lover's relationship without sexual intimacy. In view of this, the couple stated their presenting concern as 'What does it mean to "end" our relationship when we still want to be together?'

Hall (1987) describes this kind of relationship as the 'third state', a kind of relationship which heterosexual definitions of intimate relationship fail to encompass. However, it is such a common feature of lesbian relationships that it deserves to be named.

The work in the counselling sessions consisted initially of my playing the role of 'witness' for a relationship which was very close, caring and intimate but which was 'not meant to exist'. This proved to be central in enabling both women to *themselves* validate the importance of their relationship. Central to successful work with this couple was the provision of a mirror for their relationship, validating the joys of connection, the fear of loss and the sadness of change in the face of invisibility. As a result, it became easier for each woman to consider her *own* individual issues about separation in order to work out jointly what kind of relationship they wanted for the future, secure in the knowledge that I could hold on to the reality of their depth of connection as an important external witness.

## Sexuality of the therapist

Does the sexuality of the therapist have any bearing on the successful counselling of lesbian couples? There can be advantages and disadvantages associated with the choice of heterosexual, lesbian or gay therapists. Overall, however, successful therapeutic relationships depend more on the quality of relationship between therapist and client than on the sexual preference or life-style of the therapist. The problem is that a shortage of 'out' (lesbians who do not hide their sexuality) lesbian therapists means that a real choice is frequently not available.

### Lesbian therapist, lesbian clients

In a discussion of the relevance of shared background between therapist and client, Rochlin (1981/2) cites a number of studies which suggest the value of congruent background between therapist and client, including congruence of race, gender and sexual preference. Riddle and Sang (1978) support this view, seeing the therapist who is able to act as a positive role model for lesbians as distinctly advantageous. Furthermore, where lesbians do not have to explain every 'nuance and stress' of their lives to the therapist, the therapeutic process can be 'accelerated'. Liljestrand et al. (1978) found a trend towards more positive therapeutic outcomes when client and therapist were of the same gender or same sexual orientation.

Gartrell (1984), in line with Rochlin, sees appropriate communication of knowledge and information about lesbian or gay community and culture as an important part of the therapist's role. This may be particularly true in the case of isolated lesbian couples. This is supported by Riddle and Sang (1978), who see the encouragement of the lesbian to build a supportive environment for herself as one of the roles of the therapist. For many lesbians, social isolation is not only a 'personal problem' but also a reflection of the isolation experienced as a result of lesbian invisibility. Riddle and Sang caution, however, against the tendency to collapse lesbians and gay men into one 'homosexual' category. Gay males, including gay male therapists, share the same socialization as heterosexual males and are no less likely to hold sexist attitudes as a result. These attitudes can be as damaging to the lesbian client as the homophobic attitudes of the unaware heterosexual therapist.

Furthermore, having a lesbian as a therapist is also not necessarily a safeguard against homophobic practice. Gartrell (1984) emphasizes the importance of 'out' lesbians working with lesbian clients. She argues that simply being lesbian is not the sole requirement for understanding the workings of homophobia. A lesbian therapist who has not dealt with her own internalized homophobia is likely to share the same homophobic attitudes as her client, leading to a possibly damaging collusion with homophobia in the counselling process. Margolies *et al.* (1987) echo this view. While recognizing that some lesbian therapists are not able to disclose their sexuality at work, and that it is not necessarily always appropriate, they need to assess how far internalized homophobia has informed that decision. Margolies *et al.* (1987) stress that decisions about if and when the therapist should 'come out' to clients need to be examined in relation to the treatment issues of each client. However, internalized homophobia in either heterosexual or lesbian therapists will certainly have consequences in the transference relationship.

### Heterosexual therapist, lesbian clients

There may be possible advantages for clients in consulting a heterosexual therapist who is conscious of her homophobia. Such a therapist, situated outside of lesbian internalized homophobia, can act as a positive contradiction to the assumption of negative reception that many lesbian couples expect. Furthermore, such a therapist, sensitized to internalized homophobia, can be effective in challenging negative statements, modelling for the lesbian client a heterosexual response which is unexpectedly non-collusive with the client's own self-denigration. Additionally the aware and active heterosexual therapist who is the 'personification' of heterosexual society can act as a conductor for the feelings of anger lesbians may carry. It is rarely safe enough for these feelings to be expressed directly at individuals and institutions which have abused the client for being lesbian. In view of the fact that most lesbians are the daughters of heterosexual parents, the transference relationship with a heterosexual therapist may well help by raising the core of painful issues which need to be addressed in terms of rejection by families of origin.

A common defensive strategy that a lesbian couple may use to defend themselves against feared rejection or judgements by the therapist is to build an alliance against him or her. Furthermore, the couple may try to minimize the problems they are having in their relationship in an attempt to portray lesbian relationships, and therefore their *own* object choice in a positive light.

The heterosexual therapist therefore needs to be aware that interpretations of such defensive behaviour need to address the actual relationship between couple and therapist in the consulting room as well as addressing the interpersonal and intrapsychic issues which the transference relationship will inevitably raise.

Hall (1981) suggests that therapists working with lesbian couples and families need to appraise their feelings and attitudes towards their clients. For example the therapist can ask herself whether she finds her client's life-style acceptable as an abstraction, but becomes distressed to imagine her 'actually involved in those activities?'

However, if therapists have strong feelings of fear, repulsion or pity for lesbians, they should on no account take on lesbian clients until such feelings have been satisfactorily worked through. Hall also suggests that therapists need to raise such questions with themselves, their co-workers and in training workshops. Additionally they need to become more aware of the lesbian subculture. It may also be appropriate at times to use lesbian therapists as consultants when counselling lesbian couples. Lesbian relationship patterns can look very different from those of heterosexual relationships and need to be understood within their own social context. For example the lesbian communities have their own alternative framework of support systems and ethics. These have evolved as a positive response to invisibility, lack of socially sanctioned recognition, and the compounded effects of female socialization and sexism.

## Conclusion

This chapter touches on some of the issues which therapists need to bear in mind when consulted by lesbian couples. Its brevity reflects the invisibility experienced by lesbians in society. As yet, there is hardly any published research on therapeutic work with lesbian individuals, let alone the specific issues relevant to couples from a non-pathological perspective in Britain.

Therapists need to review their personal and professional beliefs about lesbians and their relationships, using lesbian and gay communal organizations as resource and consultants. Existing literature from standard textbooks sadly reinforce pathological assumptions about the 'nature' of lesbianism.

Although I have emphasized looking at the lesbian couple in the light of homophobia in this article, this is in no way meant to suggest that there are not important relational issues which arise in lesbian couples, perhaps differently from heterosexual couples. There has not been the space here to do justice to this broad topic, but I hope that there will be more opportunities to research, develop and publish information on therapeutic issues for lesbian couples over the coming years. However, the development of such a body of knowledge had to go hand in hand with increasing training opportunities for lesbians as counsellors and psychotherapists as well as willingness on the part of existing practitioners to treat the object choices of their clients with the full respect that they deserve.

Until lesbianism is taken out of the realms of pathology, lesbians will continue to find it hard to enter counselling and psychotherapy training. Without trained lesbian therapists, developments in this area of couple therapy will be severely limited.

## References

Baker Miller, J. (1976) *Towards a New Psychology of Women*, Harmondsworth: Penguin.
Duffy, S.M. and Rusblut, C.E. (1985) Satisfaction and commitment in homosexual and heterosexual relationships, *Journal of Homosexuality* 12, 2: 1–23.
Garfinkle, E.M. and Morin, S. (1978) Psychologist's attitudes towards homosexual psychotherapy clients, *Journal of Social Issues* 34, 3: 101–12.
Gartrell, N. (1984) *Issues in Psychotherapy with Lesbian Women*, Stone Center for Developmental Services and Studies, Wellesley College, Mass.
Gilligan, C. (1982) *In a Different Voice*, Cambridge, Mass: Harvard University Press.
Hall, M. (1981) Lesbian families: cultural and clinical issues, in E. Howell and M. Bayes (eds) *Women and Mental Health*, New York: Basic Books.
—— (1987) Reflections on the new lesbian (un)couple, Paper presented at conference entitled 'Homosexuality – Which Homosexuality?', Amsterdam Free University, 15–18 December.
—— (1988) Bridging the gap between mystique and mistake, Workshop presentation at International Congress on Mental Health Care for Women, University of Amsterdam, 19–22 December.
Hite, S. (1988) *Women and Love*, Harmondsworth: Penguin.
Kinsey, A.C., Pomeroy, W.B. and Martin, C.E. (1953) *Sexual Behaviour in the Human Female*, Philadelphia, Pa: W.B. Saunders.
Kurdek, L.A. and Schmitt, J.P. (1987) Perceived emotional support from family and friends in members of homosexual, heterosexual married and heterosexual co-habiting couples, *Journal of Homosexuality* 14, 3/4: 57–68.
Liljestrand, P., Gerling, E. and Saliba, P.A. (1978) The effects of social sex role stereotypes and sexual orientation on psychotherapeutic outcomes, *Journal of Homosexuality* 3:
Margolies, L., Becker, M., and Jackson-Brewer, K. (1987) Internalised homophobia: identifying and treating the oppressor within, in Boston Lesbian Psychologies Collective (eds) *Lesbian Psychologies*, University of Illinois Press.
Masters, W.H. and Johnson, V.E. (1979) *Homosexuality in Perspective*, Boston, Mass: Little, Brown.
Morin, S. (1977) Heterosexual bias in psychological research on lesbianism and male homosexuality, *American Psychologist* 32, 8: 629–37.
Oberstone, A.K. and Sukoneck, H. (1976) Psychological adjustment and lifestyle of single lesbian and single heterosexual women, *Psychology of Women Quarterly* 1, 2.
Peplau, L.A., Cochran, S., Rock, K. and Padesky, C. (1978) Loving women: attachment and autonomy in lesbian relationships, *Journal of Social Issues* 34, 3.
Richardson, D. (1987) Recent challenges to traditional assumptions about homosexuality: some implications for practice, *Journal of Homosexuality* 13, 4: 1–12.
Riddle, D.I. and Sang, B. (1978) Psychotherapy with lesbians, *Journal of Social Issues* 34, 3: 84–100.
Rochlin, M. (1981/2) Sexual orientation of the therapist and therapeutic effectiveness with gay clients, *Journal of Homosexuality* 7, 2/3: 21–9.
Rothblum, E.D. (1988) Lesbianism as a model of positive lifestyle for women: Introduction to 'Lesbianism: Affirming Non Traditional Roles', in E.D. Rothblum and E. Cole (eds) *Women and Therapy* 8, 1/2.
Surrey, J. (1984) *Self-in-Relation: A Theory of Women's Development*, Work in Progress no 13, Stone Center for Developmental Services and Studies, Wellesley College, Mass.

Turner, C.W. (1987) *Clinical Application of the Stone Center Theoretical Approach to Minority Women*, Work in Progress no 28, Stone Center for Developmental Services and Studies, Wellesley College, Mass.

Vargo, S. (1987) The effects of women's socialisation on lesbian couples, in Boston Lesbian Psychologies Collective (eds) *Lesbian Psychologies*, University of Illinois Press.

Vetere, V. (1982) The role of friendship in the development and maintenance of lesbian love relationships, *Journal of Homosexuality* 8, 2.

Weinberg, G. (1972) *Society and the Healthy Homosexual*, New York: Anchor.

# 13

# The split couple: conciliation and mediation approaches

LISA PARKINSON

## Problems of ending relationships

This chapter focuses on the difficulties which couples experience in *uncoupling* from each other during separation or divorce and the ways in which conciliators and mediators seek to help them. In a book about therapeutic work with couples, a chapter about helping couples to uncouple may sound negative, even destructive. The uncoupling process can indeed be chaotic and disruptive, lacking rules or guidelines to help former partners disengage from each other in reasonably controlled and constructive ways. The ending of a close relationship is often full of pain, guilt, depression and fear. Even those who have the support of a new partner may find the adjustment to a new relationship and living arrangements very problematic, especially if they are still partly entangled in the old ones.

In separation or divorce, individual identity and security are profoundly threatened. Crisis may follow crisis in a predictable yet unmanageable way. These crises deplete both partners' physical and psychological energy and erode the hope that things may eventually improve. What feels like a state of anarchy at a personal level may then be exposed to an alien public world – a world in which lawyers communicate with each other about their clients' personal affairs in language that is unfamiliar, intimidating and, for some people, wholly incomprehensible. In some cases, the experience of losing the whole meaning and purpose of one's life becomes a life-threatening crisis.

Professionals who work with separating and divorcing couples and their children need skills in providing counselling, non-directive support, and conflict management. Professional helpers also need to understand the extraordinarily complex range of emotional and practical adjustments that individuals and couples need to manage in separation and divorce (Bohannan 1970).

*Emotional adjustments*

Each partner has to cope with the emotional task of accepting the end of the relationship. This is often the longest and most difficult task of all, especially for those who are divorced against their will. There seem to be few couples who want a divorce equally. Much more often, the decision to end the relationship is taken by one partner and very reluctantly accepted or actively resisted by the other.

Those who feel they are the innocent victims of the other's selfish or irresponsible behaviour may get trapped inside a self-constructed cage of bitterness and hurt. Some find it very difficult to open the door of this cage, to allow other perceptions or new relationships to come in, or to walk out into a life that may still offer some positive experiences.

*Financial adjustments*

Financial problems add enormously to the emotional stresses of divorce. How can two households be supported by an income that, in some cases, barely supported one? The partner who leaves the family home may have nowhere to go and there may be no capital to buy even a small flat, if the family home is still needed by the remaining partner and the children. Some couples agree that the matrimonial home should be sold and the capital divided between them, but there is often not enough capital to purchase two homes. If interest rates are high, it may not be possible to keep up mortgage payments on one home, let alone two.

Trying to maintain a home on a greatly reduced income causes intense anxiety. Even where there appears to be enough money to support two households, disputes over its division and control often reflect deep anger about the way power was held in the marriage. We live in a society preoccupied and dominated by the acquisition of wealth or the struggle against poverty. Financial problems – and the problems many couples have in talking about their money and the way it is spent – are one of the commonest features of marital breakdown. Many women have no knowledge of their husband's earnings or business affairs and some have been dependent on their husband paying all the bills.

The control of the family's finances by one partner – often, the husband – is a major source of power imbalance in many marriages. The re-allocation of money and its control in divorce can involve major adjustments for both partners.

*Parental and social adjustments*

Many separated parents struggle to care for their children, often without adequate support from the other parent. Children's needs in divorce do not always coincide with the needs of the parent looking after them and their feelings may be misunderstood even by loving parents (Mitchell 1985; Parkinson 1987; Wallerstein and Kelly 1980). Children need extra time, reassurance and comfort from their parents just when adults may be least able to give it, because they themselves are overburdened and confused.

Many separated parents find it very hard to work out joint decisions concerning the children. They may also find it very hard to explain the arrangements to the children without putting blame on the other parent. Parents need to be able to manage their own feelings about each other and about the divorce, if co-parenting after divorce is to work in practice.

Each partner in a divorce has to deal with the psychological and social tasks of redefining their identity and social status, either as a single person or as a partner in a new relationship. Those who feel rejected and stuck in the trauma of an unwanted divorce may find it very hard to rebuild their self-esteem and reorganize their lives. Former friends of the couple or family may be lost in moving to a new home and new neighbourhood.

There are major adjustments for adults and for children if the divorce entails moving to a new, usually smaller home, in an unfamiliar environment.

## Court-ordered adjustments

The legal process of obtaining a divorce and related orders concerning children, financial provision and property is often complicated by disputes, delays and high costs. Although the UK may be moving towards no-fault divorce and joint petitions (Law Commission 1990), the partner who takes the first steps to initiate divorce proceedings is still likely to take unilateral decisions. The other partner is then often pushed into a defensive, reactive role. This polarization can be found even in consensual divorces based on two years' separation.

Most people have only vague knowledge of divorce law and find its language and procedures alien and daunting. The difficulties are even greater for those from ethnic minorities, especially if English is their second language. Solicitors are generally seen as a source of information and advice, but many people want to avoid going to a solicitor because they fear high legal costs and acrimonious legal battles.

However helpful and conciliatory the solicitors may be, the experience of legal proceedings and, in some cases, appearing in court, adds to the trauma of the divorce.

## Negotiating or fighting through solicitors

Some couples involved in separation and divorce have a sense of being at total cross-purposes with each other. The shift from marital partner to divorce opponent can happen surprisingly quickly, especially if warring partners fire at each other from opposite sides of the emotional and legal 'frontier' between them. A divorce petition based on the respondent's 'unreasonable behaviour' can cause an immediate explosion and lasting pain and anger. Although many solicitors do try to take a conciliatory approach, their involvement tends to increase the distance between husband and wife by removing the need for direct communication between them. This makes joint decision-making by the couple much more difficult.

Unilateral decisions by one party tend to lead to confrontation or passive resistance by the other. This generates negative energy: denial, frustration, anger, the desire for retaliation. Some couples ask if one solicitor can see them both, but solicitors are prevented by their professional practice rules from advising two parties who have a conflict of interest. Moreover, their legal training does not equip them to deal with complicated emotional and family problems. Many solicitors specializing in divorce and family work favour the conciliatory approach promoted by the Solicitors Family Law Association, but there are still a fair number who work in a traditional, adversarial way. Even a conciliatory solicitor may be forced into an aggressive stance on behalf of his or her client. Sharply worded letters and affidavits, making acrimonious allegations and preemptory demands, may evoke a retaliatory response from 'the other side' – and thus the battle-lines are drawn.

Vaughan (1986) illuminates these issues in a study of how – not why – people make transitions out of relationships. She found that uncoupling is primarily a tale of two transitions, one of which begins before the other. In many cases, one partner decides to disengage from the relationship while the other wants it to continue. The uncoupling process is far more difficult if each partner embarks on it at a different point in time from the other, and with contradictory objectives. The couple may then find themselves pulling in opposite directions, pursuing contrary aims, just when all their resources are needed to solve common problems. Individuals who still feel emotionally bound to their former partner, although legally divorced, may feel left in an emotional limbo and this may prevent them moving into new activities and relationships.

The legal process of divorce works rather like a conveyor-belt, picking up petitioners and applicants at one end and dropping them off at the other, with a divorce decree and related court orders, but not necessarily any feeling of resolution. At a personal and private level, individuals have to find their own route through various stages of emotional and family adjustment. These personal routes are largely uncharted and lack signposts.

The divorce rate in England and Wales increased sixfold from 1960 to 1980 and is one of the highest in Europe. Considering the very large numbers of people who divorce (often more than once) and the high levels of stress they tend to experience, the help available is scarce and poorly funded. Many marital counsellors and therapists undertake divorce counselling. However, divorce counselling is frequently not distinguished conceptually and in terms of service provision from marital counselling or from conciliation (Clulow and Vincent 1987; Parkinson 1985). Until the 1970s, when divorce became more available and widespread, there were no services concerned solely and specifically with the provision of 'conciliation' or 'mediation'. These terms are used here interchangeably, to denote a process of dispute settlement in which separating or divorcing couples are helped by neutral third parties – 'conciliators' or 'mediators' – to reach agreed decisions, instead of taking their disputes to court.

## Family conciliation services

Since the late 1970s family conciliation services have been set up in many parts of the country, mainly through local initiatives. The primary aim of these services is to reduce divorce conflicts over children. Researchers (Mitchell 1985;

Wallerstein and Kelly 1980; Maclean and Wadsworth 1988) have shown the very serious effects on children of losing contact with a parent and/or being torn between warring parents. The huge increase in divorce has brought greater awareness of the suffering involved, for adults and for children. This awareness has led many professionals to look for better ways of helping families cope with the trauma and transitions of marital breakdown and divorce – ways that do not require couples to denigrate each other in order to obtain a divorce, nor to engage in bitter wrangles over children and money.

Most divorce courts and many magistrates' courts have introduced conciliation procedures to help settle disputes at an early stage in the legal process. In-court conciliation is often confined to a single appointment with a court welfare officer acting as a conciliator. This settlement-seeking approach has value, particularly if fully contested proceedings are avoided. However, some parents have complained of being pressed into 'agreements' by welfare officers invested with the court's authority (Lord Chancellor's Department 1989; Davis 1988).

There is already a considerable literature on conciliation in Britain (Lord Chancellor's Department 1989; Dingwall and Eekelaar 1988; Parkinson 1987) which shows a great diversity of approach among practitioners. In one of the first out-of-court services, run at Bromley under the auspices of South East London Probation Service (Davis and Roberts 1988) two conciliators meet with both parents to help them work out arrangements for their children. This is normally a one-off meeting, aimed at working out access arrangements. In some cases, a follow-up appointment may be offered. The children themselves do not normally take part.

Other well-established family conciliation services, such as the Bristol and Sheffield services, use a different model of conciliation in which a single conciliator usually sees each parent separately, to start with. These separate meetings may lead to one or more joint meetings with both parents. Researchers at the University of Newcastle undertook a three-year study of selected conciliation services for the Lord Chancellor's Department. They found in their study – which included the Bristol, Bromley and Sheffield services – that the average number of conciliation appointments was just over two per case (Lord Chancellor's Department 1989).

Brief interventions with couples in the turmoil of separation and divorce can help them focus on and settle some key issues. However, the Newcastle researchers found that if major issues about the family home and financial support remain unresolved, conciliated agreements about children may be short term, as they are liable to break down under the pressure of continuing conflict on other issues.

Conciliation services, both independent voluntary services and in-court services run by the Probation Service, generally focus on parental responsibilities and arrangements for children. In practice, however, it is often difficult or impossible to work out arrangements for children without dealing with the inter-related issues of the family home and financial support. There are direct links between these issues both in practical and emotional terms. Anger and problems in one area often exacerbate the problems in other areas. Conflict is not a static substance which remains in one place. Psychoanalytic theory suggests that conflict can be transferred or projected from one person or issue to another (Dicks

1967). In divorce, conflict easily seeps from one area of uncoupling to another. But if its properties are properly understood and handled carefully, conflict can also produce beneficial changes, not only harmful ones.

## Gender issues and co-working in conciliation

When conflict is intense, there is often a need and active search for partisan support and allies. Individuals may approach helping agencies in the hope that they will provide individual support and advice, not because they offer neutral, non-judgemental help to both partners. The image projected by a helping agency – in terms of whether it caters primarily for men or women or for both equally – naturally affects take-up and referral patterns.

A number of studies have shown that men are much less likely than women to seek help with marital, emotional or family problems (Brannen and Collard 1982; Blackie and Clark 1987). It is often wives rather than husbands, mothers rather than fathers, who turn to professionals for help. In the past, professionals often responded to the female help-seeker without seeking to engage the husband or father. Now it is much more common to offer conjoint counselling, family therapy or conciliation to both partners or the family as a whole. In practice, however, it is often difficult to engage both partners in a breaking or broken relationship in conjoint counselling or conciliation. They may be very reluctant to meet face to face. Some partners suspect – with or without justification – that a counsellor, social worker or therapist has already formed, or is likely to form, an alliance with the other partner. Men are more likely to reject an offer of counselling or therapy if they see it as simply 'talking about problems'. They tend to look for practical help and concrete solutions (Brannen and Collard 1982).

Although counselling agencies tend to have a higher proportion of female clients, it is significant that self-referrals to conciliation services are different and are as likely to come from men as from women. The Newcastle researchers found that fathers were drawn towards conciliation because conciliators support both parents' continuing relationship with their children (Lord Chancellor's Department 1989: para 17.34). Fathers who contact conciliation services are usually anxious to maintain their involvement with the children. Mothers may approach a conciliation service because of similar concerns about the children, sometimes because they want to reduce visits by the father, but also in some cases because they want the father to become more involved with the children. Women may, however, question what they have to gain from conciliation if they are expected to make concessions regarding the children, without attention being given to their equally pressing financial and housing needs (Lord Chancellor's Department 1989; Davis and Roberts 1988).

One partner may be deterred from taking part in conciliation by fears that his or her position will not be sufficiently understood and supported by the conciliator. Physical violence is a very common problem leading to separation and divorce. A woman who has suffered violence may understandably feel afraid of being confronted again by the man who has been violent to her, and whom she wishes to avoid. The man, on the other hand, may fear that a female conciliator may be consciously or unconsciously prejudiced against him.

In services which use one conciliator rather than two, one of the client couple is inevitably outnumbered in the room by two people of the other sex – the conciliator and the other partner. This can increase one partner's feeling of being 'one down', however skilled the conciliator may be in maintaining neutrality and balance. It is extremely difficult to maintain neutrality and balance in situations of intense conflict. Many conciliators have a strong preference for co-working – provided, of course, that they work well together. However, the shortage of male conciliators can result in two female conciliators working together, thus compounding the problems of gender imbalance.

Informal feedback from clients suggests that conciliators' personal qualities and skills matter more to them than the conciliators' sex. However, there are a number of advantages in using a male–female pair of workers, wherever possible, particularly where there is high conflict on gender-related issues.

## Comprehensive mediation

### Terminology

Before considering the extension of conciliation into comprehensive mediation, some comments on terminology may be helpful, as there is often confusion between terms that may sound similar – 'conciliation', 'reconciliation', 'mediation', 'comprehensive mediation' and 'arbitration'.

As noted earlier, the terms 'conciliation' and 'mediation' tend to be used interchangeably. In practice, however, 'conciliation' in Britain has usually been confined to helping parents work out agreed arrangements for their children – in other words, settling disputes over custody and access. (These terms, 'custody' and 'access', will have become obsolete with the introduction of the Children Act 1989.) The National Family Conciliation Council's Code of Practice (1985), drawn up in consultation with the Law Society and the Solicitors' Family Law Association, limits 'conciliation' to child-related issues, stating that detailed negotiations over finance and property matters should be left to solicitors.

One disadvantage of the term 'conciliation' is that it is often confused – particularly by members of the public but also by some professionals – with 'reconciliation', which is defined as helping couples to stay or get back together. Other English- and French-speaking countries generally use the term 'mediation' in preference to 'conciliation', not only because it avoids this confusion with reconciliation but also because mediation covers a wider range of issues than conciliation. Mediation is increasingly used in the wider sense of dispute settlement on any issue and in any context, including neighbourhood, commercial and other non-family disputes.

'Comprehensive mediation' in separation and divorce may be defined as a process in which couples at any stage of separation or divorce are helped to explore ways of settling any or all the issues that need to be settled between them, including financial and property matters. Helping couples to settle the issues of the family home, financial support and division of capital or other assets requires knowledge and experience in relation to legal and financial issues, as well as the conflict management skills needed in conciliation.

Irrespective of the issues that are being dealt with, there is a major difference between conciliation and mediation on the one hand, and arbitration on the other. Conciliators and mediators do not have power to impose a settlement on the parties. The parties are encouraged to work out their own solutions, instead of having decisions imposed by the court. This is also known as 'private ordering'.

In 'arbitration', by contrast, the arbitrator may direct how the dispute should be settled. In binding arbitration, the parties must agree in advance to be bound by the arbitrator's decisions.

## Professional issues

There are various models of comprehensive mediation, just as there are many different forms of conciliation. In Canada and the USA comprehensive mediation is established mainly in the private sector (Haynes 1981). It is undertaken mainly by counsellors, therapists and lawyers who offer mediation separately from their professional practice as lawyers or as therapists. This separation of different areas of professional practice is essential for lawyers, because they are prevented by their professional practice rules from advising or representing two parties who have, or may have, a conflict of interest.

Lawyer mediators need to work within a different set of professional practice rules from those that apply to them as solicitors or barristers. However, the need for rules and guidelines designed specifically for lawyer mediators is not confined to lawyers. Counsellors and social workers who work as mediators will find that issues of confidentiality may be handled differently in mediation from the way they are handled in counselling and social work. The confidentiality of legally privileged discussions differs from the confidentiality applicable in counselling or social work. In mediation, it is essential for mediators and both parties to know whether information provided in mediation could be used in evidence to the court by either party, and whether a mediator could be a compellable witness.

Mediators should have professional indemnity insurance as mediators, separately from their insurance as lawyers or counsellors, as a safeguard against possible negligence claims. If mediators from a counselling or social work background undertake mediation on financial and property issues without having sufficient legal and financial knowledge, they may do so at considerable risk. They are also limited in the help they can offer if they do not know within what range a court would order a settlement, in similar circumstances.

The knowledge and skills needed for comprehensive mediation are therefore drawn from a number of different disciplines. Mediation does not, however, consist solely of borrowings from other disciplines – it has its own concepts, rules of practice and core skills. In other words, comprehensive mediation is an emerging discipline in its own right, albeit a young one.

The practice of comprehensive mediation in Britain started with a pilot project in London called 'Solicitors in Mediation', undertaken from 1986 to 1988 by five divorce solicitors and a family conciliator. This project led to an interdisciplinary association, the Family Mediators Association (FMA), being founded in December 1988 to complement and extend the work of existing counselling, conciliation and legal services (Parkinson 1989).

In the model of comprehensive mediation used by the FMA, two mediators work jointly with couples on any issues arising from their separation or divorce that both parties want to settle. One mediator is a lawyer mediator with substantial experience in matrimonial and family law. The other co-mediator is qualified and experienced in marital and family work – usually an accredited Relate counsellor, conciliator, court welfare officer, family therapist or clinical psychologist.

Co-mediators need to work within a common framework of principles and practice rules and to have common objectives. Interdisciplinary co-mediation, using a lawyer mediator paired with a family conciliator or counsellor, has the additional advantages of the co-mediators having complementary knowledge and skills. They need to be able to trust each other and to communicate easily, so that they can draw from each other's areas of knowledge and expertise and integrate their joint expertise as co-mediators.

Before beginning to practise, FMA mediators take a five-day training in cross-disciplinary co-mediation. This training involves a considerable amount of experiential learning and it is followed by a period of apprenticeship, before accreditation can be applied for. Wherever possible, a mediator in training is paired with an experienced co-mediator from the opposite discipline: supervision and consultancy are provided by the FMA.

## The scope and organization of comprehensive mediation

The issues most commonly brought to mediation are the following.

1  the breakdown of the marriage – decisions concerning permanent separation or divorce
2  arrangements for the children
3  the family home – future occupation, division of equity, etc.
4  division of other assets
5  financial provision for spouse and/or children
6  pension provisions
7  contents of the home.

FMA mediators arrange joint meetings with both parties from the outset. The first main objective is to facilitate direct communication between them so that they can gain a better understanding of each other's concerns and priorities. The second main objective is to reduce conflict between them in helping them reach joint decisions, wherever possible. Couples are helped to consider the various options available and to work out agreed decisions, as far as possible, in relation to the 'reordering' of their personal and family life.

In some cases, and only with both parties' agreement, new partners and/or children may be invited to take part in a mediation meeting, for reasons and purposes agreed beforehand with both parties. The involvement of children or new partners would normally be suggested at a later stage of the mediation, and not at the beginning.

FMA mediators meet with both parties for sessions of one and a half hours. The number of sessions is rarely less than three and there may be eight or even more meetings, particularly if there are complicated financial and property issues. Either party is free to withdraw at any time and the mediators may also terminate the sessions if they think it inappropriate to continue. For example a partner who is very depressed may not be in a fit state to take decisions. He or she may need help from a doctor or therapist and mediation may have to be ended or at least suspended. In some cases, however, it is possible for mediation and counselling to take place concurrently.

The intervals between meetings can also be varied to meet the couple's needs. If the level of crisis is high, frequent meetings may be needed. In other situations, it may be helpful to allow time for reflection and some adjustment between meetings. The mediators often propose tasks for couples to undertake before the next meeting, such as obtaining valuations and finding out about property prices. Sometimes there is a series of meetings and then a gap of several months before the couple is ready to move on to the next stage of mediation.

Both the duration of the process and its outcome vary a great deal, as may be seen by following two different couples through the process. Before describing the work undertaken with these two couples, it may be helpful to list the twelve basic stages of FMA mediation in order to give an overview of the process as a whole.

## The stages of mediation

The process of mediation starts from the point of first contact with one or both partners – or former partners – and normally ends with a written summary drawn up by the mediators.

Stage  1    Engaging both partners
Stage  2    The mediation contract
Stage  3    Identifying issues
Stage  4    Agreeing the agenda for mediation
Stage  5    Sharing and analysing financial information
Stage  6    Considering children's needs and feelings
Stage  7    Working out options and budgets
Stage  8    Negotiating towards a settlement
Stage  9    Discussing with children and new partners
Stage 10    Summarizing positions and proposals
Stage 11    Drafting the summary of mediation
Stage 12    Reviewing with separate solicitors and formalizing as necessary

### Stage 1   Engaging both partners

Mediation by definition requires the involvement of both partners, since one cannot mediate with one. The first contact, however, often comes from one partner, without the other's knowledge. One of the first tasks, therefore, is to find out whether and how the second partner can be reached.

### Case example: Martin and Jill

In the first example of a couple using mediation, the initial contact was made by the husband, Martin, who explained that he had recently separated from his wife, Jill, after a ten-year marriage. He thought that Jill would be willing to come to mediation instead of going immediately to a solicitor. He undertook to talk to her about it, as they were still able to talk, despite Jill's extreme distress.

Rather than allowing Martin to go into details about the difficulties over the telephone, the mediator who took his call asked specific questions to establish whether mediation seemed appropriate and how an approach should be made to Jill. Martin was advised to assure Jill that he had not given a one-sided account of their problems, so that Jill would be able to accept the neutrality of the mediators. This neutrality is absolutely critical in building a relationship of trust with both partners.

Jill was asked via Martin to telephone to confirm her willingness to come to mediation. Once she had done so, she and Martin were asked to complete and return referral forms giving basic personal and family information and a short statement explaining their objectives in coming to mediation. Jill wrote as follows: 'I want to sort things out with a third party who is unbiased and who is aware of the emotions and fears involved in such a situation, and who also understands the law and each party's legal rights.' Martin wrote: 'I think this process will aid the both of us as we are still very much on talking terms but things went wrong when we talked about money. Basically I resent having to channel my divorce through solicitors when my wife and I could, I believe, come to some agreement without the endless barrage and to-ing and fro-ing of solicitors' letters.'

### Case example: Fergus and Irene

Whereas Jill and Martin were still on speaking terms, albeit painfully, another couple, Fergus and Irene, had already started divorce proceedings and were communicating solely via solicitors. Irene read about mediation in a newspaper and she sent a copy of the newspaper cutting to Fergus, saying 'I'll go to this if you will'. Each of them phoned the mediation service separately and an appointment offered to them both was accepted without any direct contact between them.

### Reception arrangements

Reception arrangements need to be made with particular sensitivity and care, bearing in mind that the husband and wife may not be on speaking terms and the level of stress when they first see each other may be extremely high. They should not be left on their own in the same waiting-room, if at all possible.

### Stage 2   The mediation contract

In addition to referral forms, FMA mediators send both partners, in advance of the first appointment, a formal letter explaining the basis on which mediation is offered to them, including the nature and extent of the confidentiality provided.

It is very important that both parties fully understand the mediators' role and the ground-rules of the process. The discussions that take place in mediation are legally privileged, so that neither party need fear that an offer or comment made in mediation could be used to disadvantage them in subsequent legal proceedings. This privilege and the limits of the confidentiality provided by mediators need to be carefully explained, so that the mediators' position is clear, particularly in situations involving allegations of domestic violence or suspected child abuse.

Whereas the discussions that take place in mediation are 'without prejudice', FMA mediators explain that factual, financial information is not legally privileged. This information is open to both parties, their legal advisers and the court. Both parties are asked to give a written undertaking to provide full financial disclosure. Most couples come to mediation in a state of great tension and anxiety and it is not easy for them to grasp these legal and technical explanations. However, mediators have a responsibility to explain the basis on which discussions will take place: people seem to welcome the respect and care that is shown in providing these explanations.

When meeting Jill and Martin for the first time, the mediators took time and care to introduce themselves and to explain the help they were offering, before asking them to countersign the letter accepting the mediation contract. The main problem in starting rather slowly in this fashion is that some people may feel impatient to get going and frustrated by explanations they may find irrelevant. If, however, the explanations are given clearly and with warmth, people usually appreciate the importance of understanding whether the information they give could be used in court or not.

## Stages 3–4 *Identifying issues and agreeing the agenda for mediation*

These two stages are usually the most difficult to manage. Feelings tend to run very high, the situation may be highly volatile, and the mediators have not yet had time to develop a close working relationship with each partner and with both of them together. Even the most basic facts about their situation – such as where each partner is currently living – may be confused or disputed. One partner is often in a dominant position – on some issues, at least.

If mediators begin by asking open-ended questions without directing the question towards either party specifically – such as, 'Could one of you explain how you see the main problems?' – there is a high risk of the more powerful or emotionally dominant partner taking over and excluding the weaker or less articulate one. If the mediators permit this to happen, they will probably lose control of the mediation at this point. Tempers will rise, the partner who comes under attack may burst into tears and, in some cases, flee from the room.

Mediators need to exercise considerable control, particularly in the early stages, in order to maintain balance, neutrality and a safe environment for both parties. This does not mean that feelings are ignored: it is usually essential to acknowledge feelings and to allow some expression of them. But mediators need to control how much feeling is expressed at any one time, if its expression threatens to overwhelm one or both parties.

For example, in mediating with Jill and Martin, Jill broke down in tears at an early stage in the first meeting and found it difficult to speak at all, although Martin was visibly trying not to make things worse. The mediators acknowledged Jill's distress explicitly, gave her coffee and a box of tissues and asked her if in spite of her distress it would be useful to talk about some of the practical questions that needed to be sorted out. Jill indicated her willingness to do so, and although her grief over the ending of the marriage was profound, the reassurance Martin gave her about continuing financial support seemed to reduce the stress and panic she was experiencing.

In the second case example, Irene presented as a forceful and very angry woman who was determined to have her say. If she had been invited to explain what she felt and what she wanted, there were risks that the resulting tirade against Fergus's 'unreasonable behaviour' might have overwhelmed him, before he had a chance to make any response. It was necessary to ask closed questions to each partner in turn, such as to Irene, 'Is the house in joint names?', and to Fergus, 'How often are you seeing the children?'

The presence of two mediators helps provide balance, support and control in these fraught encounters between partners who may not have talked face to face for some time. Many couples who come to mediation fear losing control and breaking down. Both mediators need to be sensitive to non-verbal signals as well as to things that are said. Although feelings are not explored in depth, acknowledging feelings and the need to find workable solutions helps people contain destructive outbursts against each other.

Mediators tend to use focused questions, directed to each partner more or less in turn. This method of gathering information and clarifying situations maintains a balance and gives both partners an active role. In some cases, both partners start talking with each other quite easily, as well as with the mediators. In other cases, they may respond only to the mediators and may avoid looking at or speaking to each other.

One way to help non-communicating couples talk directly to each other is to ask one partner to explain something to the other, with the emphasis on future plans rather than past events. Fergus was asked to explain to Irene whether he thought it would be possible for her to remain in the matrimonial home, which she was evidently terrified of leaving. This enabled him to give her the reassurance she needed that he was not intent on selling the house immediately.

One of the mediators reframed Fergus's absorption in his business – seen by Irene as neglect of her and the family – as his hard work to support the family and provide a good education for the children. Sending the children to private schools was a priority for both parents. At this point, they looked at each other, acknowledging some agreement about their priorities for the children.

### Stage 5 *Sharing and analysing financial information*

Full information about income, debts, property, other assets and circumstances is sought from both partners in order to consider with them how their needs and their children's needs can be provided for. Towards the end of the first meeting, each partner is given a detailed financial form to fill in at home and return to the mediators before the second meeting. This systematic gathering of written information about financial circumstances is an important element of comprehensive mediation which distinguishes it from conciliation limited to arrangements for children.

In a great many cases, one partner – usually the man – knows far more about the family's financial affairs than the woman. Women are seriously disadvantaged if they do not even know how much their partner earns. Life assurance and pension provisions are often unclear to both partners. Mediators need to ask questions which help couples gather information they previously lacked. Both partners are encouraged to explain points to each other to help them piece together a full picture of their position. The mediators clarify this picture and summarize the key facts, often using a flip-chart to make the picture clearer to the couple. One woman commented, 'This is the first time we've ever talked about money.'

The focus of this stage of mediation may seem to be all about money. However, money is often charged with very strong feelings. The ownership and use of the family's financial resources generally reflect power relationships between the couple. The skills of both mediators are needed to share and analyse financial facts, while also helping couples to communicate with each other about these facts. As knowledge is a source of power, helping women to become better informed about their partner's financial affairs can be a way of reducing power imbalances between them.

## Stage 6    Considering children's needs and feelings

It may be misleading to refer to this as 'Stage 6', as mediators may need to help parents focus on their children's needs and feelings in the earliest stages of mediation, as well as throughout the process. In the second case example, Fergus was very upset when he first came to mediation because he felt that Irene had been preventing him from seeing the children. There was therefore considerable discussion about the children at the first appointment. This led to both parents accepting a short-term plan for the children to visit Fergus at weekends, on certain conditions.

In many cases, however, arrangements for the children and how parental responsibilities will be shared cannot be worked out until there are clearer plans on other practical issues, such as housing. Otherwise, parents may be planning and negotiating in a vacuum, without knowing who will be living where and the distance between the two households.

Fergus and Irene recognized that each of them needed a home where their children could spend substantial amounts of time. At the fourth meeting, the mediators proposed that the parents might find it helpful to talk about each child individually, their perceptions of each child's needs and feelings and the children's relationships with each other. Fergus and Irene had been unable to talk together when they first came to mediation. The session focusing on the children proved very valuable in drawing them together as parents and easing communication between them. They were even able to laugh at times when they talked about the children – something that would have been quite unthinkable at the first meeting.

Martin, in the first case example, was interested to know whether the children would be seen by the mediators and given a chance to express their own views. Jill was strongly against involving them, fearing that this would put more pressure on them. The mediators engaged Jill and Martin in a detailed discussion about what they saw as the pros and cons of involving the children. In the end, it was agreed that Jill and Martin would first talk with the children at home, to explain some of the things the children probably needed to hear from them both. Then, when practical arrangements had been worked out between the parents, they would bring the children to a family meeting with the mediators to talk through the proposed arrangements and look at them from the children's point of view (see Stage 9).

### Stages 7–8   Working out options and budgets and negotiating towards a settlement

There are of course wide variations between different couples in the levels of conflict between them and the complexity of the options available. Some couples come with ready-made plans that they simply want to check through with neutral, well-informed professionals. Others come with heated disputes and no idea how to move forward.

Whatever the level of co-operation or dispute, it is usually helpful for mediators to identify and look at all the various options available, however unrealistic they may be. Sometimes an important possibility has been overlooked. At other times, couples who are in fierce conflict may both reject the same options. The surprise they show when they realize that they can agree on something – even, as in this case, a negative decision – can be a turning-point. Mediators may need, however, to draw their attention to areas of agreement which can otherwise slip past unnoticed.

Fergus and Irene had got embroiled in a struggle over the children dividing their time equally between each parent. This issue was tangled up with other issues about Irene's occupation of the family home and whether and when it should be sold. Fergus pointed out that he needed to buy a home for himself so that the children could stay with him.

The mediators first sought and obtained an agreement from them both that the children should be helped to keep their relationship and spend time with both parents. They then asked Fergus and Irene to make a full list of their monthly income and expenditure and to work out provisional budgets. Irene had never done this before, as Fergus had previously paid all the bills. Costs relating to the children were listed and taken into account in each parent's budget. Housing needs were discussed in detail and a number of options were considered relating to an immediate or deferred sale of the family home – a sale in about five years' time being Irene's preferred option – and possible ways of Fergus housing himself adequately in the mean time.

If mediators succeed in engaging couples in a problem-solving approach instead of win-or-lose battles, some couples' capacity to work together on problems can improve greatly. Others may remain hostile and entrenched. At one stage, Fergus and Irene were heading towards a bitter confrontation in court.

They needed a lot of time, support and patience from both mediators to work towards jointly agreed solutions. The mediators' expertise in relation to legal and financial issues was also essential, as life assurance policies and capital gains tax needed to be taken into account.

Couples who are unable to agree at all may none the less find it useful to work through options and budgets in a rational, future-oriented way. At the very least, major points of disagreement can be identified and clarified and each party may gain a better understanding of each other's position.

### Stage 9   *Discussing with children and new partners*

If parents are themselves able to work out plans that they can both accept, they also need to consider who else will need to accept them. If children or new partners refuse to co-operate, the arrangements are likely to break down. It is important to discuss with parents how arrangements will be explained or discussed with children, and whether the children or new partners should be invited to a meeting with the mediators.

When Jill and Martin felt ready for their two children to meet with the mediators, they recognized that the children might have worries that they had not expressed to either parent. This was indeed the case: meeting first with the children on their own, and then with them and their parents together, eased communications which had got blocked and tense. Martin said afterwards: 'It reduced the stress in the family an enormous amount. Michael [their 7-year-old son] has started kissing me good night again. He had stopped kissing me because he wasn't sure if it was all right or not.'

### Stages 10–12   *Summarizing positions and proposals, drafting the summary of mediation, reviewing with separate solicitors and formalizing as necessary*

Comprehensive mediation usually involves detailed written summaries produced by the mediators at the end of the process. There are in fact two documents. The first is a 'without prejudice' summary of the proposals that have been worked out. This may be a document of several pages, signed by both mediators, which sets out the proposed settlement in considerable detail. It is prepared for both parties to take to their separate solicitors for review and advice. If they decide, having been advised on it, that they want to turn it into a legally binding agreement, this can be done with little further trouble and cost. In cases where there is partial agreement or no agreement at all, the summary sets out each party's position and explains their priorities or particular concerns. This, too, can ease the legal process and help avoid lengthy exchanges of correspondence between solicitors.

The second document prepared at the end of the mediation is 'open', in the sense of it being available to the court as well as to the parties' solicitors. It lists all the relevant financial information concerning housing, capital, income, liabilities and other relevant considerations. The drafting skills of the lawyer mediator are particularly useful at this stage of mediation. However, both co-mediators need to be involved in drawing up these summaries. Each can learn a great deal from each other's insights and skills, and the care with which the summaries is worded may be very important from the clients' point of view.

## Towards a theoretical framework for mediation

Systems theory provides a useful framework for mediation, because the issues couples bring to mediation are usually interconnected, and each issue has repercussions on others. The divorce itself and the arrangements parents make for their children are closely connected with the practicalities of housing arrangements and financial support. Emotional stability and the sense of belonging to a community depend on how the family's practical and emotional resources are used. The different parts of the whole picture need to be viewed and worked on together, like an interlocking jigsaw. Concentrating on a single piece may be wasteful if other pieces then fail to fit around it.

The way families function – or fail to function – in separation and divorce may be seen as a product of three different levels of systemic functioning. It is helpful for mediators to understand these different systemic levels so that they can help families through the stressful transitions they need to make from one family structure to another.

First, there is the marital system and the interpersonal relationship between husband and wife. The way they communicate, directly or indirectly, verbally and non-verbally, needs to be taken into account by mediators and worked with, often explicitly. For example mediators may need to ask an enraged person to pause and listen to something the other is saying. Sometimes one partner is in too much distress and despair to be able to focus on practical arrangements. Joint meetings with both parties are stressful and painful. It may be necessary, however, for each partner to witness the other's anger or distress. Although they may be shaken by its force, some ventilation of the marital conflict may be necessary and, in some cases, cathartic. Mediators need sensitivity and fine judgement in deciding when to take control and when to allow a release of feeling.

Second, marital and family systems are very closely intertwined. It may not be possible to separate them. Communication between parents and children and the reactions of other family members, particularly children, need to be taken into account in planning arrangements for the family as a whole. It is important, therefore, to understand whether and how family members communicate with each other and whether there are other relatives or non-relatives to whom the children are closely attached.

The third level of system that is relevant to comprehensive mediation is the family system in its relation to wider social and economic systems – tax, welfare benefits, employment and pensions. Mediators need to be sufficiently familiar with these wider systems so that they can help couples understand when and how to use them. Although mediators aim to help couples avoid going to court, the legal system may be needed to rubber-stamp their arrangements. Welfare benefits may be needed to supplement the family's own resources.

The concept of clients and professionals meeting together in a circular system, rather than a hierarchical one, is also relevant. In mediation, both partners and the mediators have equal status in round-table discussions. This is very different from formal court proceedings in which the couple have inferior status and are allowed to speak only when called on to do so. In mediation, communication tends to move around the table in circular fashion: mediators may put the same question to the man and woman in turn, as their answers may differ. A response may be invited from each in order to promote a dialogue between them. Co-mediators may ask different kinds of questions; they do not have to speak with one voice. Different angles can be used to stimulate fresh thinking.

The laws of physics can provide a metaphor for the organization and dynamics of co-mediation. Let us take as an illustration a table decoration seen at a friend's house, which consisted of four carved wooden horses revolving on a platform, suspended by strings twisting around a central pole. The horses' movement seemed to provide a striking metaphor for the movement that takes place in co-mediation. As the horses spun around the pole, they rose upwards on the twisting strings. One form of energy was being converted into another. The kinetic energy of the rotating bodies was converted into potential energy by the upward lift of the twisting strings. Similar energy can be generated in co-mediation, using similar elements of balance and rotation in a circumscribed space.

The work done by couples and mediators together needs to rest on a common platform – that is the basic principles of mediation – with a focus towards the centre, that is the issues on the table. As all four people become involved in working on these problems, the circular exchange of ideas and feelings can generate its own momentum. Mediators need to balance these exchanges. They also need to provide structure, support, controls and positive thinking to generate some 'lift'. Otherwise, the couple can sink into destructive attacks or repetitive, unproductive circling. Mediators need to offer a combination of positive acknowledgement, focusing and personal warmth. This combination can lift quite depressed people to work on problems they had thought insoluble. Although the deeper roots of problems are not usually unravelled and people may remain angry and distressed, problem-solving energy can be generated between them instead of destructive energy.

To take the metaphor a stage further: when the horses revolved at the lower level they spun round at a giddy speed. But when they lifted up to turn on a higher level, the speed of their revolution slowed down noticeably. Similarly when couples first come to mediation, they often seem to be spinning out of control. Mediators' techniques of gathering information in a controlled and systematic way can have the effect of slowing things down. The pace slows further as couples begin to work together in a more organized and synchronized way. A very common result is that they agree on a longer time-scale for their separation or divorce. This often seems to be beneficial for them both, because the level of stress drops and because they are able to tackle their problems stage by stage, in a jointly planned and more reflective way.

## Outcomes of mediation

Kelly (1989) found in her follow-up study of divorced couples that the reduction of individual anger owed more to the passage of time than any specific intervention by professionals. Experience of mediation was associated, however, with significantly higher levels of co-operation between former couples and better interpersonal relationships between them. There was no evidence of mediation resulting in intrapsychic change, but mediators do not, on the whole, set out to produce intrapsychic change. Kelly also found considerable differences between those couples (half the sample) who completed their mediation with a written memorandum setting out proposals for settlement on all issues, compared with those who left mediation part of the way through. The latter group divided into two sub-categories: 26 per cent who gave up without reaching any agreement, and 15 per cent who went a certain distance in mediation and then terminated for positive reasons, such as wanting to attempt a reconciliation. A further 8 per cent reached a partial settlement on some issues.

In the USA many couples coming to mediation have already taken part in marital therapy. They may have worked through some of the relationship issues and be clearer about the directions they want to take. In Britain, more couples are likely to come to conciliation or mediation without having taken part in counselling beforehand. There may be a higher level of crisis and confusion. Mediators need to be careful not to let people rush into a hasty divorce: it is important to take enough time to check assumptions and allow hesitations to be expressed.

In Kelly's study, the couples who worked out a comprehensive settlement in mediation spent a great deal less time consulting separate lawyers than those who reached only a partial settlement (the first group spent on average 8.8 hours compared with 60 hours for the second group). The legal costs for the group who settled in mediation averaged $5,000 per couple, whereas the 'partial completors' spent over $10,000 per couple. Pearson (1989) found in her national study of mediation in the USA that legal fees for couples who used comprehensive mediation successfully were about a quarter of the costs of obtaining a settlement through litigation. Consumer opinion in Pearson's study was strongly in favour of mediation, compared with using legal processes.

Mediation is obviously not appropriate in all cases. When there is severe depression or other serious psychopathology, referral should be made to other professional services. Mediators need to be alert to any signs that one or both partners cannot cope with being in mediation. If there are indications that it is not appropriate – for example where there has been violence and one party feels vulnerable in the presence of an abusive partner – then mediators should terminate the sessions and refer the couple or individuals to other services. Mediation can, however, continue in conjunction with legal advice to each party and personal protection orders if necessary.

Mediation emphasizes the values of co-operation and agreement. There is a basic paradox, however, in expecting separated couples with high levels of conflict to sit in the same room and talk together rationally. Many couples are unlikely to come to mediation, either because they do not know about it or because one of them refuses to take part. However, conciliation and mediation services do not cater only for middle-class, middle-to-high income, co-operative couples. They do cater for such couples, but also for couples with little or no ability to negotiate with each other on their own. Many couples seem poised on a knife-edge between peace and war, between caring about the other and wounding the other, between demanding everything and accepting something that seems fair to them both.

Cross-disciplinary mediation also has benefits for the professionals who take part, in developing good working relationships between members of professions who have been divided traditionally by their different training, practice, professional ethos and language. These new interdisciplinary partnerships between counsellors and lawyers need to be firm and flexible to help couples cope with the intense stress of breaking or broken partnerships. Inevitably there can be strains in co-mediating as well as benefits. Co-mediators need support, consultation and supervision, as well as learning to rely on each other.

The ties that hold couples together often have knots that are not easily untied. In divorce, these ties may be wrenched apart too fast and too harshly. One of the values of mediation is its capacity to help couples loosen these ties rather more slowly and gently than might otherwise happen. Some couples manage to retain ties of friendship and respect for each other, while also co-operating as parents. It is hard and painful work to disengage from an intimate partnership without severing parental ties as well as the marital one. Mediators can help some couples along the way, and more couples should be encouraged to consider mediation, even though the results may be limited. Mediators cannot dissolve people's hurt and pain, but they can help them manage a particularly stressful stage in their lives.

## References

Blackie, S. and Clark, D. (1987) Men in marriage counselling, in Lewis, C. and O'Brien, M. (eds) and *Reassessing Fatherhood*, London: Sage.

Bohannan, P. (1970) *Divorce and After*, New York: Doubleday.

Brannen, J. and Collard, J. (1982) *Marriages in Trouble*, London: Tavistock.

Clulow, C. and Vincent, C. (1987) *In the Child's Best Interests?*, London: Tavistock.

Davis, G. (1988) *Partisans and Mediators*, Oxford: Oxford University Press.

Davis, G. and Roberts, M. (1988) *Access to Agreement*, Milton Keynes: Open University Press.

Dicks, H. (1967) *Marital Tensions*, London: Routledge.

Dingwall, R. and Eekelaar, J. (eds) (1988) *Divorce Mediation and the Legal Process*, Oxford: Clarendon.

Haynes, J. (1981) *Divorce Mediation*, New York: Springer.

Kelly, J.B. (1989) Mediated and adversarial divorce, *Mediation Quarterly*, (24), Summer 1989, 71–88.

Law Commission (1990) *Family Law: The Grounds for Divorce*, London: HMSO.

Lord Chancellor's Department (1989) *Report on the Costs and Effectiveness of Conciliation in England and Wales*, Newcastle: Conciliation Project Unit, University of Newcastle.

Maclean, M. and Wadsworth, M. (1988) The interests of children after parental divorce, *International Journal of Law and the Family* 2: 155–66.

Mitchell, A. (1985) *Children in the Middle*, London: Tavistock.

National Family Conciliation Council (1985) Code of Practice. Swindon: National Family Conciliation Council.

Parkinson, L. (1985) Divorce counselling, in W. Dryden (ed.) *Marital Therapy in Britain*, vol. 2, London: Harper & Row.

—— (1987) *Separation, Divorce and Families*, London: Macmillan.

—— (1989) Co-mediation with a lawyer mediator, *Family Law* 19: 135–9.

Pearson, J. (1989) *The Equity of Mediated Divorce Agreements*. Paper given at the Academy of Family Mediators Conference, Breckenridge, Colorado, July.

Vaughan, D. (1986) *Uncoupling – How Relationships Come Apart*, Oxford: Oxford University Press.

Wallerstein, J. and Kelly, J.B. (1980) *Surviving the Breakup*, London: Grant McIntyre.

# PART III

# Wider issues

# 14

# Working with couples:
# educational interventions

SARAH GAMMAGE

It is no accident that there is one chapter on education in a volume otherwise devoted to therapy. This reflects the position of education in organizations with a major therapeutic goal and more generally in society at large where people are more familiar with therapy than with education. This chapter will not update the thorough accounts of such interventions as marriage preparation and Marriage Enrichment in an earlier book (Dryden 1985). Rather it will provide an overview of education work in Britain and consider the dilemmas faced by those who seek to influence educationally rather than therapeutically. Those working in the field may find the approach critical. Nevertheless, there is a clear commitment to education behind these arguments and a conviction that education in personal relationships for people of all ages has an important part to play in the struggle to be happy and worthwhile in a complex post-industrial society.

## Education and therapy

Educational interventions are different from therapeutic ones, not simply because a therapist works with one or two clients at a time and educational interventions involve working with people in groups. The teacher is called a group leader and is in the business of furthering the learning of the group members. While learning can very well be therapeutic, the style of the leader, the content and methods used are determined by the primary objective – learning. Individual therapeutic needs have to be subordinated to the learning of the group and that can be a matter of discomfort for counsellors and therapists wishing to lead groups for educational purposes. The learning objectives fall into four main categories concerned with information, relationship skills, feelings and values. Although these are inter-woven in principle they need to be addressed by the group leader explicitly in planning. Planning is very much part of intervening educationally. The group leader decides the subject of the group beforehand. It may be marriage prepara-tion, parenting, marital interaction, dealing with conflict or coping with divorce and people are invited to attend the course on that basis. The aims of the course will be outlined in pre-course material with details of the content and methods to be used, which may be group discussion, lectures, videotape material, and so on. This is in effect a contract to provide what is promised on the part of the course leader. A total renegotiation of the group content and activities is not compatible with working educationally – yet it may well be essential when working therapeutically.

Educational interventions offer people the chance to learn about aspects of their own relationships in a group by taking part in the group's activities, by listening to what the group leader and group members have to say, by observing others, by watching videos or listening to audio-tapes as well as many other ways. People attending educational groups will not usually undergo emotionally intense experiences as their particular personal problems are worked on. Indeed they should generally be discouraged from attending an educational group when they are experiencing immediate traumatic life-events. This is clearly the reverse of therapy.

Although educational intervention requires clear objective setting, planning and structure, it also draws upon many of the sources used by therapists. Group leaders influenced by the work of Carl Rogers (1965) seek to convey respect and warmth for the members of their group as well as to avoid being judgemental and overly directive. The education work in Relate draws upon several models of couple interaction, such as object relations theory outlined by Dicks (1967); family dynamics based upon systems theory outlined by Skynner (1976); and principles of learning outlined by psychologists such as Bandura (1977) in its emphasis on the importance of the model of leadership and interaction with others provided by the group leader. Active participation of group members is also essential in such work. Group leaders can and should introduce material and provide structuring principles. Experiential learning, personal involvement and clear structure are all important and are not incompatible.

## Upstream helping

Educational interventions are very important in this society but rarely recognized as such. Egan and Cowan (1979) used the metaphor of 'upstream' and 'downstream' to help in distinguishing the different kinds of interventions:

> as a society we have taken a largely downstream approach to human needs, waiting for people to develop severe problems in living and then investing enormous resources in attempts to rescue them, after which we send them back to the same human systems which were the source of their original difficulties.
>
> (Egan and Cowan 1979: 4)

Continuing with this metaphor, educational interventions are an attempt to provide upstream helping. If therapy is about rescuing people from drowning, education is about preventing people from falling or jumping into the river. Education aims to further learning about relationships by developing understanding and skill, increasing knowledge, helping people to be clear about what they value, in order that more people can deal more effectively with life's inevitable problems without needing a therapist. Like any form of preventive education which has a long-term goal, educational interventions in personal relationships have to keep on being justified since they do not offer immediate relief of suffering.

This description of intervening educationally implies more clarity than actually exists in practice. Confusions arise because different definitions of education are used by the many people and organizations working in the field. These working definitions have far more to do with the deployment of scarce resources of time, energy and money than with the philosophical and psychological underpinnings of the work. The very title 'education' is often a misleading one. To the non-expert this word is synonymous with formal education as in the work done in schools, colleges and universities and may have negative connotations. This being the case, it is entirely understandable that many people would not wish to be taught didactically by 'experts' about their personal relationships. The educator for couple relationships may have a pre-educational task as well.

## Defining the area

The public, and even counsellors working within marital agencies, assume that education in these organizations refers to teaching pupils in school about marriage. Much work is done in schools but this is an incomplete and inaccurate picture. Another confusion arises because people refer to training and education as separate activities. While it is useful to distinguish work with professionals in their occupational roles from work with people in their familial roles, people do not always adhere to this definition.

In terms of the people at whom educational interventions are aimed, it may be individuals, couples or the whole family who are the targets; intervention may also include people who are divorcing, people who are engaged, young people who are not old enough to marry, people who are in homosexual relationships, or those who have no close personal relationships. The definition explicitly adopted here is a broad one. It assumes that educational interventions involve work with people directly and indirectly with professionals who influence them and help them through a formal educational, health or welfare role. It includes education and training and is aimed at people at all stages of life from young teenagers to the retired and those in between: parents, engaged couples and those without close personal relationships at the time of contact with them. It may include homosexuals, though it is unlikely to, as well as those divorcing or preparing to marry again.

It is helpful to explain what educational interventions are, by using the organizing principle of themes. Likely themes and topics to be encountered are: marital and couple interaction, family dynamics, family life-cycle, loss, grief and dealing with change, sexuality, parenting, divorce, stepfamilies, communication skills, assertiveness, dealing with anger and conflict, negotiation, and value clarification. Particular courses for particular groups of people will of course tailor these themes to match the group. Marriage preparation courses will include material on expectations, and communication. Divorce experience courses are bound to look at loss and grief as well as communication.

The use of a broad definition of educational interventions and the organizational principle of themes is not for reasons of convenience. It reflects more accurately the work being done, reminds one that the couple is part of a wider system from which it is neither desirable nor possible to separate it and avoids making the focus too prescriptive about 'the right kind of relationship'. For instance Whitfield (1985) describes the content of preventive experiences under a sub-heading which refers to important topics in marriage-related education. Thus 'marriage' is used as a theme to draw together the list of contents. Such an approach is in danger of being prescriptive and exclusive about the kinds of relationships approved of. This raises the issue of values which will be elaborated on later. An outline of the work of different organizations will indicate the scope of the work. This outlining will begin with Relate, which is the largest national organization concerned with marital and intimate relationships.

## Relate

It surprises many that education was one of the main aims of the organization in its early days. In 1938 sixteen people formed a committee to see what could be done to help broken homes and marriages. They wished to find out what factors made for a successful marriage, what the common causes of breakdown were and what could be done to prevent it. The early approach in education was very didactic. It aimed to collect ideas and information on safeguarding marriage and to pass these on through lectures. Later specially designed programmes were developed using talks and discussions to prepare couples for marriage. This approach gave way in the 1950s and 1960s to one in which the leader facilitated discussion amongst group members rather than handing on expert information. This approach became highly influential as a particular style in running groups in personal relationships.

An educational strategy for MG (National Marriage Guidance Council 1983) set out clearly a wide range of areas in the marriage and family education field for MG to develop. It emphasized family more than marital relationships. It described courses for parents of children of different ages and projects involving pupils, parents and teachers together. This strategy clearly intended education to embrace a much wider field than simply marriage preparation. Education was for people at all stages of life and was to emphasize the 'here and now' rather than to anticipate a future 'desirable' marital state. While the approach has largely been adopted in Relate, the scope of development has been rather limited. Education is very much a subsidiary goal of the organization, consuming only about 4 per cent of its national resources.

There is a fund of wisdom about marriages, intimate communication, the impact of change and many other aspects of relationships, within the organization. This derives from clinical practice, relevant theory, debate and research. The organization has developed appropriate and efficient methods for teaching about these areas and for training others to do so. It educates not only through its personnel but also through invaluable written resources in the form of training courses and handbooks. Its work includes courses in schools, with teachers, with health visitors, doctors, clergy, social workers, probation officers, police officers as well as courses for parents, engaged couples, divorcing couples, school pupils, retired couples and others. Relate expertise and its organizational infrastructure make it the organization most credible to develop educational interventions.

## Catholic Marriage Advisory Council

The Catholic Marriage Advisory Council (CMAC) is an organization which provides remedial marital counselling and also undertakes educational work. This includes work in schools as well as marriage preparation. All CMAC counsellors are trained to run marriage preparation groups. The aim of these groups, to quote from a CMAC pamphlet (1988b), is 'to help others form a married relationship that will endure and grow in love'.

A report following a nation-wide survey prepared by the Marriage Preparation Development Department at CMAC stated

> we believe that improving a couple's mutual understanding, communication and resolution of conflicts at the time they plan to marry is the best way to improve their chances of a lasting and satisfying life.
>
> (CMAC 1988c: 21)

All CMAC counsellors are expected to be ready and willing to contribute to prepare people for marriage. It is clear that the content and method of such courses are similar to those of Relate in that couples are able to clarify their own values, improve their communication skills and their ability to deal constructively with marital conflict. Yet CMAC centres find marriage preparation a struggle. Counsellors often feel unsuited to and threatened by the work. It is feared that couples will not attend their groups willingly and the work is seen as having no measurable or achievable outcome. Consequently remedial work always takes preference, although CMAC does not have long waiting lists for remedial marital counselling.

Education is a subsidiary goal of CMAC and has modest aims: to work in schools and to provide marriage preparation. Whereas Relate is an organization not affiliated to any church, CMAC clearly is. In its statement of philosophy and values in the Annual Report (CMAC 1988a) it includes the following:

> The Catholic Marriage Advisory Council is an organisation of Catholics concerned with married life . . . it is also our purpose to promote the relationship of marriage as one that is permanent, faithful and open to life.
>
> (CMAC 1988a: 4)

CMAC is likely to occupy the more liberal end of the value spectrum in the Roman Catholic church. Yet it may well put off Catholics who fear wrongly that they will be treated in an authoritarian and judgemental way if they have marital problems. CMAC like Relate has not developed its education work extensively, despite the vigour and enthusiasm of its National Officer.

## The Church of England

Educational interventions in the Church of England are a development of the pastoral arm of the local parish. In this sense, then, working with couples educationally is a subsidiary goal of the main purpose of the church. In Britain 300,000 weddings take place each year, of which 100,000 are conducted in church. Parishes differ in size from those where one or two weddings take place a year to parishes where there might be a hundred or more. The busier the parish the more likely there is to be marriage preparation. This preparation will include much about the actual ceremony and the spiritual component of marriage. The amount of marriage education in parishes and the type of marriage preparation that is offered varies enormously.

The typical provision would be that a host couple would provide a room in their own home and another couple would act as facilitators to run the group. All those involved in the setting up and running of it would be considered as exemplars of successful married couples. The facilitator couple might devise their own programme or draw on ready-made material. How deeply the participants would consider their impending marriage as a result of such marriage preparation courses is hard to assess. Engaged couples are often in no mood to pay attention to sober considerations. The successful outcome of marriage preparation could well be that the couple decided not to marry. Running groups which are actually likely to involve people at a level deep enough to test expectations and commitment may well require a depth of training which is not available.

Another approach to running marriage preparation courses does owe a good deal to the strong link between the Church of England and Relate personnel. A considerable number of Church of England clergy are trained as Relate counsellors which is a tremendous advantage in the pastoral work of the parish. Several parishioners are likely to be Relate-trained counsellors. Courses influenced by people with this background tend to be similar to the educational approaches used within Relate. Sometimes local clergy request training from Relate to run their own groups.

Concern about marriage generally led the Church of England to set up a Marriage Education Panel which began work in 1984, an officer being appointed by the House of Bishops to develop it. This Bishops' representative sought to develop 'what was there already'. This was a number of varied initiatives and projects in the field of family life education. But this was an artificial division and it was more logical and coherent to combine marriage education with family life education. This was the desired and the actual outcome of the Family Life and Marriage Education conference run in 1989. Other educational interventions in the field of marriage other than marriage preparation for engaged couples in the church is much more *ad hoc* depending on interest at parish level. The work varies in quality – an inherent difficulty whenever individual initiative is relied upon. A great deal of enthusiasm to develop marriage and family life education comes from laymen and laywomen in the church, but it is said that many of the clergy are resistant to this work, seeing it as a distraction from the main function.

## Marriage Research Centre (now One-plus-One)

Education has been developed as a subsidiary goal in the Marriage Research Centre. The major functions of this registered charity based in Middlesex Hospital are to encourage research in the area of marriage, and clinical work with couples. It has also attempted educational work. In the mid-1980s an Educational Development Officer was appointed although it is interesting that she promptly labelled herself the Training Officer. Her brief was to develop information and training packages for health visitors, who were likely to be in contact with couples through their work. The academic argument for developing education work was very strong. The organization had a wealth of information collected from research and working with couples clinically. It seemed sensible to attempt to apply that through preventive work. One might assume the different departments of an organization might have active and regular dialogue and that in the Marriage Research Centre research and clinical practice could straightforwardly inform educational work. This was not the case. The Training Officer certainly produced course packages on many of the themes relevant to personal relationships – coping with transition, communication, confidence building and so on as well as materials to train group leaders. She developed this material from an initial assessment of the needs and concerns of nurses and health visitors in relation to personal relationship issues. The materials produced may well have owed far more to the knowledge and experience of the officer appointed than the undoubted resources residing in the Marriage Research Centre. It is another example of the difficulty of developing education as a subsidiary goal. While theoretically it makes absolute sense to link such different concerns within one organization, it seems extremely difficult to do so in practice.

## Marriage Enrichment

The Marriage Enrichment Association has education as its primary goal. David Mace, who was involved in the setting up of the National Marriage Guidance Council, studied and wrote extensively on the importance of educational interventions to strengthen couples early in their marriages. He was instrumental too in setting up the Association of Couples for Marriage Enrichment out of which the Marriage Enrichment Movement in this country developed. The Association is a registered charity, technically non-denominational, although many people in the Marriage Enrichment Movement are Christians. Marriage Enrichment does not have a problem in competing for resources within its organization since it has been set up to pursue one goal – Marriage Enrichment. As a small organization it charges a very modest fee for its residential courses. It selects, trains and accredits its support leader couples though this would not compare in depth or quality with the training that is given to counsellors or tutors in Relate. These courses are usually run as a weekend residential workshop for couples who wish to improve their marriage but whose problems are not of a scale to threaten that marriage. Marriage Enrichment offers couples the opportunity to take an honest look at their present situation. In recognizing and valuing the strengths that they each bring to the marriage they come to accept and trust one another more deeply and begin to see how further growth is possible.

(Association for Marriage Enrichment 1983: 2)

The problem of the Marriage Enrichment Movement is not whether the goal should be pursued but how to extend its influence to more people. The organization does not have a high public profile. It seeks to address what it perceives as a general social problem through working directly with couples in their marriage in order to strengthen them. Yet it is doubtful whether Marriage Enrichment can have any significant impact on marriage as an institution. More likely it is a harmless and possibly beneficial activity for a few couples who already enjoy a good marriage by most standards. There seems an unfortunate circularity in the whole approach. Couples who could contemplate and survive a weekend where they are prepared to talk about their marriage with other couples must have a reasonable relationship already. Marriage Enrichment has a distinctively middle-class Christian flavour to it and its appeal seems to be to the 'converted'.

Several assumptions seem to lie behind Marriage Enrichment. First, marriage is seen as under a strain in modern times: in response Marriage Enrichment aims to increase communication and openness between marriage partners. A second theme in Marriage Enrichment is the lastingness of the relationship: Marriage Enrichment is about people staying as a couple and being open and available to each other. Third, Marriage Enrichment sees a good marriage as one based on democracy and companionship – a very attractive notion. Its strength as a movement is that it can have such a clear value position and embody these in its methods and its goals. This is also its weakness. It is clear about what it has on offer but it does not seem to appeal to the population at large. The Marriage Enrichment Movement draws together people of very similar value positions both as organizers and subscribers. Unfortunately people who agree to such an extent about basic values connected with families and intimate relationships seem to be a small minority. In embodying a clear educational approach to marriage Marriage Enrichment may be too exclusive and self-limiting.

## Other organizations

There are other organizations whose work has some importance for education in personal relationships. The **Family Planning Association** (FPA), which works with many professionals in personal relationships and sex education, has an indirect influence through training and their approach to running groups is very similar to that adopted by Relate. They are committed to giving clear information about sexuality and opportunities for people to discuss such matters openly. The Education Unit at the FPA has achieved financial success over the years which means their courses are in demand and people are willing to pay for them.

Another independent but more local organization is the **Community Education**

**Development Centre, Coventry**, which undertakes a considerable amount of family education and has developed many significant projects. Their work tends to be directed at parents, toddlers and children rather than at 'couples' and it has attracted private funding for many of its projects. Working in the area of family life may attract both sponsors and consumers more readily than work focusing on couples in intimate relationships.

An interesting and fairly recent voluntary organization has been set up in London. **Parent Network** is an organization for parents and it is mentioned here because it exemplifies the strengths of a clear focus in educational work while avoiding exclusivity. Funded from a private trust, it has established a programme for parents to improve communication with their children based on the parent effectiveness course outlined by Thomas Gordon (1976) and is rapidly establishing a network for these courses throughout the country.

Another marital organization, the **Jewish Marriage Council**, which provides a confidential counselling service for couples, also undertakes preventive work. Its courses are

In the form of group discussions for schools, youth clubs, engaged couples and newlyweds. In content they are carefully balanced between personal relationship aspects and traditional Jewish values and attitudes.

(Jewish Marriage Council 1989: 1)

Thus we have an example of an organization which is developing a subsidiary goal in its educational work which has no problem about value clashes. The council aims its education at a particular religious group.

## Other educational work

It is difficult to estimate the scope or evaluate the quality of other work that may be included as educational interventions. The Norwich Centre for Personal Professional Development runs courses on 'Self-knowledge and close relationships', 'Masculine and feminine workshops', 'Ongoing encounter groups' and other courses. These are likely to have impact on people's relationships. An organization advertised as LRT (Loving Relationships Training) based in London runs courses claiming to transform the quality of relationships or create ideal relationships. These courses seem to run on a strictly commercial basis and make claims that one might think would appeal only to the gullible. However, such organizations make money out of people's desire for happier and more satisfying relationships and show that education need not be an uncommercial enterprise.

Many courses which can help people in their personal relationships appear on the brochures of adult education institutes run by both universities and local education authorities. These depend upon local allocation of resources and will no doubt be increasingly squeezed by financial stringencies. Such work cannot be co-ordinated or standardized in its approach. It would be idealistic to hope that adult education in personal relationships could become as available and popular as car maintenance or woodwork classes. Relate centres in some areas have

persuaded adult education institutes to run courses on parenting skills, assertiveness training and other related areas.

## Working in schools

Personal relationship education in schools is vital and important. Any society
genuinely concerned about the quality of marriage and the family might seize
the opportunity of the school curriculum to educate for it. Schools contain a cap-
tive audience of impressionable young people who are receptive to learning about
themselves and relationships. They may have been damaged by their experience
of family life and may well be confused and ignorant about sexual matters. Marriage and family education as such would rarely, if ever, be found under this title
on the school curriculum. However, personal relationships will be undertaken
within a whole range of subjects in school such as social studies, community
studies, citizenship, child care, health education, general studies, liberal studies,
humanities, English, or religious education. There is a more detailed discussion
of this in Gammage (1986).

Schools had until recently a great deal of autonomy over the shape and content
of their own curriculum. This meant that many schools devoted much time and
attention to personal relationships and some schools devoted very little. Our present concern should be with the possibilities of the National Curriculum, which
could potentially extend the best teaching of personal and social education
to all. Personal relationship education will occupy a place within health education described grandly but unconvincingly as 'a cross-curricular theme'. This
means in effect that it will be neither a core nor a foundation subject and must
occupy the leftover space to be competed for by many non-traditional but highly
worthwhile subjects. Some will argue that personal and social education will take
place in many subjects across the curriculum. Teachers know that this is more
likely to mean that no one will have responsibility for the subject. Despite the
rhetoric it seems that in practice, marriage and family education will have less
chance of being addressed as the National Curriculum becomes implemented.

## Examples of the work

It must be evident, given the range of organizations providing education in this
field, that to select one course to provide an exemplar of the work cannot truly
represent any one of them. Nevertheless the reader will be given a flavour of the
content and style from an outline of a course called 'Why people marry'. The
course would be run for adults for about eight sessions of one and a half hours
on two consecutive days. It would be aimed at a wide range of people. In the
first session the group leader would convey basic information about the course
content, find out what course members hoped to gain from it, establish a pur-
poseful, open and non-threatening atmosphere and provide activities to enable
the course members to get to know each other. Before the end of this session the
group would 'invent' a man and a woman in two small separate groups. Much

fun is to be had from such an activity despite the serious underlying purpose. In the next two sessions the leader would 'marry' the individuals and the group would be invited to assess their potential strengths and weaknesses as a couple. Brief input would then be provided by the leader on ways of understanding how couples 'fit'. The leader would refer to unconscious processes and collusive patterns of interaction as outlined by theorists such as Dicks (1967). Following this the members would be asked to apply these principles to case studies, presented in written form. The group would split up to work in twos or threes to be ready to report their analyses and prognoses later. These would be reported back to the whole group.

After sessions which have included substantial input and intensive discussion the course leader would need to provide a much more unstructured period of time to allow individuals to relax, consolidate their learning so far, and have an opportunity to give more personal and emotional reactions. The material would inevitably have evoked strong feelings. While there would be no intention to allow the group to become a therapy session leading to intense examination of these emotional responses, members would be encouraged to express their thoughts and feelings. The group leader's task would be to summarize and link individual contributions in a way relevant for the group as a whole. It would be essential that the leader affirm the value contributions of everyone while keeping the course purposefully moving.

In the latter stages of the course, work would be focused on the resources and skills that people bring to relationships. This could be done very simply by asking people to discuss it in twos or threes and report back to the whole group. This would tend to emphasize positive aspects of relationships to counteract what might have been more negative earlier on. Before the final session it would be necessary to hold an application session. This simply means that course members would be invited to think through what they have learned and how that would be applied when they leave the course and go back to their daily lives. As always this would be a very valuable opportunity to learn from others. The course would end with a summary of what has been covered, comments from each person on the good and bad aspects of the course and a review of whether the expectations outlined by members in the first session had actually been fulfilled or not. A standard evaluation form would be given to everyone to fill out.

This very brief outline of the programme and content of a course on marriage should demonstrate some of the differences between therapeutic and educational groups. It should be clear that there is a high degree of participation by group members and many of the activities are structured to obtain that. There is also clear input from the group leader. The input is followed by time to digest and apply that material. The course outlined here is more typical of a course for professional people. The same kind of programme, with its characteristic style of leadership and balance of participation and input, can be modified for courses more suitable for the general public. For instance one might run a publicly advertised course on 'Couple communication'. In the same way the leader would establish an optimal learning atmosphere at the beginning, with a warm, welcoming, open and business-like approach; give members the opportunity to express their doubts and hopes early on; provide an outline of what will happen in each session; and conduct a 'getting-to-know-each-other' exercise. As before the leader would have a set of concrete objectives to inform the plan. The course would be designed according to principles about where, when and how much information to provide, about the balance of group activity to small group work and personal contribution, and about the variety and pace suitable for the membership. The content would include consideration and practice of direct communication, assertiveness, dealing with conflict, blocks to communication and more. Good courses will not overload members to the point of indigestibility but will give them something to go away with apart from what they have contributed. All courses will end with an invitation for comments and reactions from group members and a standard evaluation form to complete when there has been a chance for reflection.

## Resources

Commercially produced packs of materials on personal relationships are not strictly speaking 'interventions'. Nevertheless resources are a means of education in personal relationships and inspire and reflect much of the philosophy, style and content of the work that is done. The Community Education Department of the Open University has produced a variety of study packs on health choices, first years of life, pregnancy and birth, parents talking, family relationships, and more. However, there are no packs directly on intimate relationships. The Family Planning Association has produced excellent written materials on AIDS, assertiveness, and more. Relate has published a series of study guides on aspects of relationships. The Health Education Authority supplies annotated lists on videos, books, films, pamphlets and other materials for personal relationships education. A fascinating and comprehensive review of learning materials in personal relationships skills for adults was compiled by the Open University for the Health Education Authority by Shakespeare (1987). There is a plethora of materials for use in schools. Yet another curriculum development project called Foundations has been set up by the National Family Trust. The project aims to 'develop, evaluate and publish curriculum units and schemes of work promoting understanding of human development and its expression in personal relationships'.

Launching another pack of materials will create interest in personal relationships in educational circles. Unfortunately commercially produced resources are no substitute for skilled practitioners. Learning about personal relationships is an enterprise requiring face-to-face personal interaction. Running programmes with small groups of people is highly expensive. Not only is it expensive to write and mount a course but also it is expensive to train people to be competent and even more expensive to train tutors to supervise that work and to maintain an organizational superstructure to support it. These are the problems encountered by organizations such as Relate and CMAC. But it is only by this direct route that one can seriously claim to have any impact on helping people learn about their relationships in a deep and meaningful way.

## Dilemmas

There are clearly dilemmas for organizations and individuals in promoting and developing educational interventions. Relate, CMAC, the Church of England and the Marriage Research Centre (One-plus-One) share similar ones. Educational work in these four organizations has a marginal status, lacks resources, is ambivalently regarded and can encounter resistance from personnel engaged on the major goals. Despite this there has been sufficient commitment from a hardy minority to keep education going in all of these organizations. One way out of the dilemma might be to establish a secure and separate funding base for educational developments. If such work were financed as a separate enterprise it might thrive without affecting the organizations' main goals. One major and obvious source of funding is from central government but there has been a major shift away from direct government subsidy to voluntary organizations. Other sources of funding are independent private trusts but they tend to look to fund specific initiatives in particular problem areas such as sex abuse, deprivation, and so on, often depending on 'topical' concerns. Such trusts are not as keen to fund initiatives which have more general educational aims.

Another source of funding would be from charging the public and the professionals at a commercial rate for courses. While it remains to be seen whether courses for professionals can be self-funding in an organization such as Relate, it would be unrealistic to expect the same for courses directly for the public. In Britain, where even formal education is undervalued and where a smaller proportion of people attend higher education than any other European country, it would be optimistic to assume that the public would pay for education in personal relationships at a sufficiently realistic rate to cover costs. While people will approach an organization such as Relate when they are in distress, more women than men attend and those people that do present themselves are a minority of even those couples who are in trouble. It may be alien to many people to learn formally about an area that clearly belongs to the informal and private domain. It is unfortunate that education (Relate/CMAC/Church of England style) falls between two stools, that of personal self-growth or self-development, which seems to be an expanding industry in this country and that of community education. The former include people who will pay private organizations which offer courses in Transactional Analysis, Gestalt work, Encounter, and more. Voluntary organizations have failed to attract these people. Yet to the more deprived sections in the community our work must seem at best a luxury and at worst a total irrelevance. Market forces may solve the problem. Voluntary organizations may learn to convince people of the value of what they have to teach. If this happens there will be plenty of highly committed, thoughtful and well-intentioned people who want to provide it.

## Values

Financial dilemmas are not the only ones facing organizations undertaking education in personal relationships. The question of the values underpinning educational work is a problem for organizations where education is a subsidiary goal. For instance it is a problem for the Church of England, which must maintain its commitment to the ideology of monogamous lifelong marriage, but it cannot afford to be harsh, condemning or reactionary towards its constituents in the face of inevitable changes in society. It is not surprising that there is a half-hearted attitude to promoting marriage education. CMAC faces a problem particularly when so many members of the Catholic Church marry non-Catholics. Its marriage education approach is not prescriptive, yet the Catholic Church is the least liberal in its attitude to divorce. Both organizations then have the dilemma of not compromising the very clear values that they represent without alienating their congregation.

Relate is a secular organization and unapologetically offers divorce experience courses. There are good arguments why such courses are educational. Many people divorce, remarry and divorce again. Divorce experience courses can help people learn from marriage failure and help to prevent future marriage breakdown. Nevertheless all organizations in the relationship business steer an uneasy course where values are concerned. Groups criticize them on the one hand for being too reactionary and rigid in their approach by focusing on marriage or ignoring homosexuality, and on the other for being too tolerant and permissive about family breakdown.

There are bound to be a very wide variety of values underpinning education in personal relationships. Broad trends in our society such as the changing status of women, the democratization of the family, the ideology of personal fulfilment, the decrease of extended family networks, the decline of influence of the Church, the increasingly multi-racial, multi-cultural composition of communities, all have profound implications for couples. Few would disagree that adults and children have basic personal and social needs. Organizations differ in the way they shape the work they do with couples in response to broad societal trends.

For instance the Marriage Enrichment Movement is committed to helping couples stay together. Whitfield (1985) says we should teach people how to be more committed and less transient in their promises and to work at their marriages. The approach of Relate is to help people work out their own salvation and to equip them educationally with a better repertoire of interpersonal skills to deal with the greater personal demands made on them. The variety of basic beliefs is a problem for any individual running a course in personal relationships. Selecting topics for a course programme is in itself highly revealing of a value position. The course leader has to show his or her hand in a way not required of a therapist. This may be a reason why people are more reluctant to be educators than therapists in these organizations.

**Evaluation**

Questions of values lead logically and finally to the issue of the evaluation of educational interventions. Joy Ross (1985) describes the area as neglected and this is still the case six years later. Fielder and Fielder (1985) can refer only to American research on Marriage Enrichment. Evaluation is a term often used very loosely to mean the subjective reactions of course members. While seeking such reaction and comment is an essential part of good group leadership it is no more than a subjective gauge. Evaluation of educational work has to be addressed in terms of its internal and external effectiveness. One is achievable, the other is very problematic. The first refers to evaluating educational work in terms it has set for itself. Thus an individual course must be evaluated in terms of whether it has achieved its own objectives. Educational work needs to be evaluated as part of the overall organizational objectives as well. This presupposes there is clarity about such objectives in the first place.

Evaluation can be carried out by people within an organization or by outsiders who may be relied on to provide objective assessment. The depth or thoroughness with which such evaluation can be carried out will depend on resources available. Since these are in particularly short supply for educational work it is not surprising that very little evaluation is done. Addressing the external effectiveness of educational work is highly problematic because of the variety of views on what effectiveness would mean. Organizations such as Family and Youth Concern would probably disagree fundamentally with the aims of much educational work done by organizations such as Relate and the Family Planning Association. Interestingly there is much consensus in the style and approach used in running educational groups by organizations outlined in this chapter despite the difference in emphasis on values concerned with the family and individual. The Sex Education Forum, a committee co-ordinated by the National Children Bureau to develop and support initiatives in Sex Education, has demonstrated that it is possible to achieve a working consensus in a very controversial area. The group includes a very broad spectrum of organizations such as the CMAC, Brook Advisory Centre, Relate, Family Planning Association, the Health Education Authority and many more.

## Conclusion

Voluntary organizations working in the personal relationships field receive grants from central and local government and are increasingly being required to account for the spending of this money in terms of value for money. It is not easy to establish that marital counselling is value for money in this sense and it is almost impossible to do this for educational interventions. It is extremely difficult to link immediate action in groups with long-term effect. Practitioners of the work are often inspired by their preferred philosophies of individual and couple development. Evaluation does require a more rigorous and down-to-earth approach in terms of what may be useful and acceptable to the public at large. It may well be that to begin with research resources should be targeted at market research into what people require. This approach was exemplified by the Parent Network organization, who commissioned research before they set up their organization. This may be the most fruitful way to target scarce resources. It would at least enable providers to match people's stated needs more clearly and realistically with what they have on offer. I hope it is clear by now that a great deal is on offer in terms of knowledge, expertise and experience of working with people struggling with their relationship problems as well experience of training and teaching others in the field. These resources need an educational as well as a therapeutic outlet. It would be sad if 'upstream' helping did not develop as a thriving part of the range of services on offer to the general public. Such a service could help people to enjoy their personal relationships far more in this rapidly changing society.

# References

Association for Marriage Enrichment (1983) *Focus on Couples*, London: Westminster Pastoral Foundation.

Bandura, A. (1977) *Social Learning Theory*, Englewood Cliffs, NJ: Prentice-Hall.

CMAC (Catholic Marriage Advisory Council) (1988a) *Annual Report*, London: CMAC.

—— (1988b) *Preparing Couples for Marriage*, Pamphlet, London: CMAC.

—— (1988c) *Prepared for Marriage prep* Report prepared for CMAC, London.

Dicks, H.V. (1967) *Marital Tensions*, London: Routledge & Kegan Paul.

Dryden, W. (ed.) (1985) *Marital Therapy in Britain*, Milton Keynes: vol. 2, Open University Press.

Egan, G. (1986) *The Skilled Helper*, Monterey, Calif: Brooks/Cole.

Egan, G. and Cowan, M. (1979) *People in Systems*, Monterey, Calif: Brooks/Cole.

Fielder, H. and Fielder, R. (1985) Marriage enrichment, in W. Dryden (ed.) *Marital Therapy in Britain*, vol. 2, Milton Keynes: Open University Press.

Gammage, S. (1986) Education for marriage with secondary school pupils, in P. Brindley and S. Saunders (eds) *Learning for Life*, Study Day Publication, Rugby: National Marriage Guidance Council.

Gordon, T. (1976) *P.E.T. in Action*, Toronto: Bantam.

Jewish Marriage Council (1989) *Annual Report*, London: JMC.

National Marriage Guidance Council (1983) *An Education Strategy for MG*, Recommendations to the NMGC Executive, Rugby: NMGC.

Rogers, C. (1965) *Client Centred Therapy*, Boston, Mass: Houghton-Miflin.

Ross, J. (1985) Marriage preparation, in W. Dryden (ed.) *Marital Therapy in Britain*, vol. 2, Milton Keynes: Open University Press.

Shakespeare, P. (1987) *The Contribution of Learning Materials to Personal Relationships Skills of adults*, a study commissioned by the Health Education Authority, Community Education, Open University, Milton Keynes.

Skynner, R. (1976) *One Flesh: Separate Persons*, London: Constable.

Whitfield, R. (1985) The prevention of marital distress, in W. Dryden (ed.) *Marital Therapy in Britain*, vol. 2, Milton Keynes: Open University Press.

# 15

# Couple therapy: the agencies approach

DAVID BARKLA

Agencies are a means of organizing the delivery of professional services. They may employ some or all of the workers in a profession, and they may influence or govern entry into the profession, and/or its standards of training and professional discipline. At the same time they provide the public with acceptable ways of recognizing reputable professionals and consulting them.

The term 'couple therapy' includes a variety of substantially different treatments for a variety of substantially different problems: it is not surprising that different agencies sometimes choose different words and adopt different definitional boundaries in describing their work. Discussion of these words and definitions has sometimes become heated; for instance there has been dispute about whether there is a distinction between 'therapy' and 'counselling', and if so, what the distinction is. No general distinction is assumed in this chapter.

Another important ambiguity in the notion of 'couple therapy' is whether it can be said to occur when the therapist is working with only one of the partners. Agencies may differ in how they describe this situation. In this chapter it is not assumed that both partners have to be present with the therapist; on the other hand it is not assumed that *all* therapy undertaken by couple-orientated agencies is couple therapy.

## The established professions

We could reasonably expect to find specialized parts of the established health and welfare professions acting as agencies engaged in couple therapy. Because couples' problems are so widespread and so damaging, we could expect to find these specialized services very widely available. In fact we find no such thing. There does not appear to be any effective institutional support for couple therapy in Britain, either from the principal professional bodies, or from the managements, of the health and welfare services. This is not because these services manage to steer clear of couples with problems. But there are forces in couples, in professional workers and their agencies, and in the community in general, that hinder identification and treatment of problems in the relationship. These forces are vividly described by Mattinson and Sinclair in a local authority social services setting in their book *Mate and Stalemate* (1979). Their study made no claim to be quantitatively representative of social services departments in general, but their main findings would probably hold good in most places.

Only a very small proportion (about 3 per cent) of the cases referred to the department were considered at the outset as having a problem in the couple's relationship, and hardly any were referred *because* of such a problem. On the other hand, among couples who were involved with the department long enough to be allocated to a particular worker's caseload, about 60 per cent were definitely seen as having a problem in the relationship, and of those described as 'priority' cases, nearly 90 per cent had such a problem. However, the main focus of the social worker's attention was not couple therapy, but some kind of policing and/or coping with crises. Work with these couples took up time out of proportion to their number, and in many cases the couple appeared to get no lasting benefit from it. The workers were well aware of this and consequently felt frustrated. So there was reason to believe that couple therapy could be a sound investment of effort. Mattinson and Sinclair (1979) describe work with selected cases where a definite focus on the couple's relationship appeared appropriate. They claim demonstrable improvements in the capacity of couples to sustain and develop their own relationships, and consequent reduction in their dependence on social services. Although the work was time-consuming it was not more expensive than the department's customary range of interventions.

But the capacity of the department to undertake couple therapy on a larger scale was still severely limited at the end of the project, for several reasons. First, the duties imposed by the community on social workers – particularly in relation to children – lead many clients to be deeply suspicious of the department's intervention in their lives and to evade it as much as they can. There are other clients who positively seek help, but do so in a profoundly dependent way. Obviously starting serious couple therapy is difficult with either sort. Second, the volume of resource is in many places so small in relation to need, that it is all used up in responding to crises; however inefficient a strategy that may be, departments have no option but to treat immediate problems as their first priority. Third, the specific skills required for couple therapy are not given much emphasis in social work training. (These three limitations were recognized as very serious at the time of the project – the mid-1970s – and there is no reason to suppose they are less serious now. There was then also some hostility within the department to couple therapy on the ground that the only proper response to social problems was a more politically radical one; this view is perhaps less widely advocated now.) So the upshot was that although Mattinson and Sinclair (1979) thought there could and should be more couple therapy in social work, they were left sadly uncertain whether it would actually be developed. In the decade since they wrote, there seems to have been little progress.

In other services the forces at work are sometimes very different, but have a similar final result. For instance, general medical practitioners may have a very long-term relationship with their patients and one that is on the whole free from policing responsibilities. GPs may even call themselves family practitioners. But there is even less in medical training than there is in social work training about the dynamics of behaviour in couples and families. And probably patients are even more deeply imbued than doctors with the assumption that the causes of suffering lie within individuals rather than between them.

Couple therapy could be provided in association with general medical practice, rather than being an integral part of it. There are general practice teams – though still a very small proportion – which include a practice counsellor. The work of these counsellors is by no means all couple therapy, or even relationship counselling. The nature and extent of the working relationship between the GPs and their practice counsellor (or 'surgery counsellor', which may not be the same thing) varies considerably from place to place, and there appears to be little published evidence to show how much couple therapy is done, or how it is influenced by having originated in a medical setting.

There are also individuals in other sectors of the Health Service who are engaged in providing couple therapy of one sort or another, though usually this is only a fairly small part of their professional work. In a few places dedicated individuals have succeeded in setting up operational units for sex therapy or relationship therapy, or both, and have kept these units in existence for a number of years.

Admirable though they are, these units could hardly be described as agencies, because they appear to be totally dependent on individual principal workers and have no certainty of surviving the departure of those individuals. While they exist, the units may deliver a very substantial service in their area. For instance the Whiteley Wood Clinic in Sheffield (which is among the oldest-established and largest units) takes on approximately 500 new couple cases per year. Such units also carry out important training functions, most frequently for concerned individuals working in a wide variety of settings, and with many different kinds and levels of professional involvement with couples.

As well as operational units, there are professional associations whose members include a number interested in couple therapy, and these might in principle have a considerable influence on the professional development of couple therapy. These associations include the Institute of Psychosexual Medicine, the Association of Sexual and Marital Therapists, the British Association for Counselling, the British Psychological Society Special Group in Counselling Psychology, and several associations of psychotherapists and social case-workers. In fact none of these associations has been in a position to devote much attention directly to couple therapy, because of other pressures on them. This is not only a matter of their institutional circumstances; there also appears to be a relatively slow development of the knowledge base for couple therapy. None of the journals published by these bodies carries many articles on couple therapy.

## Agencies working across the boundaries of couple therapy

There are several different kinds of agencies that do in fact serve couples. Some of these kinds of agencies do not claim to provide couple therapy, but they nevertheless merit brief attention here.

The first group consists of self-help agencies. They tend to suffer severely from transience of membership, but a number have become well established. Some of them are concerned not with extant couples, but with the survivors of couples broken by death or divorce. Others are concerned with couples as parents, rather than as partners in their own right. In spite of apparently widespread concern about 'the state of marriage' in general, and individual anxieties about people's own marriages, there has been no sign of a major self-help movement for marriage. Of course a self-help movement might not wish to become an agency; it might adopt a strongly anti-professional stance. But those self-help movements that do take on the task of establishing and managing therapy services for their members are well placed to prevent those services from being dominated by the interests of their professional workers.

There are some organizations to serve couples who have not identified themselves as having 'a problem', notably the Association for Marriage Enrichment and the (Catholic) Marriage Encounter. These are part of the wide and very diverse 'growth' movement, which undeniably contains elements of therapy, since it always aims to make its participants better, by more-or-less specific methods, even when it also asserts that they are already OK at the outset. But for every couple who try to improve their relationship with the help of Marriage Enrichment or Encounter, or any other sort of 'growth', there are hundreds who do nothing about it until it is intolerably bad, or even 'irretrievably' broken down. Nevertheless it is a rather arbitrary judgement to exclude these organizations from a discussion of couple therapy, and is to be justified only by their own disclaimers of professional authority.

There are agencies which provide therapy to couple relationships within a framework of therapy to the whole family (or as many of the whole family as they can muster). The exclusion of these agencies from a discussion of couple therapy can hardly be made on any rational grounds. It is quite possible to contend that a couple relationship has very little psychological meaning and very little social importance if it is separated from other relationships in the family group. At the very least, the couple relationship is heavily influenced by them. On the other hand it can be argued that the salience of these other relationships may leave insufficient room in the practice of family therapy to deal adequately with the couple relationship. Besides, people play a part in the diagnosis and treatment of their own problems, and those who choose to approach a family therapy service may well be asserting that their problems do not lie in the couple relationship. These are issues of great theoretical and practical importance, but beyond the scope of this chapter.

We exclude the family therapy agencies from further consideration here, not out of ignorance or prejudice or envy (who could imagine such things?), but simply because the relationship between couple therapy and family therapy is discussed in Chapter 5.

Finally, there are agencies providing conciliation or mediation for separating couples – usually divorcing, and often at a late stage in the proceedings (see Chapter 13). The primary aim of conciliation is to enable the couple to make an agreement that will last, about potentially very difficult 'practical' issues, especially the care and control of the couple's children, and access to them by the non-custodial parent. The conciliation services are well aware that such agreements can work satisfactorily (which chiefly means 'in the best interest of the child') only if the residual relationship between the separating partners is not too hostile. 'Civilized' attitudes say little if anything about the real relationship, which may well need a good deal of therapy. Some conciliators, though not all, are personally well qualified to provide such therapy, but unfortunately the resources of the service may be insufficient to permit it. This is partly because of time pressures arising from the legal proceedings, but more because the services are mostly very poorly funded. So, although conciliators clearly bring a therapist's outlook to their work, and may bring a therapist's skills as well, the conciliation services are not at present major providers of couple therapy.

## Specialist agencies

There are six or seven agencies for which the provision of couple therapy is a major function. In total they provide about 320,000 face-to-face therapeutic interviews a year, of which about 40 per cent are with both partners together; they take on about 60,000 new cases a year. They all carry out other activities as well, and even their provision of couple therapy differs greatly one from another, so it is almost impossible to generalize about them, except to make the point that they are all charities, not commercial enterprises or statutory agencies. They all receive some financial support from public funds, but neither central nor local government is obliged, under current legislation, to maintain any service to couples. These agencies fall naturally into three subgroups.

1   Two small specialized units whose distinctive contribution lies beyond their own clinical work, through research and teaching: the Tavistock Institute of Marital Studies and 'One-plus-One'.
2   Two 'national' organizations devoted to delivering services as widely as possible throughout the community: Relate and the Scottish Marriage Guidance Council.
3   Two or three organizations set up to meet the special needs of a particular part of the community: the Catholic Marriage Advisory Council, the Jewish Marriage Council and the Asian Family Counselling Service.

### Research and teaching agencies

#### Tavistock Institute of Marital Studies
The Tavistock Institute of Marital Studies (TIMS) provides a small London-based service of psychotherapy for couples, but has for many years exerted a world-wide influence on couple therapy, through a long line of important publications, and training activities involving practitioners in the other couples therapy agencies and in the principal health and welfare professions. The work of TIMS is deeply rooted in the object relations tradition of psychoanalysis. This has enabled it to insist steadfastly on the importance of two features of couples' relationships which are often disregarded: first, the 'unconscious' and apparently

profoundly irrational nature of much of the interaction between partners, and second, the powerful significance, for both partners, of many couple relationships that appear superficially to have no life in them. Although these insights came originally out of psychoanalytic psychotherapy and continue to be informed by it, TIMS couple therapy is brief by psychoanalytic standards, consisting on average of less than six months of once-weekly appointments, with two therapists. Moreover, TIMS workers devote effort, through their research and training consultations, to demonstrating that the effects of psychodynamic forces can be recognized and worked with in ordinary counselling and case-work practice.

The professional staff of TIMS consists of about twelve psychotherapists, nearly all full-time, and mostly from backgrounds in social work. In 1988–9 about one-third of the total cost of their couple therapy was borne by clients, on a sliding scale of fees; most of the other two-thirds was met by a central government grant. Heavy dependence on grants is hard to avoid, because of the high proportion of research and development in the work.

*One-plus-One*

The Marriage Research Centre, now operating under the name One-plus-One, also provides a small London-based service of couple therapy but makes its principal contribution to the field through research and teaching. Its emphasis has been on the exploration of overt values and attitudes in couples' relationships, based on research among people who have not been clients of therapy services as well as among those who have. The organization's change of name reflects a concern to take proper account of recent alterations in publicly mediated images of couple relationships, and the resulting impact on individuals. The Marriage Research Centre was founded much later than the Tavistock Institute of Marital Studies, and is much smaller, but it occupies an important position. Its research on the social evolution of couple relationships forms a widely valued complement to the TIMS work on the homeostatic forces within such relationships.

**The 'national' agencies**

*Relate*

The National Marriage Guidance Council, now under the name Relate (and Cyd-ddeall in Wales), operates in England, Wales, Northern Ireland, the Channel Islands and the Isle of Man, but from the outset the organization in Scotland has been separate and independent. Relate is not a unitary organization. It is a federation of about 150 local Marriage Guidance Councils (now called Relate Centres) which have a substantial degree of autonomy. They determine the scale of recruitment of people to run services in their area and how the services are to be deployed, and they acquire the resources needed to support those services. However, they have committed themselves, as members of the federation, to achieve and if possible exceed a set of standards for various aspects of quality, quantity, and range of service, and they have delegated to a central organization the selection, training and in-service support of their practitioners. So Relate's local services to couples conform, broadly speaking, to national standards.

Relate operates services of education for the public, and training for other organizations, but about 95 per cent of its work is described as counselling or sex therapy.

The adoption of the name 'Relate' has given rise to an assumption in some quarters that the organization now claims a general competence to deal with problems in all kinds of close relationships. This is not so. The most substantial reasons for the change were specific misconceptions arising from the original name, in relation to the original aims and structures; these misconceptions had been recognized for decades. The main problems arose from the words 'marriage' (which has often been taken to imply that the service is intended only for people who are legally married and fully intend to remain so) and 'guidance' (which has often been taken to imply that the organization's counsellors are – or think they are – moral authorities). Because of increases in divorce and in cohabitation it gradually became more important to find a title that had no tendency to deter any category of marital or quasi-marital couple, at whatever stage in their relationship. The relationships of homosexual couples show not only important similarities to those of heterosexual couples, but also important differences from them, and it is not clear how much specialization is required in order to provide a satisfactory counselling service for homosexual couples. In fact, some do receive counselling from Relate, but only a very small number (see Chapters 11 and 12).

Relate has an interest in the possibility of developing family therapy, especially to deal with problems arising from impending separation of the parents, and problems in 'reconstituted' families. The development of this interest is at an early stage, and not incorporated into Relate's basic structure. Apart from this, no extension of Relate work is currently envisaged into fields of counselling outside couple relationships.

It cannot be said unreservedly that practically all Relate's work is couple therapy. The number of cases in which both partners attend has been increasing gradually for many years (in 1990 about 40 per cent of the total) but obviously that means that most cases are still conducted with only one partner. (This does not apply to Relate's sex therapy service, which is almost entirely with couples.) It could certainly be claimed that much of Relate's work with only one partner is directed towards improving the couple's relationship, but some individual work is probably not couple-related.

Another complication is that about one-third of Relate's clients attend for only one interview; it is clear that some of these are seeking services that Relate cannot provide, while for others, the one visit provides what they require at that point. However, in many cases it is impossible to assess at the end of a single interview what has been achieved.

The content of the couple therapy offered by Relate counsellors depends heavily on how much a client is willing and able to engage with it. At the least, the counsellors will offer a therapeutic environment through their personal qualities of non-possessive warmth, accurate empathy, and genuineness, and will attempt to help clients to strengthen these qualities in their couple relationship. Some clients have such a poor valuation of themselves that the counsellor's demonstration of acceptance is a major therapeutic intervention – and may be all the client can take. Others may be able to embark on a strenuous exploration of how their present relationships are repeatedly distorted by assumptions derived from earlier ones. Others (and this applies especially but not exclusively to those with sexual problems) may benefit from specific guidance about how to dismantle mutually unsatisfactory patterns of interaction and start to build better ones.

It would be naive to suppose that the value of therapy is a simple function of its duration, but duration has some importance. A survey in 1982 showed the following distribution:

| | |
|---|---|
| 1 interview | 31 per cent of cases |
| 2 interviews | 12 per cent of cases |
| 3–5 interviews | 27 per cent of cases |
| 6–10 interviews | 21 per cent of cases |
| 11–15 interviews | 6 per cent of cases |
| 16–20 interviews | 2 per cent of cases |
| over 20 interviews | 2 per cent of cases |

More recent but less systematic data are broadly consistent with these figures.

Of course the effectiveness of the therapy also depends on the counsellor's skill – a point to which we must return. But Relate's selection, training and in-service support system is intended to ensure that *all* its practitioners of couple therapy gain a sufficient general grounding in the principles and practice of client-centred counselling, and in the elements of object-relations theory, behavioural learning theory, and family systems theory. Many Relate counsellors go on to take further training, especially in psychodynamic psychotherapy. Relate services are aimed at strengthening couple relationships where possible, and where that does not appear possible the work is aimed at helping clients to separate with as little damage as possible to their families, their partners, and themselves.

Serious critical evaluation of this kind of work is extremely time-consuming and expensive, but Relate is planning to engage in it as far as resources will allow. The very small studies carried out hitherto, while exposing some weaknesses, have been on the whole encouraging.

A more specialized service of behavioural therapy for sexual problems is available in about a hundred Relate Centres. The therapists are trained Relate counsellors who have received further training in sex therapy. This staffing policy reflects the service's experience that not many sexual problems are simply the result of poor learning at a behavioural level: there is usually some fragility in other aspects of the couple's relationship too. The success rates claimed by pioneer sex therapists have rarely been achieved since. However, Relate's follow-up interviews three months after completion of therapy provide assessments of outcome by clients which are reasonably satisfactory.

In the early stages, the geographical development of Marriage Guidance Council (MGC) services depended on where the pioneers lived, but for many years it has been possible to regard everywhere in England and Wales as 'covered' by a local MGC. Over 90 per cent of the population lives within about six miles of a place where Relate couple therapy is available. The volume of the service has grown fairly steadily for many years.

In 1988–9 about 49,000 new cases were opened in England and Wales, and about 270,000 counselling or sex therapy interviews given. But there are very large variations in volume of service from one area to another, partly attributable to variations between individual centres, and partly to variations in local and regional wealth. Even the best resourced areas have the equivalent of only one or two full-time practitioners per 100,000 population (i.e. about 24,000 couples); in the North of England, the Midlands and Wales, the service is even more understaffed.

Relate's counsellors are nearly all volunteers who give a minimum of three hours' client contact time per week for a minimum of forty weeks a year. The actual average time worked in 1988–9 was almost 50 per cent higher than this minimum: a little under 180 hours in the year. It has grown steadily over many years in response to three kinds of pressure. The first is actual demand from clients, which has persistently grown ahead of Relate's resources. The second pressure is the concern of the in-service support system to ensure that counsellors gain enough work experience to attain the highest level of skill they can – and rising expectations about what is attainable. The third pressure is financial incentive. For several years Relate's policy has been that all work over an agreed minimum *should* be paid at realistic rates, and gradually schemes of sessionally paid counselling have been introduced by one Centre after another. Most of these schemes still pay very modest rates, and the bulk of Relate's couple therapy is still given without payment to the counsellors, but there is a trend towards paid work, at a proper rate.

It is natural to ask why Relate originally chose to depend on a volunteer work-force, and having so chosen, why it later decided to introduce payment into the system. The original choice, made over forty years ago, was easy. Wartime experience appeared to show that there was always a strong supply of volunteers willing and able to meet any need, for the common good. Moreover, while the government was willing to offer some financial support for a scheme for selecting and training volunteers, it was not willing to fund a statutorily established body of professional workers for couple therapy (i.e. marriage guidance) and there was no other apparent source of funds for payment of professional workers.

The subsequent change began at least as far back as the early 1970s, simply because the organization was beginning to look for a greater time commitment from its voluntary workers than they could be expected to give without payment. (The minimum voluntary commitment amounts to about a day's work a week, when training and other ancillary activities are taken into account.) The pressure for increased time commitment was felt first by trainers and in-service supervisors, but worked rapidly and inexorably through to practitioners before the end of the 1970s.

Apart from the direct financial implications, the professional and organizational consequences of operating with a volunteer work-force are immense. It requires the setting up of a self-contained system of selection and training and in-service support, because the time at the disposal of volunteers does not fit the schedules or the location of traditional training courses. So a large component of the training has to be carried out locally, which requires a relatively large geographically dispersed body of trainers and supervisors, each responsible for working with a relatively small group of trainees. Such a system has the great advantage that once it is set up, it can fairly readily deliver a programme of continuous monitoring and skill development and even 'retraining' of local counsellors throughout their service with the organization, not just during an initial training period. This departure from the habits of the wider training world has many incidental advantages, for instance it allows Relate to avoid the strait-jackets of the examination system and a single annual intake of trainees. But some of these advantages have unintended side-effects: for instance the absence of examinations and diplomas can hinder recognition of merit, both from the outside looking in, and from the inside looking out.

There are two very obvious unintended consequences of using a volunteer work-force pushed to the limit of acceptable voluntary commitment. First, it makes for perennial problems in recruitment at local level. The time commitment is not the only problem; selection for personal suitability is also necessary, and since this depends ultimately on the national work-force of trainers and supervisors, it is frequently a source of tension between the centre and the periphery.

Second, the requirements make it differentially hard to recruit men. Of the 1,900 practitioners between 25 and 65 currently working for Relate, only about 15 per cent are men. It is not clear what the effect of that is, but in an organization primarily concerned with interaction between a man and a woman, this proportion of men is an apparent oddity.

Because of the federal structure of Relate, its finances are complex, but the main features are simple.

1  The real cost of Relate couple therapy is increasing – possibly at an accelerating rate – principally because of attempts to remedy long-standing understaffing throughout the organization and underpayment in the largest sectors of it. However, it is worth noting that in 1988–9, despite increased costs, the average *total* cost of delivering an hour's service, including the current costs of the whole training system, was about £15.40, far lower than the costs of a paid service.

2  The proportion of total costs met from public funds has been decreasing for several years. The largest element of this decrease up to now has been in central government grants to Relate National. Local government grants to Relate Centres have decreased in some areas but not overall. It is unclear whether they will decrease under the government's proposed funding structures for local authority services, or whether there will be pressure on Relate to alter its services in order to attract grant support.

3  It is not easy to obtain a large volume of charitable funding for Relate's work.

4  The main funders of the growth in the costs of the service are the people who use it. It has always been and still is the policy of the organization that people should not be denied its service if they are unable to contribute towards the cost. For many years that led to very low average contributions, but the point has been reached where clients *in aggregate* must make substantial payments if the service is to survive. (In 1988–9 clients paid just over 30 per cent of the total costs.)

This section has been long, not only because information is ready to hand, and because Relate is the largest and probably the most complex of the agencies, but also because much of its experience has relevance for the other voluntary agencies, whether or not they develop in the same direction as Relate.

### Scottish Marriage Guidance Council

The Scottish Marriage Guidance Council (SMGC), since 1990 known as Marriage Counselling Scotland, has a position in Scotland closely analogous to that of Relate in the rest of the UK. Its constituent local MGCs offer broadly the same kinds of services to couples, though not at present a separate sex therapy service; the counsellors are selected, trained and supervised in a fundamentally similar system, although there are significant differences of organizational detail. The separate existence of Relate and SMGC appears to owe more to the facts of British geography than to any differences of social or professional aims.

Nevertheless, that geography, and the economy built on it, have produced very substantial quantitative differences between the SMGC and Relate services. The decline both in general wealth and also in Relate services, from the South of England to the North, is continued into Scotland so that the SMGC volume of service in relation to the population is lower than the Relate volumes for the northern regions. But whereas in northern England there is a shortage of counsellors, in Scotland the deficit takes a different form: the average client contact time delivered by SMGC's counsellors appears to be less than half of that delivered by Relate's. There are several possible explanations, of which the most obvious is that SMGC is attempting to serve areas of extremely high and extremely low population density. Both these conditions have been found very difficult in England and Wales, even though variations of population density are much less than in Scotland.

The financial implications of a relatively low-volume and widely dispersed service are complex, and information on the total effect is not readily available. But having very few if any colleagues within easy reach must constitute a significant problem for counsellors and supervisors.

### Agencies to meet special needs

### Catholic Marriage Advisory Council

The Catholic Marriage Advisory Council (CMAC) was established at about the same time as the National Marriage Guidance Council, to provide services, mainly but not exclusively for Catholics, in the light of the teaching of the Roman Catholic Church about the institution of marriage and the relationship between husband and wife, and about related matters. It runs counselling services and an advisory service on natural family planning. The CMAC statement of philosophy and values includes a general acceptance of the uniqueness and autonomy of each client 'without discrimination of race, colour, or creed', backed by more specific statements of a client-centred orientation, for example 'we believe that people should have free access to the knowledge that will enable them to make conscientious decisions'.

The service is provided through local centres, whose distribution reflects that of the Catholic population, with marked differences from the general population. There are CMAC Centres in most cities, but not all, and not in all counties. (The organization of CMAC in Scotland is separate from that in England and Wales, but they are treated together in this section.) The size of the service is not straightforward to assess, because it relates to a potential clientele larger than the number of active Catholics, but smaller than the general population. In 1988–9 CMAC opened about 5,200 new cases, including its services of psychosexual counselling and natural family planning, which are staffed by specialists, separately from its counselling service; the volume of these services is low. The counselling service, which is growing, provided about 24,650 interviews in 1988–9 – an average of 5.3 per case (the Relate average is 5.5).

Like the national agencies, CMAC staffs its counselling service by selecting, training, and giving in-service support to a volunteer work-force, but there are some important differences from Relate's practice. The most obvious is that the target work-load for a counsellor is sixty interviews per year, and the actual average in 1988–9 was a little under fifty. The volume of training and in-service support received by CMAC counsellors is approximately the same as in Relate, and it is directed towards equipping them with a similar range of skills. Perhaps less emphasis is placed on object relations theory in CMAC work.

In 1988–9 there were about 540 CMAC counsellors, working in 82 Centres. There is a body of tutors responsible for in-service training and for supervision of counsellors, but some post-probationary counsellors are supervised by experienced counsellors within the Centre. In general, the individual work-loads of those operating the training and in-service support system are considerably lower than in Relate.

The financial position of CMAC is substantially different from that of the national agencies. The main reason is that unpaid voluntary work forms a much greater proportion of the total in CMAC, including the in-service training and support system. There are a number of other features that make comparison difficult. However, like the national organizations, CMAC finds problems in increasing its income to match the demands on it.

*Jewish Marriage Council*

The Jewish Marriage Council provides services of couple therapy as well as a number of other services related to marriage and family life in the Jewish community. The aims of its counselling service are similar to those of the other 'general practice' couple therapy services mentioned in this chapter. The service is based principally in London and Manchester, and its total volume is naturally very much smaller than the others, amounting to about 250 cases in 1988–9, of which about half were for one interview only. There are about thirty therapists, all unpaid volunteers, selected and trained in a system structurally similar to those of the other agencies. The average client contact time per year per therapist appears to be about forty hours.

*Asian Family Counselling Service*

As a postscript, and a reminder that all is flux: the Asian Family Counselling Service has not been examined here because it *is* a family counselling service, not a couple therapy agency. But one of the main reasons for setting it up was to help Asians to deal with marriage problems, particularly problems related to the stresses of settling in Britain, and it appears that in the course of time a larger proportion of its clients are coming to locate their problem in the couple relationship, not in the family as a whole. So, in the next edition of this book, perhaps this chapter will include an Asian couple therapy agency.

## In conclusion

What can we say in summary about the agencies' approach to couple therapy? Ideally we should outline its origins by reference to well-known landmarks in the history of 'the helping professions', indicate the state to which developmental forces have brought it so far, and estimate where it would be at some future point if present trends were to continue unchanged.

This chapter has shown that the agencies are a very disparate set of bodies. They have arisen from a variety of professional backgrounds, and some originated in social concern rather than any particular professional expertise. Throughout their history, their ethical principles and social goals have differed in some important respects. Their therapeutic methods have also been diverse; they were originally opportunistic initiatives, and because of the heterogeneity of the agencies, there has hitherto been little systematic cross-fertilization of techniques between them.

However, all the agencies exist in the same social environment, characterized by increasing expectations of personal well-being among consumers – coupled with a much greater flow of messages to them about where well-being is to be found – and by increasing efforts among producers to strengthen their economic position against their competitors. One way producers can strengthen their position is to improve their products, and accordingly, most if not all couple therapy agencies are taking more interest in critically evaluating their own work, and in alternative ways of working. This is still at an early stage, and is still hindered by their hand-to-mouth financial positions. But it could gradually lead to a millennium in which the couple therapy agencies have a common armamentarium of therapeutic methods, continually extended by the sort of competitive-collegiate culture that already exists in scientific medicine.

There is certainly scope for this kind of development, but it is by no means inevitable. Apart from the general possibilities of doom which are too well known to need repetition here, it could happen that technical and organizational developments lead to fission rather than fusion of the couple therapy agencies. That outcome does not appear to be indicated by present trends, but existing specialisms within the field of couple therapy have obvious affinities with services outside the field, for instance family therapy, or social skill training, or individual psychotherapy, or psychosexual medicine.

One feature of couple therapy will remain constant, whatever organizational framework it is set in: it will always be hard, often agonizing, and even dangerous work. There are and always will be easier ways of earning a living; although couple therapists undoubtedly have reasons of self-interest for undertaking the work, few could survive long in it without a personal concern to help others in need. That concern, rather than any particular technical skill, may prove to be the essence of the couple therapist's power to heal.

## Reference

Mattinson, J. and Sinclair, I. (1979) *Mate and Stalemate*, Oxford: Basil Blackwell.

# 16

# Research in therapy with couples: an overview

## KATE WILSON AND ADRIAN JAMES

Although the extent and range of research into therapy with couples is impressive, any review must begin by acknowledging certain [inherent] characteristics which may limit its usefulness or at least make its interpretation more difficult for the practitioner. These problems are over and above those relating to the design of the studies themselves and we begin by exploring them in turn.

Practice guides and reviews of research tend to consider marital therapy as a sub-species of family therapy, on the basis that both attempt to modify the inter-actions between components of 'natural systems'. Nonetheless it is frequently unclear whether or not the two are being treated as synonymous, or whether couples issues alone are being addressed. Two major reviews (Gurman and Kniskern 1978; Gurman, Kniskern and Pinsof 1986) do not resolve this ambiguity, considering marital therapy as a sub-species, but nonetheless separating marital from other types of therapy with family relationships. Clearly, it is not always necessary to consider the relationship between the two; but the extent to which, for example, findings concerning intervention in one system may be generalized to another is surely relevant. Given the close scrutiny which researchers have accorded both marital and family therapy, it is surprising that this ambiguity has not received greater attention and the extent to which the two should be treated as different entities still requires clarification.

A further uncertainty lies in the extent to which it is accurate to use the terms 'couple therapy' and 'marital therapy' interchangeably. It might have been anticipated that by now some distinction would be emerging in the research literature between therapy addressing problems between couples who are mar-ried, and therapy with unmarried couples or with gay or lesbian couples. However, we found no research which made a distinction between the different groups, or indeed which focused specifically on the problems of non-marital couples. The research studies which we discuss in this chapter by and large refer to marital therapy and although it is not always explicitly stated, it is usually evi-dent that the data are drawn from married couples. We have therefore tended in the chapter to use the term 'marital therapy' rather than 'couple therapy' as this reflects the terminology in the literature. We are, however, aware from anecdotal evidence that the problems encountered by non-marital couples may be very different from those of married couples and would hope that a future research review might be in a better position to elaborate on the distinctions than we are at present.

Although British studies into marital therapy are beginning to form a distinctive literature, and British writers have contributed significantly to the theoretical understanding and treatment of marital problems, the majority particularly of outcome studies in this field are American in origin. This relative imbalance is so familiar that the UK reader is probably innured to it, but the problems of cross-cultural generalization remain. It is worth noting that here, as in other fields, the number of consumer studies published in Britain is proportionately far greater than it is in North America. These studies tend to report lower levels of satisfaction with treatment than do the range of studies from the other side of the Atlantic, but it is difficult to draw any conclusions from this because of the very problems of comparison referred to above.

Although there have been numerous reviews of the research in this field and indeed reviews of reviews and critical reappraisals of review findings (e.g. Williams and Miller 1981; Wells and Giannetti 1986) the content and manner of presentation of much of the research may limit its use to the practitioner. Colapinto (1979), writing over a decade ago, questioned the value of traditional research methods and the ability of what he describes as linear (i.e. cause–effect) approaches to address systems issues. Schwartz and Breunlin (1983), on the basis of interviews with clinicians in the field of family and marital therapy, report that the majority found most research papers to have little relevance for their clinical practice. Gurman and colleagues (1986), acknowledging the problem, suggest that these reactions principally derive from four features relating to the research – practitioners' reactions to outcome research, the dominance of outcome over process research, the type of measures used to assess effectiveness, and the conventional manner in which findings are reported. They are, however, in no doubt that traditionally designed studies can yield useful information about the efficacy of different forms of marital therapy, a view with which we would concur. None the less, the issues of both accessibility and usefulness are clearly ones which researchers need to address, and are to some extent linked to issues concerning the kind of research which is undertaken, and by whom and in what settings the research is conducted.

Studies evaluating behavioural marital therapy (BMT), and particularly studies addressing its effectiveness, far outweigh in number those concerning other approaches to therapy. The relative paucity of non-behavioural research must raise some critical questions about practice, since it clearly indicates that progress, changes and developments in practice are not necessarily influenced by considerations of effectiveness. Thus, for example, Bennun (1986a) has commented on the relatively recent impact of cognitive interventions on the practice of couple therapy and the development of related theories, but on the almost complete absence of outcome literature related to such developments. This view is shared by Bagarozzi and Giddings (1983) who comment, for example, on one such approach (rational-emotive therapy) that its 'effectiveness as a treatment for marital distress has yet to be demonstrated' (1983: 11). A recent study by Huber and Milstein (1985) of seventeen couples, nine of whom were offered a cognitive restructuring programme, with positive results, was the only small example of research into rational-emotive therapy that we found.

It seems particularly paradoxical that the current interest in such innovations as cognitive therapy and rational-emotive therapy which stress, for example, the systematic assessment of clients' evaluative beliefs about perceived events and have led to the development of valid and reliable schedules to assess these (Epstein 1986), should not yet have led to the publication of a body of systematic evaluative studies of such methods. As Bagarozzi and Giddings (1983), in their review of research on marital violence, have argued, the lack of empirical data raises 'a number of substantive issues . . . which require some consideration and further exploration before practitioners elect to employ one or more of the treatment approaches' (1983: 9) which they discuss.

Finally, in considering some of the problems and limitations inherent in these studies, we must acknowledge the difficulty in writing this review of deciding which studies would 'count' as acceptable when it came to reporting and evaluating their findings.

In our search of the literature, we came across a large number of publications, both books and journal articles (predominantly American), which were more than just theoretical expositions and which often referred to or were based upon an empirical component consisting of an analysis of clinical practice or case studies. We would concur with the view that much useful information can be gleaned from the study of work with individual couples in practice settings (Barlow *et al.* 1984; Baucom and Hoffman 1986). Accounts such as the vivid one provided by Clulow (1985), of sustained work undertaken with a couple at the Institute of Marital Studies, are often rich in detail, and may resemble treatment as it is usually conducted in practice settings more closely than the carefully controlled studies which we describe below. As Haldane (1987) comments of Mattinson and Sinclair's (1979) study *Mate and Stalemate*, 'For me this is the account of marital work which rings most true to my experience of National Health Service general psychiatry and child and family psychiatry services and of private practice'. (Haldane 1987: 7).

Such studies are often presented as essays in objective, scientific analysis. However, with the exception of some of the consumer studies to which we refer later in the chapter, they are seldom analysed with sufficient rigour to be classed as research studies and probably could not be said to meet any of the six simple criteria of acceptability on which Gurman (1973) rated research reports in the first of his major reviews. We have therefore, with some regret, excluded them from the present review.

Baucom and Hoffman (1986), discussing the limitations of existing empirical research on marital therapy, suggest that research could be made more applicable to clinical settings, and could more easily be carried out by practitioners themselves, if case studies or single case evaluations were used in a more structured way. As in controlled-outcome investigations, they consider the goal in a case study must be 'to provide data suggesting that therapy is responsible for treatment change and to rule out as many alternative explanations as possible'

(1986: 610). The content to be assessed (for example the couple's communication patterns) must be specified, and they suggest that one of a number of standardized assessment instruments may be used to establish a base line and evaluate change and the extent to which any changes are attributable to the treatment itself. They highlight the need to consider a variety of potential sources of the assessment data (for example the extent to which self-reports or ratings by the couple, or outsiders' ratings, might be used) and the frequency and timing of its collection. They also stress the importance of clearly defined intervention procedures rather than a vague 'what seemed to work', although as we see from studies such as that of Crowe (1978), which we discuss in the next section, isolating the characteristics of a particular approach is far from straightforward.

Given the expense and difficulty of conducting more orthodox research in clinical settings, and the difficulties of interpreting the results of such research, it seems to us that these suggestions offer one useful way forward. Practitioners working with specific couples could thereby provide information in a systematic rather than anecdotal way about treatment changes and be in a better position to attribute changes to specific interventions or to match clients with certain kinds of problems to particular approaches to treatment.

With these caveats concerning the nature and limitations of the research in mind, we shall now turn to the research studies themselves. We consider first the evidence concerning the effectiveness of different forms of marital therapy, following this with a section on factors which have been found to have some bearing on outcome. The ensuing section considers special issues in marital therapy, a broad grouping in which we have included studies relating to marital therapy where there are problems of addiction, conciliation and divorce research and research relating to sex therapy. Inevitably there is considerable overlap between the different sections, and to some extent the divisions must reflect the need for clarity of access rather than absolute distinctions between the kinds of research under consideration. Thus, for example, one of the British consumer studies considers the effectiveness of treatment measured at a post-treatment follow-up, in addition to reporting levels of consumer satisfaction. None the less we consider it along with other consumer studies rather than extracting these findings and considering them in an earlier section on effectiveness, taking the view that in this case the distinction along the lines of type of research was more easily understood.

## The effectiveness of marital therapy

As we indicated above, there have been since the early 1970s a number of major reviews of marital therapy research, most importantly those conducted by Gurman and various co-authors. The earliest review (Gurman 1973) found the number of research studies which met an acceptable standard of rigour so few that it was difficult to draw from them any firm conclusions, although it appeared that about 66 per cent of the couples concerned could be said to have improved as a result of a variety of therapeutic interventions. A second major review (Gurman and Kniskern 1978) considered over 200 outcome studies, and demonstrated not only that the quality of the research undertaken had improved enormously, but also that research had become an established part of the marital therapy landscape.

The third and latest review (Gurman *et al.* 1986) summarized the major findings from the earlier review, and considered those issues which appeared to warrant further exploration as a result of more recent studies. Those findings which relate to marital as opposed to family therapy (where this distinction is valid) are reproduced here.

1  Non-behavioural marital and family therapies produce beneficial outcomes in about two-thirds of cases, and their effects are superior to those receiving no treatment.
2  When both spouses experiencing marital difficulties are involved together in therapy (commonly described as conjoint therapy) there is a greater chance of positive outcome than when only one spouse is treated.
3  Positive results of both non-behavioural and behavioural marital and family therapies typically occur in treatment of short duration, that is one to twenty sessions.
4  A deterioration in the individual (identified patient) and/or in the relationship may sometimes occur in association with marital and family therapy.
5  A therapist 'style' of providing little structuring of early treatment sessions and little confrontation of highly affective material may be reliably associated with observed deterioration effects. Such a style is clearly more deterioration promoting, in general, than a style of stimulating interaction and giving support.
6  There is no empirical support for the superiority of co-therapy compared with marital or family therapy conducted by a single therapist.
7  A reasonable mastery of technical skills may be sufficient for preventing worsening or for maintaining pre-treatment family functioning, but more refined therapist relationship skills seem necessary to the yielding of genuinely positive outcomes.

The second of these findings, namely that concerning the greater efficacy of work conducted with both spouses rather than with one, had a substantial impact on practice when it was reported in the original survey. The data on which this conclusion was reached has, however, attracted subsequent critical comment, and we shall return to it as an issue later in the chapter.

### Behavioural and non-behavioural marital therapy

In common with other fields, research into behavioural approaches to marital therapy far outstrips that into other approaches, so that although, as Gurman *et al.* (1986) point out, this probably does not reflect the balance of clinical practice, any review must acknowledge that 'there are two quite distinct marital therapy research literatures' (1986: 582). The literature dealing with behavioural approaches contains numerous outcome studies, while very few deal with the outcome of other approaches (for example psychodynamic, rational-emotive, strategic, systemic).

None the less, a number of studies have attempted to compare the outcome of different therapeutic approaches. For example Crowe (1978) randomly assigned forty-two couples to BMT, group-analytic couple therapy or a control group. He found no significant differences on individual or sexual adjustments or target complaints between the two kinds of treatments at post-test or at an eighteen-month follow-up. Boelens *et al.* (1980) compared behavioural contingency contracting and strategic therapy, and found no differences between the two treatments, save that the 'strategic' couples showed greater evidence of relapse at follow-up. Baucom and Lester (1982: quoted in Gurman *et al.* 1986) compared BMT with cognitive therapy plus BMT, and again found little significant difference. Finally, Johnson and Greenberg (1985a) in an impressively designed study which they later partially replicated using novice therapists (1985b), compared the use of emotionally focused (EF) therapy with cognitive behavioural marital therapy. Both forms of treatment led to an improvement in the quality of marital relationships, but EF therapy was found to be superior on marital adjustment, intimacy and reduction of target complaints post-test, and these higher scores were sustained at an eight-week follow-up.

This last study excepted, there are, as Gurman *et al.* (1986) point out, a number of problems with these accounts, largely arising from the fact that the non-behavioural treatments delineated in them often depart in important characteristics from the models which they purport to investigate. To take but one example, Crowe (1978) excludes from psychodynamic therapy non-directive interventions, although the latter would be consistent with the approach. The studies are also typically conducted by researchers from behavioural and communication orientations, and this may have some bearing on the design of the studies. None the less, on the basis of these studies it can be concluded that the efficacy of BMT over other forms of marital therapies has not been established, and in the most satisfactory study emotionally focused therapy was found to be more successful.

There are numerous studies which compare BMT to no-treatment, characteristically using waiting-list couples as control groups. In general, these studies demonstrate to varying degrees significant improvements in marital functioning amongst the couples receiving treatment. However, as Baucom and Hoffman (1986) comment in a critical integrative analysis of these studies, although decreases in negative verbal behaviour and improvement on self-report measures of marital satisfaction and adjustment were established, increases in positive communication and problem-solving behaviour have not been consistently demonstrated and appear to be more difficult to establish.

## Factors affecting outcome in marital therapy

A small number of studies have examined the relative efficacy of different kinds of interventions within one form of treatment. We consider these in the ensuing section, together with the evidence on the effect of treatment mode, and the evidence of the implications of predisposing factors (for example depression in one partner, commitment to the marriage, communication patterns) for successful or unsuccessful treatment outcomes. Finally, we consider in this section the findings of a number of consumer studies, although, as we indicated above, many of these studies address other issues in addition to those relating to factors which may affect outcome.

## Intervention strategies in non-behavioural approaches

It is possible, drawing on the admittedly scanty outcome studies which investigate non-behavioural approaches, to draw certain conclusions about what strategies are likely to be more effective. These relate largely to the need to link the exploration of feelings and unconscious (or 'out of awareness') experiences with concrete active therapist interventions directed towards changing behaviour. Thus, for example, in the Johnson and Greenberg studies (1985a; 1985b), the linking of inner experience with behaviours, and therapist suggestions directed at changing those behaviours, is found to achieve a greater degree of positive change than intervention where these links are not made. Such conclusions are supported by the findings of the consumer studies, which we review later.

## Intervention strategies in behavioural approaches

A few studies have attempted to measure the comparative efficacy of different treatment methods within a behavioural approach, for example, problem-solving training, communication training and contingency contracting. No consistent outcome differences have been established in the effectiveness of different procedures, either when used in combination or in isolation, or when the order of presentation is varied. There is some evidence (Turkewitz and O'Leary 1981) to suggest that behaviour exchange training is more effective when used with contingency contracting than without it. Baucom and Hoffman (1986) comment that in their clinical experience, some couples find contracting appealing and others find it unhelpful, but that there is no evidence to support these observations or to identify which couples might benefit from such procedures.

## Couple characteristics

Attempts have been made to identify couples' characteristics which may be linked with successful treatment outcomes, and it is to these studies that we now turn.

Beach and Broderick (1983) studied a sample of forty-two couples seeking marital therapy in order to explore the relationship between commitment to the marriage at the start of therapy and any changes during therapy. The study builds on the insights of social exchange theory and related areas of study, which suggest that level of commitment can have a major impact on people's social behaviour and that high commitment couples should be more amenable to therapeutic intervention. The study demonstrated that for women, pre-therapy commitment was clearly related to marital satisfaction at intake and to changes in marital satisfaction following therapy, but there were no such findings for men. This study also showed, however, that communication ability was predictive of marital satisfaction and that changes in communication ability as a result of therapy were also predictive of increases in marital satisfaction for women. The authors conclude, however, that further research is needed to investigate the process which links commitment to gains in therapy.

A subsequent study sought to develop these findings further. Beach *et al.* (1985) studied 120 couples seeking marital therapy, assessing levels of depression, levels of commitment, as well as key demographic variables. They found that all couples where extramarital sex was identified as a problem showed either lowered commitment to the marital relationship, higher levels of depression, or both. Moreover, they found that it was the spouse who was engaging in extramarital sex, regardless of their gender, who was most likely to show these symptoms. They suggest that the depression may result from the ambivalent commitment of that spouse to the marriage, which may also be a factor leading to extramarital sex. The authors conclude that conventional couple therapy programmes (e.g. communication training, behavioural contracting) fare poorly in such situations and that individual therapy with the spouse concerned, in which the issue of commitment can be explored, should be considered as a precursor to couple therapy. In concluding, they raise the question of why the spouses of persons engaged in extramarital sex do not also show lower levels of commitment and higher levels of depression.

The relationship between depression and marital problems has also been the focus of research and Kuipers (1987) usefully summarizes the background research on depression, the family and on the effectiveness of treatment. Hinchliffe *et al.* (1978) comment on the basis of their study of depression and marriage: 'There is consistent evidence that the marital situation is crucial to the understanding of a depressed spouse' (1978: 107) and conclude on the basis of their own and other research that conjoint marital therapy combined with drug therapy is more effective than either conjoint marital therapy or drug therapy alone. They do not prescribe either the amount or form of therapy however, or rule out concurrent individual therapy and the authors conclude that 'Obviously more research evaluation of such methods is needed' (1978: 107) and that the absence of this should not discourage therapists from using conjoint methods of their choice. Kuipers (1987), however, nearly ten years later, is still forced to conclude that 'evidence for the effectiveness of . . . marital treatment is mainly descriptive or limited to small numbers' (1987: 208).

Corney (1987) reported the results of a clinical trial involving eighty depressed women patients in general practice, who were randomly allocated to an experimental group for treatment by social workers attached to the surgeries, or to a control group for treatment only by their GPs. During follow-up investigations at six and twelve months, it was found that women with major marital problems were more likely to be depressed than those with good relationships, but that those who had received social work help had made more improvement than the control group. It was also found that women with major marital problems also tended to have poorer social contacts and that these women benefited more from the additional social work help. The effectiveness of this intervention was not related to the number of interviews and no standard programme of treatment was used. Social workers gave information and practical help where needed, using some behavioural interventions and, in 90 per cent of the cases, using sustaining and exploring techniques in order to increase the clients' awareness and understanding of their situation.

Corney (1987) concludes that her findings relating the quality of the marital relationship to clinical outcome in the treatment of depressed women are consistent with other research, such as that by Gibbons *et al.* (1978), whose study of task-centred social work with self-poisoners in a hospital setting also showed improvements in marital and interpersonal relationships. Corney (1987) notes, however, that there was no evidence from her study that conjoint therapy was more effective in work with marital problems than help given to wives only, and that the provision of practical help may have been of particular value. This possibility would receive broad support from consumer research in social work and would also tend to support the studies of Relate clients reported below, in which disappointment was expressed about the lack of more concrete assistance such as advice and information.

Another study by Cline *et al.* (1984) is worth mentioning, not least because it seems to sum up the current state of research into couple therapy in its findings. The study involved seventy-seven distressed middle- and lower-class couples who were treated by nineteen therapists using conjoint therapy. A variety of tests were used to assess marital satisfaction and communication skills and both couple and therapist behaviour were assessed although the type of therapeutic approach employed is not made clear. The study revealed the importance of socio-economic status as a factor influencing client responses to therapist behaviour, suggesting that directive forms of therapy were not related to positive outcomes for middle-class couples, while reflective therapist behaviour led to decreases in positive social behaviour for working-class husbands and wives and directness led to increases. The overall thrust of the findings according to Cline *et al.* (1984) is that no one approach to marital therapy will be necessarily appropriate for the different sexes and for those with different socio-economic backgrounds and that social class is a more significant variable than the gender of the spouse. Such conclusions, although adding another piece to the already existing jigsaw of research findings, also serve to highlight the need for the addition of further pieces before a clear picture begins to emerge.

Finally, the issue of couples' characteristic communication patterns and their relevance to marital problems and marital therapy has been the subject of much research. Boland and Follingstad (1987) have undertaken a comprehensive methodological review of the US literature focusing on the assessment of the relationship between marital satisfaction and communication. They considered a total of forty-eight studies, dividing these into broad categories of studies which look at the content of communication and those which look at process. On the basis of this research, they concluded that both content and process elements are important predictors of marital satisfaction. In the content studies, high levels of self-disclosure – e.g. expressions of love, support and affection – and greater depth and breadth of disclosure consistently emerge as being positively related to marital satisfaction. Process research studies have consistently shown the importance of positive communication patterns and skills and clarity of speech in increased levels of marital satisfaction. On the basis of these findings, Boland and Follingstad (1987) conclude that, while good communication is not a universal panacea, treatment packages would be wise to include training for couples in these aspects of communication.

As with most such reviews, however, the authors are critical of many of the studies on methodological grounds. The studies reviewed varied between those using samples as large as 731 wives, to those with samples as small as 14 couples, and poor sampling methods are identified as a weakness in many studies. The studies also employ a wide range of research strategies and instruments which, as Boland and Follingstad (1987) point out, makes effective comparative research or replication studies difficult, thereby limiting the cumulative value of this body of research.

### Treatment mode

A number of studies have addressed the question of the relative efficacy of different modes, as opposed to theoretical approaches to treatment. These studies have looked at the differences in outcome between conjoint/individual treatment, treatment with one/two therapists and treatment in a group as opposed to individually. The findings concerning the number of therapists (that it makes no difference) are relatively unproblematic, although more subtle research instruments which tested also, for example, for levels of experience, might reveal discernible differences.

As Wells and Giannetti (1986) point out, Gurman and Kniskern's (1978) earlier finding concerning the negative outcome of individual marital therapy (IMT) has serious implications, since exclusive reliance on a conjoint mode of treatment means that 'potential clients who . . . do not have an available or co-operative spouse, run the risk of being refused treatment, or offered a treatment the therapist believes inferior' (1978: 43). They, among others, reappraised the research studies which were purported to demonstrate the relative inferiority of IMT and criticized the methodology used in the review. Gurman and Kniskern (1986) subsequently modified their position somewhat, acknowledging that there is little empirical evidence of the inefficacy of IMT. However, they point out that while the efficacy of conjoint marital therapy has been satisfactorily established, there is no similar evidence of the efficacy of IMT. They therefore conclude that 'there is ample warrant for the position that conjoint therapy can for now, be considered the treatment of choice for marital problems' (1986: 59).

Since this question must be of considerable concern to practitioners, particularly those in non-specialist settings where it may be especially difficult to engage both partners, it is to be hoped that further research will clarify the issue.

As Bennun (1986b) in a review of group marital therapy comments, 'the growth of the group marital therapy literature has not been paralleled with an increase in empirical investigation' (1986b: 71). There have been few acceptable outcome studies, and crucial decisions concerning, for example, group composition, structure and therapist style have had to rest for the most part on clinical judgements and intuition.

Gurman and Kniskern (1978) reviewed fifteen group marital studies, and concluded that of the nearly 400 patients concerned, 66 per cent showed improvement after treatment, with 30 per cent no change, and 4 per cent deterioration, a figure comparable to other forms of marital therapy. In a separate study, they concluded that deterioration occurred more often in group marital and individual therapy than in therapy which involved some form of conjoint work. Later studies have provided a no less equivocal picture: Hahlweg *et al.* (1982) randomly assigned eighty-five couples to one of two treatments (BMT or communication skills training) and one of two modalities (conjoint or conjoint group) or a waiting-list control group. Both kinds of BMT, but only the conjoint mode of communications training showed improvement when compared to the control group. However, Bennun (1984) found no difference between these treatment modes or in a comparison with BMT undertaken with one partner alone.

Group therapy research, particularly that which tries to use more than a simple outcome measure, is notoriously problematic, and the paucity of studies into outcome and process issues in group marital therapy, let alone those which are methodologically acceptable, shows that marital group therapy research is no exception. Group therapy as an approach to marital problems has been gaining in popularity, and it is to be hoped that research in the next decade will be available to guide this practice.

### Consumer studies

Gurman (1973), in a review of research into the effectiveness of marital therapy, rightly expresses caution about the reliability of client self-report studies. However, although evidently distinctive from the other studies we have considered in this section, such studies and the issues they raise about practice clearly deserve attention as part of a growing body of consumer research and for the insights they provide into the impact of marital therapy upon clients. Moreover, in drawing attention to factors which are outside the therapeutic encounter, and locating the client/worker exchanges in a wider context, they provide a useful counterbalance to many of the evaluative studies which focus exclusively on these. A number of recent studies conducted under the auspices of the National Marriage Guidance Council (now Relate) evaluate aspects of the work of the agency through the use of clients' accounts of their experiences of counselling. Although many of the findings link with data that we have considered elsewhere in this section (for example those relating to the importance of a structured approach to intervention), for ease of access, we consider these studies as a group.

Hunt (1985) undertook a study of former Marriage Guidance (Relate) clients to consider why they chose the agency, what expectations they had, their experience of counselling, what it achieved and what had happened since its conclusion, using responses from a sample of fifty-one people from forty-two marriages, involving twenty-one counsellors, both groups being broadly representative of Relate clients and counsellors. She found that 49 per cent of clients had been satisfied by the experience, with 25 per cent being satisfied in some respects and 25 per cent being dissatisfied. In addition, 49 per cent felt positive about the counselling they had received, although 41 per cent sounded negative and 10 per cent had mixed feelings. Overall, only 46 per cent felt they had benefited from counselling, 4 per cent feeling neutral and 50 per cent feeling they had not benefited at all. As Hunt observes, in comparison with the Gurman and Kniskern (1978) review of research which concludes that the main forms of non-behavioural marital therapy appear to produce beneficial effects in 61 per cent of cases (or more, if individual therapy results are excluded) these figures are not encouraging and do not support the optimism expressed by counsellors in assessing their work. If anything, given the numbers of those who declined to participate in the research, the figures suggest that the overall rate may be even lower, although, as Hunt rightly argues, the assessment of the relationship between quality of counselling and client satisfaction is problematic since

> their opinion of the help they received may very well be affected by their feelings about the situation they are currently in, as is their view of all the other events in their lives.
>
> (Hunt 1985: 17)

Hunt also concludes, on the basis of her evidence, that joint interviews do not necessarily produce a more satisfactory outcome and that the more interviews held, the more clients felt they had been helped, although few cases had more than ten interviews.

The study does reveal various aspects of the counselling experience with which clients were satisfied. Many valued being able to express their feelings, acquiring some understanding of themselves and their problem, and confiding in a neutral person. However, nearly half indicated that they had felt disappointed by the lack of advice and suggestions given and virtually none of the clients could recall forming an explicit agreement with their counsellor concerning the nature, aims or frequency of sessions which 'often led to misunderstandings and ambiguities and uncertainties about how to proceed' (1985: 70). Similarly 65 per cent of clients felt puzzled, distressed and dissatisfied after their first interview, particularly those seeking advice or a more structured, more focused response from the counsellor as opposed to simply the opportunity to ventilate their feelings. Thus the reflective, non-directive approach by counsellors was felt by many to be unproductive during initial interviews.

Following from Hunt's research and a recognition of the problem of 'engaging' clients in the helping process, Gaunt (1985) did a further study of first interviews. She argues that a wide range of client and counsellor characteristics may be related to the fact that nearly one-third of all Relate clients attend for only one interview, and reviews the research on this. Her findings are based on a study of ninety first interviews from a sample of Relate referrals, in which she adopted what she describes as an experimental approach. One group of counsellors conducted interviews according to a set of guidelines prepared for the research (stressing, in particular, the importance of a more structured approach, of effective time management in the interview, and a more active approach to counselling. This included clarifying clients' expectations, explaining the purpose of counselling, and seeking agreement about the issues to be worked upon and the number of sessions to be offered). The control group interviewed as normal, although subsequent analysis revealed that some of this group incorporated some of these elements in their interviews without instruction.

Clients in the experimental group tended to rate their interviews more highly, but while finding them valuable and/or useful, they also tended to find them more difficult and uncomfortable, with counsellors being perceived as slightly less warm and friendly. Overall however, in contrast to Hunt's (1985) survey, most clients rated their interview highly, over 60 per cent rating them 4 or 5 on a scale of 0–5. Gaunt (1989) concludes on the basis of this that counsellors should be encouraged to develop the use of contract-making techniques in first interviews, and to exercise greater control over the process of the interview in order to increase client satisfaction levels and the number of counselling sessions attended.

These studies are complemented by another piece of research into the experiences of counsellors and their clients by Timms and Blampied (1985), based on intensive tape-recorded interviews with fifty clients and seventeen counsellors from two Catholic Marriage Advisory Councils and one Relate Centre in the north-east of England. This study identifies and addresses a significant problem in assessing the effectiveness of marital therapy and in evaluating research in this area namely that generally, with the exception of important studies such as that by Brannen and Collard (1982), little attention is given to the experiences of clients before they reach the helping agency. In addition, it must be recognized that clients are not always seeking 'help' *per se*, a factor which has clear implications for evaluative research, and that even where 'help' is sought, it can be of different kinds. As Timms and Blampied observe

> Many of our clients wanted to place their experiences, to evaluate them in the context of other people's behaviour, so that causal or moral attributions might be made. Others were more concerned with problem-solving and carrying through a decision, whilst others were content to come to some accommodation. These purposes . . . were clearly envisaged in many cases long before the client arrived at the agency's door.
>
> (Timms and Blampied 1985: vii)

These findings clearly dovetail with those of Hunt (1985) and Gaunt (1985) about the significance of clients' expectations in determining their satisfaction with marital counselling and how discrepant these can sometimes be with counsellors' perspectives.

Timms and Blampied (1985) are therefore concerned to explore clients' experiences and the purposes they begin to entertain before reaching the marriage counselling agency; the impact of these factors on the subsequent interactions between clients and counsellors; and the impact of the organizational context of counselling for both clients and counsellors. They found that counsellors were keen to distinguish themselves from social workers and that they needed the agency as an organizational framework in which to give expression to their principal motives as counsellors – beneficence, and 'the opportunity to exercise, on a small scale, some virtuoso skills' (1985: 65). Simultaneously clients were seeking counsellors to act as 'a kind of tribunal in which clients would receive a hearing impartial and fair' (1985: 62), in the course of which they could get a picture or a 'version' of their problem (cf. Hunt's (1985) findings above). Again, the organizational context of the encounter was important since once there, clients felt they could tackle the difficult key problem of the public disclosure of painful and private sorrows, without this going beyond the agency. This points to the need for agencies with characteristics which both facilitate disclosure and can guarantee confidentiality, characteristics which are generally missing from informal social networks and possibly, too, from statutory agencies. One of the main conclusions which Timms and Blampied draw from their research therefore is that the notion of agency function is central to an understanding of marriage counselling.

## Special issues in couple therapy

Within the field of marital research there are distinctive groupings which focus on marital intervention with particular kinds of problems in marriage. We consider in this section intervention in marriages where there is a history of violence and substance abuse, sexual problems, the distinctive field of conciliation and divorce research, and finally therapy in remarriages.

It is evident that when couples seek help over their marital difficulties, the problems may be located within the family. Such situations might include couples where there is mental illness in the family, where there are mentally handicapped children, elderly relatives or physical disability. The literature relating to this from a family perspective is vast and cannot be reviewed here, and readers are referred to source books such as Orford (1987) for further discussion. Some of these issues have been explored with particular reference to couple therapy, however, and merit more detailed consideration here.

### Violence and substance abuse

Bagarozzi and Giddings (1983) review US findings on conjugal violence and consider the usefulness of these for therapeutic practice. They point out that in the USA, much as in Britain, research into conjugal violence suffered from 'selective inattention' until the late 1960s as part of the preservation of the myth of the loving and nurturing family but that subsequent research has demonstrated the widespread nature of marital violence. This view is confirmed by Dobash and Dobash (1987) in a review of the British evidence.

Bagarozzi and Giddings (1983) highlight a number of problems in these studies of marital violence, including weaknesses in research methodology, statistical analysis, the conceptual limitations of sociological approaches which locate the causes of marital violence outside the immediate confines of marriage and the family, and the practical and clinical utility of their findings. They identify three broad categories of therapeutic response – the reduction of aggression through periodic cathartic release, the reduction of anger through cognitive restructuring, and the management of anger and the learning of non-aggressive conflict management skills – but conclude that the relative merits of these approaches cannot be assessed at present because of a lack of empirical data. While they offer a theoretical critique of the different approaches, based partly upon other research studies, they conclude that 'no empirically based procedures are available which have been developed expressly for the treatment of conjugal violence' (1983: 12).

Because of the association between alcohol abuse and violent behaviour, the issue of marital violence leads almost inevitably to a consideration of alcohol abuse in marriage. Dominian (1986) refers to a study of battered wives by

Gayford, published in the *British Medical Journal* in 1975, which showed that alcoholism was present in 75 per cent of the cases. In such cases, violence might be viewed as effect and treatment may be aimed at a presumed cause, alcohol abuse. Nace (1982) reviews various treatment approaches to the alcoholic marriage. Although somewhat dated in its adherence to the disease-model of alcoholism, the article stresses the importance of being prepared to diagnose alcoholism when evaluating marital problems. While Orford's (1987) critical review of alcoholism and marriage warns against the dangers of focusing only on the drinking problem in the alcoholic marriage, and argues that marriages stressed by alcoholism should not be regarded as wholly different from other marriages under stress, Nace (1982) points out that in practice, it is necessary to emphasize the particular contribution of alcoholism to marital dysfunctioning. On the basis of his review of the research, therefore, Nace recommends that the alcoholism must be treated first, to be followed by marital therapy, and that treatment will be more successful if the spouse or family are included in the initial evaluation and subsequent treatment plans.

Such recommendations are consistent with other reviews of research (e.g. Janzen 1977; Steinglass 1976) which are on the whole fairly positive about the value of family-orientated treatment approaches. More recently, Pearson and Anderson (1985) have sought to link such research to the broader practice questions of family systems dynamics, considering the functions which alcohol may serve in a family – to signal stress and strain, to stabilize a chaotic system by acting as a scapegoat for hidden problems, and to regulate emotional intimacy. Such perspectives clearly indicate that alcohol abuse can also be viewed as effect rather than cause and that once the functions of alcohol abuse in a family are known, and family or marital therapy has been provided, the drinking behaviour is likely to become dysfunctional to the family and to be replaced by more adaptive behaviours. In a survey of the use of such methods in 146 agencies in Massachusetts, however, Regan *et al.* (1983) found that the families of alcohol abusers remained on the periphery of the treatment process and that despite their growing popularity elsewhere, conjoint couple therapy, group couple therapy and family treatment were seldom used. Where families did receive help, this was usually in the form of individual counselling. No similar research appears to have been undertaken in Britain.

A further US study worth mentioning is that by O'Farrell *et al.* (1985), who report the results of an experiment using behavioural marital therapy on couples in which the husband had recently begun individual alcoholism counselling. A total of thirty-four couples were involved, ten of whom received weekly sessions of behaviour therapy, a further twelve receiving weekly sessions of interactional group therapy, and twelve being allocated to a control group where no marital treatment was offered to the couple. The study concluded that those couples involved in the behavioural programme improved significantly in terms of certain criteria of marital functioning such as marital stability, communication skills when dealing with marital problems, and overall marital adjustment, and that such treatment produced better outcomes in these areas than the interactional programme, while the control group showed no marital relationship improvements. While this study is based on a small sample, it lends further credence to the view that it is important to work with the marriage and not just with the individual. It also further confirms the value of behavioural approaches.

## Sexual problems

A review by Thompson and Cranwell (1984) of the sources used in the US literature on sex therapy confirms the dominant influence of the work of Masters and Johnson (1966) in the practice of sex therapy, a picture which is reflected in Britain, where in general sex therapy is less readily available.

Hawton (1985) provides a comprehensive review of research on sex therapy with couples, an area which (even in Britain) is relatively well-researched in comparison with couples therapy in general. In Hawton's view, 'sufficient research has been conducted for clinical practice to be based on a more substantial footing' (1985: 200). He distinguished between studies of the outcome of sex therapy, both short- and long-term studies which compare sex therapy with other treatment modalities, and studies in which modifications to key components in the Masters and Johnson model (single therapists instead of co-therapists, frequency of treatment sessions, and the use of self-help methods) have been evaluated.

Most outcome studies suggest that the immediate results of sex therapy are not as good as Masters and Johnson originally reported, a view shared by Scharff (1988) on the basis of his work. Masters and Johnson reported an overall success rate of 80 per cent with only a 5 per cent relapse during a five-year follow-up. Their research has subsequently been criticized on methodological grounds, however, and Hawton (1985) concludes that although results are reasonable, later research generally shows that only approximately two-thirds of couples have a satisfactory outcome. This general picture receives further confirmation from a recent British study by Warner *et al.* (1987) of 1,194 cases seen in a three-year period by services forming part of the Edinburgh Human Sexuality Group, in which a moderate or even better outcome was achieved in 68 per cent of cases. Exceptionally, also, Renshaw (1988) reports an 80 per cent improvement in her study of treatment outcomes among 1,188 couples over fifteen years at the Loyola Sex Clinic. However, a recent British study by Hawton *et al.* (1986) of 106 couples suggests that after three years some of the gains evident immediately after therapy (particularly in relation to disorders such as premature ejaculation or low female desire) may have been lost. In general, however, few studies address the issue of long-term outcomes.

Hawton (1985) also concludes from his review that amongst couples who respond poorly to sex therapy a fairly large proportion will eventually separate, although his own research (Hawton *et al.* 1986) found only a 13 per cent separation rate. Studies identifying factors predictive of treatment success have mostly been limited by being retrospective. They suggest, however, that several factors are related to the successful treatment of sexual difficulties: the overall quality of the marital relationship; motivation, especially of male partners; the existence of any psychopathology; the degree of sexual attraction between partners; and the progress made in the early stages of treatment.

Comparative studies have commonly shown the superiority of sex therapy to other forms of treatment for sexual problems. Those studies evaluating variations in the Masters and Johnson model suggest that, in general, co-therapy is no more effective than single therapist treatment, weekly treatment is more effective than the intensive approach advocated by Masters and Johnson, and that although self-help may have a part to play in the treatment of some straight forward problems, it is often insufficient and that regular brief therapist contact is necessary.

In a slightly different vein, Schover and LoPiccolo (1982) report the results of a study of 152 couples, where one spouse had either low sexual desire or an aversion to sex, who were dealt with at a sex therapy clinic between 1974 and 1981. They argue that desire-phase dysfunctions began to be recognized as a separate diagnostic entity only in the late 1970s and were not therefore addressed by Masters and Johnson. The couples received fifteen to twenty weekly sessions of conjoint behavioural sex therapy, with homework assignments between sessions. The study provided clear evidence of an increasing prevalence of desire-phase sexual dysfunctions, particularly amongst men. The authors comment that 'There have recently been new societal pressures to engage in frequent sexual activity' (1982: 194) which may be leading couples to identify more readily lack of sexual activity as a problem needing professional help. They also comment on the perception on the part of many clinicians of the difficulty of treating such problems, a view confirmed by Hawton *et al.* (1986) who found a high recurrence of low female desire problems in their follow-up study. This difficulty is also commented upon in a study by Schreiner-Engel and Schiavi (1986), who found a strong relationship between desire problems and histories of major and intermittent depression. However, Schover and LoPiccolo found significant treatment gains which were largely maintained during the follow-up period, although they conclude that 'sex therapy probably had only a limited effect on overall marital adjustment' (1986: 195).

Hawton (1985) observes that sex therapy is yet another form of couple therapy in which clinical practice and enthusiasm have tended to outstrip research findings. The overall conclusions of his review are confirmed by Scharff (1988) who comments that 'Sex therapy is a valuable tool, but it is not the miracle it seemed it might have been' (1988: 234). Couples often seek help with a sexual problem when there are serious underlying relationship problems, which may considerably limit the success of any treatment focused solely on the sexual problem (Clegg 1980; Nadelson 1983; Watson 1984). As Scharff concludes, commenting on the complexity of individuals, couples and their relationships:

> Success in one area, such as sexual satisfaction, is often blocked until other areas are approached. Sex therapy itself can work and for many couples is all that is needed. But for many others, it is one part of a larger path.
>
> (Scharff 1988: 234)

### Conciliation and divorce research

Timms and Blampied (1985) argue, in the research study quoted earlier, that

> we should not assume that either the efforts or the effects of counsellors constitute homogeneous phenomena. Because 'counsellors' share a name, they are not necessarily doing the same thing.
>
> (Timms and Blampied 1985: v)

This observation has particular significance in evaluating the recent major research study into conciliation in England and Wales (Conciliation Project Unit 1989), which examined the effectiveness of conciliation, the schemes studied being classified according to whether they were court-based or independent, and whether they had a high or low degree of judicial control. It is difficult to summarize succinctly such a large research project, but the main findings concerning effectiveness include the view that conciliation 'is at least as effective as other, more traditional procedures in generating satisfactory settlements' (CPU Summary Report 1989: 11) and that 'there were few significant differences in the effectiveness of services' (1989: 9), with the exception of court-based services with a high degree of judicial control which were less successful.

As Timms and Blampied (1985) warn in relation to counselling, however, it should not be assumed that because activities or individuals share a name, they are necessarily doing the same thing. Despite this, the Conciliation Project Unit

> considered it inappropriate to apply any preconceptions . . . concerning the meaning of 'conciliation' and . . . approached all known schemes which identified themselves as providing a conciliation (or mediation) service in connection with family disputes.
>
> (Conciliation Project Unit 1989: 3)

In evaluating the findings of this study, therefore, it is important to bear in mind that the fact that schemes *identified themselves* as providing conciliation cannot be taken to mean that they were necessarily undertaking the same activity. In addition, the categories described above into which the schemes were divided were identified *not* on the basis of what they did but at least partly on the basis of 'intuition supported in some measure by other research' (CPU Summary Report 1989: 4). Had these categories been devised on the basis of empirical inquiry into the schemes a different categorization might have emerged and, through altering the grouping of the data, produced very different results. It should also be noted that two areas were selected for study, for the purposes of comparison with the main sample, on the basis of a formal acknowledgement that conciliation was not available in those areas. This was to allow the comparison of conciliated with non-conciliated cases. The validity of this comparison must, however, be open to question, since a number of the cases in those areas will have been dealt with by court welfare officers, who frequently adopt a conciliatory or settlement-seeking approach. Thus settlement-seeking work with couples may have occurred even if no formal conciliation scheme could be said to exist (see James and Dingwall 1989). Therefore in spite of the interesting data generated by this research, its conclusions concerning effectiveness must for these reasons be treated with great caution.

This argument is echoed by Pearson and Thoeness (1988) in relation to US research on divorce mediation. Their findings, based on two major research projects, suggest that mediation provides a valuable complement to formal court processes, engendering a greater sense of commitment to abide by agreements reached in mediation, increasing co-operation, and reducing re-litigation. Their findings confirm other research suggesting strong consumer satisfaction, but producing only ambiguous evidence concerning more basic behaviour changes. As with the situation in Britain, however, in spite of a rapid growth of schemes and a high level of enthusiasm for and commitment to the use of mediation in divorce, there have been few empirical studies of the efficacy of mediation and research to date has also suffered from methodological weaknesses or limitations. This view is endorsed by Sprenkle and Storm (1983) in their review of research. As Dingwall and Eekelaar (1988) comment: 'There is a lack of clarity in defining what constitutes mediation so that the commensurability of findings cannot be established . . . there is uncertainty about the outcomes to be measured' (1988: 171). As a consequence, there is a need for caution in interpreting existing studies, and a need for more sophisticated, fundamental and wide-ranging research. Their conclusions are notably more conservative than Sprenkle and Storm's (1983) earlier review which suggested impressive evidence for the superiority of mediation.

Such issues are again highlighted by another recent consumer study of mediation in family disputes in the South-East London (Bromley) Conciliation Bureau. Davis and Roberts (1988) conclude that the effectiveness of mediation should be assessed in terms of any changes in the parties' capacity to negotiate, rather than outcome measures such as 'agreements'. This view is supported by their research, which indicated that in some cases, mediation improved considerably parties' negotiating capacities. The implications which this carries for the resolution of access disputes and consequent benefits for children must be clear. Other research studies, such as those by James and Wilson (1984), Lund (1984) in the UK, and Wallerstein and Kelly (1980) in the USA support this view.

Interesting similarities between marital counselling and mediation do none the less emerge from this research. For example Davis and Roberts (1988) make the point that

> one of the strongest messages to emerge . . . was that these couples regarded their disputes as arising from unique personal circumstances. They felt that these special elements had to be taken into account – something the legal process . . . had failed to do.
>
> (Davis and Roberts 1988: 147)

This perspective, highlighting as it does clients' personalized construction of their problems and the importance of individualized responses to these is similar to that observed by Timms and Blampied (1985) and draws attention as they do to the significance of agency setting, as we have argued elsewhere (James and Wilson 1986). It is interesting to note that, on the basis of this and other research referred to, a consistent case emerges for the establishment and maintenance of independent, non-statutory agencies for providing both marital counselling and conciliation. Similarly as far as conciliation is concerned, the overall conclusion which can be drawn from research is summed up by Davis and Roberts, who argue that

> it may genuinely be said that parents have *nothing to lose* . . . for some couples, there may also be a great deal to gain.
>
> (Davis and Roberts 1988: 151, italics in original)

In general, it must be acknowledged that in spite of the rationale and enthusiasm for the development of alternative approaches to resolving divorce-related disputes, and the evidence of a shift in policy and family law which broadly supports such developments, the research evidence does not provide the clear and unambiguous evidence of effectiveness which their proponents have hoped for and which they believed would be forthcoming.

## Therapy in remarriages

Finally, it is also worth commenting briefly on the issue of problems in marriages and families where one or both parents have remarried. We have commented elsewhere on the extensive research into the nature and extent of stepfamily problems (James and Wilson 1986), but in view of the prevalence of divorce and subsequent remarriages, such problems are increasingly likely to appear as issues in couple therapy. Glenn and Weaver (1977), from a study based on a substantial questionnaire, concluded that difficulties were particularly intense in the first year or two of remarriage and that the failure rate during this period of adjustment is considerable. However, they also found that couples who survived this period had a good chance of an enduring relationship. Goldberg (1985) concluded that remarried families often do very well with counselling or therapy, which is particularly effective if intervention takes place early on. However, problematic remarriages are still proportionately in the minority, and in view of the relative paucity of research into marital therapy, it is scarcely surprising to find an absence of studies focusing specifically on the effectiveness of therapy with remarried couples.

## Conclusion

It would be foolish to attempt to summarize in a concluding paragraph the findings from the extensive and diverse research which we have considered in this chapter. We have attempted in each section to report findings which seemed to us to have the greatest significance for practice, to point out the perhaps inevitable limitations of even the best-designed research studies, and to indicate aspects in relation to each topic where further research seems particularly to be called for.

However, as we suggested in our opening discussion of the research into marital therapy, there are certain issues which in our view need to be given priority in any future research if the problems of clients, and those who seek to help them in this country are to be properly addressed. We conclude by briefly mentioning these.

Other writers (Gurman *et al.* 1986: Haldane 1987) have commented upon the failure of a good deal of the existing research to address issues which are of real concern to practioners and their clients. Taken with the finding which we discuss elsewhere (James and Wilson 1986; 1987) of the difficulty which clients may have in obtaining any help at all with their marital problems, this suggests a need both to adopt research designs which may be more readily incorporated into existing clinical practice, such as the single-case evaluation mentioned earlier, and also to focus on providing information which will enable agencies to make best use of limited resources, in order to increase the availability and effectiveness of marital therapy. This focus needs to take account, too, of the fact that in Britain many (or indeed most) of the professionals whom couples are likely to encounter in primary health and social services settings are not specialists, and that a good proportion of those who do work almost exclusively with couples, although they have received specialist training, still work as volunteers (notably in Relate).

Therefore, there seem to us to be two areas of research which should be given priority: one that looks to providing information to quite basic but still unanswered questions, as Haldane (1987: 27), suggests, about the 'use of time in relation to outcome' that is such topics as the number, frequency, regularity and duration of sessions. The other relates broadly to organizational issues – the structure and dynamics of those organizations whose activities involve, or could potentially be developed to involve, marital work, the targeting and delivery of services, and the most effective ways of training competent practitioners.

Reviews of research traditionally end with an indication of where more research needs to be done, and it is perhaps inevitable that reviewing a great number of research studies produces a particular consciousness of their limitations and of what further questions they raise or fail to address. None the less, it is important too to acknowledge that there are a number of areas where practice issues have been considerably clarified, as indeed we hope that this chapter has demonstrated.

## References

Bagarozzi, D. and Giddings, C. (1983) Conjugal violence: a critical review of current research and clinical practices, *American Journal of Family Therapy* 11, 1: 3–15.

Barlow, D.H., Hayes, S.C. and Nelson, R.O. (1984) *The Scientist Practitioner: Research and Accountability in Clerical and Educational Settings*, New York: Pergamon.

Baucom, D.H. and Hoffman, J. (1986) The effectiveness of marital therapy: current status and application to the clinical setting, in N. Jacobson and A.S. Gurman (eds) *Clinical Handbook of Marital Therapy*, New York: Guilford Press.

Baucom, D.H. and Lester, G.W. (1982) The utility of cognitive restructuring as a supplement to behavioural marital therapy, Paper presented to the Association for the Advancement of Behaviour Therapy, Los Angeles.

Beach, S. and Broderick, J. (1983) Commitment: a variable in women's response to marital therapy, *American Journal of Family Therapy* II, 4: 16–24.

Beach, S., Jouriles, E. and O'Leary, K. (1985) Extramarital sex: impact on depression and commitment in couples seeking marital therapy, *Journal of Sex and Marital Therapy* II, 2: 99–108.

Bennun, I. (1984) Evaluating marital therapy: a hospital and community study, *British Journal of Guidance and Counselling* 12: 84–91.

—— (1986a) Cognitive components in marital conflict, *Behavioural Psychotherapy* 14: 302–9.

—— (1986b) Group marital therapy: a review, *Sexual and Marital Therapy* 1: 61–74.

Boelens, W., Emmelkamp, P., MacGillavry, D. and Markvoort, M. (1980) A clinical evaluation of marital treatment: reciprocity counselling vs system-theoretic counselling, *Behavioural Analysis and Modification* 4: 85–96.

Boland, J. and Follingstad, D. (1987) The relationship between communication and marital satisfaction: a review, *Journal of Sex and Marital Therapy* 13, 4: 286–313.

Brannen, J. and Collard, J. (1982) *Marriages in Trouble: The Process of Seeking Help*, London: Tavistock.

Clegg, H. (1980) Marital sexual dysfunction, *Marriage Guidance* 19, 4: 185–90.

Cline, V., Mejca, J., Coles, J., Klein, N. and Cline, R. (1984) The Relationship between therapist behaviours and outcome for middle and lower-class couples in marital therapy, *Journal of Clinical Psychology* 40, 3: 691–704.

Clulow, C. (1985) *Marital Therapy: An Inside View*, Aberdeen: Aberdeen University Press.

Colapinto, J. (1979) The relative value of empirical evidence, *Family Process* 18: 427–41.

Conciliation Project Unit (1989) *The Costs and Effectiveness of Conciliation in England and Wales*, London: Lord Chancellor's Department.

Corney, R. (1987) Marital problems and treatment outcome in depressed women: a clinical trial of social work intervention, *British Journal of Psychiatry* 151: 652–9.

Crowe, M.J. (1978) Conjoint marital therapy: a controlled outcome study, *Psychological Medicine* 8: 623–36.

Davis, G. and Roberts, M. (1988) *Access to Agreement: A Consumer Study of Mediation in Family Disputes*, Milton Keynes: Open University Press.

Dingwall, R. and Eekelaar, J. (1988) *Divorce Mediation and the Legal Process*, Oxford: Clarendon.

Dobash, R.E. and Dobash, R.P. (1987) Violence towards wives, in J. Orford (ed.) *Coping with Disorder in the Family*, London: Croom Helm.

Dominian, J. (1986) *Introduction to Marital Problems*, London: Fount.

Epstein, N. (1986) Cognitive marital therapy: multi-level assessment and intervention, *Journal of Rational-Emotive Therapy* 4, 1: 68–81.

Gaunt, S. (1985) *The First Interview in Marriage Guidance*, Rugby: NMGC.

—— (1987) *Reception Interviews in Marriage Guidance*, Rugby: NMGC.

Gibbons, J.S., Butler, J., Unwin, P. and Gibbons, J.L. (1978) Evaluation of social work service for self poisoning patients, *British Journal of Psychiatry* 133: 111–18.

Glenn, N.D. and Weaver, C.N. (1977) The marital happiness of remarried divorced persons, *Journal of Marriage and the Family* 39, 2: 331–37.

Goldberg, M. (1985) Remarriage: repetition versus new beginnings, in M. Goldberg (ed) *Contemporary Marriage: Special Issues in Couples Therapy*, Harewood, Ill: Dorsey Press.

Greenberg, L. and Johnson, S. (1986) Emotionally focused couples therapy: an integrated affective systemic approach, in N. Jacobson and A.S. Gurman (eds) *The Clinical Handbook of Marital Therapy*, New York: Guilford Press.

de Groot, H. (1985) *Marriage Guidance Counsellors in the Medical Setting*, Rugby: NMGC.

Gurman, A.S. (1973) The effects and effectiveness of marital therapy: a review of outcome research, *Family Process* 12, 2: 145–70.

Gurman, A.S. and Kniskern, D.P. (1978) Research on marital and family therapy: progress, perspective and prospect, in S. Garfield and A. Bergin (eds) *Handbook of Psychotherapy and Behaviour Change: An Empirical Analysis*, 2nd edn, Chichester: Wiley.

—— (1986) Individual Marital Therapy: Have reports of your death been somewhat exaggerated?, *Family Process* 25: 51–62.

Gurman, A.S., Kniskern, D. and Pinsof, D. (1986) Research on the process and outcome of marital and family therapy, in S. Garfield and A. Bergin (eds) *Handbook of Psychotherapy and Behaviour Change: An Empirical Analysis*, 3rd edn, Chichester: Wiley.

Hahlweg, K., Revenstorf, D. and Schindler, L. (1982) Treatment of marital distress: comparing formats and modalities, *Advances in Behaviour Research and Therapy*, (4) 57–74.

Haldane, J.D. (1987) *Marital Therapy: Research, Practice and Organization*, Aberdeen: Aberdeen University Press.

Hawton, K. (1985) *Sex Therapy: A Practical Guide*, Oxford: Oxford University Press.

Hawton, K. Catalan, J., Martin, P. and Fagg, J. (1986) Long-term outcome of sex therapy, *Behaviour Research and Therapy* 24, 6: 665–75.

Heisler, J. (1987) *Dropping Out*, Rugby: NMGC.

Heisler, J. and Applegarth, G. (1985) *Salaried Counselling: The Salford Scheme*, Rugby: NMGC.

Hinchliffe, M., Hooper, D. and Roberts, F. (1978) *The Melancholy Marriage: Depression in Marriage and Psychological Approaches to Therapy*, Chichester: Wiley.

Hooper, D. (1985) Marital therapy: an overview of research, in W. Dryden (ed.) *Marital Therapy in Britain*, vol 2, London: Harper & Row.

Huber, C. and Milstein, B. (1985) Cognitive restructuring and a collaborative set in couples' work, *American Journal of Family Therapy* 13, 2: 17–27.

Hunt, P.A. (1985) *Clients' Responses to Marriage Counselling*, Rugby: NMGC, pp. 72–83.

Jacobson, N. and Margolin, G. (1979) *Marital Therapy: Strategies Based on Social Learning and Behaviour Exchange Principles*, New York: Brunner/Mazel.

James, A. and Dingwall, R. (1989) Social work ideologies in the Probation Service: the case of civil work, *Journal of Social Welfare Law* 6: 323–38.

James, A. and Wilson, K. (1984) The trouble with access: a study of divorcing families, *British Journal of Social Work* 14, 5: 487–506.

—— (1986) *Couples, Conflict and Change*, London: Tavistock.

—— (1987) 'An ultra-sensitive area', *Community Care* February: 19.

Janzen, C. (1977) Families in the treatment of alcoholism, *Journal of Studies on Alcohol* 38. 114–40.

Johnson, S.M. and Greenberg, L. (1985a) Differential effects of experiential and problem-solving interventions in resolving marital conflict, *Journal of Consulting and Clinical Psychology* 53, 2: 175–84.

—— (1985b) Emotionally focused couples therapy: an outcome study, *Journal of Marital and Family Therapy* 11, 3: 313–17.

Kuipers, L. (1987) Depression and the family, in J. Orford (ed.) *Coping with Disorder in the Family*, London: Croom Helm.

Lund, M. (1984) Research on divorce and children, *Family Law* 14, 7: 198–201.

Masters, W. and Johnson, V. (1966) *Human Sexual Response*, London: Churchill.

McCrady, B. and Hay, W. (1987) Coping with problem drinking in the family, in J. Orford (ed.) *Coping with Disorder in the Family*, London: Croom Helm.

Mattinson, J. and Sinclair, I. (1979) *Mate and Stalemate*, Oxford: Basil Blackwell.

Nace, E. (1982) Therapeutic approaches to the alcoholic marriage, *Psychiatric Clinics of North America* 5, 3: 543–64.

Nadelson, C. (1983) Problems in sexual functioning, in C. Nadelson and D. Marcotte (eds) *Treatment Interventions in Human Sexuality*, New York: Plenum.

O'Farrell, T., Cutter, H. and Floyd, F. (1985) Evaluating behavioural marital therapy for male alcoholics: effects on marital adjustment and communications from before to after treatment, *Behaviour Therapy* 16: 147–67.

Orford, J. (1975) Alcoholism and marriage: the argument against specialism, *Journal of Studies on Alcohol* 36: 1,537–63.

—— (ed). (1987) *Coping with Disorder in the Family*, London: Croom Helm.

Orford, J. and Harwin, J. (eds) (1982) *Alcohol and the Family*, London: Croom Helm.

Pearson, D. and Anderson, S. (1985) Treating alcoholic family systems: interviewing in the marital subsystem, *Family Therapy* 12, 3: 211–20.

Pearson, D. and Thoeness, N. (1988) Divorce mediation: an American picture, in R. Dingwall and J. Eekelaar (eds) *Divorce Mediation and the Legal Process*, Oxford: Clarendon.

Regan, J., Connors, G., O'Farrell, T. and Jones, W. (1983) Services for the families of alcoholics, *Journal of Studies on Alcohol* 44: 1,072–82.

Renshaw, D. (1988) Profile of 2,376 patients treated at Loyola Sex Clinic between 1972 and 1987, *Sexual and Marital Therapy* 3, 1: 111–17.

Scharff, D. (1988) *The Sexual Relationship: An Object Relations View of Sex and the Family*, 2nd edn, London: Routledge.

Schover, L. and LoPiccolo, J. (1982) Treatment effectiveness for dysfunctions of sexual desire, *Journal of Sex and Marital Therapy* 8, 3: 179–97.

Schreiner-Engel, P. and Schiavi, R. (1986) Lifetime psychopathology in individuals with low sexual desire, *Journal of Nervous and Mental Disease* 174: 646–51.

Schwartz, R.C. and Breunlin, D. (1983) Research: why clinicians should bother with it, *Family Therapy Networker* 7: 23–7, 57–9.

Sprenkle, D. and Storm, C. (1983) Divorce therapy outcome research: a substantive and methodological review, *Journal of Marital and Family Therapy* 9, 3: 239–58.

Steinglass, P. (1976) Experimenting with family treatment approaches to alcoholism, 1950–1975: a review, *Family Process* 15: 97–123.

Thompson, A. and Cranwell, F. (1984) Frequently cited sources in human sexology, *Journal of Sex and Marital Therapy* 10, 1: 63–70.

Timms, N. and Blampied, A. (1985) *Intervention in Marriage: The Experience of Counsellors and their Clients*, Sheffield: Sheffield University/Community Care.

Turkewitz, H. and O'Leary, K.D. (1981) A comparative outcome study of behavioural marital therapy and communication therapy, *Journal of Marriage and Family Therapy* 7: 159–69.

Wallerstein, J. and Kelly, J. (1980) *Surviving the Breakup: How Children Cope with Divorce*, London: Grant McIntyre.

Warner, P., Bancroft, J. and members of the Edinburgh Human Sexuality Group (1987) A regional clinical service for sexual problems: a three-year study, *Sexual and Marital Therapy* 2, 2: 115–26.

Watson, J. (1984) Appraisal of marital problems in the context of psychosexual disturbance, *British Journal of Guidance and Counselling* 12, 1: 52–61.

Wells, R. and Giannetti, V. (1986) Individual marital therapy: a critical appraisal, *Family Process* 25: 43–51.

Williams, A.M. and Miller, W.R. (1981) Evaluation and research on marital therapy, in G.P. Scolevar (ed.) *The Handbook of Marriage and Marital Therapy*, Jamaica: N.Y. Spectrum.

# 17

# Training for couple therapy

BRIDGET HESTER

## Introduction

Earlier chapters have looked at different theoretical approaches and specific areas of work in couple therapy. In this chapter on training I shall attempt to embrace these differences and identify necessary components, whatever theoretical background is employed. Nevertheless, my own personal bias will inevitably underpin what is presented. This bias is that to be an effective couple therapist one should have some understanding of how past impinges on present, and of the human need for attachment.

There is a gap between what training should be available to equip a couple therapist fully, and what is available. The reasons for this vary. One considera- tion is the need to be realistic about what can be covered in a reasonable length of time at a manageable cost. Established courses tend to be those delivered by agencies adhering fairly strictly to a well-established theoretical approach, with a marital or family focus. However, there is increasing pressure on practitioners to become more eclectic to meet the needs of an apparently increasingly diverse client population. The increased diversity is the inevitable result of the growing acceptability of therapy in the various social and cultural groups.

I shall look first at issues concerning the selection of therapists. The following section 'What to learn' will focus on topics which should be covered in the train- ing of a couple therapist. This will be followed by a section 'How to learn'. Finally, the section on 'Where to learn' will give a brief outline of some of the training which is currently available, together with some addresses. This list is not comprehensive. Established available training (as already mentioned) tends to be in marital and family therapy. There are other training opportunities to be found throughout Britain, which are usually well publicized.

## Selection

It is difficult to evaluate training without addressing the subject of selection: one affects the other. Selection itself has two aspects. One aspect is the choice made by applicants: what criteria do applicants use when choosing a therapy course? The other aspect is the choice made by trainers: what criteria do trainers use when choosing course members?

Since the focus of this book is on therapy with couples, it is necessary to ask whether there are specific qualities needed to be able to work with couples which are different from those required of psychotherapists working in individual therapy. It is conventionally considered to be desirable, if not a necessary prerequisite, that those training to work with couples should have had experience of being in an ongoing committed intimate adult relationship. However, there are practising couple therapists who have not had this experience. There appears to be no empirical evidence confirming that competence in couple therapy depends on such experience. Much of what is required of a therapist demands an empathic response to a way of relating which one has not experienced. Thus it seems logical that other experience of loving relationships could be enough for a particularly gifted couple therapist.

It is not necessary to have trained as an individual therapist before training to work with couples. In fact it could be argued that this is a disadvantage, because of the need to maintain a relationship focus in couple work. This is a difficult skill, perhaps because culturally the western world appears to over-simplify individualism and minimize attachment needs.

Selection for training in couple therapy, apart from the comments just made, embodies the same criteria as selection for other modes of psychotherapy. Inevitably when selecting or being selected for a course of study, the question of academic ability must be addressed. Sometimes this is measured by requiring applicants to have specific academic or professional qualifications, such as those required, for example, by the Institute of Family Therapy, or the Institute of Psychiatry. Other agencies, for example Relate (National Marriage Guidance), use a less formal way of assessing intellectual ability.

Some courses specify particular professional experience as a prerequisite. Relate does not require particular professional experience, but will vary selection procedures and training requirements for applicants with relevant professional experience. Thus, this agency also recognizes the advantage of experience at the point of selection.

Another requirement of a therapist is the ability to cope with anxiety and function well under stress. These qualities are assessed at selection interviews, commonly using evidence from how the candidate copes with the stress of the selection procedures.

Evidence from outcome studies shows that therapists in any field of therapy, whose clients find them empathic, warm and accepting, are the most effective. This seems to suggest that one should select trainees with specific personal qualities demonstrating empathy warmth and acceptance to train as couple therapists. Perhaps this is the 'psychological good health, flexibility, open mindedness, positive attitudes between people, and interpersonal skill' which

Matarazzo and Patterson (1986) say are associated with success as a therapist. There appear to be no outcome studies comparing therapist competence with personal qualities or level of competence shown at selection. However, one's intuitive response would be that there is as strong a relationship between this and the ability to form a satisfactory therapeutic alliance as there is between the latter and favourable outcome to therapy (Gurman *et al*. 1986; Hunt 1985). Matarazzo and Patterson (1986) quote a study by Whitely *et al*. (1967) showing that the best students were better therapists at the start of a course than the poorest students had become at the end. They say, however, 'There are no established measures to predict differential student response to clinical skills training' (Matarazzo and Patterson 1986: 822).

It is important to look at self-selection. The applicants' own choice of a particular training programme and a particular orientation is an important factor. As Gurman pointed out 'the choice of favourite method of psychotherapy . . . is always very personal'. 'It is likely to reflect an intuitive and at times consciously arrived at sense of a good fit between the demands of working in a particular way and . . . how we work as individuals' (Gurman *et al*. 1986: 613). In other words, we do best what we most like and feel most attuned to. This is referred to by Mattinson (1988) who says, 'Choice of work . . . when choice is available, reveals many aspects of personality and indicates how a person is attempting to form his adult identity' (1988: 35). She goes on to say 'The external environment and internal environment of individuals . . . need to be relatively compatible' (Mattinson 1988: 38). This apparent need for a good personal fit with a method of working is probably as important a factor in choice of couple therapy training as are factors such as time available, costs, and professional environment.

## What to learn

### The therapeutic alliance

The most useful way of approaching the question of what trainees need to learn in order to practise couple therapy is to start with the results of outcome studies. It is becoming increasingly evident that what matters most, regardless of theoretical approach, is the nature of the therapeutic alliance between the couple and the therapist (Gurman *et al*. 1986). The client's contribution to and perception of this therapeutic alliance is, according to Stiles *et al*. (1986), the best predictor of outcome. The relationship skills of imparting warmth, understanding and acceptance which are partially tackled in the micro-skills training mentioned later, are clearly an important part of this, but as is pointed out by Hunt (1985) the therapeutic alliance, i.e. collaboration in working together, also needs agreement between clients and therapist as to the tasks and goals of therapy. In addition her research showed that how the therapist managed the timing and structure of the session was very important to clients. She also showed that clients frequently wanted more intervention and more direction from their therapist. The implication of this last is that the therapist should be well grounded in knowledge about relationships, particular human problems, the social/cultural environment affecting clients, and his or her own social/cultural bias. As has been pointed out by Grunebaum (1988), there needs to be more study as to 'what therapeutic approach works with what couple . . . who have which particular problem, . . . and more attention needs to be focused on ethics and values' (1988: 198). I would suggest that all the factors mentioned above are important ingredients of the facilitative therapeutic alliance. I would agree with Stiles *et al.* (1986) that the therapeutic 'alliance construct is a conceptual umbrella for uniting a number of client and therapist contributions; the exact operation of these constituent factors remains to be clarified' (1986: 174).

## Fundamental range of knowledge

In order to help couples who come with problems therapists need to know about the interplay between emotional/social/cultural factors, and how the social and cultural factors shape problem definition. They need to know about their own social/cultural and emotional bias, and how reframing of problems must suit the social/cultural environment of the clients. Therapists need to know about different theoretical approaches, and to know which is likely to be the most appropriate for a particular couple, given the time and resources they have available. They need to have a range of intervention techniques. It is necessary to know about human sexuality, and to be comfortable talking about sexual matters. There are a range of particular problems, such as the nature of some psychiatric conditions, physical and sexual abuse, and addiction which a therapist should learn about.

## Pattern repetition

Whatever approach is used, the effect of past on present is indisputable. Whether the approach is behaviourist or psychodynamic, therapists will know that people build on previous experience and that one's behaviour and belief about oneself is shaped by what went before. Thus, even if the therapy with a couple concentrates solely on present patterns of relating, it is important for the therapist to know how patterns are perpetuated.

## The nature of couples

It is important when training as a couple therapist to learn that the nature of a couple in an intimate relationship is more than the sum of those two individuals. Together they create an entity which they have an investment in keeping going. This is implicit in the systems approach. It is necessary to understand the nature of their intimate relationship to begin to understand what value to place on the individual's wishes and aspirations. Too often therapists fail to recognize the fantasy nature of so much which is expressed, and that to balance out the constraints and forced intimacy of relationships it is often necessary to have an emotional world of escape, of dreams which are not necessarily to be acted upon. There is constant tension between being part of something and being an individual in the present, just as there is tension between being in the present and how one was in the past.

## Ending of a couple relationship

Couple therapists will frequently be working with the ending of a couple relationship. Relate has variously estimated that 10–25 per cent of cases at any one time are people who are divorcing or separating. Working with an intimate relationship which may be ending is an important task for new therapists to learn. The major difficulty is uncertainty. Many couples precipitate the ending of a relationship because of the discomfort of uncertainty. Likewise, some therapists find it hard to stay with uncertainty, and become zealous in assisting a partner to make a decision one way or another, at a time when the most appropriate work would be to help the clients cope with uncertainty, until the most appropriate longer-term outcome becomes apparent.

## Alliances

It is important to learn strategies of control and intervention for working with a couple. How do you build up an alliance with both while avoiding a coalition with one or other partner? In some respects working with a couple focus makes this easier to learn because of awareness that as a therapist you are outside the bond and it is the relationship that you are assisting. The dynamics of some cases can inappropriately entangle the therapist in the relationship if there is a slip to an individual focus. However, the difficulties of being outside and making effective interventions cannot be minimized. The essential skills of confronting and containing a couple are not easy for beginning therapists. Some schools of therapy deal with these potential problems by always working in co-therapy, for example the Tavistock Institute of Marital Studies. An alternative approach as used by the Institute of Psychiatry makes it clear to couples that the single therapist is part of a team of therapists working on their case. Some approaches reflect the established power and authority of the profession in which the method developed. Thus the perceived authority of that profession creates its own distance. An example would be therapies developed within the medical profession. Therapists who work singly and are outside such established professions, or particular schools of therapy, need to find different strategies for establishing power and control which rest in the therapeutic relationship itself.

## Ethics

If training is to ensure adequately that the therapist does not inappropriately intervene in the clients' lives there needs to be input on the ethics of intervention. Much work has been done in drawing up codes of ethics for professional therapists. Emphasis on this in training goes together with teaching that when working with emotional issues the therapist, as well as the clients are likely to experience strong emotions. These may be understood to be transference of feelings about significant figures from early life, or trainees may learn more pragmatically that in the intimacy of therapy, feelings of warmth, love and sex merge and flow and can be misinterpreted thus tempting the therapist to break professional boundaries.

### Achieving aims

Whatever therapeutic approach a trainee learns, the aims are the same. They are to find an effective way of achieving goals, whether you use the three-stage model of exploration, understanding, action (Truax and Carkhuff 1967), or a different facilitative framework. As the pressure increases to undertake short-term work, it is becoming increasingly important that therapists learn how to move clients on effectively within the structure they are using. Thus therapists need to keep a sharp focus, be clear about the goals, and always work in close consultation with the couple, ensuring that the progress of therapy matches their aims and abilities, while moving the process on.

### Self-awareness

There is no question that to become a competent therapist it is necessary to learn about self in relation to others. Therapists should be aware of how they cope with their own unwanted emotions, and know what situations will cause them to have a particular emotional reaction. They should also be aware that they are shaped by particular social and cultural influences, as much as by their emotional experience of being in loving relationships.

### Evaluation

Trainees must learn how to evaluate their practice. While ongoing supervision does ensure a degree of evaluation, case-work needs to be evaluated in the light of research findings into the efficacy of couple therapy. It is also important for trainees to learn to question the relevance of their own personal, social or cultural values for different client populations.

### Social and cultural issues

Therapists need to discover *from* clients what their problems mean to them culturally and emotionally. It is not possible to divorce feelings from the cultural environment in which they are experienced. The whole concept of working with people in relationship involves the awareness of the pressure of that relationship upon the individual and the pressure of the larger social group on that couple, and ultimately the culture within which they live. There is no way someone can change drastically without it having implications on their relationships in the wider world. When one acknowledges this one can work with the pros and cons of change and understand what decisions have to be made given that the individual's position in the pair and the couple position in the family and community are important to their well-being. Social and cultural factors matter, particularly for a couple relationship and training needs to address these issues much more than is done at present. In some couple therapy training, there has been a tendency to over-emphasize the psychological aspects of human functioning, and in the process minimize other social factors. Trainees can complete a training course without being made aware of the effect of shift-work patterns or unemployment on a relationship.

Many couple problems can be solved at a practical level if the therapist recognizes the validity of these pressures. It is not necessary always to search for antecedents to solve a couple's problem. Conversely, in the face of some present-ing behavioural problems, it is necessary to look deeper and tackle the underlying emotional difficulty of which the behaviour is a symptom. Thus the therapist does need to be well trained in assessment and to know what questions to ask about past and present so as to make the judgement of where to intervene. It requires a high level of training and experience to be able to assess the different factors in a particular case, and a good awareness of cultural and theoretical frameworks to know what is most likely to work. As Tseng and Hsu (1979) note: 'The clients' familiarity with, orientation to, and expectation from treatment will greatly deter-mine the course of therapy and its effectiveness' (1979: 338). Thus, if one is work-ing with a varied population one needs also to know that the success of a particular approach is limited to certain client groups. For example the cultural influences on psychoanalysis are European Judaeo-Christian (Tseng and McDermott 1981; Grosskurth 1986). LeVine (1973) points out that these techniques suit highly literate individuals with a highly developed capacity for abstract thought and self-description along western lines. Similarly person-centred therapy with its non-directive approach promoting the client's autonomy, equality and independence reinforces the American cultural norms of self-determination (Meadow 1964).

By contrast in some cultures people somatize emotional problems with the result that there will be little within the cultural framework which identifies emo-tional stress related to a relationship problem. It will be experienced by one or other partner as a physical problem and the new therapist will need to adopt a very different stance to link the emotion with the 'symptom'. Clients will also expect their relationship to the therapist to mirror general attitudes to authority within the culture. Some will look for treatment along autocratic instructive authoritarian lines, while others will seek a more egalitarian relationship with the therapist.

Couple therapists need to learn about their own social and cultural biases as well as their emotional predilections and prejudices. This is particularly impor-tant when approaching working with couples from a different social or cultural background, or with gay or lesbian couples (see Chapters 11 and 12). For example there is a clear cultural bias in the western tradition that marriages resulting from the free choice of the individuals concerned must be better than marriages which have been arranged by the couple's families. It has also been found that there is heterosexual bias in people's perception of loving relationships (Testa *et al.* 1989): 'For many heterosexuals the notion may be foreign that two gay men or two lesbians can be as loving, affiliated, and committed as two heterosexuals' (1989: 171). It is important for couple therapists to learn that with homosexual relationships societal attitudes are an important factor in the breakup of relation-ships (Peplau *et al.* 1982). Stigmatization forces a group to play the role laid down for them (Goffman 1963). People in the stigmatized group internalize the negative stereotypes. This will be true for Blacks and other minorities as well as for gay men and lesbians and for people with disabilities. Therapists will not necessarily be personally familiar with the relationship patterns which clients pre-sent, and may well need help to identify appropriate therapy approaches.

Much of the available training focuses on marriage or quasi-marital relationships between heterosexuals, using psychological theories which have developed within a western Judaeo-Christian culture. These theories are then applied to couples who differ culturally, racially or in terms of sexual preference. More work is needed in developing theoretical frameworks which can explain a couple bond across these differences. As an example, the concept of unconscious choice of marital partner to explain similarities between a wife and a man's mother is less useful than the concept of self and self's ability to perpetuate patterns in behaviour in intimate relationships when we embrace arranged marriages.

## Eclecticism or specialization

To train to become a therapist competent in working with a variety of couples, it is necessary to become familiar with several theoretical approaches. Theoretical approaches are all derived from someone's attempt to understand the nature of humanity. Some of them aim to illuminate processes which are subconscious; others are restricted to overt behaviour. Some assert that you cannot change without understanding, while others assert that by changing behaviour you can change the experience and hence solve the problem. The reality is that both are true and the therapist has to learn which approach will suit the particular couple and particular problem which they present. Amongst the population are a diversity of couples who all make sense of the world in a particular way. To be able to help anyone who comes, it is essential that the therapist has the ability and training to use methods of intervention suitable for a variety of couples.

This is not necessarily an argument for integration of approaches, although therapies can usefully learn from each other. Therapy is a creative process. Effective therapy arises from creating an environment including a series of constructs which have meaning for a couple, and which they can trust. This may most effectively happen for a particular couple within a traditional therapeutic approach. Hence the suggestion that therapists should learn several theoretical approaches. We shall look to future comparative outcome research to learn about the relative advantages of integration or specialization. Since much of current training does follow a particular theoretical standpoint, trainees must realize that the framework used governs the effectiveness of their work, their client population, and the level of interaction at which they intervene.

## How to learn

This section will look at the methods used in training for couple therapy. These methods are widely employed in counselling and therapy training, with the possible exception of sculpting, a technique used to illustrate the hidden emotional pressures of the relationship on different members in a family or other close-knit group. This type of simulation is commonly employed as a tool for helping trainees understand more clearly the nature of relationships.

Training courses are frequently re-evaluated and methods changed as a response to feedback from trainees. However, Matarazzo and Patterson (1986) point out that we still seem to lack consensus on the basic issue of what and how we should teach . . . or how well we are doing it. . . . Until we deal more satisfactorily with measuring the complex outcome variables we have inadequate means to evaluate the teaching programmes.

Matarazzo and Patterson 1986: 822)

Training courses on offer do not necessarily use the combination of methods outlined below. Reasons for this vary. It can be because of the orthodoxy of a particular theoretical approach, or relate to the existing level of expertise of the trainees, or to the aims of a specific course.

Training courses whose structure, development and attitude model the structure, development and attitude of the method of intervention they teach are the most effective. It is fair to say that most trainers aim to model what they are teaching at the micro-level but may not necessarily pay enough attention to the need for congruence at the macro-level of course structure.

Training needs to be a mixture of academic input; simulation, whereby trainees take on the role of therapist or client in therapy, or improvise a scene involving a couple; observation of therapy; therapeutic skills practice; supervision; ongoing practice; and discussion. Much of the writing on training emphasizes skills and practice rather than academic input. This is not to deny the importance of the academic aspect of being a therapist, but rather to emphasize the importance of experiential learning so that an effective balance is achieved. Reading and didactic teaching about the theoretical basis for the practice are a necessary part of training. However, it is insufficient to learn in an academic way without personal and practical experience to reinforce the learning. Training is inadequate without ongoing supervised practice. The more therapy practice a potentially competent trainee can experience, the more competent he or she becomes.

Truax and Carkhuff (1967), who developed Carl Rogers's client-centered approach, identified three central elements of training:

1  a therapeutic context in which the supervisor himself provides high levels of therapeutic conditions
2  a highly specific didactic training in the implementation of the therapeutic conditions of empathy, warmth, genuineness
3  a quasi group therapy experience where the trainee can explore his own existence and his own individual therapeutic self can emerge.

(Truax and Carkhuff 1967: 242)

They said

Trainees can learn to implement accurate empathic understanding, non possessive warmth and genuineness much the same way that people learn to drive a car . . . can be told concretely and specifically some things to do or try, and some things not to do, can be given practice in role playing, can observe, . . . and learn from own experience.

(Truax and Carkhuff 1967: 239)

They acknowledge that trainees will feel self-conscious and artificial at first.

## Micro-skills training

Egan (1982) developed from Truax and Carkhuff (1967) a systematic programme of micro-skills training which has since been used extensively in many courses for beginning counsellors and therapists. Micro-skills training is the breaking down and learning of techniques, such as attending, paraphrasing and confrontation, which are essential ingredients of effective counselling. The therapeutic process is also broken down for trainees to learn which techniques are effective at different stages in the process.

The National Marriage Guidance Council introduced Egan's micro-skills training into their basic counsellor training in 1984. It has been found, as Matarazzo and Patterson (1986) commented, that micro-skills training is demonstrably effective at producing immediate training effects for those who are relatively inexperienced. It has also been found that the specificity of feedback in micro-skills method is appreciated by trainees (Toukmanian and Rennie 1975). However, micro-skills training does need to be offset by other methods. It does not in itself produce a good therapist. In fact there is a danger that a too-rigid adherence to the instructions given could result in incongruence between the behaviour adopted, and the therapist's natural style. Another danger of such rigid adherence is that individual and cultural differences in personal space needs are not accommodated. As pointed out by Hunt (1985) 'Technical skills themselves do not necessarily lead to a good counselling outcome because the most important ingredient is the relationship' (1985: 62). If you approach learning from the position of teaching micro-skills the trainees' concentration on the minutiae can result in their becoming lost. To continue the analogy with learning to drive a car, used by Truax and Carkhuff (1967: 239), learner drivers cannot also take in their surroundings, nor plan their route. Learning to drive does not show them the way across town. Thus the early confidence induced by this method can rapidly vanish in unfamiliar territory, and leave the trainee anxious. Alternative methods of training whereby trainees are encouraged to develop their broader response with clients without naming the skills can give an underlying confidence that a direction will emerge. But without skills training as well, this can be anxiety provoking, and can encourage a disregard for focus, the maintenance of which much couple therapy research has found to be important.

## Small group learning

Training for couple therapy is commonly effected in small groups, of up to twelve members. This group is then subdivided into twos, threes and fours according to what is to be practised or simulated. It is particularly important when learning to work with relationship problems that trainees experience and observe relating within a group. A group which has the same membership throughout the course, and also examines the relating within the group, re-creates the difficulties of belonging and being separate which are inherent in intimate couple relationships. Egan (1982) outlines the benefits of small group learning for counsellor training:

1  observing own behaviour and receiving feedback
2  developing observation skills

3 lowering defences
4 experimenting with new behaviour
5 exploring social influence
6 discovering models
7 giving and receiving help
8 seeing the principle of learning and behaviour in action.

(Egan 1982: 25)

## Simulation

Simulation techniques are widely employed and are an important part of training. Trainees practise micro-skills in simulated situations acting as therapists with fellow trainees as clients, and vice versa. These are frequently video-recorded to enable trainees to evaluate their own performance. Role-play is used not only to practise being a therapist, but also to help therapists understand the situation their clients find themselves in by playing the roles of the partners in the particular situation they present, and spontaneously developing their interaction. This is a valuable technique for developing understanding of the relationship problems of others, and of learning how the personality of the trainee affect the role-play. So there is self-learning as well. As mentioned earlier, an extension of this technique is sculpting, whereby fellow-trainees are placed into static positions illustrative of the underlying pressures in the relationship as perceived by the trainee therapist concerned. Role-play and sculpting are powerful techniques, and should be used carefully. The process of absorbing the emotions and situations of people in difficult relationships can trigger personal issues for trainees which makes it difficult for them to shed the role they played. Hence, trainers need to take care to de-role trainees after such events. However, role-play and sculpting are important bed-fellows for micro-skills training, ensuring that the imagination and creativity of trainees develops alongside techniques.

## Modelling

Trainees value modelling of good therapy, whether live or on video. Several training programmes incorporate observation of real practice as part of the training. Modelling also occurs within supervision and by trainers in training sessions, and it is important that supervisors do model the attitudes and techniques that trainees are expected to acquire. Truax and Carkhuff (1967) say 'If trainees could not experience high levels of warmth, regard, understanding, genuineness from the supervisor they could not be expected to function at high therapeutic levels themselves' (1967: 271).

## Case discussion

Case discussion in small groups is a component of many training courses. This method has been criticized. As Matarazzo and Patterson (1986) say 'it is a relatively ineffective method of teaching interviewing skills' (1986: 823). However, it is a good way of learning about different aspects of the case and underlying dynamics of the interaction. Different group members highlight different issues. A group which has a stable membership can usefully use the additional knowledge gained from the relationship patterns shown in the group to illuminate a therapist's working with a particular case. Reflections from the case can be seen within the dynamics of the group. Thus such a group can be helpful. However, there needs to be firm and able leadership of such a group to ensure that issues to do with dynamics of the group are not interpreted as belonging to the clients.

### Awareness groups

These groups have various titles, such as experiential groups, study groups, discussions groups. These are quasi-therapy groups which have a closed membership throughout a course and focus on personal or emotional difficulties experienced by trainee therapists as they develop their role. 'They allow the trainee the chance to explore himself, others and his surroundings in the hope of finding more constructive resources within himself and more rewarding relationships with others' (Truax and Carkhuff 1967: 284). This is precisely what the therapist tries to provide for the client couple. These groups are a particularly useful forum for preparing couple therapists for understanding about themselves in relationship. But they do need strict boundaries and careful leadership to be fully effective.

### Supervision

Supervision, whether one to one or in groups, is an essential part of training. Supervised practice is where much learning is initiated, and certainly where it is consolidated. Supervisors do need to be able to impart specific knowledge and skills. It is also recognized by Ivey (1983) that personal involvement between supervisor and trainee is necessary in order for the trainee to learn to apply the separate skills meaningfully, and to help the student through emotional issues. Buhrke (1989) stresses the importance of a supervisor's attitude in helping trainees overcome homophobia to enable them to work effectively with lesbian and gay couples. Thus the supervisor's attitude teaches the trainee to view a problem in a specific way, at the same time as modelling the effective helping techniques the trainee is expected to practise.

Courses vary as to whether trainees receive individual or group supervision. There are some issues, mostly to do with personal susceptibility to case material, which are more effectively addressed in individual supervision, away from the dynamics of the peer group. Not all courses require trainees to provide video- or audio-tapes of therapy sessions, or require live observation of the trainees' practice. It is extremely useful for supervisors to have access to the trainees' actual practice by one of these methods, as an alternative to seeing the trainees' notes on sessions.

## Length of training

Training courses aimed at producing competent therapists out of inexperienced applicants need to extend over a considerable period of time. For a part-time course, two years is probably a minimum. This is because it is only in extended practice that trainees experience and can thus learn about effective intervention in later stages of the therapeutic process, and have enough experience of different cases. Relate requires trainees to complete three years and 360 hours of therapy before receiving accreditation. Courses provided for trainees who already have some experience in working with couples have other requirements. The Tavistock Institute of Marital Studies specifies a minimum of six couples in eighteen months. The Institute of Family Therapy specifies 100 hours of therapy practice in the year of their Part I Family Therapy training.

## Where to learn

This chapter ends with information about some available training courses, with names and addresses of the training organizations concerned, who will give further information about the training on offer. This is not a comprehensive list. Readers who are interested in obtaining training should also make enquiries in their locality. Some Psychotherapy Diploma courses also have a substantial couple therapy content.

### Family Institute

The Family Institute specializes in the practice, teaching and research of family therapy. They practise brief therapy using a problem-focused approach based on systems theory. They offer a variety of training courses, short workshops, agency-based training, and an introductory course, and the University of Wales Diploma in Family Therapy.

Further information from
Barnados Family Institute
105 Cathedral Road
Cardiff, CF1 9PH

### Institute of Family Therapy

The Institute of Family Therapy introductory course in Family and Marital Therapy is a one-year part-time course, which takes place on Tuesday afternoons. The course, based on systems theory, is aimed at professionals interested in working with families in any setting. It does not train participants to be therapists but is a requirement for applicants for the Part I Clinical Family Therapy Training. The closing date for applications for the introductory course is 30 May each year.

Part I Family Therapy Training is a part-time (Wednesday evenings) Certificate Course run in conjunction with Birkbeck College, London. Entrance requirements are the completion of the Introductory course (or its equivalent) and therapeutic practice with families of at least 100 hours throughout the course year. The closing date for applications is 30 May each year.

A two-year advanced clinical training is available which is designed for professionally qualified practitioners with at least one year post-qualifying experience. The course is part-time, consisting of weekly supervision, and teaching blocks twice per term on Thursday evenings and all day Friday. Additional requirements are attendance at specialist modules and day workshops provided by the Institute from their teaching programme.

The Institute of Family Therapy and Birkbeck College MSc in Family Therapy is designed for professionally qualified practitioners who wish to pursue their careers concurrently. The majority of teaching is provided out of working hours or organized in discrete blocks. Entrance requirements for this course are a degree in psychology, education, medicine, social work or nursing studies (other degrees or relevant qualifications may be considered) plus the completion of an approved two-year introductory training in Family Therapy, and a satisfactory standard in the Institute of Family Therapy and Birkbeck College Joint Certificate Examination.

The Institute also offers agency-based training, offering programmes tailored to meet the particular requirements of the agency concerned.

Further information from
Institute of Family Therapy
43 New Cavendish Street
London, W1

## Institute of Psychiatry

The Institute of Psychiatry offer a one-year part-time introductory foundation course Therapy with Couples. This course in marital and sex therapy uses the behavioural/systems approach and leads to a Certificate in Therapy with Couples using a Behavioural Systems Approach. The course takes place on Mondays.

Admission requirements are professional experience of working with couples, together with relevant recognized qualification in such disciplines as counselling, psychiatry, psychology, social work or psychotherapy. The closing date for applications is 31 May each year.

A one-year Diploma course is being developed starting in October 1990. Applicants for the Diploma course are required to hold the Certificate in Therapy with Couples.

Further information from
Institute of Psychiatry
DeCrespigny Park
Denmark Hill
London, SE5 8AF

## Relate (Marriage Guidance)

Basic counsellor training is provided part-time over a period of two years for applicants who have been selected at a day selection conference to train to become Relate counsellors. Trainees are required to carry a minimum case-load throughout, as defined by the Relate Centre for which they work. The training consists of three modules delivered in six forty-eight-hour blocks at Rugby, plus regional training, fortnightly case discussion attendance, and regular case-work supervision. The approach is client-centred, with an emphasis on psychodynamic concepts and systems theory. Trainees are given training in therapeutic skills using Carkhuff's three-stage model of the counselling process. The advanced training for marital sexual therapy is a behavioural therapy training, and behavioural techniques are increasingly becoming part of basic counsellor training. Training is being redesigned into a Certificate course and an advanced Diploma course, which should be available in 1991 and 1992.

Relate offers a variety of non-specialist courses throughout the country for professionals wishing to acquire skills for working with couple relationships.

Further information is available from any local Relate Centre and from
Relate National Marriage Guidance
Herbert Gray College
Little Church Street
Rugby, CV21 3AP

## Tavistock Institute of Marital Studies

The Tavistock Institute of Marital Studies (TIMS) offers two levels of training for practitioners wishing to undertake psychotherapy with couples.

The Diploma in Marital Therapy equips the successful student to practise as a specialist marital/couple psychotherapist, alongside other psychotherapists who work with individuals, families or groups. It is an intensive course extending over two, three or four years (dependent on whether it is undertaken full-time or part-time). The theoretical orientation is psychoanalytic. Training consists of theoretical lectures and seminars, individual, co-therapist and group supervision. An apprenticeship model of practice training is used. The trainee's clinical work is undertaken in co-therapy with a TIMS staff member.

Admission requirements include a previous qualification and practice in one of the welfare professions, relevant clinical experience, and the willingness to undergo a minimum of three times a week personal psychoanalytic psychotherapy throughout the duration of the training.

Non-specialist training on marital interaction theory is taught to a wide range of professionals who seek to have the marital dimension as part of their broader primary professional task. This training tends to be based on either regular weekly seminars over a period of a year, or intensive block periods of three or four days with follow-ups. The theoretical orientation is psychoanalytical, but applied to the particular setting, role and task of the individual practitioner. Training consists of a mixture of theoretical seminars and clinical supervision of back home clinical work which is undertaken in small groups. This training does not equip people to specialize in marital psychotherapy but rather gives an important perspective to a more generic role.

Further information from
Tavistock Institute of Marital Studies
The Tavistock Centre
120 Belsize Lane
London, NW3 5BA

### Westminster Pastoral Foundation

The Westminster Pastoral Foundation do not offer a pre-qualification in couple therapy but do offer an advanced placement.

Further information from
Westminster Pastoral Foundation
23 Kennington Square
London, W8 5HN

## References

Buhrke, R.A. (1989) Lesbian related issues in counseling supervision, *Women and Therapy* 8: 195–206.

Egan, G. (1982) *The Skilled Helper*, 2nd edn, Monterey, Calif: Brooks/Cole.

Goffman, I. (1963) *Stigma: Notes on the Management of a Spoiled Identity*, Englewood Cliffs, NJ: Prentice-Hall.

Grosskurth, P. (1986) *Melanie Klein*, London: Hodder & Stoughton.

Grunebaum, H. (1988) What if family therapy were a kind of psychotherapy? A reading of the *Handbook of Psychotherapy and Behaviour Change*, *Journal of Marital and Family Therapy* 14, 2: 195–9.

Gurman, A.S., Knoskern, D.P. and Pinsoff, W.M. (1986) Research into the process and outcome of marital and family therapy, in S.L. Garfield and A.E. Bergin (eds) *Handbook of Psychotherapy and Behaviour Change*, 3rd edn, New York: Wiley.

Hunt, P.A. (1985) *Client Responses to Marriage Counselling*, Rugby: National Marriage Guidance Council.

Ivey, A.E. (1983) *Intentional Interviewing and Counseling*, Monterey, Calif: Brooks/Cole.

LeVine (1973) *Culture, Behaviour and Personality*, Chicago: Aldine. Matarazzo, R.G. and Patterson, D.R. (1986) Methods of teaching therapeutic skill, in S.L. Garfield and S.E. Bergin (eds) *Handbook of Psychotherapy and Behaviour change*, 3rd edn, New York: Wiley.

Mattinson, J. (1988) *Work, Love and Marriage: The Impact of Unemployment*, London: Duckworth.

Meadow, A. (1964) Client centered therapy and the American ethos, *International Journal of Social Psychiatry* 10: 246–59.

Peplau, L.A., Padesky, C. and Hamilton, M. (1982) Satisfaction in lesbian relationships, *Journal of Homosexuality* 8, 2: 23–5.

Stiles, W.B., Shapiro, D.A. and Elliot, R. (1986) Are all psychotherapies equivalent?, *American Psychologist* 41, 2: 165–80.

Testa, R.J., Kinder, B.N. and Ironside, G. (1987) Heterosexual bias in the perception of loving relationships of gay males and lesbians, *Journal of Sex Research* 23, 2: 163–72.

Toukmanian, S.E. and Rennie, D.L. (1975) Microcounseling versus human relations training: relative effectiveness with undergraduate trainees, *Journal of Counseling Psychology* 22: 345–52.

310                                                                                   *Bridget Hester*

Truax, C.B. and Carkhuff, R.R. (1967) *Towards Effective Counseling and Psychotherapy*, Chicago, Ill: Aldine.

Tseng, W.S. and Hsu, J. (1979) Culture and psychotherapy in A.J. Marsella, Tharp R.G. and Gborowski T.J. (eds) *Perspectives on Cross Cultural Psychology*, New York: Academic Press.

Tseng, W.S. and McDermott, J.F. (1981) *Culture, mind and therapy: an Introduction to Cultural Psychiatry*, New York: Brunner/Mazel.

Whitely, J.M., Sprinthall, M.A., Mosher, R.L. and Donaghy, R.T. (1967) Selection and evaluation of counselor effectiveness, *Journal of Counseling Psychology* 14: 226–34.

# Index

Davidson, B., 39, 45
Davis, G., 221, 222, 288
De Amicis, L. A., 162
death, separation and, 45
defeat, attitudes of, 126
definitions, 18–19
depression, 45–6, 277–8
desire, lack of, 141, 286
determinants (issues for therapist), 62–3
development, families and, 91–6
developmental
    crises, 130, 131
    model (gay relationships), 199–201
    transitions, 100
'deviant' relationships, 19, 28
dialogue (therapist/sociologist), 12–15
Dicks, H. V., 83, 221–2, 242, 251
Dingwall, R., 221, 287–8
distraction technique, 132
divorce, 4, 20–21, 40, 45–6, 254
    relationships after, 41–2
    research, 286–9
    *see also* ending relationships
Dobash, R. E., 283
Dobash, R. P., 283
Dominelli, L., 179–80, 183
Dominian, J., 16, 283
drug abuse, 115
drug therapy, 277
drugs, sex therapy and, 155
Dryden, W., 5, 18, 64, 102, 142, 161,
    184, 241
Duck, S., 29
Duffy, S. M., 208
Duvall, E., 73
dyadic focus, 18–19, 45, 99–100, 114,
    117–20, 122

eclecticism, 140, 301
economic relationship, 23
Edinburgh Human Sexuality Group, 285
education
    by gender, 168
    partner similarity, 40
    staple intervention, 81
    violence and, 48, 50
educational interventions
    Catholic Marriage Advisory Council,
        245
    Church of England, 246
    conclusion, 255–6
    defining the area, 243–4
    dilemmas, 253
    education and therapy, 241–2

evaluation, 254–5
    examples of work, 250–52
    Marriage Enrichment, 247–8
    Marriage Research Centre, 247
    other educational work, 249–50
    other organizations, 248–9
    Relate, 244–5
    resources, 252
    upstream helping, 242–3
    values, 253–4
    working in schools, 250
Edwards, J. N., 40
Eekelaar, J., 221, 288
efficiency, lowered, 126
Egan, J., 242, 303–4
Ellis, A., 142
emotion, expressing, 175–6
emotional adjustments (ending
    relationship), 218
emotional health, 43
emotionally focused therapy, 64–5, 72,
    275
emotions, distorting, 153
empty chair technique, 116
Encounter, 253
ending relationships
    conciliation, 220–23
    mediation, 223–6
    problems, 217–19
    solicitor's role, 219–20
    training, 298
    *see also* divorce; separation
Epstein, E., 38
Epstein, N., 272
'equifinality', 73
erectile problems, 143, 148–9, 154, 161,
    202
Erickson, E. H., 73
established professions, 257–9
ethics of intervention, 298
ethnic clients
    specific sex therapy, 184–5
    *see also* transcultural issues
ethnic intermarriage, 179, 181, 192
ethnocentrism, 28, 179, 182
evaluation
    of education, 254–5
    single case, 272, 289
    of trainees, 299
Evans, M., 139
expectations
    of clients, 282–3
    of gay couples, 196, 197
    modifying, 151

split couple (*continued*)
  negotiation/fights through solicitor, 219–20
  outcomes, 235–6
  problems of ending relationship, 217–19
  stages of mediation, 226–33
  theoretical framework (mediation), 233–4
Sprenkle, D., 288
'squeeze technique', 139
stage discrepancy, 201
Stanley, E., 142, 144, 151, 158, 161
Stanworth, M., 168
staple interventions, 77, 80–83
status, therapist's, 191
status inconsistency/incompatibility, 50
Steinglass, P., 284
Steinmetz, S.K., 48
stepchildren, 42
stigmatization, 300
Stiles, W.B., 296–7
stop-start technique (sex therapy), 160
Storm, C., 288
strategic interventions, 86, 113, 115
Straus, M.A., 48, 49, 50
Street, E., 103, 104, 105
stress, 126
Strube, M.J., 46–7
structural crises, 130
structural interventions, 85, 113, 115
structural relationships, 117
Suarez, L., 39
substance abuse, 283–4
Sue, D., 191
Sukoneck, H., 211
supervision (of trainee), 305
supportive therapy, 70–71
'surgery counsellor', 259
Surrey, J., 208
surrogate therapy, 138, 139, 142
systems theory, 7–8, 64–5, 72–3, 264, 284
  mediation framework, 233–4
  working with individuals in, 111–15, 121–2
Szapocznik, J., 112, 115, 117, 122

Tavistock Institute of Marital Studies, 261–2, 298, 306, 308–9
teaching agencies, 261–2
Teismann, M., 114
termination (of therapy), 86–8

Testa, R.J., 300
theoretical framework (mediation), 233–4
therapeutic alliance, 61, 76–7, 78–9, 116, 296–7
therapeutic approaches
  to couple therapy, 59–66
  to couple therapy in family context, 89–108
  to couples in crisis, 125–37
  gender issues, 165–77
  to homosexual men, 196–205
  to individuals, 110–23
  to lesbians, 207–15
  sex therapy, 138–63
  split couples, 217–36
  transcultural issues, 179–93
therapeutic contract, 76–7, 79–80
therapeutic goals, 79
therapeutic intervention, 200–201
therapeutic strategies, 198–203
therapeutic tasks, 79–80
therapist
  attitude, 172–5, 189–90
  as determinant, 62–3
  language use, 170–71
  neutrality, 119–20
  responses, 101–3, 196–7
  roles, 103–4, 131–2, 209–11
  selection, 295–6
  sexuality, 203–4, 212–14
  skills, 104–8
  training, *see* training (of therapists)
  use of, 41, 75–6
therapy
  barriers, 185–8
  boundaries, 129, 188
  concept, 5–6
  education and, 241–2
  implications for, 3–4
  main focus/purpose, 70–71
  research, *see* research in therapy (overview)
  social context, 16–17
  termination, 86–8
  unfolding, 76–86
Thiessen, D., 38
'third state', 212
Thoeness, N., 287
Thompson, A., 285
thoughts (focus of therapy), 71
time-limited crisis, 126
time out, 133
time together, 152
Timms, N., 282–3, 286–7, 288